McGRAW-HILL SERIES IN POLITICAL SCIENCE
Joseph P. Harris, CONSULTING EDITOR

THE UNITED NATIONS
IN ACTION

McGRAW-HILL SERIES IN POLITICAL SCIENCE

Joseph P. Harris, CONSULTING EDITOR

✓ ✓ ✓

THE UNITED NATIONS
IN ACTION

EUGENE P. CHASE

Professor of Government, Lafayette College
Secretary, Trusteeship Committee
San Francisco Conference on International Organization

FIRST EDITION

McGRAW–HILL BOOK COMPANY, INC.

NEW YORK   TORONTO   LONDON

1950

THE UNITED NATIONS IN ACTION

To My Wife
and to all other persons
who have worked with or for
The United Nations

PREFACE

The United Nations is an effort to organize the world for the maintenance of peace and the promotion of general well-being. Many things about it are easy to condemn. But it is the current experiment, full of possibilities. It deserves our intelligent understanding, if we think that international organization is better, on the whole, than international chaos. I have tried to explain it without being too technical.

The point of view of the author is that of an individual American citizen interested and trained in international affairs and international organization. Since I served for some years as an officer of the Department of State, as one of the experts who made plans for the Charter of the United Nations and who subsequently were engaged in interpreting the Charter and adjusting United States policy to it, my point of view is inevitably influenced by the positions which I held, and by my colleagues in the Department. As a member of the Department who was lent to the international secretariat of the San Francisco Conference, I had the experience of working for all the nations represented at that conference, and my nationalism is tempered, I hope, by that experience. It should be possible to be both a good citizen of one's own country and a good citizen of the world. When I have followed American policy, as I usually have in this book, it is because I have agreed with it. When I have ventured to disagree, my disagreement is also my own.

It will be plain that, like all Americans, I have been greatly influenced by the questions that have been raised since the Charter of the United Nations went into effect. Our national habit is to demand immediate attainment of a goal. We are possessed by what Emerson called "the hunger for sudden performance." But it is too soon to lament weaknesses in the United Nations. Though the United Nations is new and experimental and will no doubt be different in the future, it already has an independent

vii

life and character of its own. Halting and clumsy as its first
attempts have been, it has been no different from most great
experiments in government. Even the United States was not
created in a day.

Here a word must be said about the most important political
issue in the United Nations—the negative attitude of the Soviet
Union toward so many United Nations activities. My references
to Dumbarton Oaks and to San Francisco will show that the postwar position of the Soviet Union is not essentially different from
its position during the war. We must remember that the West-
erners at San Francisco were confronted by the same problem
that they face now. They were sure that the cooperation of *all*
the great powers was essential to world peace and to any general
international organization. The United Nations could not have
been created without the Soviet Union. When the recurrent
"walk-outs" of Soviet representatives have seemed to indicate the
possible withdrawal of the Soviet Union and its satellites from
the United Nations, the other members have perhaps been prepared to go ahead without them. The resultant organization
would be useful, no doubt, but it would no longer be the "general
international organization" foreshadowed in the Moscow declaration of 1943 and established at San Francisco. Even in the midst
of the Korean war, the United States representative to the Security Council has reiterated the position that Soviet participation in the United Nations is desirable, though he quite properly
points out that it should be in accordance with the principles of
the Charter. For believers in international organization, the
choice still remains: something, though not exactly what they
want, or nothing. This book is written on the theory that something is better—a great deal better—than nothing.

This volume tries to cover most of the essential activities of the
United Nations up to December, 1949. It went to press during
the lull before the Korean crisis broke, and the critical develop-
ments of 1950 can be mentioned only briefly here.

In June, 1950, North Korean forces marched across the thirty-eighth parallel, which since 1945 has separated Korea into two zones, and attacked the Republic of Korea, which had been established in the South under the auspices of the United Nations and recognized by the General Assembly to be the only legitimate Korean government.

This clear case of aggression was discussed by the Security Council in a hurriedly called meeting on June 25. The Secretary-General opened the meeting by reporting the invasion, of which he had received official notice from the United Nations Commission on Korea. The Council adopted a resolution calling for the cessation of hostilities and the withdrawal of North Korean forces to the thirty-eighth parallel. This resolution, introduced by the United States, was approved by nine votes, Yugoslavia abstaining and the Soviet representative being absent.

Two days later, since the attack continued, the Council passed a further resolution recommending that member states "furnish such assistance to the Republic of Korea as may be necessary to repel the armed attack and to restore international peace and security in the area." With the United States taking the lead, forces of member states at once began to assist the Korean government. A further resolution, of July 7, recommended that the forces of member states be made available "to a unified command under the United States."

The brilliant improvisation by which the Security Council, having no forces of its own, made a call for volunteers has subsequently received the approval of most members of the United Nations. It would seem to be entirely in accordance with the Charter. The resolutions were passed in the absence of the Soviet representative, who had failed to attend since January because the Council had refused to unseat the representative of the Nationalist government of China. But on his return to the Council in August the Soviet representative could not persuade the Council that actions taken in his absence were void.

While the military operations grew in intensity, repeated efforts were made by the Indian government, a member of the Council, to initiate a settlement by mediation. As of the end of August, these efforts had not met with success nor with much apparent consideration by the major powers figuring in the Korean case. Military action drowned out all other voices.

I can repay only by this brief general acknowledgment my obligation to my colleagues in the Department of State and in the Secretariat at San Francisco, and to all the delegates of foreign countries from whom I have learned so much about their problems and their policies.

I cannot mention by name my friends and former colleagues who have read chapters of this book and kept me straight on many points. The reader may take every significant statement in the volume as being backed up by documents (which are described in the Bibliographical Note) or by the statements, sometimes private, of responsible officials. This is true, at least, except where the author is obviously expressing his own opinion. In these latter situations the reader should weigh the value of the author's judgments against those of whatever authorities he has learned to trust. I suspect that the text contains errors, but not for want of care in the effort to avoid them.

EUGENE P. CHASE

HEBRON, CONN.
August, 1950

CONTENTS

PART ONE

The Drafting of the Charter

Chapter 1. PURPOSE AND PREVIOUS EXPERIMENTS IN INTERNATIONAL ORGANIZATION

THE PURPOSE OF THE UNITED NATIONS

Two wars in one generation are, as the Preamble to the Charter of the United Nations indicates, too much. If the future is to be worth living in—if, perhaps, there is to be a future at all—there must be peace. Peace in this sense and for this purpose does not mean a complete absence of armed conflict, but it does mean an absence of large-scale wars, and it means also the limitation in number as well as in size of small and individual wars.

Peace in this sense has always been the world ideal, at most times and in most places. But before the war of 1914 the choice between war and peace was more a matter of preference than of social necessity. The war of 1914 indicated what the war of 1939 seems to have proved, that in the modern world large-scale war is universal war, and that universal war is universal destruction.

Out of a clearly felt recognition of this situation the United Nations Organization arose. Its purpose is to make large-scale war impossible, or at least unlikely. Though all the nations at San Francisco could think of things which they would like to gain, and might be able to gain, by a future war, all of them feared such a war as too destructive for themselves. The great, and the original, purpose of the United Nations Organization is to preserve the peace—to maintain what the Charter calls "international peace and security."

In addition to preserving the peace, the United Nations was created to be an instrument of general welfare, in a sense a world government, to do certain things by collective action which needed to be done and which could only be done collectively. To make life not only more safe and more secure but also more productive and even more comfortable was the second, but not a secondary, purpose of the drafters of the Charter.

The older, and the primary, purpose of government has been security. The community was organized to protect its members from attack while they went their own individual ways. The newer, and nowadays the equally important, purpose of government, is to perform, by the central agency of the community, functions which cannot be performed by the individual members of the community going their own separate ways. The Charter, and actions taken under it, have a duality of purpose—the same duality of purpose that can be seen in the functioning of national governments—the negative purpose of protection or security and the positive purpose of affirmative action to promote the general well-being.

The United Nations Organization cannot be understood without the realization that it is intended to serve these two purposes. It is a security organization first of all. But it is also—and correlatively—a welfare organization. Indeed, in view of the contemporary, positive conception of government, it can hardly perform properly its first, or security, function without performing its second function of promoting the general welfare.

Since it attempts to perform both of these functions, the United Nations resembles, indeed is, a world government—not a government so closely integrated and so all-powerful as that of the Soviet Union or of France or of the United Kingdom or even of the United States, but world government nevertheless. Of course, as a world government it is infinitely more inefficient and ineffective than are the governments of most of its members, but the purpose of the United Nations is clear, however incomplete its organization or ineffective its action.

Every modern government of a national state has failed from time to time, and most of them fail daily, to perform their presumed functions. They continue to exist, nevertheless, and to command respect and allegiance because their constituents are better off with them (however ineffective and inefficient) than they would be without them. The United Nations Organization is peculiarly subject to criticism as ineffective and inefficient, but—as in the case of so many national states—it is probably better to have the United Nations with all its inefficiency than not to have it at all. It is extremely unlikely that any sort of "world government" which required the surrender of any appreciable amount of national sovereignty would be accepted by the governments, or even the peoples, of most of the larger countries whose support would be necessary for it to succeed.

Previous Types of World Organization

The United Nations Organization was not created out of nothing. It was based on many ideas, many institutions, and many practices of the past.

The idea of world peace is as old as the world, and the idea of world government is as old as government itself. In the history of our Western culture (of which the United Nations is a product) the idea of a conscious world community, peaceful and civilized, is as old as the Stoics, whose philosophy prevailed in Rome, and as Christianity, which gave ethical leadership to those whom Rome governed. The Stoics and the Christians alike believed that all men are members of one universal community, which is as wide as the world, or indeed the universe, and which has common principles and laws. The actual world of the Stoics and of the Christians was, it is true, a divided world, but the ideal was an ideal nevertheless. Men should be brothers, whether they behave as such or not.

Perhaps nothing in the past of our civilization has influenced our thinking in international affairs so much as the empire established by the Romans. Though the Roman empire was despotic and cruel, at its height it had all the characteristics which we desire in world organization. The Roman empire was universal. It had one government—*Senatus Populusque Romanus.* It had one law—*jus civile.* It had peace—*pax Romana.* And it included the entire known world—*orbis terrarum*. There may have been harshness and cruelty; it is true that in some corners of the world the Romans, as the historian said, did make a desert and call it peace. But the instrument could not be reckoned too unworthy, because of the great end which it served. Dante could justify the empire on religious grounds by pointing out that Christ was born during the reign of Augustus, *when all the world was at peace.*

Rome fell, but Christendom remained. Christianity had been accepted as the Roman religion by Constantine. The Church had been organized, and its center, Rome, was the center of the empire. When the empire fell, the Church eternal remained. Though the empire was broken up into barbarian kingdoms by the Teutonic invaders, the Church retained a sovereignty over all. Rome—the Empire—dissolved and ceased to be the center and the source of unity. Rome—the Church—remained as the center and the source. Christendom, the body of all believers, took the place of the Roman empire as a world state. Like the empire it was all-inclusive. Like the empire it had one government and one law. Like the empire it maintained one peace. Like the empire it handed down an ideal of unity and concord to succeeding generations.

The Reformation shattered the Church, as the barbarians had shattered the empire. The seamless robe was rent. Unity, peace, and concord ceased to dwell among men. The "wars of religion" were the most devastating and the most cruel since the early days of Rome; they were not equaled in cruelty again until the twentieth century. For a century or so civilization lapsed. There was chaos of ideas and of allegiances. It was at this time that the national states arose, developing from the barbarian tribal kingdoms. France, Spain, and England among the earliest, and then a series of many others, became separate kingdoms with their own sovereignties, their own territories, and their own peoples. The theory of sovereignty, the unchecked and uncontrolled rule of the monarch over his subjects, developed. The single world of the Empire and of the Church was broken into fragments, but the fragments developed a tough and resilient life of their own. Nationalism in the sense of a feeling and a dogma has increased in strength since then, but the nation-state is only as old as the Reformation. "The Kingdom of England is an empire" said a famous law of Henry VIII; that is, it is self-sufficient and a law to itself. Ever since the rise of the nation-state the world has been an international world, made up of separate self-contained units, as distinct from each other as pebbles in a basket. This world of entirely separate units—"sovereign states"—is the world by which the United Nations was created and into which it was born.

It would be going too far to say that this world of separate sovereign states lacked common beliefs and principles, even in its early days. "The law of nations" or "international law," a set of principles and practices based on the common belief of enlightened mankind, was acknowledged as binding on all civilized rulers and peoples. When Grotius wrote his *Law of War and Peace* (1625), he set forth the rules that should govern the relations of states with each other. When the nations of Europe gathered to sign the Peace of Westphalia after the Thirty Years' War in 1648, they went so far as to lay down new rules for their own future guidance.

Since that time, for three hundred years, the civilized world has been organized on the basis of certain assumptions.

ASSUMPTIONS AT THE BASIS OF WORLD ORGANIZATION

The Family of Nations

The first assumption has been that of the existence of a "family of nations." At first the family consisted of the more mature nations of Western Europe, all of them Christian, though some Catholic and some Protestant. As civilization of the Western European pattern spread and as one state after another attained its nationality and individuality, the family of nations grew larger. At first the world of international law was no wider than the old world of the Western church, but soon the Russian empire, with its Eastern Christianity, was recognized as a part of the civilized world, and in the eighteenth century all of Europe, except the Turkish empire (which was not Christian), was considered part of civilization. The colonial empires, geographically outside Europe, were culturally a part of this European world. When the United States and the other European colonies in the Western world attained their independence, they were accepted automatically as junior members of the family to which they belonged. When non-Christian countries, like Turkey, conformed sufficiently to the standard pattern, they were accepted as members of the family of nations. The Mohammedan states, Japan, and China came very late into the family. Not, indeed, until the First Hague Conference in 1899 was the family of nations geographically a world family.

The Law of Nations

The principles and rules—the law—of the family of nations was the "law of nations" or, as we call it, "international law." When the family of nations was exclusively Christian, the principles and laws were supposedly founded on principles accepted by Christians. As a matter of actual fact most of the traditional rules of international law, though no doubt consistent with Christianity, are borrowed from Roman law in the form in which that law governed a world state. Custom, the accepted principles of morality, and some sense of right and justice as absolutes are the bases of international law, and international law is the system of rules which is conceived to be binding on all states that belong to the family of nations.

International Conferences

Conferences of the members of the family of nations were held from time to time. They occurred most often when a war had been fought and it was necessary to restore peace and try to promote stability for the future. There has been a recent tendency to make the conferences universal, that is, to include in them all members of the community of nations; but in their earlier history they usually included only those states which in one way or another were directly involved in the war just fought or in the situation which was to exist. Admission to a peace conference was a privilege of the belligerents. Other interested states, strong enough to gain admission, might be admitted. The Congress of Westphalia was a peace conference of those states which fought the Thirty Years' War. The Wars of the Spanish and Austrian Successions resulted in the Treaties of Utrecht. The nineteenth century was the great century of conferences, of which the greatest was the Congress of Vienna in 1814–1815, which not only restored the peace after the wars of the French Revolution and Napoleon, but also attempted to organize a future peaceful world. Consciously and intentionally some of the Vienna powers held smaller and lesser conferences to deal with more limited problems. This congress system did not last long, for it broke when England withdrew in 1822, but it established a pattern for the future. In 1856 in Paris a conference was held to draw up the peace treaty to end the Crimean War. Although limited in membership, this conference, in the Declaration of Paris, acted as a legislative body for the family of nations. The Berlin Congress of 1878 was a similar gathering. The largest and most ambitious of conferences of that century was the conference which met at The Hague in 1899 to codify laws of war and peace and which included most of the independent states of the world. The Second Hague Conference in 1907 was equally universal. Lesser conferences, like those held in London on Balkan questions, were part of the pattern.

During the first decade of the twentieth century it was finally assumed that all sovereign independent states belonged to the family of nations, which acknowledged the authority of international law. No widespread war had disturbed the civilized world since the Congress of Vienna had been held. Many men believed that large-scale war had grown unnecessary. The war of 1914 was an unexpected interruption to the development of world cooperation through the conference system. But, in a sense, it was only an interruption. The Peace Conference of

Paris in 1919 was even larger and more widely attended than its precursor in Vienna a century before and addressed itself to even more problems. From then until 1939 the conference system was merged with the League of Nations.

Universality

The Conference of Paris in 1919 shows the assumptions of the world system in their clear form. The international world was tangible and definite and it was made up of all states that accepted the principles of international law. The defeated powers were absent, for they were assumed, by having fought on the enemy side in the war, to have put themselves in the wrong and to have outlawed themselves, at least temporarily. (Such an arrangement was nothing new. France had been an outlaw when the Congress of Vienna began, though the skill of its plenipotentiaries restored it to good standing, and France was one of the effective forces in drawing the final treaties.) And though the neutrals were absent at Paris, for this was a conference to draw up treaties of peace, the neutrals were few and inconsiderable.

The "Great Powers"

Another assumption of the international system was that, though sovereign independent states were legally equal, certain great powers had a position of prominence and of moral (as well as physical) superiority. In the old European world of the eighteenth century, by general acknowledgment Great Britain, France, Austria, and Russia were "great powers" with a controlling voice in the affairs of all the nations and with considerable power, if not authority, to settle things by themselves. Spain had been, but no longer was, of this circle. Prussia was establishing its position within the group. The nineteenth century saw the general acceptance of a German empire (grown out of Prussia) as second to no other power, and a united Italy which was a great power, though the least among them. When the United States defeated Spain in 1898, it became the first non-European state recognized to be a great power, with all the implications of that status. When Japan defeated Russia in 1905, Japan also entered the circle. In 1919, Germany and Austria, as defeated powers, were shorn of territory and demoted to the ranks of lesser powers. The Soviet Union was also outside because it had made peace with Germany in 1918 and had withdrawn from its normal relations with the rest of the world.

In the Covenant of the League of Nations, Great Britain, France, Italy, Japan, and the United States were given a privileged position as permanent members of the Council. (The United States never took its seat.) The German republic and the Soviet Union, during their few years as members of the League, shared this position of privilege. In 1937 one would have said, apart from political prejudices, that five European states (the United Kingdom, France, Germany, Italy, and the Soviet Union), one Asiatic state (Japan), and one American state (the United States) were great powers. China might become great in the future, but was not so at that time. The war of 1939 broke the power of France. Germany, Italy, and Japan were defeated. The three surviving great powers had become allies. The United States, the United Kingdom, and the Soviet Union determined most questions from 1941 to 1945 in concert. They admitted formally, if not actually, that China and France were of their company.

Lawmaking

The final assumption of the international community is that it possesses the authority to make rules which shall be binding on the members of the society. At first, international law, like early systems of national law, was derived from custom. But at least as early as the Congress of Westphalia, international conferences began to codify old rules and to invent new ones. Many conferences, like those at The Hague in 1899 and 1907, have been held for the specific purpose of drawing up great lawmaking treaties. Others, like that of Paris in 1856, have made law consciously but incidentally. The international world should be, as in many ways it has begun to be, a world of law.

THE LEAGUE OF NATIONS

All these elements combined in the creation of the League of Nations at Paris in 1919.

The League of Nations possessed no originality of either purpose or structure. Its purpose was the maintenance of peace by the two means accepted as essential and supplementary—by machinery designed explicitly to prevent, or at least to minimize, war and by various general and specific methods for ameliorating international difficulties and for promoting the general international welfare. The League structure was merely a codification and a standardization of the institutions and practices of the family of nations in the world of international law.

The family of nations appears in the League Covenant and in the "League system" in the form of the membership of the League. At first this membership was limited to the ex-Allies in the war against the central powers and to those neutrals whom the ex-Allies accepted as sufficiently of their way of thinking in international affairs. For example, one of the neutrals left out at the start was Mexico. Its name was not included in the annex to the Covenant as a state invited to accede to it, for the United States maintained that Mexico did not sufficiently accept the obligations of international law. The Soviet Union, likewise, was omitted in 1919, because of the belief that its revolution had put it outside the world of accepted international law and practice.

Potentially, however, the membership of the League was universal. Any and all states might be voted into membership if they convinced the original members that they accepted and were capable of satisfying the necessary obligations of membership. In fact, before the League came to an end, all the great powers, including Germany and the Soviet Union but excepting the United States, had been members at least for a time, as had all the other states in full standing according to international law, except Iceland, Saudi Arabia, and the tiny entities of Liech-

tenstein, Monaco, and San Marino. The members of the family
of nations, accustomed to meeting in occasional conferences, composed the Assembly of the League, which met regularly once a
year and was, in fact, the international conference institutionalized.

The Concert of Powers, the steering or the dominant group of
great powers, was institutionalized in the Council of the League,
wherein the great powers, as defined in 1919 and as redefined
from time to time subsequently, were permanent members. The
League was to do the various things that the powers, either great,
or great and small together, were accustomed to doing—to settle
disputes, to codify the existing rules of international law, to make
new rules. The League also had positive, though not clearly
defined, functions of acting for the general welfare. Much of
the time of the Assembly was devoted to this purpose and so
was its whole paraphernalia of commissions, committees, and
special conferences (as on transportation or on double taxation
or on opium control). In this aspect the League resembled a
rudimentary world government.

It was by institutionalizing existing practices that the League
made an advance over the previous international world. The
League was certainly not a superstate. It contained, however,
certain elements of world government. The Council, which included not only the great powers but also representatives of
the smaller powers, developed into an executive committee of the
League, responsible for the most part to the Assembly. The
Assembly became not only a parliament of the nations but also
to some extent an international governing body and exercised a
limited budgetary authority. The Secretariat of the League,
which was far from being an international executive, furnished
continuity to the machinery. Under the old system the Family
of Nations and the Concert of Powers were active only when
specially called into action. Under the League system there was
always something there, at the League headquarters in Geneva.

Furthermore, the League system included two other organs
of international government, created by separate conventions or

agreements—the International Labour Organisation and the Permanent Court of International Justice. The ILO resembled a department of labor in a rather individualistic national government. The World Court was an international court. Like the League itself, these organizations possessed no power to force their decisions on their members, but their accomplishments were none the less real. Citizens of highly organized national states, in which the coercive element of government is conspicuous, denied that the League was a government, because it lacked the power to coerce. But students of history, as well as of the art of government, saw the League performing functions of government in a way precisely like that of national states in earlier times or that of contemporary states where rule must be by consent rather than by fiat and enforcement.

The League "failed," that is, it stopped performing its functions, after the special meeting of the Assembly in December, 1939, which "expelled" the Soviet Union. But its "failure" was not unlike the breakup of previous loosely coordinated governments which went to pieces through internal revolution or outside pressure or a combination of the two. Rome fell. The Polish kingdom disintegrated. The Holy Roman empire simply ceased to be. Nineteenth-century Spain would have disappeared many times had it not been contained in so separate a geographical package. The Ottoman empire, after centuries of disintegration, is now completely gone.

INTERNATIONAL ORGANIZATION DURING THE WAR

The war of 1939 was fought on one side by an alliance of powers so close in itself as almost to be one government—Germany and Italy and their satellites—who, with Japan, constituted the "Axis." On the other side an *ad hoc* wartime coalition became a new expression of the old principles of world law and organization. The Atlantic Charter was a restatement of crucial principles of international justice; its incorporation in the Declaration by United Nations of January 1, 1942, created what was from one point of view merely a new wartime alliance but from another a new family of nations. Twenty-six governments signed the Declaration by United Nations. Between June 5, 1942, and March 1, 1945, twenty-one other members adhered to it.

The members of the "United Nations" never met collectively, all of them, until the San Francisco Conference in 1945. But the steering group of great powers of the United Nations met from time to time during the war. In October, 1943, the foreign ministers of the United States, the United Kingdom, and the Soviet Union met in Moscow and were joined by the Chinese ambassador in signing the Declaration of Four Nations on General Security, which foreshadowed a "general international organization." In November, 1943, the heads of the governments of the United States, the United Kingdom, and China met in Cairo, and of the United States, the United Kingdom, and the Soviet Union in Teheran. Finally, Churchill, Roosevelt, and Stalin met again at Yalta in February, 1945.

At Yalta a new form of the concert of great powers came into being. A three-power Conference of Foreign Ministers, to meet every three or four months, was created. At Potsdam later in 1945 the three powers decided to include China and France in this Conference of Foreign Ministers. It was also decided to invite China and the Provisional Government of the French Republic to join in sponsoring the United Nations Conference at San Francisco. This latter decision, though France refused to become a "sponsoring power," created the Big Five conference that met during the San Francisco Conference. This five-power steering group met frequently during the San Francisco Conference, just as a similar group had met during the Paris Conference of 1919 or as the Council of the League had met from 1920 to 1939. The ILO, the World Court, and indeed the League itself continued in quiescence throughout the war. Changing in membership but not in basic pattern, the institutions of international cooperation had survived the League and were ready to be incorporated into the United Nations.

Looked at in historical perspective, the ideas and the institutional arrangements which are incorporated in the United Nations are not new. Indeed they are old and conventional. A world of nation-states, sovereign but held together by a mutual obligation to legal principles and practices, had developed patterns of mutual action. Over three centuries, but particularly since 1814, the development of institutional arrangements became more intensified. The League system was an attempt, and a reasonably successful attempt, to bring the rules and the practices together as the basis for a more constant collaboration of the nations. The United Nations is another attempt, more carefully concerted, to do the same things. Each experiment, whether large or small, is based on the experience of the past.

Chapter 2. PLANNING FOR THE UNITED NATIONS ORGANIZATION

PLANNING IN THE UNITED STATES

No international agreement has ever been more carefully prepared for than the Charter of the United Nations. The work of preparation proceeded first and most intensively in the government of the United States. It began as soon as President Roosevelt agreed, early in the war, that the establishment of a general security organization would be desirable as one of the products of an allied victory. Indeed it is fair to say that the United Nations owes its existence to American initiative. The "Atlantic Charter," enunciated in 1941, by the American President and the English prime minister, is the only statement of general war objectives made before the Moscow Declaration of 1943, and the Atlantic Charter made no reference to any international organization, though it refers, as it were incidentally, to a possible future "establishment of a wider and more permanent system of general security."

The American Secretary of State Mr. Cordell Hull had always been a confirmed and uncritical believer in a general international organization; indeed, Mr. Hull had been a believer in the League of Nations. Though this uncritical faith may not have been shared by his immediate superior, the President, or by some of his subordinates like Mr. Sumner Welles, Mr. Hull always gave full and complete support to planning for a general international organization and to the plans that his subordinates made. A planning group was created in the Department of State early in the war.

It was acutely remembered in Washington that preparations

for the Peace Conference of Paris of 1919 were made by a semi-private group, the Inquiry, organized under the direction of Colonel House. The Department of State had been left completely outside in planning for a conference whose decisions it would be required to carry out. Other departments, like the Navy and War Departments which had at least a contingent interest, were similarly excluded. It is true that the Inquiry enlisted many eminent men whose knowledge was full and sound and that the American representatives received all the competent advice that they desired. But the legitimate and important complaint remained that the business of the Department of State should be done by that Department and by no one else.

This mistake was not to be repeated after the Second World War. The planning for the peace treaties to be made after that war and for the security or general international organization which was to replace the League was to be carried on by the Department of State.

The planning was begun on a small scale before the United States entered the war and was developed seriously at a time when the war was going badly. Because the attitude of the public toward an international organization was considered doubtful, the planning work of the Department was conducted in the utmost secrecy. Indeed, many officers of the Department itself were not certain what problems the planners were handling. The secrecy, perhaps excessive, was firmly insisted on by the persons immediately responsible for the work. Mr. Leo Pasvolsky, Special Assistant to the Secretary of State, was given direct and complete charge of the work. He advised the Secretary himself and was completely trusted by Mr. Hull. Mr. Stettinius, who succeeded Mr. Hull, had almost as great confidence in him. Mr. Pasvolsky continued to have direct and effective responsibility until his resignation in 1946 after the United Nations was in operation.

In February, 1941, a Division of Special Research was created within the Department to explore all problems related to the peace settlement, to collect information and compress it within the covers of handbooks to be used by negotiators, and to indicate possible lines of policy. This division was soon divided into two, a Division of Political Studies, which contained the specific planning work related to the peace settlement and to international organization, and a Division of Economic Studies, which was to do similar planning in the economic field. The officers assigned to the latter division were obviously miscast, since the Department as a whole, high American officials generally, and most foreign governments, looked upon the war and a possible future peace as a purely political matter. The Division of Economic Studies worked largely in a vacuum until it was abolished in the "first Stettinius reorganization" of the Department, that of January 15, 1944. Its personnel, however, formed the nucleus of most of the new divisions of the very important and greatly expanded economic offices of the Department.

The Division of Political Studies, under the direction of Mr. Harley Notter, recruited its officers largely from outside the Department. They included a large number of men and women of academic attainment. The entire country was represented. Their point of view was, for the most part, that of fervent believers in international organization. Most of the experts recruited had been strong supporters of the League of Nations, and a few of them had been employees of the League. They were also, for the most part, believers in moderation and rationality in international affairs, hoping that intelligence and good will could reorganize a shattered world. Almost nothing that the planners did in regard to general questions (such as those of German boundaries or economic organization) was accepted even by the Department as its firm policy. But much of what they did in planning for a general international organization was at least discussed on higher levels.

When Mr. Stettinius became Under Secretary of State, he arranged a reorganization of the Department which became effective on January 15, 1944. There was created an Office of Special Political Affairs in charge of political "postwar" planning, responsible through its director to Mr. Leo Pasvolsky as Special Assistant to the Secretary of State. Within this office two divisions were created (largely out of the existing personnel), a Division of International Security and Organization Affairs, responsible for planning related to the general international organization and particularly for Dumbarton Oaks, and a Division of Territorial Studies, responsible for the planning related to the peace settlements. In December, 1944, the latter was abolished, and three divisions were created for the international planning: International Security Affairs, International Organization Affairs, and Dependent Area Affairs. These three divisions did the immediate planning for the San Francisco Conference.

In the American system of government, technicians, however competent, are never allowed to have their way. All questions, however abstruse, must be settled by the plain sense of the political representatives of the people. The sooner that Congress is brought into the discussion of technical matters, the greater the amount of approval that the plans of the experts will receive. This was true even in the Roosevelt administration when the prestige of the President was great enough to cause Congress to accept policies which not all its members may have understood. The introduction of members of the Senate and the House, or of distinguished and presumably competent members of the public, into the discussion and decision of matters of technical complexity is a practice which may discourage the experts without illuminating policy. Nevertheless the gap between the expert and the public and political point of view must be bridged. To that end a series of committees was set up in the Department of State. The committees were composed of high departmental officials, occasional high officials from other Departments, and representatives of Congress and of the public. Senator Warren Austin and Representative Charles Eaton, early members of the so-called "political subcommittee," gained there an acquaintance with the problems of the Department which greatly helped their effectiveness, one as United States representative to the Security Council and the other as ranking Republican member of the House Committee on Foreign Affairs. The public was represented by publicists and public figures like Myron Taylor, Anne O'Hare McCormick, and Hamilton Fish Armstrong. The various committees discussed all sorts of subjects and from time to time considered and revised policy documents prepared by the experts in the Department. When approved by one of the policy committees, the document could go forward not merely as the work of the expert staff but as work provisionally acceptable from a political point of view. Clumsy as the committees were, they gave a sense of reality to the work of the experts which would have been otherwise lacking. Furthermore, though the very existence of the committees was secret, individual members of the committees served as channels through which departmental thinking could more easily reach the public.

The last meeting of any of the committees occurred in the fall of 1943. With the first Stettinius reorganization of 1944 a new and more formal set of policy committees was established: the Post-war Committee and the Policy Committee, both composed of top officials of the Department and of no one else and both practically identical in membership. From January, 1944, on, the departmental approval of the work of the experts in the planning divisions was given by these committees. A special "Agenda" Committee was created in the Department to review and approve the plans for a general international organization later presented at Dumbarton Oaks.

Representatives of the Army and of the Navy were brought in, through methods considered appropriate, in regular and *ad hoc* committees concerned with planning. The Interior and other Departments interested in particular matters likewise took part.

The administration in Washington is not, nor has it ever been, coordinated. It comprises a series of rival departments, just as much now as in the days of Hamilton and Jefferson. Just as Hamilton tried to control foreign affairs though Jefferson was Secretary of State, so heads of other departments have tried to assume the functions of the Secretary of State in modern times. Hull was hard to supplant or to by-pass because of his prestige with the Cabinet, the President, the Congress, and the country. But always the Secretary of State, whether in a Cabinet meeting or in conference with the President himself, must compete with other Secretaries perhaps equally in favor and more readily listened to. The Department of State may be entrusted with the special function of giving advice on foreign affairs, but that does not prevent other Departments from using their personnel, granted them by Congress for other purposes, for trying to perform the functions of the Department of State.

Above the executive departments, and supreme in enunciating the policy of the administration, is the President. He makes the final decisions on the advice of whatever advisers (official or private) he wishes to consult. President Roosevelt, once committed to the support of an international organization, remained steadfast, though he took no special interest in its nature except that it must further his military advisers' requirements for "security."

In the United States planning for the United Nations, as well as in the League previously and in the United Nations which was to follow, the difference and possible conflict between two types of international organizations existed. What was foreshadowed in the Atlantic Charter was a "security organization," *i.e.*, some sort of international agency which would minimize war, or at least cause it to be won by the right people—an organization which would ensure the "security" of the allies and in particular the national security of the great powers among the United Nations. The official planning started with the concept of a security organization, an agency which would try to ensure that the allies, when they had won the war, would be able to maintain their consequent international position, without, it was hoped, being obliged to fight future wars. Those members of the United Nations who were strong enough would put their national security ahead of any sort of limitations on their independence which might contribute to an effective world organization. For instance, the security of the United States was to be served by an

international organization which would help the United States
to maintain its position and would not limit that position in any
important respect. The phrase "international peace and security," the maintenance of which is placed as the first purpose of
the United Nations in the Dumbarton Oaks Proposals, was a
phrase invented to signify the concept we have been outlining—
a system or situation the first aim of which is to safeguard the
national security of the great allies and incidentally to minimize
international armed conflict, since peace on the whole contributes
to security.

Because the Dumbarton Oaks Proposals were drafted by the
big powers which were to be the permanent members of the
Security Council, they were able to stake out their claim to a
predominant position in the prospective organization.

As soon as the first proposals for a security organization were
developed, it became clear that other functions and activities besides security would have to be entrusted to the new international
organization.   It became known in departmental planning as the
"general international organization." If the proposed organization had been limited to a league to keep the peace, the other
international functions performed within the League of Nations
system would have gone unsupervised and undirected. No one,
least of all internationally minded Americans, wished that. The
general international organization was then to be *first of all* a
security organization but, second only to that, a general organization capable of being entrusted with a great variety of collective
international functions.

Planning in the Department of State seemed to be largely in a
vacuum until the foreign ministers of the United Kingdom, the
United States, and the Soviet Union met in Moscow in October,
1943. To that meeting the American delegates carried a paper
stating their policy toward the creation of a general international
organization, and from the meeting emerged the Declaration of
the Four Nations on General Security of October 30, which said
among other things:

That they recognize the necessity of establishing at the earliest practicable date a general international organization, based on the principle of the sovereign equality of all peace-loving states, and open to membership by all such states, large and small, for the maintenance of international peace and security.

This statement, signed by the British, American, and Soviet foreign ministers and by the Chinese ambassador, was the pronunciamento on the basis of which the organization later known as the United Nations was created. This statement (into which the term "peace-loving" crept, in Moscow, into a generally acceptable American draft) includes also the basic references to "sovereign equality" and to "international peace and security" which were to be such essential features of the international organization as finally formed. After the acceptance and promulgation of this Moscow statement, the American planners could proceed to elaborate their outlines and to prepare for the next stage in securing acceptance.

The Dumbarton Oaks Conversations

The government of the United States, still pushing its project, initiated the Dumbarton Oaks Conversations, which took place in the summer of 1944. These Conversations were held to discuss plans for the general international organization proposed at Moscow. They were held between the four powers responsible for the Moscow Declaration. The Soviet Union refused to participate in four-power group conversations on the ground that it was not at war with Japan. Consequently, two sets of conversations were held, the first set between the United States, the United Kingdom, and the Soviet Union, and the second set between the two former and China.

The British-Soviet-American conversations came first. Plans were put forward by the three governments, and a jointly acceptable set of "proposals" was agreed upon by the tripartite conference. When this set of conversations was over, the representatives of the Chinese Republic were welcomed and engaged in conversations with the Americans and the British. Though the Chinese put forward many proposals differing from those already agreed to by the other three delegations, the Chinese delegation did not press its own ideas and accepted what had been approved jointly by the other three delegations. The Chinese proposals were oriented less toward a security organization and more toward a general welfare organization than those of the other three powers. Some of the Chinese proposals had a better fate at San Francisco and were included in the final Charter.

When the Conversations, and the accompanying secrecy, were over, the Proposals were released to the public and became the subject of intensive governmental propaganda in the United States and, to a lesser degree, in other nations. They met with a mixed reception. Rather to the surprise of the American planners, they were cordially received by the so-called "nationalistic" or "isolationist" press in the United States because they yielded no national sovereignty and because they emphasized the problem of "security." Americans who had been supporters of the League of Nations were disappointed in the Proposals because they seemed to sacrifice the general welfare to this very concept of security. But most persons in most countries approved the proposed project of reestablishing a general international organization.

The Dumbarton Oaks Proposals seem bare and bloodless today in comparison with the expanded form, much modified in emphasis, which they assumed in the Charter of the United Nations. The Charter (excluding the lengthy Statute of the International Court of Justice) is two and one-half times as long as the Proposals and far more specific. Dumbarton Oaks was an awkward sketch, the Charter a fully elaborated plan.

The United Nations, as proposed at Dumbarton Oaks, was clearly in its primary function an organization "to maintain international peace and security," although it was also intended "to achieve international cooperation in the solution of international economic, social and other humanitarian problems." It underscored the fact that it was to be composed of, and open to, "peace-loving" states. This meant in fact that it was open to those states making war against Germany; it was clearly intended to be the continuation of a wartime alliance. The "sovereign equality" of these states was carefully stated.

The principal organs of the organization were to be a general assembly, a security council, an international court of justice, and a secretariat. The general assembly, composed of all members, was to be merely a body for discussing international problems. The security council received the emphasis. The key provision in the Dumbarton Oaks Proposals is that which says that "members of the Organization should by Charter confer on the Security Council primary responsibility for the maintenance of international peace and security and should agree that in carrying out these duties under this responsibility, it should act on their behalf" (Chapter VI. B.1). A long and complicated procedure was provided, with the security council as the focus.

A much shorter and briefer summary statement was made of the arrangements for an economic and social council, which was to be subsidiary to the general assembly and was concerned with "international economic, social and other humanitarian matters."

A court and a secretariat were provided for without much detail.

And everything (as in the Charter later on) was subject to the right of the warring governments to act as they saw fit in regard to their enemies, either now or in the future. "No provision of the Charter should preclude action taken or authorized in relation to enemy states as a result of the present war by the governments having responsibility for such action" (Chapter XII. 2).

Several questions, including "the question of voting procedure in the Security Council," were left for "future" (*i.e.*, three-power) decision. No agreement was reached at Dumbarton Oaks as to the extent to which the great powers were to have the "veto," *i.e.*, to be able to block decisions or actions of various sorts agreed to by the rest of the proposed security council. The Dumbarton Oaks Proposals did not attempt to resolve the question as to how great-power prominence might be reconciled with the "sovereign equality" of the "peace-loving states" that were to be members of the organization.

An omission at Dumbarton Oaks was a program for mandates and colonies. This also would have to be considered later.

In so many respects the proposals of the United States formed the basis for the agreed draft which came out of Dumbarton Oaks that the United States might be blamed for the overattention to security in the narrow sense. But it should be remembered that the American draft proposed at Dumbarton Oaks was not necessarily what the United States might be willing to agree to later on. It was the maximum that the United States government was willing to commit itself in 1944 to support.

PLANNING IN OTHER COUNTRIES

What plans for an international organization were under consideration by other governments, the secrecy of foreign offices does not yet permit us, for the most part, to know. The British government instituted in its Foreign Office a small group which was to concern itself with problems of international organization. Prof. C. K. Webster, a veteran adviser from the 1919 Conference of Paris, was entrusted with the direction of its work. His brochure on the procedure of the Conference of Vienna had been a handbook at Paris; his experience at Paris was to be a handbook for the new conference to come.

The British government was more limited in its resources than was the United States, in men, in time, and in facilities, for planning of the sort in which the American Department of State was so extensively engaged. Other governments, including those in exile, were more limited still. The Soviet Union and China made careful preparations for Dumbarton Oaks. France was occupied until 1944, and its provisional government, headed by General de Gaulle, had to rely largely on the already existent ideas of persons who had been officials before 1940. Most other governments devoted at least a part of the time of some of their able officials to problems of international organization, and certainly the amendments to Dumbarton Oaks which they suggested showed that a great amount of intelligence and ingenuity was expended even by small governments. Such comparatively unhampered governments as those of Canada and Australia had strengthened their departments of external affairs and were devoting increasing attention to problems of future international organization.

Most of the nations which were to gather at San Francisco had been members of the League of Nations and had found the League satisfactory as a general international organization (until the point where it foundered on the pusillanimity of some of its great powers) and were disposed to plan with a view to a United Nations that would be a continuation, in a somewhat more rational and effective form, of the old League. The planners in the United States government also were greatly affected by the League system. All of them were familiar with it, and some of them had been officials in it. The new international organization was to be superior to the League, but the friendliest of critics could see a great similarity.

When the foreign officials began to plan, they realized that they must plan in consideration of the Dumbarton Oaks Proposals. By fiat of the Big Four of the United Nations, the Dumbarton Oaks Proposals were put before the world as the plan on which the great powers had agreed.

Yalta

The Yalta Conference is already stigmatized as a conference at which the United States bought too little for too much. In early 1945, however, generous gifts to the Soviet Union seemed calculated to stimulate the Soviet government to cooperate more fully with American plans, by pushing to a speedy conclusion the war with Germany, by entering and helping in the war with Japan, and by sharing in the establishment of the international organization. If Yalta looked like hard bargaining on one side, it may have looked like hard bargaining on the other also. The Soviet Union was certain to be important in the Pacific, whether it actually fought Japan or not.

As far as the general international organization went, the Yalta Conference took, rather painfully, three decisions supplementary to Dumbarton Oaks. The first was on voting in the proposed security council, where the Yalta conferees put forward the subsequently notorious veto, though their statement on this point was intentionally ambiguous. In brief, the veto meant that any one of the permanent members of the security council could block any action and many discussions which it disliked.

The second important decision of Yalta was to strengthen the voting power of the Soviet Union by giving the White Russian and the Ukrainian republics separate membership in the United Nations, though they were parts of the Soviet Union.

The third significant decision at Yalta was to set up as part of the organization an international trusteeship system which might be applicable to three categories of territories: (a) former mandates under the League of Nations, (b) territories to be detached from enemy states as a result of the existing war, and (c) other territories which the authority responsible for their administration wished to place under trusteeship.

At Yalta also it was decided to send out invitations to a United Nations conference to establish an international organization. This conference was to meet in San Francisco on April 25, 1945, and was to have the Dumbarton Oaks Proposals as its agenda. Invitations were to be sent to all the original signatories of the Declaration of United Nations and to governments associated with them who had gone to war with the "common enemy" by March 1, 1945.

It is useful to note in addition that the Yalta Conference decided that regular consultations between the three foreign secretaries should continue to be held at intervals of three or four months. This institutionalized group meeting was much like the Supreme Council of the Allied Powers following the Paris Peace Conference of 1919. Like the latter, it was intended to be a body dealing with the problems of the war just ended, while the United Nations was to deal with the problems of the future. At the tripartite conference at Berlin (Potsdam) in August, 1945, the Council of Foreign Ministers was expanded to include all the Big Five.

Chapter 3. THE SAN FRANCISCO CONFERENCE:
ORGANIZATION

The San Francisco Conference was sometimes referred to by the Americans there as the conference to end all conferences. It was the greatest international conference ever held, and it was hoped that no conference so large need ever be held again. And perhaps no great conference has ever been so successful in attaining its objectives. For in spite of all difficulties it did draw up a Charter which commanded the general approval and support of all the nations represented.

PLANNING THE CONFERENCE

The Call

The Yalta conferees decided that the Conference should be called. The Chinese government, which had taken part in Dumbarton Oaks, agreed to join the three Yalta governments as a "sponsoring power" of the Conference. The French government refused. The nature of the invitation and those to be invited had been decided at Yalta. Since the Conference was to be held in the United States, the American Secretary of State Mr. Stettinius and the ambassadors of the other three sponsoring powers approved the detailed plans.

The Date

The Conference was to meet on April 25, 1945. The position of the United States government had been that plans for a new league of nations should not (like those for the old League of 1919) be made during the peace conference. The plans for the League had become entangled in the negotiations for peace terms and consequently (as in the American Senate) become blurred with those terms in the eyes of the peoples and legislatures of the world. This time the United States government wanted a separate conference devoted exclusively to plans for a general international organization. Further (again thinking of the Senate and the League), President Roosevelt wanted the plans for the general international organization made *during the war* so that the enthusiasm for the war would guarantee their acceptance in the United States and in other nations. Consequently, the sooner the Conference could be held, the sooner the plans could be ratified, and the international organization instituted. At the time of Yalta the European war was apparently expected to last much longer than it did—to the end of the summer campaigns of 1946 was the common estimate; and the Japanese war was expected to last a year after the surrender of Germany. Consequently, April 25, 1945, was a reasonable date to select for a United Nations conference on international organization. It was certainly never thought that V–E Day would come long before the Conference finished its deliberations or that the surrender of Japan would come long before the Charter was ratified. A going world organization while the war still continued was the aim.

As sometimes happened during the war, no sooner had a clear decision been made by the Big Three than the difficulties of carrying it out seemed overwhelming. There was a strong "unofficial" movement favoring the postponement of the proposed conference. It was encouraged by the sudden death of President Roosevelt on April 12. But the government of the United States, suspecting that a postponement even for a short time meant no conference at all, went ahead with its plans, and the delegates arrived without difficulty at the appointed time and place.

The Length of the Conference

The Conference was intended to be short—six weeks at most. It was to be a demonstration of allied might and solidarity and of the effective leadership of the sponsoring powers. Since the sponsoring powers' proposals were well-known, and the powers had agreed upon them, the other members of the Conference could propose amendments and could press them but would obviously have to agree to what the big powers wanted. Consequently it was believed that the Conference need not last long. A few weeks would satisfy diplomatic amenities and national pride, would allow for the necessary speech making, would give the great powers time to polish their proposals, and would allow the lesser powers time to accept them gracefully. As it was, the Conference lasted longer than had been intended, and its work was actual and not nominal. But it did a great deal of work in a short time and eventually did not stretch out to a much greater length than had been contemplated.

The Place of Meeting

San Francisco proved to be an admirable site for the Conference. Its choice was determined by the fact that the United States was not only the chief initiator of the project of the United Nations but was the only one of the Big Five on whose territory a conference could be held in comfort. Perhaps also only the United States was in a position to bear the expenses of a great conference. Otherwise the competition might have been keen between Paris and some Eastern European city. The United States was safe and comfortable. Washington, the obvious choice, was too official, and it was hoped that the governments would send, as they did for the most part, other delegates than those who were accredited to the American government and stationed in Washington. San Francisco was on the West Coast, relatively near the far eastern war, near China, the Soviet Union, and Australia and New Zealand.

San Francisco had the disadvantage of distance from the old established centers of power. But the governments and the public utilities cooperated on methods of rapid communication. Personnel could fly in United States Army planes. Telephone and telegraph were as rapid as the governments concerned desired. The distance had the very happy effect of compelling the delegates to forget their daily preoccupations at home and think about international organization.

San Francisco, a metropolis noted for its hospitality, accommodated its visitors gracefully. To men and women from beleaguered or devastated countries, the Conference city provided not merely comfort but luxury. From the point of view of personal liking, delegates to the San Francisco Conference would have agreed to choose San Francisco as the permanent seat of the United Nations.

MEMBERSHIP IN THE CONFERENCE

The conferees at Yalta decided that the signatories to the Declaration by United Nations of January 1, 1942, plus those other states that became eligible by declaring war on the Axis by March 1, 1945, should be invited to attend the Conference. As the Yalta Agreement on World Organization expressed it: "The nations invited to this conference should be (*a*) the United Nations as they existed on 8 February 1945; and (*b*) such of the Associated Nations as have declared war on the common enemy by 1 March 1945. . . ."

A number of states which had no doubt been friendly to the United Nations but had preserved a neutrality during the course of the war were influenced by the Yalta statement to declare war and to make themselves available for an invitation to San Francisco. Among these were a number of Latin-American states, whose interest in one way or another may not have been a matter of general concern. Among those who qualified at the eleventh hour were also Turkey, Egypt, Saudi Arabia, Syria, and Lebanon —all of them vocal at San Francisco. The complete list of sponsoring and invited powers included forty-six governments.

There were doubtful cases. At Yalta the Soviet representative, presumably afraid that his government would not have sufficient friendly support at the Conference, secured the approval of Mr. Roosevelt and Mr. Churchill to the proposition that the Byelorussian and Ukrainian republics (integral parts of the Soviet

Union) should be separate members of the Conference.   The conference of American republics at Mexico in the spring of 1945 had agreed to support the admission of Argentina to good standing in United Nations affairs if Argentina fulfilled certain conditions. These conditions having been fulfilled, they supported Argentina for membership in the San Francisco Conference.   Poland had not yet achieved one united government which was recognized by both the United States and the United Kingdom on one hand and the Soviet Union on the other, and so no invitation was issued to the Polish government.

In accordance with their agreement, the United States and the United Kingdom sponsored the admission of the two subsidiary Soviet republics, and the Conference was prepared to agree.   The Soviet delegation led a slightly disingenuous opposition to the admission of Argentina.   Mr. Molotov hinted at a bargain.   Argentina should not be admitted, he maintained, because its government was fascist.   But if the Conference admitted delegates from the Soviet-recognized government of Poland, perhaps the Soviet government would no longer object to the admission of Argentina.   The actual bargain, if there was one, comprised Byelorussia and the Ukraine vs. Argentina.   At any rate, these three entities were admitted to the Conference on April 30.   The Conference refused to admit delegates of the Soviet-sponsored government of Poland, but a place was left for subsequent Polish signature to the Charter.   A Danish delegation was admitted to the Conference as soon as Denmark was liberated.   The total number of delegations which finally were present amounted to fifty.

A number of the governments represented at San Francisco were far from democratic in character.   A number of them had been reluctant to take any clear stand with the United Nations against the Axis powers.   The Soviet government was not at war with Japan and during the latter part of the Conference was not actually engaged in any war at all, though the United States, the United Kingdom, and China were girding their loins for an effort equal to that which had ended in Europe.   Furthermore, two governments represented, those of India and of the Philippines, were not legally independent. Nevertheless all the delegations took their places and maintained their points of view, as delegates of independent governments should. The least important question, in evaluating the suggestions of a delegation, was its government's recent or past political service to the United Nations as a wartime ally.

The Conference, compared with other past international conferences of comparable size, had a large representation of Latin-American states, a scant representation of European states, and was attended by representatives of African and Asiatic states which had never appeared internationally before (see list of delegations on page 37).

The Agenda

The invitation to the Conference had been to attend a conference "to prepare a charter for a general international organization for the maintenance of international peace and security" and suggested that the Dumbarton Oaks Proposals serve as a basis for the Charter. The formal agenda for the Conference was agreed upon at a meeting of the Heads of Delegations on April 27, 1947. This meeting decided that the agenda should be "the Dumbarton Oaks Proposals, as supplemented at the Crimea [Yalta] Conference, and by the Chinese proposals agreed to by the Sponsoring Governments, and the comments thereon submitted by the participating countries."

When issued as a Conference publication, the agenda had attained the size of a large volume. It was not, at any rate, restricted to the text of Dumbarton Oaks.

The Framework of the Conference

The Conference was a group of people who met under certain conditions, physical, diplomatic, and political. The physical arrangements were adapted to the political. The organizers de-

THE FIFTY DELEGATIONS AT SAN FRANCISCO

Sponsoring states and France (Big Five):

China
Soviet Union
United Kingdom
United States
France

European:

Belgium
Byelorussian S.S.R.
Czechoslovakia
Denmark
Greece
Luxembourg
Netherlands
Norway
Ukrainian S.S.R.
Yugoslavia

Arab Union:

Egypt
Iraq
Lebanon
Saudi Arabia
Syria

British Commonwealth:

Australia
Canada
India
New Zealand
Union of South Africa

Other African:

Ethiopia
Liberia

Other Asiatic:

Iran
Philippine Commonwealth
Turkey

Latin-American:

Argentina
Bolivia
Brazil
Chile
Colombia
Costa Rica
Cuba
Dominican Republic
Ecuador
El Salvador
Guatemala
Haiti
Honduras
Mexico
Nicaragua
Panama
Paraguay
Peru
Uruguay
Venezuela

cided how the Conference would work, and then the physical arrangements were made to fit these needs.

Preliminary arrangements for the Conference were approved by a four-power group consisting of the American Secretary of State representing the United States and the British, Soviet, and Chinese ambassadors to Washington representing the other sponsoring powers. The detailed arrangements for the pattern of organization of the Conference were in the hands of the American Department of State. This was because the United States was the host country, and a long tradition of international practice determines that the country in which a conference is held shall make the arrangements and provide the services necessary for the conference.   Since planning for the establishment of a general international organization had been in the hands of the Office of Special Political Affairs and of its divisions of International Organization Affairs, International Security Affairs, and Dependent Area Affairs, the Director of the Office, Mr. Alger Hiss, was designated by Mr. Stettinius, the Secretary of State (who would be temporary president of the Conference), as the temporary Secretary-General.   Mr. Hiss, with the help of the staff of the office and the divisions, and with much aid from other parts of the Department, began the organization of a conference staff on a large and inevitably increasing scale.   The personnel involved was either lent by the Department of State or was paid for by the generous appropriation for international conferences which had been farsightedly inserted in the United States budget for the year.   Other Departments in Washington also lent a limited number of persons.   The armed services and the local and state authorities in San Francisco were generous in providing personnel for technical and housekeeping jobs.

The United States had been host to no important international conference since the Washington Conference of 1921–1922, which, after all, had been attended by only a few states.   The largest conferences in which it had participated were the Inter-American conferences, for which a long and distinctive tradition, not capable of transplantation, has grown up.   No general international conferences of moment had been held since 1933, and the United States lacked the experience common to much of the civilized world of participation in Council and Assembly meetings of the League of Nations.

Many members of the staff of the part of the State Department directly concerned possessed a vast amount of information on international conferences, though few of them had had much experience.   Other parts of the Department, notably the Division of International Conferences, gave their expert help.   A recent publication of the Carnegie Endowment for International Peace, Vladimir D. Pastuhov's A *Guide to the Practice of International*

Conferences, served as the text for the officers of the Department. No doubt some of the formalism and intricacy of the San Francisco Conference was due to the fact that an amateur group of directors tried to do everything in the most traditional way. But if the persons responsible for the organization of the Conference, from the Secretary of State down, were amateurs, certainly the conduct of the Conference was one of the most brilliant amateur feats of diplomatic history.

Perhaps only Americans, with a gift both for organization and for improvisation, could have created so quickly and so effectively a large new group to do an almost unprecedented thing: to hold a gigantic conference in wartime and to make it run smoothly.

The Delegates and the Secretariat

Conference personnel consists of two parts. The most important part, indeed the essential part, consists of delegates of the states participating in the conference. It is they, or their governments, who will make the decisions of the conference. They will be accompanied, in modern times, by large numbers of advisers. The first task of those who arrange a conference is to try to facilitate the self-directed activity of the delegates and their staffs, whether their contentment and satisfaction is a matter of food, drink, or carbon paper. But delegates cannot perform their functions as conferees without a conference secretariat, composed of people who will help the delegates to do their work in a reasonably efficient and effective way and who will provide them with all sorts of technical assistance to promote this efficiency. It is not the function of the secretariat to make the decisions of the conference. Its function is to facilitate the making of decisions. In accordance with diplomatic tradition the Secretariat of the San Francisco Conference was provided by the United States. Though a few persons were detailed to it by other delegations, the Secretariat consisted almost entirely of American personnel. It organized and guided the Conference with skill, graciousness, and effectiveness.

Delegates, particularly those coming from countries with small professional classes, often assume that their relative importance is such that all who facilitate their activities are servants, much as a doorkeeper is a servant.   Members of the Secretariat at San Francisco sometimes had the experience of being treated like servants by delegates of lesser education, social standing, and even wealth than themselves.   Most delegates, however, and particularly those with a wide international experience, made good use of the help afforded by excellent technical assistance. Many chairmen of committees, statesmen in their own right at home, found themselves assisted as secretaries of committees by distinguished political scientists or experts in international law and they relied on them not merely for housekeeping arrangements but for expert advice.   An interesting example of the services performed by the Secretariat was in the preparation of rapporteurs' reports from the Conference Committees.   These reports are a reasoned summary of the work of the Committee, the most important record of its work, and the channel through which it exerts its effect.   In all cases the members of the Secretariat assisted in the drafting of these reports.   In many cases the reports were almost entirely written by members of the Secretariat.

To surround the delegates with services, including that of technical information and help, and yet to allow them their initiative was, then, the function of the Secretariat.   To plan a procedure for the Conference, always subject to the approval (or disapproval) of the Conference itself, was part—an important part—of this function.

The major decisions as to the organization and procedure of the Conference, with the exception of the question of the presidency, had been made in advance, but were ratified by the Conference itself in the appropriate ways.

CONFERENCE PROCEDURE

A conference consists of delegations which are autonomous and which cannot be coerced. By international custom each has one vote. At San Francisco it was decided that decisions should be made by a special majority of two-thirds of the delegations voting.

The Conference was elaborately organized. In addition to the inevitable Credentials Committee, the Conference had three general committees. Two were to guide the Conference: the Steering Committee, consisting of the heads of all delegations, and the Executive Committee, comprised of the heads of the Big Five and nine other delegations (Australia, Brazil, Canada, Chile, Czechoslovakia, Iran, Mexico, the Netherlands, and Yugoslavia) which prepared business for the Steering Committee. The third, the Coordination Committee, was composed of delegates of the states represented on the Executive Committee. These delegates were chosen for their technical competence and had the responsibility of consolidating into one coherent charter, properly phrased, the texts as agreed upon by the several technical committees. The Coordination Committee was advised by the Advisory Commission of Jurists, who examined the drafts on legal points and reported back to the Coordination Committee.

The Conference must also have a president, who according to custom would be the head of the delegation of the host country, in this case Mr. Edward Stettinius, Secretary of State. There was a contrary precedent, however, the Lausanne Conference of 1922, which was called jointly by three powers and presided over in rotation by the chairmen of their three delegations. The Soviet delegation at San Francisco insisted that this precedent be followed. Since the four sponsoring powers were in the position of joint hosts, they should consequently share the presidency. This contention was accepted, and therefore the chief delegates of the four powers took turns in presiding over the plenary meetings of the Conference, session by session. Mr. Stettinius, however, was continuously the chairman of the Steering Committee and of the Executive Committee.

The actual work of drafting the chapters and articles for the Charter was assigned to four commissions, each of which was in theory to direct the work of several "technical" committees, of which there were twelve. Each state that was a member of the Conference was represented on each commission and committee. Commission I was concerned with General Provisions, Commission II with the General Assembly, Commission III with the Security Council, and Commission IV with Judicial Organization. The various sections of the Dumbarton Oaks Proposals were divided among the technical committees, and Committees II/4 (on Trusteeship) and IV/2 (on Legal Problems) had additional subjects assigned that were not covered by the Dumbarton Oaks Proposals.

The commissions were created to determine the general principles to be included in the Charter, to give directions to the committees under them, to receive and coordinate the reports of the committees, and to pass them on to the Conference in plenary meeting, where the Conference would give final approval to them. In fact, the commissions served no real substantive purpose in the Conference, though they did provide a spectacle for the public, since their meetings were open and were held in the Opera House, and a number of honorary positions for delegates. Early in the Conference each commission met formally and then remained quiescent until it met again toward the end to receive and to approve the recommendations of its committees. The technical committees had done such a thorough job that there was no need (and no time) for substantive work by the commissions.

The twelve technical committees did the drafting of the Charter. On the basis of that portion of the Dumbarton Oaks Proposals assigned to them, they each drafted one or more sections of the Charter, using complete freedom to revise, to add to, or to subtract from the Proposals. Though the work of the committees was uneven in both substance and form, their drafts were a comprehensive rewriting and expansion of the Proposals.

When once an article for the Charter had been accepted by two-thirds of the committee (on which each delegation was represented), it was bound to go through to the end and to appear, except as revised verbally by the Coordination Committee, in the Charter itself. Some of the organizers of the Conference had expected that the Steering Committee, as directed by the Executive Committee, would intervene in major questions of policy and give orders to the technical committees, but the great majority of delegations saw at once that they could express themselves most effectively in the technical committees. As a result, the powers that would have preferred a more tightly controlled Conference were obliged to yield and to fight their battles in the committee rooms themselves. This meant that the vital struggles in the Conference occurred at the drafting stage. Many committee rooms, each in its time, became the center of the struggle over essential questions such as expulsion of members, the veto, or the purposes of the Economic and Social Council.

Politically, of course, no committee was left to do exactly as it liked, since a clear indication on the part of any one of the three Yalta powers that it would insist on its own point of view was in every case eventually accepted by the committee, for fear that otherwise the Conference would break up and no Charter be signed. The great powers yielded, however, much more than they intended, and much of the tone and temper of the Charter was the result of free discussion and decision at San Francisco.

Each committee had its chairman and its rapporteur. These positions were assigned to distinguished delegates from nonsponsoring powers. Most chairmen were competent; a few really directed the work of their committee. The rapporteurs were responsible for the drafting of the committee reports to the commissions but had no other actual function since they did not personally present or support their reports in the commission meetings. Each committee had a secretary, assigned from the Conference Secretariat, who provided technical advice and assistance when called on by the committee and who was responsible for the preparation for the committee meetings and the reporting from them. Otherwise, the committee was its own master. Large delegations assigned individual delegates and advisers to the work of individual committees. Small delegations were sometimes in the position where one delegate must cover most or all of the entire field of the Charter.

The committees met at irregular intervals; one held twenty-nine meetings during the five weeks devoted to committee work; one held only six. Many subcommittees existed. Many references (behind the scenes) to the Big Five and some references to governments themselves hindered the work and prolonged the Conference. From the headquarters of the United States delegation, which was also the meeting place of the Big Five, came incessant pressure, exercised in many indirect ways, to hurry. As inevitably happens, as soon as the political disputes that had held up the work of the committees were resolved, the big delegations wished to sign the Charter and go home. The enormous final burden of completing the drafts and "coordinating" the Charter had to be accomplished under great pressure at the end, mostly by the Coordination Committee, the chairmen and secretaries of the committees, and the Conference Secretariat. The final deadline was met. The Conference gave formal approval to the Charter on June 25, 1945, and it was signed the next day.

THE DELEGATIONS

Each government represented in the Conference appointed a delegation at its discretion. A few delegations were small. Many of them were extremely large and contained a vast number of advisers, assistants, supernumerary politicians and military people, as well as clerks and stenographers. For example, the official list of May 28 gives 3 persons in the delegation of Luxembourg, 8 in that of Panama, 58 for the United Kingdom, 74 for France, and 174 for the United States. In a number of cases distinguished political leaders came as part of the delegation but returned to their home capitals when it was clear that the work of the Conference would be prolonged. There was, and under wartime conditions could be, little going back and forth. Each delegation was self-contained. The leading delegates were ordinarily accompanied not only by their personal secretaries but by their chief personal advisers as well.

The delegation of the United States was naturally the largest and, except in the nature of the actual delegates themselves, illustrated the composition of a great international delegation of today.

Since the United States has a "presidential" government in which authority in foreign affairs is shared between the President and Congress, the delegation itself was selected by the President and approved by the Senate. It consisted of former Secretary Hull as senior adviser (but Mr. Hull was not well enough to attend); the Secretary of State, Mr. Stettinius, who was chairman of the delegation; the chairmen and ranking minority members of the Senate and House Foreign Affairs Committees, Senators Connally and Vandenberg, and Representatives Bloom and Eaton; Commander Harold E. Stassen, former governor of Minnesota, who was a Republican distinguished for his interest in international organization; and Dean Virginia Gildersleeve of Barnard College representing women. An equal number of alternate delegates of equal ability, though less high position, came next. There followed a long list of advisers, most of them from the Department of State, and special advisers, mostly from the Army and Navy but also from other government departments. These persons represented the United States; they were assisted by dozens of assistants, lesser officers, clerks, and a large administrative staff. The quality of the delegates of the United States was good but not uniformly distinguished. President Roosevelt had wished to secure a delegation politically influential with the Senate and had relied on two things to supplement any diplomatic weakness: the ability of the professional advisers who accompanied the delegation and his own presence in the White House. The President died two weeks before the Conference met. As soon as the government caught its breath after this irreplaceable loss, President Truman requested the United States delegation (then holding preliminary meetings in Washington) to make its own decisions on matters of undecided policy. The delegates did well enough in the Conference; but because they were unskilled in international negotiation, they did not exercise that leadership of the Conference which might have been expected.

The delegation of the United Kingdom, perhaps the next in importance, was organized in much the same way. It was led by Mr. Anthony Eden, the Foreign Secretary, with Mr. Clement Attlee, leader of the parliamentary Labour party, present during the early part of the Conference. The other delegates and assistant delegates were chosen from the parliamentary leaders of the parties which made up the coalition government that was in power. The advisers were chosen from the government departments.

The Soviet delegation worked and lived as a unit in the headquarters on the tenth floor of the St. Francis Hotel, and its spokesmen in committees were spokesmen and not negotiators. Its head, Mr. V. M. Molotov, People's Commissar for Foreign Affairs, was not only the most important delegate at the Conference but also, because of his skill and strength, one of the great personal forces.

The Chinese and French delegations were also large and representative of their governments. Mr. V. K. Wellington Koo, perhaps the most experienced diplomat at the Conference, was in effect the head of the Chinese delegation and added his personal skill to his position. Mr. Georges Bidault, Minister of Foreign Affairs, led the delegation from the Provisional Government of France. This delegation, though able, was somewhat lacking in coordination and uneven in character—a natural enough condition for a great country undergoing the strains of *épuration* and reorganization.

For the most part the lesser governments were represented by the best that their countries possessed. As a result many small delegations contained members who outshone their colleagues from the larger delegations in their ability, knowledge, and diplomatic skill.

Europe, shattered by an essentially European war, was greatly underrepresented at the Conference. The three Soviet states and those states which have come to be called the Soviet satellites sent able delegates who were tied and bound by the political conditions which controlled their governments at home. The smaller states of Western Europe that were present were the Netherlands, which sent a strong delegation; Belgium, whose delegation was liberal and cosmopolitan, especially in the persons of Spaak, Rolin, and De Schryver; Luxembourg, the smallest of all, ably spoken for by Bech and le Gallais; Norway; and, during the latter part of the Conference, Denmark.

The Arab states, for all of whom even independence was a comparative novelty, came to their first great conference well-represented and effectively advised.

The Latin-American states were numerous. Their delegates, mostly chosen from the educated elite, held their own with the delegates of the older states in the European tradition.

The political freedom of the British dominions, their happy political and economic position, and their complete acceptance of the principles of Western European civilization gave them a tremendous advantage in San Francisco. Each of them present (Ireland, a neutral, was not invited) was thoroughly well represented. The Canadians had one of the ablest delegations in San Francisco. The prime minister Mr. Mackenzie King was one of the unpublicized "big men" of the Conference. He was supported by Mr. L. S. St. Laurent as active head of the delegation and by the whole group of brilliant younger men who, under Mr. King's leadership, have made Canada's policy strong and effective. Australia had a delegation which represented its socialist government and also its freedom from conventional prejudices. It had cochairmen, Mr. Forde and Dr. Evatt, but Dr. Evatt, as Minister of External Affairs, had been the originator of Australia's wartime foreign policy and, in particular, of the Canberra Agreement of 1944, which foreshadowed a new Pacific policy. He became the leader of the smaller powers in the Conference. He was seconded and supported by his great friend Peter Fraser, prime minister and Minister of External Affairs of New Zealand, a more conventionally minded but equally fearless leader. Field Marshal Jan Smuts of South Africa led an able delegation which made a less spectacular contribution to the work of the Conference.

Organization of the Secretariat

It is customary for the host country at an international conference to provide the secretary-general of the conference and such other staff as the conference needs. They serve the whole conference and not their own delegation. At San Francisco the Conference, or "international" Secretariat, consisted of hundreds of persons. Most of them were provided by the United States. A few other nations, the British, French, Belgians, Chinese, and Lebanese, lent members to the Secretariat.

Members of the Secretariat served the Conference and its delegations impartially. They were "international civil servants" for the time being. The inevitable loyalty to one's own government felt by all government servants appears to have biased almost not at all the members of the Secretariat in the performance of their functions.

The Secretariat might be analyzed as consisting of groups performing various special functions. The "working" secretariat consisted of a relatively small group of seventy or more persons who served as secretaries of commissions and committees. They worked directly on the substantive business of the Conference. They were obliged to possess knowledge of the problems with which they dealt and of conference procedure. They were recruited largely from the Department of State and the foreign service of the United States and from academic experts in international organization and law.

Next in importance for the substantive work of the Conference were the many officers concerned with the processing of documents. The Conference was almost too well-documented. Every paper officially related to the work of any committee or commission was made a Conference document. The numbers ran into thousands, and the number of copies produced and distributed was usually in the hundreds. It is said that the entire original allotment of paper for the work of the Conference was exhausted in the first ten days.

A large number of Secretariat officials performed many supplementary activities, serving as librarians, transport and housing officers, security officers, and officers of the day.

The Conference early decided on two "working languages," English and French (the latter as a courtesy to the great liberated ally), and five official languages, English, French, Russian, Chinese, and Spanish. All speeches were interpreted into the other of the two working languages—into French if made in English, into English if made in French. If made in a third language, they were interpreted into both English and French. All documents were immediately produced in both English and French and as soon as possible in the three other official languages.

Chapter 4. THE SAN FRANCISCO
CONFERENCE: POLITICS

A WARTIME CONFERENCE

The achievement of the San Francisco Conference can be correctly estimated only if it is realized that it met during the greatest war of modern times, that most of the governments represented were seriously involved in that war, and that, while the Conference was in session, country after country in Europe was being liberated. The victory in Europe occurred unexpectedly on June 10 during the Conference itself, but the Pacific war, an even greater war to those participating in it, showed no signs of termination, though actually it ended before the Charter could be ratified.

A conference in wartime to discuss matters that confessedly will not take place until after the war is over was an anomaly in itself in those days of "total war." It would not have been held without pressure from the United States, as the delay between Dumbarton Oaks and Yalta shows. Except for the United States, every important nation represented at San Francisco was under the handicap that its leading representatives were concerned either with the war or with the immediate problems of liberation. Many leading statesmen were unsure whether they were needed most at San Francisco or at home. Some important political figures attended for a brief time and then left their representation to subordinates. Others had to rule a nation at night after attending the Conference all day. Furthermore, the peculiar pressures of a wartime situation cramped the vision of many delegations. The Conference was not free to do its best. On the other hand, most of the member states considered its work so essential that they

50

did their very utmost at the Conference. Perhaps only the American, British, and Soviet delegations proceeded as calmly as if there were no war, though even so, Mr. Attlee had to return to London and Mr. Stettinius had to fly to Washington.

Examples of the difficulties are innumerable. For instance, Mr. Joseph Bech, the chief delegate from Luxembourg, learned from the newspapers that the government of his country (in which he was foreign minister) had resigned, but was unable to communicate with his government because the headquarters of SHAEF lay in between. He finally decided that he would have to return to find out what was going on. The prime minister of New Zealand, the chief delegate of his country, performed his work as prime minister in the late evening and early morning hours from his desk in the Sir Francis Drake hotel. But his Parliament met before he could return, and his later days at San Francisco were a conflict between duties. Mr. Georges Bidault, the French Minister of Foreign Affairs, was badly needed in Paris during the entire Conference; he finally returned. The chief Dutch and Belgian chairmen left in the middle. It might be added that Mr. Stettinius found his resignation timely the moment the Charter was signed.

The "psychology of wartime" did not completely overwhelm the Conference, but it was present. Its most noticeable form was the insistence on the part of some of the great powers that the lesser allies should do what the great powers wished, because the latter were winning the war for them. For this reason the small powers were not completely free.

On one occasion late in the Conference the Soviet member of a committee said, in effect, that the small powers should accept what the great powers wanted because the great powers were winning the war for them. Dr. Evatt of Australia rose to point out that Australia had been in both wars (European and Pacific) from the beginning. He remembered that the Soviet Union had not been in the European war from the beginning and was not, at the moment, in the Japanese war at all.

NATIONAL POLICIES

The national policies of the states involved determined many issues in the Conference. "Power" in the current sense of available resources and force was not the sole basis on which issues were decided. Strong convictions, well expressed, often won victories. In the late spring of 1945 it could not be questioned that the United States represented power, yet the Soviet Union on the one hand and little Australia on the other had more to say about the final form of the Charter than the greatest country in the world.

The general policy of the United States was somewhat contradictory. As in 1919 and 1920, the administration and its supporters were in favor of a general international organization and of American membership in it. More of the "opposition," *i.e.*, the Republicans in Congress, were now in agreement with the administration. Indeed, practically all educated and respectable opinion in the United States was ready to approve the results of San Francisco, whatever they might be. Senator Vandenberg (once somewhat isolationist) was as strongly in favor of the United Nations Organization as Senator Connally. Yet the United States delegation was still fearful that any charter to which the United States was a signatory would meet strong opposition in the Senate and in the country. The policy of the United States in San Francisco was, then, to favor wholeheartedly the strongest and most effective international organization that was possible, but always remembering, or at least believing, that if the organization were too strong and too powerful, the American people and Senate would reject it. The American policy consequently included the preservation of the right of the United States to be able to check the organization if it seemed about to pursue a policy contrary to the policy of the United States.

In other words, the earliest plans of the United States included the great-power veto on all coercive efforts of the international organization. Americans had just about reached the position of accepting a League of Nations, but not of yielding any sovereignty to any superstate. At the same time, American policy insisted that the international organization should have coercive power and should exercise force clearly and bluntly to keep the peace. The contradiction was something which the delegation—and Americans generally—were apparently unable to perceive.

Within the limits of general American policy, the delegation of the United States was sympathetic with the emphasis on the general welfare sections of the Charter. It wanted a manifold and broad world organization, as long as the organization could not coerce the United States. In regard to details where some American interest might seem to be involved, as on the questions as to whether "independence" should be stated as a goal for trust territories or "full employment" as a general social and economic objective, the American position was sometimes not liberal at all.

It is perhaps comprehensible that the American delegation, being thus divided in intention, did not exercise much leadership in San Francisco, except in the very important function of trying to get some sort of a charter framed and agreed upon.

The British delegation, which was perhaps next in importance to that of the United States, was the choice of Winston Churchill, then prime minister of a "national" government predominantly Tory and imperialist in point of view. A few members of the Labour party were included, and Mr. Attlee spent a short time in San Francisco, but the delegation was essentially Conservative. During most of the Conference the Foreign Secretary, Mr. Anthony Eden, headed the delegation more than adequately.

Since the United Kingdom had been, all in all, the leading member of the League of Nations, it might have been expected to desire a restored League of Nations. But neither the Conservative party nor Mr. Churchill had ever been very enthusiastic about the League. In consequence, British policy was committed to the creation of a new league, but not disposed to go too far in making it strong. The British in San Francisco were most successful in mediating between conflicting interests and in sponsoring Big Five policy. But when crises arose, they always—

still considering themselves as the great world power—were on the side of international prestige and not international democracy. Had the Labour party been in power, as it was soon to be, the English position would have been more confused, but it would undoubtedly have been somewhat more international.

The position of the Soviet Union in San Francisco was always clear to those who were willing to listen and understand. The Soviet Union had been dismissed from the League of Nations in 1939 for its attack on Finland and was initially disposed to reject any conception of an international organization as an attempt at general world government. The Soviet Union was, however, impressed with the convenience to itself of the type of general international organization in which the great powers, particularly the United States and the United Kingdom, would join with it in a mutual maintenance, after the war, of the same supreme position in the allied world of which Teheran and Yalta had been examples. The Soviet Union was heartily in support of a general security organization over which the great powers would have complete control. Even more, if possible, than the United States, it was unwilling to put itself in the position where any other power, either great or small, could exercise any control over its policy. In the final speeches that ended the public sessions of the Conference, the Soviet spokesman, and he alone, referred to the United Nations as a "security organization." Apart from the arrangements for a security council, with the veto, which would protect the position of the Soviet Union and give it, with its colleagues, a certain coercive power over the small nations, the Soviet Union had little interest in the details of the Charter. So long as it had the power, as a member of the Security Council, to prevent any important action under the Charter, the Charter might say what it liked. On the other hand, any general statement in support of the position of the underprivileged nations or peoples received the strong support of the Soviet Union.

It was, of course, the possibility that the Soviet Union might withdraw from the Conference or fail to sign the Charter which caused the Conference to respect the rigid claims of great-power

authority staked out at Dumbarton Oaks and at Yalta.   The other
nations at San Francisco, and particularly the other great powers, wished the Soviet Union to be in the Organization and were
willing to make any sacrifice to that end.   The Soviet Union
understood this position and required the sacrifices.

China, the fourth sponsoring power, was so conscious of its
political weakness that it made no insistences of its own.   Its
policy was to support an international organization with strongly
democratic features, but more than anything else to work with
the United States and the United Kingdom who were guaranteeing its position at home.

By early agreement of the sponsoring powers, the Provisional
Government of liberated France was given the position of a great
power.   The French delegation represented, however, a government newly established in a country so weakened by the war
that its actual strength and authority were less than that of many
other governments represented at the Conference.   The French
habit of international importance sometimes conflicted with other
delegations' views of reality.   The French received little encour-
agement for their particular views from the rest of the Big Five
and carried very little weight at the Conference.

The smaller states in the Conference fell, from a political point
of view, into groups.   The Soviet member states and neighbors
(Byelorussia, the Ukraine, Yugoslavia, and Czechoslovakia) had
little policy except to follow Soviet lead.   The liberated states of
Northern and Western Europe, though ably represented, exhibited
less initiative and less constructive force than in the old League
of Nations which they had influenced so greatly.

Three other groups showed distinctive qualities—the Arab
states, the Latin-American states, and the members of the British
Commonwealth.

The Arab states were newly united in the Arab League, formed
on March 22, 1944.   In San Francisco they held frequent caucuses
and worked together to secure their position as new and ambitious
claimants to international power.   Five of the seven signatories
of the Pact of the Arab League were at San Francisco—Egypt,

Syria, Iraq, Lebanon, and Saudi Arabia. Transjordan was still part of the British mandated territory of Palestine and is still outside the United Nations. Yemen was not admitted to the United Nations until September 30, 1947.

The Latin-American states were much the most numerous group in the Conference. When they voted as a bloc, their votes counted heavily in the necessary two-thirds majority. They sent capable, if not always active, delegations. Brazil was well-represented. Argentina, whose delegation appeared late because of the dispute over its admission, was uneasy in the Conference. Mexico had been expected to take the lead among the Latin-American states, since it was not only the largest Spanish-American state, but was on excellent terms both with the United States and with its colleagues to the south. Its delegation helped, however, rather than inspired or directed. Colombia, and its chief delegate Señor Lleras Camargo, therefore stood out among the Latin-American states. But the remoteness of the Latin Americans from the war and from the other great political problems of the day, except those of the American hemisphere, caused them to contribute less than might have been expected from the ability of their delegates and their genuine understanding of problems of international organization.

The British dominions played a far greater part in the Conference than their number and size would indicate. The Union of South Africa sent as its chief delegate the great veteran of international cooperation Field Marshal Smuts. His prestige was great, since he was the only statesman present who had played a major part in the Paris Conference of 1919. His delegation, however, was cautious and conservative and followed the lead of the Big Five. The delegations of Australia, New Zealand, and Canada were impressive and influential. The leadership of the smaller powers in the Conference was quickly assumed by the cochairman of the Australian delegation, Dr. Herbert Vere Evatt. His determination that the small powers should obtain as much as they possibly could, combined with his tireless energy, knowledge, and force of personality made him at once the detestation of the Big Five and the champion of the little forty-five. If an award had been made for the ablest and most effective delegate to the Conference, it would have gone without question to Dr. Evatt. His position was ably supported by the forceful prime minister of New Zealand, Mr. Peter Fraser. The Canadian delegation, if more quietly, maintained the same small-power point of view.

Among the most significant and surprising manifestations of the Conference was the delegation of the Philippine Commonwealth. It was headed by Gen. Carlos P. Rómulo, an orator as well as a conspicuous patriot. Still legally subject to rule by the Congress of the United States, the Filipinos showed independence, intelligence, and initiative. The situation illustrated what freedom and democracy can mean when cultivated by a nation honestly determined to set its subjects free.

GREAT POWERS VERSUS SMALL POWERS

The San Francisco Conference was inevitably the scene of politics. With all that variety of opinion which is found in any truly deliberative body, the Conference was, nevertheless, divided into two political groups—the great powers and their satellites on the one hand, and the smaller powers on the other.

Canada tried to maintain the contention that there were "middle powers" which did not claim the position of the great powers and did not have the strength the latter possessed, but which were entitled to a semiprivileged status in a general international organization. This contention was recognized in the provision that "due regard" should be "specially paid" in the elections to the Security Council "in the first instance to the contribution of members of the United Nations to the maintenance of international peace and security and to the other purposes of the Organization."

It was hard to decide precisely which states, besides Canada, were "middle powers," and in general policy Canada and the other possible "middle powers" were to be classed as small powers.

Canada was to be greatly disappointed a year later when

Australia rather than Canada was elected to the Security Council in the first election of nonpermanent members.

The Small Powers

The smaller states in general agreed in opposing the extreme claim of authority which the great powers had written into Dumbarton Oaks for themselves and fought the "veto" where they could. They also worked to expand the power of the General Assembly and of the Economic and Social Council so as to make the United Nations as much as possible an international organization with a general commission to work for the well-being of the world. The small states had mostly been strong believers in the League of Nations and sometimes particular beneficiaries of it. They wanted peace among all nations. They saw the general as well as the specific values of an international organization. Differing in detail, they agreed in principle. Furthermore, the smaller states had the least to lose and the most to gain from the creation of an effective international organization. Their delegates understood what such an organization must be and pressed hard for it.

The Great Powers

On the other hand, the original expectation of the sponsoring powers seems to have been that the lesser members of the Conference would be given a chance to consider and discuss the Dumbarton Oaks Proposals and then would, of necessity, accept them with merely verbal changes. The whole organization of the Conference was calculated to that end: commissions and committees with universal representation, but the Steering Committee (steered by its Executive Committee) which would bring back to reality, *i.e.*, Dumbarton Oaks, the wandering thoughts of the delegates, and the Coordination Committee which would put into satisfactory form such wandering thoughts as accidentally slipped by this machinery. The technical committees which actually drafted the Charter were expected to be subject to Executive Committee control. Indeed, one difficulty in understanding the

Conference from its documents arises from the fact that, according to the original instructions to the Secretariat, the "summary reports" of the meetings of the technical committees were to be as brief and formal as possible.

In fact, however, the technical committees showed every inclination to discuss and to act on the subjects assigned to them, in their own way and without attempting to get their recommendations into any general pattern. The issue of their freedom from control was finally fought out in the Steering Committee. The freedom of the technical committees was insisted upon by the smaller powers, led by Dr. Evatt of Australia, and when Field Marshal Smuts, usually on the big-power side, came out persuasively for their autonomy, their position was supported. It was decided that the Steering Committee should not make a practice of giving orders to the technical committees. The Coordination Committee, after attempts to streamline what the committees did, found that its revisions had to be satisfactory to the committee which had done the original drafting.

The Big Five, nevertheless, acted as a political steering committee for the Conference. They met frequently to decide their joint attitude toward small-power amendments and usually worked in concert in the subsequent meetings of the technical committees. The small powers were not organized in a caucus. It had been expected that they would be led by some Latin-American delegate, probably the chief delegate of Mexico, but Evatt of Australia, by his enterprise, persistence, and clear sense of what was desired, carried Australia to the position of their leader. In the crucial battle, that of the extent and meaning of the veto, the issue seemed to be Evatt against the United States, the United Kingdom, and the Soviet Union; and the liberalization of Dumbarton Oaks owes more to Evatt than to any other person. Nevertheless other delegations, notably that of Canada, and other delegates, such as Paul Boncour of France and Henri Rolin of Belgium, gave strong help.

Politics in the Conference finally became the balancing of concessions to the smaller powers against the maintenance of the

great-power veto at all essential places in the machinery of the
United Nations. The Charter was so greatly liberalized that all
delegates of small powers could sign it with good will, yet it was
not modified so as to decrease the coercive power, or the power
to block, of the permanent members of the Security Council.
The fight was conducted all along the line—as to membership,
suspension, expulsion, as to election of the Secretary-General, as
to enforcement procedure, and as to possible amendments of the
Charter. On the issue of great-power control, the small powers
were forced to yield when an appeal to Moscow (on enforcement procedure) found Moscow determined to maintain its position. On many lesser points the small powers won. When the
struggle was over, Dr. Evatt, like a good politician, though defeated on the major issue, rejoiced sincerely in the amount that
he had secured for Australia and for its associates.

On Chapters XI, XII, and XIII, which dealt with trusteeship
and colonial questions generally and concerned intimately the
national interests of three of the Big Five and of several other
Western European powers, the Big Five were almost as intransigent as on the veto. On colonial questions the Conference considered the susceptibilities of the colonial powers to a great degree. Even here Australia and New Zealand, with a good deal
of help from the Americans, were able to liberalize the general
tone of the Charter provisions. The trusteeship system and the
Declaration on Non-Self-Governing Territories were essentially
the product of Americans, Australians, and New Zealanders.

Studies of previous great international conferences always show
the stronger powers of the moment attempting a dictation over
the conference. The principle of unanimity (modified in San
Francisco to a requirement of a two-thirds vote) has always conflicted with the fact that at the end of any war states are unequal
in their possession of readily mobilizable power and in their disposition to use it. At San Francisco, as at Vienna or Paris, two
things were in conflict in determining the conference decisions.
One was power and the disposition to use it. The other was a

belief that the world must be organized on the basis of justice if it was to be worth organizing at all.

PROCEDURE AND POLITICS

The procedure of the Conference gave a reasonable opportunity to those delegates who wanted to liberalize the Dumbarton Oaks Proposals.

Each member of the Conference had one vote. It was decided that a two-thirds majority of the delegations present and voting would determine any substantive question. There was consequently a margin for the interplay of interest, and few decisions made in the Conference were clearly predictable in advance.

Again the Dumbarton Oaks Proposals set forth the agenda of the Conference, but they had already been supplemented by comments forwarded by the governments invited to attend. Indeed, the sponsoring powers themselves had put forward a series of modifications of the Proposals, largely based on suggestions made by China. New proposals had to be received even during the Conference itself, though there was a time limit on them. Furthermore, as soon as the discussion of the various chapters of the Dumbarton Oaks Proposals was begun in the committees, it became clear that the delegates intended to express themselves freely and that the Conference had a bigger task than had been expected. Everything was discussed at the complete discretion of a two-thirds majority.

The Conference moved slowly. The first seven working days were spent in the usual statements of national policy by representatives of all the governments. Meetings of the commissions followed. Finally the committees got down to work and, for the most part, discussed as freely and as lengthily as if time were already merged with eternity. Constant efforts were made by the Secretary of State, as representing the sponsoring powers, to hurry the Conference to a conclusion. Public opinion everywhere, and not least in the United States, objected to Conference delays. Eventually a deadline was set for the signing of the Charter, because of the promised attendance of President Truman, and this deadline was kept. The Conference lasted longer than had been intended, but it was not a long Conference.

RESULTS OF THE CONFERENCE

The San Francisco Conference achieved a general international organization. It drew up a Charter which was signed by all the members of the Conference, and the Charter was quickly ratified. The delegates went home satisfied on the whole, if not always pleased with the details. The new United Nations Organization would work out, it would grow, it would become adequate to its tremendous tasks.

In the first place an international security organization had been set up which would, if the great powers continued in agreement, keep the peace in the future. It would be able to suppress a Germany or a Japan which might try to revive its military position. This was perhaps the greatest, yet at the same time the most illusory, of the things the Organization proffered, for the impotence of both Germany and Japan after their surrender had not been anticipated. At least the United Nations would protect everyone against a recurrence of the war. And as to other threats to the peace, the security machinery would deal with them also.

Concerning cooperation for improving the economic and social conditions of the world and of the individual nations, the Charter promised well. Also a restored and renewed international court was created as an integral part of the structure of the Organization. A much better integrated machinery than that of the League of Nations had been established with the widest of mandates.

It is true that Chapter XVII entitled "Transitional Security Provisions" gave the warring allies permission to pursue their aims, whether collective or individual, until the least traces of the Second World War were eliminated. But this was peacemaking, with which the United Nations had nothing to do; it was to take over after peace had been made.

PUTTING THE CHARTER INTO EFFECT

What was to be done actually to bring the machinery of the United Nations into existence? The first step was the ratification of the Charter. This presented, in fact, no difficulties. The United States ratified the Charter as a treaty with the almost unanimous approval of the Senate on September 20, 1945. The Big Five and a majority of other signatory states had deposited ratifications by October 24, 1945, and the Charter was in effect. All signatories had ratified and deposited their ratifications by December 27, 1945.

At the same time that they signed the Charter, the delegates at San Francisco signed an additional agreement, the "Interim Arrangement" by which the actual machinery of the United Nations would be organized. In this document they agreed that a Preparatory Commission of the United Nations should make arrangements for the first sessions of the General Assembly, Security Council, Economic and Social Council, and Trusteeship Council, and for the establishment of the Secretariat and of the Court. The Preparatory Commission, consisting of representatives of all the member states, was to meet in San Francisco (as it did) on the day after the signing of the Charter. It was to reconvene in London as soon as possible after the Charter went into effect. An Executive Committee of the Preparatory Commission was created, composed of the same fourteen states that constituted the Executive Committee in San Francisco. This Executive Committee was to meet in London and prepare for the meeting of the Preparatory Commission.

The Executive Committee met in London on August 16, 1945. The Preparatory Commission met on November 24, 1945. The First Part of the First Session of the General Assembly met in London on January 10, 1946.

Chapter 5. THE CHARTER AS WRITTEN
AT SAN FRANCISCO

PREAMBLE AND PRINCIPLES

The San Francisco Conference established an organization, that is to say, a piece of political machinery, by means of a charter or constitution. In trying to see what the Organization actually is, it is necessary first to disregard the impressive verbiage which precedes and accompanies the constructive portion of the Charter. The preamble, the "purposes," the "principles," and constant references in the Charter to standards of international conduct are in the tradition which has characterized all constitution making since the time of the French Revolution. They are proclamations of intent, or at least of good will. They indicate a political atmosphere within which, it is hoped, the activities of the Organization will be performed and they suggest large purposes which it should serve. They direct or orient its activities.

These statements of principle and purpose are not to be confused with anything of the nature of a bill of rights. For a bill of rights, such as the English Bill of Rights of 1689 or the first ten amendments to the Constitution of the United States, is less a statement of general principles than a set of specific and enforceable guides to the rulers. The general statements in the Charter of the United Nations are guides, but not enforceable. In American constitutional terms they all are "preambulary" material. The Organization could function without them in precisely the same way as with them, and there is no reason to suppose that any member of the Organization will feel specifically restrained by them. This is not to say that they serve no useful

purpose.   They can be referred to in any appeal to the opinion
of a United Nations organ or to the general public opinion of the
world.   India, for instance, in the Second Part of the First Session
of the General Assembly made much of the Charter references to
race equality in its dispute with the Union of South Africa.   But
the propagandist and the doctrinaire will find more value in these
general statements than will the legislator, the administrator, or
the judge.

These statements, however, were not mere "window dressing."
As expressions of deep conviction on important matters they were
close to the hearts of most of the delegates.   They were well
worth stating with all the weight that their incorporation in the
Charter gives them.   They will have their effect.   But they can
never be more than a standard set before the nations which will
be enforceable, if ever, only when it does not actually need to
be enforced.

The effective parts of the Charter create an organization.   It is
an organization intended to do two things: "to maintain international peace and security" (Chapter I. 1. 1) and "to achieve
international cooperation in solving international problems of
an economic, social, cultural, or humanitarian character" (I. 1. 3).
A third purpose of the Organization is implied: the creation of
a structure that shall be lasting.   The Organization is so constructed that it has the elements of life in it.   It should en-
dure; there is no provision for its termination.   Whether it ac-
complishes much or little, it will continue to exist.   The three
purposes or interests—security, welfare, and organization—sometimes conflict with each other in the Charter, but they are all
there.

What then, is the United Nations Organization as the Charter
establishes it?

MEMBERSHIP

In the first place, the United Nations is a membership organization.   Like any other club to which one pays dues and assumes

obligations, the Organization is exclusive, or at least selective. The original members were the fifty-one "United Nations" as defined in April, 1945. Members cannot withdraw, constitutionally at any rate, though they can be expelled. Presumably in that respect they resemble states in the American Union and not members of the British Commonwealth of Nations. The Organization, once established, is not a league freely entered and freely relinquished. It is permanent.

Further admission to membership is open to all "peace-loving states" which will carry out the obligations of the Charter. The attainment of membership was not planned to be too easy, but most of the San Francisco conferees hoped for the time when all states in the world could or would become members. Membership *should* be universal. Meantime the Security Council, acting as a membership committee, might well exercise (as it has done) a close scrutiny over applicants. The League precedent worked both ways. The League was at first a wartime alliance, but became almost universal before its end. States came in and out, however, on political and ideological grounds; perhaps the League was only an alliance after all, and the United Nations Organization might not try to go beyond that stage too soon. At any rate the United Nations with its original membership of fifty-one (now fifty-nine) need not fear the rivalry of any numerous or powerful counteralliance.

The equality of the members, once in, is an essential part of the Organization. It might have been possible to have created an organization based on a graduated membership, with voting strength proportioned to population or resources. The only differentiation between the members of the United Nations, however, is the special position of the five powers that are permanent members of the Security Council. Their special position is undoubtedly great. In some respects it is overwhelming. But it is functional; they have a special position for certain purposes, particularly the maintenance of international peace and the stability of the Organization itself. It is for this latter purpose that they serve as a membership committee, screen candidates for the position of Secretary-General, serve on the Trusteeship Council, have a veto over amendments. In other respects (as, for example, voting in the General Assembly or the Economic and Social Council and the Trusteeship Council) they are like all the other members.

PRINCIPAL ORGANS

The management of the affairs of the Organization is entrusted to six "principal organs"—the General Assembly, the Security Council, the Economic and Social Council, the Trusteeship Council, the International Court of Justice, and the Secretariat.

The General Assembly

The General Assembly is composed of all members of the United Nations. Each member nation has one vote. Decisions "on important questions," some of which are listed in Article 18.2, are made by a two-thirds majority, and on other questions by a simple majority, in both cases a majority of the members present and voting. The General Assembly is to meet in regular annual sessions and, in addition, may hold special sessions.

The General Assembly is the one organ in which all members are represented; it is consequently the conference of all members, the primary and fundamental gathering which focuses the manifold activities of the United Nations. Unlike the Assembly of the League of Nations, whose competence extended to any matter that concerned the League, the General Assembly is limited by intent, so that it may not make recommendations on matters which the Security Council is considering as part of the Security Council's peculiar functions.

The competence of the General Assembly was much more limited at Dumbarton Oaks than finally at San Francisco. It emerged from San Francisco, as any general assembly of the members of a league or association is bound to be, the central body which is expected to exercise general control. Its method of achieving results goes no further, however, than the power of making recommendations; its authority and power is clearly limited, and this limitation shows the looseness of organization of the United Nations considered as a world government. But unlike the Assembly of the League, or any traditional international conference of sovereign states, such decisions as it makes need not be universally agreed upon. Furthermore, in the two-thirds majority necessary, the great powers need not be included, nor does abstention serve as a negative vote.

With the limitation of its competence admitted, the area of the General Assembly's activity is vast and its functions are manifold. It may, according to the crucial Article 10, "discuss any questions or any matters within the scope of the present Charter" and, except that it cannot make recommendations on matters which the Security Council is dealing with, it "may make recommendations to the Members of the United Nations or to the Security Council or to both on any such questions or matters." In other words it may discuss anything and may make recommendations on anything except a question of international peace and security which is at the particular moment under consideration by the Security Council. It is government by resolution, a primitive and non-coercive sort of government, but it may be considered government nevertheless.

In addition to the authority to discuss and recommend, the General Assembly has specific authority over the Economic and Social Council (and indirectly through the Economic and Social Council over the specialized agencies), it has specific authority over the Trusteeship Council, and it makes regulations governing the Secretariat. Furthermore, all the organs of the United Nations, including the Security Council, make annual reports to the General Assembly.

The General Assembly possesses a further power. It elects the members of the Economic and Social Council, some of the members of the Security Council and of the Trusteeship Council, and on recommendation of the Security Council the Secretary-General. The Secretary-General and the General Assembly act concurrently to elect the judges of the International Court of Justice.

And on recommendation of the Security Council the General Assembly admits new members to the United Nations. This electoral function of the General Assembly is of the utmost importance.

Finally, the General Assembly possesses the authority to approve the budget of the United Nations.

The General Assembly resembles a one-chamber parliament of a popularly governed country in that it represents the constituents, determines policy, supervises administration, selects administrators, controls the budget, and serves as an arena for discussion. It is unlike such a parliament in that in all these matters its activity is limited, though in differing degrees, and that it is completely lacking in either authority or power to enforce its will on member states.

This concentration of powers in the General Assembly makes it the parliament of the United Nations. Though the framers of the Charter tried to keep the security functions of the Organization for the Security Council, even these functions seem to be shared with the General Assembly. Just as in the case of the League Assembly, it seemed quite likely that the General Assembly would increase in power, since such an increase is to the interest of most of the member states.

The Security Council

The distinctive difference in machinery between the San Francisco Charter and the Covenant of the League of Nations is the special position given in the Charter to the Security Council, a position greater than that which the League Council had held. The Security Council is to have "primary responsibility for the maintenance of international peace and security," and all the members of the Organization are to entrust it with the authority to act, in this respect, on their behalf.

The Charter reads as follows:

In order to ensure prompt and effective action by the United Nations, its Members confer on the Security Council primary responsibility for the maintenance of international peace and security, and agree that in carrying out its duties under this responsibility the Security Council acts on their behalf (Article 24.1).

The Members of the United Nations agree to accept and carry out the decisions of the Security Council in accordance with the present Charter (Article 25).

The General Assembly may discuss, and indeed recommend, in the area of international peace and security, but it was not to have the power either to act or to interfere. The Security Council was to be the efficient and active agent of the United Nations. This is, indeed, the peculiar and distinctive characteristic of the Security Council. It is organized to act. It is supposed to act. It alone can act. If the conferees at Dumbarton Oaks and at San Francisco had thought in such terms, they might have said that the Security Council was to be "pure act."

In spite of the priority of position given to the General Assembly in the San Francisco Charter, the Security Council was intended to be the most important organ of the United Nations. If there were six "principal organs," there was to be one efficient organ. The degree to which this assumption was made has varied. One extreme position was taken by Soviet conferees at Dumbarton Oaks and maintained, by and large, by the Soviet government ever since: that only the Security Council was worth taking seriously and that the other organs were to be kept in a place of complete subordination. The other extreme position was that of Evatt and other representatives of lesser powers who maintained that any special position of the Security Council was a bad thing in itself and that its position in the Charter or in subsequent activities under the Charter should be minimized to the fullest extent possible.

The peculiar Charter position of the Security Council—and the essence of its nature—consists of two things: its control over other organs of the United Nations and its special authority in the field of international peace and security.

It is a focus of control. Its recommendation is necessary before the General Assembly may elect any state as a new member of the Organization (Article 4. 2). Its permanent members are members of the Trusteeship Council (Article 86). It approves the creation of trusteeships of strategic areas (Article 83). Its recommendation is necessary for the appointment of a Secretary-General (Article 97). It has conjoint authority with the General Assembly to elect judges of the International Court of Justice. It has conjoint authority with the General Assembly in calling a general conference to review the Charter.

As an efficient agency responsible for the maintenance of peace and security, the Security Council has distinctive characteristics and powers. It is small, five permanent members and six non-permanent members, the latter elected for terms of two years by the General Assembly. It is "so organized as to be able to function continuously" and for this purpose "each member . . . shall . . . be represented at all times at the seat of the Organization" (Article 28. 1). It makes decisions, in all matters of any importance, by a special majority of seven members, in which majority the five permanent members must be included. It may meet anywhere. It is provided with the Military Staff Committee to advise and assist it (Article 47), and may establish subsidiary organs at its discretion.

As to its powers, a considerable portion of the Charter outlines them. These powers extend both to the use of force and also to the calling on member states for certain types of action. The Security Council, alone among the organs of the United Nations, is specifically given authority and power to coerce.

Since the organization of the Security Council in January, 1946, it has seemed, in the eyes of impatient observers, to be the least efficient and effective action agency that could be conceived. Its behavior will be analyzed below, in Chapters 10 and 11. The fact that for political reasons a piece of governmental machinery does not behave as some of its observers had expected does not, however, change the intentions of its creators or the nature of the machinery created. What the Security Council was intended to be, what in the Charter it remains, are points clear and easy to understand.

The Economic and Social Council

The Economic and Social Council was provided for in Dumbarton Oaks and raised to the status of a principal organ at San Francisco. It is entrusted with plans for international economic and social cooperation. It is the focus in the United Nations Organization for those functions of contemporary government relating to the general well-being of the people. Just as the General Assembly is, on the whole, deliberative and the Security Council is regulatory and repressive, so the Economic and Social Council is to be constructive in plans and in recommendations for action. As broadly stated in the Charter, its functions include all the positive actions that modern man demands of modern government.

The Economic and Social Council is composed of eighteen members elected by the General Assembly for terms of three years. The great powers have no special prominence. As a matter of fact, the great powers have all been elected to the Council and will, no doubt, continue to be reelected, but as members of the Council they are merely five among eighteen, with no favored position. Decisions in the Council are made by a simple majority of members present and voting. The Council may meet at its discretion and has decided to meet in two sessions yearly.

In some areas of its activity the Economic and Social Council is responsible to the General Assembly; in most areas it does things on its own initiative. It acts by consideration, inquiry, making of recommendations, and preparation of draft agreements. It creates commissions and committees. For certain purposes it supervises the "specialized agencies." Nothing that the Economic and Social Council does is spectacular, but nothing that it does is unimportant.

If one can make a comparison with national governments, the Economic and Social Council is somewhat similar to a subsidiary legislature dealing with economic and social matters and to an economic and social cabinet or small body of policy makers. It acts through its own commissions and subcommissions. But it also serves in a tremendously important and vital capacity as the fulcrum of relationship between the United Nations Organization and the other United Nations organizations known as the "specialized agencies." These specialized, functional organizations are, in many respects, like separate departments in a national government. The International Labour Organisation is a department of labor, the Food and Agriculture Organization is a department of agriculture, UNESCO (The United Nations Educational Scientific and Cultural Organization) is essentially a ministry of education, the International Civil Aviation Organization is a ministry of aviation. The Bank and the Fund have certain functions that national treasuries exercise. The World Health Organization is a ministry of health, the International Refugee Organization an emergency ministry of resettlement, the International Trade Organization a ministry of trade or commerce. The Universal Postal Union and the International Telecommunications Union will perform certain functions of ministries of communications or of posts and telegraphs. The International Maritime Consultative Organization will perform other functions of national ministries of trade or commerce.

The Trusteeship Council

The Trusteeship Council is a very special body for a very special purpose. It represents the United Nations in the supervision of such dependent areas or non-self-governing territories as, under the Charter, are made "trust territories" and thereby placed under international supervision.

The Trusteeship Council includes automatically all the permanent members of the Security Council and all members of the United Nations which administer trust territories. In addition, the General Assembly elects, for three-year terms, a sufficient number of member states who do not administer any trust territories, to create a numerical balance between administering and nonadministering states.

It acts under the general control of the General Assembly and in relationship for certain purposes with the Security Council.

Its function is to exercise a limited supervision over the trust territories which are administered by specific members of the United Nations.

The International Court of Justice

The International Court of Justice occupies a special legal position. Chapter XIV of the Charter provides for its existence as part of the United Nations Organization, but a separate Statute of the Court is appended to the Charter and was signed as part of the Charter in San Francisco.

The Court is a slightly modified form of the Permanent Court of International Justice which it replaces. The latter, though part of the League of Nations system, was a distinct international organization, owing its existence to a separate protocol drawn up in December, 1920, and effective in September, 1921. The new Court is an integral part of the United Nations and one of its principal organs.

The Court is composed of fifteen judges elected concurrently by the General Assembly and the Security Council. Its jurisdiction is still largely voluntary over cases submitted to it by members of the United Nations, by the organs of the United Nations, or by nonmember states. Its seat is The Hague, and it is administratively independent. It deals with international questions, which it determines according to accepted principles of international law. It is the judicial arm of the United Nations.

The Secretariat

A sixth principal organ of the United Nations is the Secretariat. According to the Charter a Secretary-General is appointed by the General Assembly on recommendation of the Security Council. He is the "chief administrative officer of the Organization" (Article 97). In accordance with regulations laid down by the General Assembly, he appoints a staff who assists him in his administrative and secretarial duties.

Under the League system the first Secretary-General of the League, Sir Eric Drummond, served as an administrator and, to some extent, as a political focus for all the activities of the League. Like the League, the United Nations has avoided the creation of any central executive, either single or multiple. But the establishment of the Secretariat as a principal organ of the United Nations gives the Secretary-General and his staff a position of authority which is essential in the absence of a chief executive. They are the one organ of the United Nations which is not only always in existence but always functioning, not authorized to determine policy, but charged with facilitating and encouraging its formulation. The Security Council, it is true, is organized "so as to be able to function continuously," but the Secretariat, which serves the Security Council as well as the rest of the Organization, must function not only when the Security Council is functioning but also between such times; it *does* function continuously. Furthermore, it has the characteristics of continuity of personnel; this it shares with the Court. In the General Assembly, Security Council, Economic and Social Council, and Trusteeship Council the members are states. Of the Secretariat the members are individual human beings.

To sum up, it can be said that the United Nations Organization possesses all the machinery of a world government, although there is no effective coordination between its organs, the authority and powers of which are to a large extent noncoercive. For the most part, that is with the exception of the coercive authority which the Security Council possesses if it wishes to use it, the members of the Organization are free either to conform to its mandates or to resist them. The machinery of world government, nevertheless, is there.

PART TWO

*The Establishment of the Organization and the Work
of the General Assembly*

Chapter 6. ORGANIZING THE UNITED NATIONS

INTERIM ARRANGEMENTS

The San Francisco Conference had decided that the steps preliminary to the actual creation of the Organization should be taken in London in the fall of 1945. Each delegate who signed the Charter at San Francisco signed also a document on "interim arrangements" outlining the things to be done in order to translate the words of the Charter into a functioning organization. The interim arrangements provided that a preparatory commission should be established to make "provisional arrangements for the first sessions of the General Assembly" and for the establishment and meeting of the other principal organs. The Preparatory Commission held its first meeting, a purely formal one, in San Francisco on the morning after the Charter had been signed. It determined to meet next in London on the call of its Executive Committee (composed of the fourteen states which were members of the San Francisco Executive Committee), "as soon as possible after the Charter of the Organization comes into effect."

The Executive Committee

The Executive Committee met in London on the call of the government of the United Kingdom on August 16, 1945. The Charter went into effect on October 24, 1945. The Preparatory Commission met at the call of the Executive Committee in London on November 24.

The agreement on interim arrangements included a provision that the Preparatory Commission should "make studies and prepare recommendations concerning the location of the permanent

79

headquarters of the Organization." The designation of London as the headquarters was therefore temporary. The government of the United Kingdom became the host of the United Nations for the moment, in the same way that the government of the United States had been the host in San Francisco. In London the government of the United Kingdom supplied the facilities and furnished a gifted member of its Foreign Office staff, Mr. Gladwyn Jebb, who had served as adviser to its delegation in San Francisco, to be the Executive Secretary of the Executive Committee and the Preparatory Commission. The governments which were members of the Executive Committee, fourteen in all, and of the Preparatory Commission, fifty-one in all, sent delegations just as they had sent them to San Francisco. London was the most convenient capital in Europe, and the United Kingdom government made arrangements with its traditional skill. The Executive Committee met in Church House, Westminster. The large meetings of both the Preparatory Commission and of the First Part of the First Session of the General Assembly met in the Central Hall, Westminster.

Before even the Executive Committee met, the war in the Pacific as well as in Europe was over. Furthermore, the member governments had been able to study the Charter as finally drafted and to prepare proposals to put the Charter into effect. The fourteen-member Executive Committee was a highly competent group of officials (most of whom had been at San Francisco) who had been gathered to build the framework of an effective and functioning organization. Mr. Stettinius was the American delegate and Mr. Adlai Stevenson (later governor of Illinois) the alternate delegate. Mr. Benjamin Gerig, as principal adviser, served as the first head of the United States delegation. He was Chief of the Division of Dependent Area Affairs of the Department of State and had been Deputy Secretary-General of the United States delegation at San Francisco.

The report of the Executive Committee deals entirely with questions of organization, in regard to which it showed great judgment and skill.

The Preparatory Commission

The next step was a meeting of the Preparatory Commission to receive the report of the Executive Committee and, on the basis of this report, to make definite plans for the General Assembly. Perhaps the greatest difference between the Executive Committee and the Preparatory Commission was that representatives to the latter were largely diplomats, whereas the work of the smaller and less conspicuous Executive Committee had been accomplished by experts.

The report of the Executive Committee served as a foundation on which the Preparatory Commission built. There was greater agreement in the Executive Committee than in the Preparatory Commission; national politics reentered when the governments had had a chance to study what the Preparatory Commission suggested. In particular, the Soviet representatives opposed the making of suggestions by the Executive Committee to the Security Council, though the terms of reference of the Preparatory Commission seemed to include such suggestions.

If the United Nations was to be immediately useful, it had to organize without delay. Nor was it desirable to protract meetings in the difficult conditions of postwar London. Yet disputes, which arose as soon as the Preparatory Commission met, indicated that the work of establishing the organs of the United Nations might be slow and, in some respects, difficult. All member states intended to share appropriately in the planning and to take time to demonstrate their importance. Delay often made it possible for the minority to accept what it could not accept at first. In actuality, the establishment of the United Nations as a functioning organization took place with reasonable speed, if one compares its efficiency with that of national legislatures.

The United Nations has constantly functioned in situations where it has been the desire of the majority, or of the dominant part, to move swiftly and of the minority to delay, though the majority and minority have not always been composed of the same members or of the same interests. All in all, the Preparatory

Commission performed extremely well, though as a result of its disagreements the General Assembly could not meet in 1945 as had been hoped.

FIRST MEETING OF THE GENERAL ASSEMBLY

One of the limiting factors in the United Nations is the time at which, by general agreement, the General Assembly must hold its annual sessions. Since national legislatures customarily meet in the winter and spring and since the summer is the holiday period for those situated north of the equator, as most of them are, the General Assembly, like the Assembly of the League of Nations, is obliged to hold its regular meetings in the autumn; and the provisional Rules of Procedure of the General Assembly provide that it shall meet every year "commencing on the third Tuesday in September." In order to establish the pattern as quickly as possible, it was determined to hold the first regular annual session of the General Assembly in two parts: the first part for purposes of organization immediately after the Preparatory Commission had adjourned, this part to be as short as possible, and a second part of the same first annual session to be held at the normal time beginning in September. This part was to concern itself with problems of substance. The First Part met on January 10, 1946. The Second Part was twice postponed because of the Peace Conference in Paris and began its meetings on October 23. And as might have been expected, it was impossible to keep questions of substance entirely out of the First Part, and therefore the First Part lasted from January 10 to February 14.

The First Part dealt, however, primarily with questions of organization, and as a result of its actions all the principal organs of the United Nations, except the Trusteeship Council, were promptly brought into being.

Organization

The provisional organization of the General Assembly itself, which in its essentials became permanent, was the first task of the

General Assembly. The General Assembly elects a president, who serves throughout the session and until his successor is chosen, and seven vice-presidents. The first session chose Mr. Paul-Henri Spaak of Belgium as president, and seven vice-presidents, of whom five were representatives of the great powers. A "general committee" to serve as an agenda and steering committee was instituted, composed of the president and vice-presidents of the General Assembly and the chairmen of its six main committees. It was decided that this committee should not consider political questions. Six main committees were established, dealing with large segments of the General Assembly's functions. In these main committees items on the agenda are normally discussed before they come to the floor of the General Assembly for decision. The committee members choose their own chairmen. Each member state is represented on each of these committees. Voting in the committees is by simple majority. In the General Assembly itself, most decisions require a two-thirds vote.

In addition to the General Committee and the six main committees, which are a permanent part of the General Assembly organization, the First Part of the First Session established a Headquarters Committee, to make recommendations on the site of the United Nations, and a League of Nations Committee, to deal with the transfer of certain League matters to the United Nations. With the adoption of the Rules of Procedure, the General Assembly took definite form and could function effectively.

The Rules of Procedure were, in fact, based largely on the procedure of the Assembly of the League of Nations, modified when necessary to fit the Charter. They are an acceptable compromise between the Anglo-Saxon and the Continental rules for doing business and proved their utility from the first moment. Only one question, that of languages, remains seriously inconvenient. After San Francisco it was impossible to accept only English as a working language, and it was impracticable to add any working language to English and French. Consequently, the General Assembly and the other organs accepted English and French as working languages and the five languages of the Charter as official languages. The amount of necessary interpretation and translation remained large, but appeared to be unavoidable.

Elections

The General Assembly's next task was to play its part in the establishment of the other organs of the United Nations. It had to elect members of the councils and of the Court, and in these first elections it had to choose the total number of elected members, though for terms of varying length. It was authorized to elect six members of the Security Council and did so promptly. Australia, Brazil, Egypt, Mexico, the Netherlands, and Poland were elected. The Security Council was therefore able to hold its first meeting on January 17. With more deliberation the General Assembly chose eighteen members of the Economic and Social Council and then joined with the Security Council in electing a total of fifteen judges for the International Court of Justice.

In all these elections the normal forces of political association and combination played their part, no matter what the exact Charter stipulation might be. The Security Council included two Latin-American states, one from the Arab League, one from Western Europe, one from Eastern Europe, and one British dominion. This distribution is regional and political and seemed to set a pattern for the future. The Economic and Social Council naturally and inevitably includes the five great powers, and the rest of the eighteen are chosen on the basis of their economic importance, but also as a result of previous selection by "blocs." From the beginning there have been three geographical blocs in the United Nations—Eastern European or Soviet, Latin-American, and Arab. The latter two, which have often worked together, control almost half the votes of the General Assembly. The United States does not control a bloc and has sometimes attempted to oppose the Latin-American bloc. The British Commonwealth members do not vote together, nor do they necessarily follow the lead of the United Kingdom.

The election of the Secretary-General was the most important political act of the session. He is chosen by the General Assembly on recommendation of the Security Council, but his selection was delayed until the General Assembly committee had reported on appropriate terms of employment for him. Most members felt that he should not be a citizen of any of the Big Five. Yet the political impartiality of each small power was challengeable. In preliminary conferences between the Big Five many names were suggested. Perhaps the ablest candidate, who was thoroughly acceptable to four of the five, was Mr. Lester Pearson of Canada, then ambassador to the United States. To please the Soviet Union, however, and to prevent a Soviet veto, the great powers preferring Pearson accepted Mr. Trygve Lie, the foreign minister of Norway, who was readily accepted by the rest of the Security Council and by the General Assembly.

Because no trust territories had as yet been created, the General Assembly was unable to elect members to complete the Trusteeship Council. It did, however, pass a resolution urging that trusteeship agreements be negotiated so that they could be approved in the Second Part of the First Session. On the related question of non-self-governing territories, it requested the Secretary-General to incorporate in his annual report to the Assembly a summary of information transmitted to him under Article 73e of the Charter by members administering non-self-governing territories.

Creation of the Atomic Energy Commission

All these steps to bring the organs under the Charter into existence were clearly indicated by the Charter itself. The General Assembly created also an additional body of the first importance when it established a "commission to deal with the problems raised by the discovery of atomic energy." It gave to this Atomic Energy Commission wide terms of reference and made it responsible to the Security Council to which, once created, it was to make reports and recommendations and from which it was to take instructions. This Commission was to be composed of one representative of each member of the Security Council plus a representative of Canada.   It met first on June 14, 1946.

Secretariat and Budget

To complete the structure of the United Nations, the General Assembly passed a resolution providing for the organization of the Secretariat, which is under the direction of the Secretary-General, and authorizing negotiations to secure for the United Nations and its staff the legal privileges and immunities necessary for carrying out their functions.

Finally, the General Assembly authorized a provisional budget for 1946 of $21,500,000 and a capital fund of $25,000,000, both based on contributions assessed on members.

ESTABLISHMENT OF THE SECURITY COUNCIL

The Security Council was brought into existence when the General Assembly elected the Council's nonpermanent members on January 12, 1946.   The Council held its first meeting on January 17 at Church House, Westminster.   At its first meeting it adopted provisional Rules of Procedure recommended by the Preparatory Commission but referred them at once for review to the Committee of Experts.   The Committee was slow in making its recommendations: their final working form dates from June 26, 1946.   As a result, the Security Council began to concern itself with substantive business under some uncertainty as to how it was supposed to act, and its procedure was worked out from almost daily experience.

The Security Council was faced at once with requests to attend to a series of matters, many of which came to have a long and continuing life in the Security Council.   At its second session it received complaints on the Greek question under Article 35 and on the Indonesian situation under Article 34 and has never since failed to have simultaneously many questions under possible consideration.

At the same time it was obliged to perform various miscellaneous functions under the Charter not directly related to its position as chief caretaker of international peace and security. At its first meeting it created the Committee of Experts to advise it on questions of procedure and other technical questions. At its second meeting it adopted a directive in accordance with which the Military Staff Committee, which is under its control, met first on February 4, 1946. On February 6, 1946, it shared in the election of fifteen judges of the International Court of Justice. Preparatory to the meeting of the Second Part of the First Session of the General Assembly, it considered applications for membership in the United Nations and made recommendations to the General Assembly.

ESTABLISHMENT OF THE ECONOMIC AND SOCIAL COUNCIL

The Economic and Social Council was brought into existence by the election of its eighteen members by the General Assembly on January 12, 1946. Of the eighteen members one-third were to serve each for one, two, and three years. The six elected for one year ceased to hold office on January 1, 1947, and the Second Part of the session elected six states for three years to replace them. Retiring members are eligible for reelection.

The Economic and Social Council met three times in 1946. Since then it has met twice annually. Its first president, who was reelected for 1947, was Sir A. Ramaswami Mudaliar of India, who had been the able chairman of Committee II/3 at San Francisco.

The Preparatory Commission had recommended that the Economic and Social Council should set up eight commissions to deal with different aspects of its work. At its first session five "nuclear commissions," composed of experts serving in their personal capacity, were established to plan five of the commissions, and at its second session five commissions were consequently set up:

Economic and Employment
Transportation and Communications
Statistical
Social
Human Rights

The Commission on Narcotic Drugs was set up at the first session. The Commission on the Status of Women (previously a subcommission) was set up at the second session. Population and Fiscal Commissions were set up at the third session. These nine (instead of eight) commissions vary in size from twelve to eighteen members.

ESTABLISHMENT OF THE ATOMIC ENERGY COMMISSION

The Atomic Energy Commission, a special body unforeseen in the Charter, was created by the General Assembly and made dependent on the Security Council. It appears to be the only example so far of the creation of a "subsidiary organ" of the United Nations "which may be established in accordance with the present Charter." It was established by vote of the General Assembly on January 26, 1946. Its first meeting was held on June 14, 1946. Article 7.2 of the Charter is the general grant of authority under which its exists. Article 22 permits the General Assembly to "establish such subsidiary organs as it deems necessary for the performance of its functions," and Article 29 gives identical power to the Security Council.

ESTABLISHMENT OF THE TRUSTEESHIP COUNCIL

The Trusteeship Council was established by vote of the General Assembly in the Second Part of the First Session. The General Assembly approved trusteeship agreements for eight territories. Then it elected two states, Mexico and Iraq, to make up the required Charter balance between administering and nonadministering states and directed the Secretary-General to summon the first meeting of the Council not later than March 15, 1947. The Council met for the first session at Lake Success on March 26 and adjourned on April 28. During the session it adopted rules of procedure, drew up a draft questionnaire, considered petitions, and considered relations with other organs of the United Nations. It elected the United States representative Mr. Francis B. Sayre as president for one year without the privilege of reelection. The Soviet Union, which had opposed the General Assembly resolution on Trusteeship, did not attend the sessions of the Trusteeship Council until April 27, 1948, when the Council was concerned with Jerusalem.

ESTABLISHMENT OF THE INTERNATIONAL COURT OF JUSTICE

On February 6, 1946, the General Assembly and the Security Council joined in the elections of fifteen judges of the Court of International Justice. In accordance with the Statute of the Court (which is appended to the Charter of the United Nations and is juridically part of the Charter) the seat of the Court is established at The Hague, where the president and registrar of the Court are to reside. The Court met at The Hague on April 3. It elected Mr. J. G. Guerrero of El Salvador as president and Mr. Jules Basdevant of France as vice-president, and appointed Mr. Edvard Hambro of Norway as registrar. It held its inaugural sitting on April 18 and sat until May 6. During this period it prepared rules of procedure and formed the Chamber for Summary Procedure.

The first business brought before the Court was the Corfu Channel mine dispute referred to it on April 9, 1947, by the Security Council.

ORGANIZATION OF THE SECRETARIAT

A Secretariat was improvised in London to serve the General Assembly and the Security Council. As soon as a Secretary-General was elected on February 1, 1947, the members of the Secretariat became, according to the Charter, subject to his direction and control. In recruiting and directing his staff, the Secretary-General is obliged to follow "regulations established by the General Assembly" (Article 101.1). Such regulations were made by the First Part of the First Session of the General Assembly on recommendation of the Preparatory Commission.

Two factors rendered difficult the selection of the original staff of the Secretariat. The staff had to be chosen speedily. Furthermore, according to the Charter, it had to be recruited "on as wide a geographical basis as possible." The eight positions of Assistant Secretary-General were given to nationals of eight nations, including all the Big Five. As was inevitable, the governments of the members of the United Nations looked upon positions in the staff as patronage which they should all share and also as opportunities for exercising influence over the work of the Organization. The Secretary-General could not resist such pressure. Many early members of the Secretariat were, therefore, unskilled in their functions or unwilling to perform them. At the same time large numbers of the staff who were engaged in essentially administrative duties were naturally recruited in the United States. As of November 6, 1946, when the Secretary-General reported on its organization, the Secretariat consisted of 2,992 persons—including 1,611 Americans, 448 citizens of the United Kingdom, 297 French, 121 Swiss, and 121 Canadian. By the summer of 1949 the Secretariat contained almost 4,000 persons.

The necessarily rapid recruitment made a certain amount of inefficiency inevitable, and the need for economy, so noticeable after the budgetary actions of the Second Part of the First Session of the General Assembly, made it difficult to secure good candidates. But the inefficiency, resulting chiefly from the element of patronage, had been foreseen, and the Secretariat from the first functioned adequately, if not exceptionally well, and has continued to improve.

THE SECOND PART OF THE FIRST SESSION OF THE GENERAL ASSEMBLY

The Second Part of the First Session of the General Assembly met at the temporary headquarters in New York—Lake Success and Flushing Meadows—on October 23, 1946, and continued through December 16. Between the two parts all the organs of the United Nations, except the Trusteeship Council, had been active.

The session reconvened after half a year of intense and varied experience.

In legal theory the Second Part was an adjourned meeting, so that no organizational changes occurred. But it was, already, the great forum of the United Nations, the sounding board of humanity, and immediately acquired the character of a public inquest into the affairs of the world.

PROBLEMS OF ORGANIZATION

From the point of view of organization and administration, the most important questions before the General Assembly in 1946 were the permanent headquarters and the budget.

The Headquarters

The question of the permanent Headquarters was undoubtedly, next to the selection of the Secretary-General, the most important one before the Assembly of 1946. Accessibility, local influence, and freedom of publicity condition the work of the organs of the United Nations. Geneva is accessible to Europe and the Near East and has a tradition of tolerance, and the League was about to transfer its more than adequate buildings to the United Nations. But the Soviet Union was opposed to a United Nations which looked like a new League. Since many of the problems of the United Nations were to be European problems, the United Nations might well have been in Europe, and a site not too "Western" in location might have been found. Europe, however, was voted down, though by a very small majority. Eventually, the decision against Europe was followed by a decision in favor of the United States.

One great reason for the choice of the United States for the headquarters was to maintain the interest of the United States in the Organization. Some delegations felt that the people of the United States might regard the United Nations as too foreign and too distant if, as in the case of the League of Nations, its headquarters were in Europe.

After the United States had been decided on, most delegations preferred a site in the East, and near New York City because of its cosmopolitan and metropolitan character. After lengthy study by the special Headquarters Committee the General Assembly, while still in London, voted that the permanent Headquarters of the United Nations should be in Westchester County, New York, or in Fairfield County, Connecticut, or in both of them. The Headquarters Commission was to make more specific recommendations to the Second Part of the session. Meanwhile it was decided that the temporary Headquarters was to be in New York City.

A temporary headquarters for the Secretariat was secured by Mr. Lie in buildings of Hunter College in the Bronx. During the summer of 1946 a move was made to Long Island. The City of New York opened its building at Flushing Meadow as a meeting place for the Assembly, and part of the Sperry Gyroscope building at Lake Success was secured for the Secretariat and for smaller meetings than those to be held at Flushing Meadow. The various national delegations were housed in hotels and other buildings in New York City. The provisional arrangements lacked convenience in every way. Hunter College was found to be inconvenient and inaccessible. Long Island was more so.

Since the proposed permanent site in the most expensive of New York's outer suburbs appeared to be impracticable, the Commission examined other possible locations. Eventually, Mr. John D. Rockefeller, Jr., offered a gift of a site in midtown Manhattan on the East River, and New York City agreed to facilitate the location. The General Assembly gave its approval on December 14, 1946.

The Budget

In the Second Part of the 1946 Assembly, the budget underwent examination and was reduced. The Working Capital Fund was cut to $20,000,000, and the final budget for 1946 was fixed at $19,390,000 and for 1947 at $27,740,000. The Committee on Contributions drew up a scale of contributions to the budget to be levied against the members, related partly to the estimated economic capacity of the member state and partly to such political considerations as whether the country had been invaded or not. The minimum contribution was very small. The United States was proposed for a contribution of 50 per cent. The latter figure was protested by the American representative and others and was cut to a maximum of 39.89 per cent with the provision that this proportion was to be considered exceptional, temporary, and resultant from war conditions and that normally no nation should pay more than one-third of the budget.

The location of the Headquarters in New York City, the necessity of making contributions in dollars, and the consequent expensiveness of the United Nations were considerations which made it seem reasonable to most member states that the American contribution should be very large. At the same time the objections to having an organization located in the United States and paid for predominantly by American money were almost as great. There were indications that some member states looked upon the United Nations as a nonessential which might be provided for them by their rich friends. At the same time the unexpected activities of the organs of the United Nations carried unexpected expense, and the Secretary-General was constantly obliged to urge economy.

A problem arose as to the budgets of the "specialized agencies." If these agencies were to be closely integrated with the United Nations, their budgets might properly be made part of the budget of the United Nations itself. If, on the other hand, their budgets were separate, some of the agencies might receive money which would be used better by the United Nations. And yet, since the membership of most specialized agencies differed from that of the United Nations, budgetary centralization would be unpredictable and unfair. There was no doubt that in the future the United Nations, like all national governments, would have serious and recurrent disputes over its budget.

As a temporary measure the Secretary-General was authorized to lend money to specialized agencies for two years, and the

General Assembly voted specifically to lend $1,300,000 to the Interim Committee of the World Health Organization.

POLITICAL PROBLEMS

Political questions were brought to the General Assembly, which had to be handled by that body.

Ending the League of Nations

The 1946 Assembly was obliged to deal with certain problems relating to the League of Nations. Since the United Nations was to replace the League of Nations (which maintained a formal existence until the summer of 1946), a negotiating committee was appointed by the General Assembly to arrange with the League authorities to take over properties of the League. The General Assembly also determined to take over and continue nonpolitical activities of the League, so that there might be as little interruption as possible in these activities. In particular, it recommended that all treaties be registered, not merely those made since the ratification of the Charter but also those unregistered with the League.

Membership

On the recommendation of the Security Council the General Assembly admitted four states to membership in the United Nations—Afghanistan, Iceland, and Sweden in November and Siam in December, and asked the Security Council to reconsider other applications for membership which the Council had rejected.

Spain

Franco Spain, as a wartime associate of the Axis powers, came under condemnation. In December the General Assembly voted that the Franco government should be excluded from the United Nations and from its agencies and its conferences, and that if within a reasonable time there did not come into existence a popular and free government in Spain, the Security Council should consider measures to remedy the situation. Furthermore, all members of the United Nations should immediately recall from Madrid their ambassadors and ministers plenipotentiary accredited there.

Voting in the Security Council

The problem of the veto had already arisen in the Security Council. On this question the General Assembly recommended that the Security Council adopt practices which would reduce the difficulties arising from the Charter requirement of a special majority for any substantive action taken by the Council.

Indians in South Africa

The problem of discrimination in South Africa against the Indian population of the Union was brought before the Assembly by the delegation of India, who maintained that discrimination impaired friendly relations between the two countries. In spite of the South African insistence that the problem was a domestic matter, the General Assembly passed a resolution expressing the opinion that the treatment of the Indians should be in conformity with agreements between the countries and with the provisions of the Charter.

Trusteeship and Non-Self-Governing Territories

The Second Part of the 1946 session was able to establish the international trusteeship system, since trusteeship agreements had been made for eight formerly mandated territories. These agreements were approved by the General Assembly. Thereupon the Assembly elected two nonadministering states, Mexico and Iraq, to the Trusteeship Council. Since this election produced the necessary Charter balance between administering and nonadministering members, the Council could come into existence. The Soviet Union stated its belief that the trusteeship agreements were contrary to the Charter and failed to take its seat in the Trusteeship Council until 1948.

On the question of non-self-governing territories, the Assembly created a committee to examine the Secretary-General's summary of the information transmitted in regard to non-self-governing territories and to make recommendations "regarding the procedure to be followed in the future." It also recommended a conference of representatives of non-self-governing peoples to carry out Chapter XI and to express the aspirations of non-self-governing peoples.

Armaments

In January, 1946, the General Assembly had established the Atomic Energy Commission. In December it passed a comprehensive resolution on armaments, looking toward a study of the whole problem under the direction of the Security Council.

Miscellaneous

Already, in July, 1946, the Secretary-General had made the first of his annual reports on the work of the Organization. The Security Council and the Economic and Social Council reported likewise. Before it finished its sessions, the General Assembly of 1946 had begun consideration of many problems relating to international well-being which were to concern the United Nations in the years to come. When it adjourned on December 16, the work of organization of the United Nations had been concluded, and the status and effectiveness of the General Assembly as the principal organ of the United Nations was established.

Chapter 7

THE GENERAL ASSEMBLIES OF 1947
1948, AND 1949: PROBLEMS OF
ORGANIZATION AND MEMBERSHIP

NUMBER AND LENGTH OF MEETINGS

It had been expected that the meetings of the General Assembly would be limited to a few weeks and that they would be concerned with reaching fairly easy decisions on largely agreed-upon matters. The Security Council, which meets even while the General Assembly is in session, was to relieve the General Assembly of concern with problems of international peace and security. The Economic and Social Council and the Trusteeship Council were to handle the other large areas of business. Though the General Assembly could consider many questions of international peace and security, and though it has complete authority over the Economic and Social Council and the Trusteeship Council, its authority was considered residual. But the democratic instinct, the soundest instinct in the affairs of human organization, has been too strong. The General Assembly is the center of the United Nations. It can neither abdicate nor share its position.

In fact, the General Assembly has met far too often and far too long. Obliged to meet twice in 1946 to complete the work of organization, it also met twice in 1947 and in 1948. And since an adjourned session in the spring of 1949 was needed to finish the work of the regular 1948 session, the Assembly met twice also in 1949. A special session (the first) to consider the problem of Palestine was held from April 28 to May 15, 1947. The second regular session met from September 16 to November 29, 1947. A second special session, again on Palestine, was held from April 16 to May 14, 1948. The regular session of 1948 began on

September 21 and adjourned on December 12 with so much business still to do that a Second Part of the session was held from April 5 to May 18, 1949. The Assembly reassembled again on September 20, 1949.

The reasons for many and lengthy sessions are comprehensible and for the most part valid.

The agenda of the General Assembly consists partly of matters of organization which must be handled at least once a year (such as elections to the councils and the budget) and partly of items proposed by member governments, by organs of the United Nations, or by specialized agencies.

The political questions on the agenda are seldom disposed of in one session. Many of them are problems long recognized as perennial and probably insoluble. Most of them are bound to be discussed annually, even if a solution is known to be impossible. Even a question like Palestine or Indonesia, which seems in the process of settlement, will be mentioned again and again. The General Assembly is the supreme forum.

LEADERSHIP IN THE GENERAL ASSEMBLY

About the only leadership which the General Assembly has been able to provide officially for itself lies in the General Committee. This arranges the agenda and acts as a steering committee—subject to the General Assembly itself. But the General Committee cannot keep off the agenda any item whose discussion meets a considerable demand nor can it force the Assembly to accept any plan of work.

If effective great-power leadership had appeared, the business of the General Assembly would proceed more rapidly. When the five great powers have been in agreement, delay has been slight. On the one question on which the United States and the Soviet Union were in substantial agreement, the partition plan for Palestine in November, 1947, and the admission of Palestine to the Organization in May, 1949, two-thirds of the Assembly agreed quickly, even if reluctantly. The fundamental differences be-

tween the United States and the Soviet Union, which were noticeable in the autumn session in 1947 prolonged the autumn session
of 1948, in spite of the fact that the United States was usually able
to secure a two-thirds vote in favor of measures of which it was
the chief sponsor. Even so, many of the two-thirds accept slowly,
reluctantly, and with reservations. Perhaps the United States
and the Soviet Union, who sometimes seem to be trying to lead
the United Nations in opposite directions, have clear-cut long-
term policies, but the other members of the United Nations are
not always sure what they are.

In default of the great-power leadership that the Charter assumed, leadership has been left to the ordinary political processes.
The General Assembly assumes some of the characteristics of a
legislature where policy and politics are mingled. Blocs are
formed. Factions and almost parties develop.

Regional blocs began to appear early. The communist or
Soviet bloc was the first to show itself, though it has not been
unchanging, since it has added Czechoslovakia and (in 1949) lost
Yugoslavia. The Latin-American states and the Arab League
states have shown a constant tendency to work as groups and even
to caucus and bargain as similar blocs do in national legislatures.
The Asiatic nations tend to vote together. The colonial powers
generally stand together on issues involving colonial problems.
And so do the anticolonial powers. On Palestine, on the Italian
colonies, on Indonesia, on Spain, the large voting strength of such
blocs has hindered quick conclusions. Furthermore, there is a
latent antagonism between the great powers and the lesser powers,
who may be weaker but are much more numerous. Anti-Semitism is sometimes noticeable. Most delegations are anticommunist, but most are socialistic, or at least strongly in favor of
the "welfare state." Field Marshal Smuts has suggested that
the General Assembly is opposed to segregation of races because
the majority of member governments represent colored populations. On the position of women, some delegations are conservative, some radical.

Some delegations are leaders because of the importance of

their country. Some lead through ideas, others by personality. A delegation representing a government with definite ideas has an importance far beyond its vote or its national strength. The most conspicuous example of influence arising from ideology is shown by the Soviet bloc, but the Arab states are hardly second in this way, since their position on most things is firm and unchangeable. Part of the effectiveness of South Africa, the Philippines, Australia, and India come from their firm, clear, and uncompromising policies.

Speeches for the constituents at home, for propaganda, or for personal advantage are common, just as they are in national legislatures. Filibustering occurs, as it does in the American Senate or the English House of Lords. Arguments are repeated again and again, as in any free parliament. Irrelevancy sometimes seems to be the rule. The General Assembly "wastes" most of its time, as does the American House of Representatives or the French National Assembly. All these things are true because the General Assembly is composed of the same sort of people who compose national legislatures, and because the General Assembly, like national legislatures, cannot be more wise than the people it represents. Part of the price of free, popular, representative government is to support legislatures which are so free and so uncontrolled that they are superficially inefficient.

Personal leadership is just beginning to emerge. Such leadership must come from the statesmen of the smaller powers. The great powers will seldom spare the time of their highest officials for continuous attendance at the General Assembly. Furthermore, they change their representatives of ministerial rank frequently and can do so because the man, whoever he may be, is less than the nation he represents. It matters little whether a Bidault or a Schuman, a Molotov or a Vyshinsky, a Byrnes or a Marshall represents France, the Soviet Union, or the United States. But representatives of lesser powers are often more important than their country. Evatt of Australia, Rómulo of the Philippines, Fraser of New Zealand, Spaak of Belgium, Aranha of Brazil, Malik of Lebanon, Bramulgia of Argentina are examples of men who have exercised personal leadership. A good deal used to be said, in the old League of Nations' days, about the "Geneva atmosphere," which softened the intransigence of nationalists, encouraged the internationalism of the weakhearted, and offered a worthy forum to the greatest of statesmen. Such an atmosphere does not yet exist at Lake Success, but such men as these are creating it.

Some of these problems of leadership are bound to lessen with time. The General Assembly has been underrepresentative of the European states, whose experience in international negotiation is historically greatest. It has been overrepresentative of the newer states. Already in 1949 it included five states not independent in 1945—India, Pakistan, the Philippines, Burma, and Israel—and even if one excludes the British dominions, nine others that did not exist in 1919—Iraq, Byelorussia, Egypt, Iceland, Lebanon, Saudi Arabia, Syria, the Ukraine, and Yemen. A considerable proportion of member states and their representatives is composed of novices. Because of political and social change, individual representatives of even the older states must sometimes be novices also.

On the other hand, it cannot be overemphasized that the General Assembly has conducted itself with a degree of decorum and effectiveness which is astonishing in so divided and so difficult a world. The Secretary-General in his annual report of 1946–1947 pointed out as a difficulty that "the growth of the Organization had been somewhat impetuous and not always sufficiently subject to over-all planning" (page *vii*). But in his report for 1947–1948 he commented that the United Nations "has become the chief force that holds the world together against all the conflicting strains and stresses that are pulling it apart," and that the "organs of the United Nations are now virtually the only places where regular contact and discussion have been maintained on a continuous basis between the Western Powers and the Soviet Union" (page *ix*). Though a limited good, this is better than nothing. The General Assembly *is* the "town-meeting of the world" if not yet quite the "parliament of man." For this reason even the fruitless and exasperating wrangles over disarmament or over human freedoms have their value, though they may temporarily exacerbate feelings already too easily stirred up.

THE ORGANIZATION OF THE GENERAL ASSEMBLY

The pattern of organization of the General Assembly was suggested by the Preparatory Commission and adopted in 1946. It still works effectively. The Assembly elects a president for each session and seven vice-presidents. These eight officials, together with the six chairmen of the six main committees (each elected by his committee) serve as a general committee which exercises such guidance and direction as the Assembly chooses to receive. The General Committee is a steering committee, but precluded from deciding any political question. It has useful powers of coordination but no control.

A second committee concerned with procedure is the Credentials Committee of nine elected members.

The six main committees are each composed of one representative from each member state. The areas of their jurisdiction have come to be well defined. They are:

First Committee: Political and Security

Second Committee: Economic and Financial

Third Committee: Social, Humanitarian, and Cultural

Fourth Committee: Trusteeship (and problems of non-self-governing territories)

Fifth Committee: Administrative and Budgetary

Sixth Committee: Legal

Most of the conspicuous problems which go to the Assembly are referred to the First Committee, and sometimes an *ad hoc* political committee has been created to supplement it. The main committees often use subcommittees. The delegates who represent their governments in the main committee may often be experts and technicians rather than political heads of delegations. Except in the First Committee, there is a good deal of continuity of personnel from one session to another.

There are two standing committees of the General Assembly whose members are elected by the Assembly but serve in their personal capacity. The first is the Advisory Committee for Administrative and Budgetary Questions which examines the budget as drawn up by the Secretary-General. The second is the Committee on Contributions which decides annually how the contributions to the budget shall be assessed.

The General Assembly uses *ad hoc* committees dealing with individual matters of substance, such as the special committees on Palestine and the Balkans. The Interim Committee, or "Little Assembly" discussed below, is perhaps more than a committee in the usual sense.

The president of the General Assembly has become a person of greater importance than would be implied in his election for a session and his functions as presiding officer in plenary meetings and in the General Committee.

The first president, Mr. Spaak of Belgium, who presided over the two parts of the 1946 session, had the honor of interpreting the Provisional Rules of Procedure as an effective code of parliamentary conduct. Based on Continental rather than Anglo-Saxon precedents (for they are derived largely from the rules of the League of Nations Assembly), the rules give so much freedom to delegates as to require an effective president to be a strategist as well as a chairman. The president of the first special session was Mr. Oswaldo Aranha of Brazil. His effectiveness caused him to be elected as president of the regular 1947 session. The second special session on Palestine, in 1948, was a body of diplomats and technicians rather than of major governmental representatives, and was guided effectively by a relative newcomer to United Nations meetings, Dr. Arce of Argentina. The third regular session of 1948 chose Dr. Evatt of Australia, whose energy and effectiveness had been known from the days of the San Francisco Conference. General Carlos Rómulo of the Philippines, who had been chairman of his delegation at San Francisco, was the president of the 1949 session.

During the sessions of the General Assembly, most of the time is occupied by meetings of the main committees. Plenary meetings of the Assembly begin the session and permit the inevitable political pronunciamentos. They occur also later in the session when it is necessary to record decisions, or even to reargue cases on which committees have already voted. Not infrequently, a close issue will not be determined until it has been discussed in plenary meeting, though for the most part the speeches in plenary meetings are for the record only.

CONTINUING THE ORGANIZATION

Whatever else the General Assembly fails to do, it has never yet failed to perform the acts which are annually necessary to keep the United Nations and its organs functioning.

Elections

In each annual session there must be elections to the Security Council and the Economic and Social Council, and there may be elections to the Trusteeship Council or the Court. The Court is planned to change slowly in membership, and the only elections of its judges held since the Court was constituted in 1936 were to the five places which fell vacant on December 31, 1948. To these five places were reelected the judges whose terms had expired. For the councils, the practice has developed that the five permanent members of the Security Council and the Trusteeship Council will be elected members of the Economic and Social Council also. Otherwise, the principle of rotation seems to have been adopted. When a member of a bloc or grouping is to retire, its successor is chosen by the other states in the group and is ordinarily elected by the Assembly.

This practice may conflict with the principle (or practice) of geographical distribution. In 1947 when Australia, Brazil, and Poland were retiring from the Security Council, Australia as a member of the British Commonwealth was replaced by Canada, Brazil as a Latin-American state by Argentina, and Poland as a member of the Soviet bloc by the Ukraine. This was bloc representation. An attempt had been made to upset it. The United States wished to secure the election of Czechoslovakia instead of the Ukraine. This effort failed, since the Ukraine was the choice of the other Eastern European members. A more nearly successful attempt to elect India instead of the Ukraine also failed, though the failure left the entire southern and eastern area of Asia unrepresented.

In 1949 Czechoslovakia was the choice of the Soviet bloc to replace the Ukraine and was strongly backed by the Soviet Union. Yugoslavia, because of its dispute with the Soviet Union, received the support of the United States, though not that of all the important anticommunist powers. Yugoslavia was elected by 39 to 19, precisely the necessary two-thirds.

The Budget

The budget must receive annual approval. Advised by its two technical committees, the Committee on Administrative and Budgetary Problems and the Committee on Contributions, the Assembly need spend little time on the matter. It seems satisfied so long as the budget as drawn up by the Secretariat is cut on the advice of the committees, and so long as the scale of contributions is maintained without essential change. Though some millions of the budget go to pay the expenses of bodies like the committees and commissions concerned with Palestine, there has been little objection so far to the specific items included in the budget. In 1948 the United States secured the approval of the Assembly to a statement that normally there should be a ceiling of 33⅓ per cent on national contributions to the budget. The 39.89 per cent contribution of the United States of 1948 was levied, however, for 1949 and was cut only slightly for 1950.

Other Problems

A number of problems of the effective establishment of the United Nations have continued. The first is that of the headquarters. The 1946 Assembly determined on New York, and a site on Manhattan was secured, but permanent buildings had to be constructed. Eventually, a loan was arranged with the United States and approved by Congress in the summer of 1948. The cornerstone of the first of the buildings, the one intended for the Secretariat, was laid on United Nations Day, October 24, 1949.

The Convention on Privileges and Immunities of the United Nations has not yet been widely ratified and lacks the ratification of the United States.

The problem of a United Nations guard has arisen. To Palestine Mr. Lie had sent fifty guards from his headquarters staff to assist United Nations officials there. In his report for 1947–1948 he speaks of a small United Nations guard force which might be at the disposal of the General Assembly and the Security Council "not as a striking force but purely a guard force." It could be used as a constabulary in such places as Jerusalem and Trieste. Such a force might be useful, even if the Security Council had at its disposal forces under Article 43, since the availability of the latter would be limited to emergencies.

In 1948, over the protest of the Secretary-General, the General Assembly voted to add Spanish as a working language. The decision was to go into effect for the fourth regular session.

The General Assembly adopted an emblem in 1946 and in 1947 a flag and flag code.

Two major subproblems of continuing the Organization are the question of membership and the question of the Interim Committee.

Membership

New Members Admitted

From the beginning it seems to have been assumed that action on applications for membership must go through two stages. The Security Council must "recommend" favorably. After the favorable recommendation is made, the General Assembly can admit to membership by a two-thirds majority. From the beginning the recommendation of the Security Council has been considered the type of action which requires the special majority of Article 27.3. In other words the veto applies.

In 1946 four new members were admitted to the Organization—Iceland, Sweden, Afghanistan, and Siam. In 1947 Pakistan (on its separation from India) and Yemen were admitted. In 1948 Burma was admitted, and late in May, 1949, Israel. There are, however, many other states which have applied for membership.

The Continuing Problem of Membership

Up until the General Assembly session of 1949 applications received from thirteen other states had been examined by the Security Council's Committee on the Admission of New Members and had failed to secure the favorable vote of the Security Council. They are Albania, Ireland, the Mongolian People's Republic, Portugal, and Transjordan, all of which applied in 1946; Austria, Bulgaria, Finland, Hungary, Italy, and Romania, which applied in 1947; Ceylon, which applied in 1948; and Nepal, which applied in 1949. In 1949 the Korean government, established in the American zone and voted by the General Assembly to be the only legal government of Korea, applied. So also did the government in the Soviet zone. These applications had not yet been acted on by the Security Council.

The thirteen applicants for admission which have failed of favorable action have received varying votes. Some of them received seven or more favorable votes but were vetoed by the Soviet Union. (They are Austria, Ceylon, Finland, Ireland, Italy, Nepal, Portugal, and Transjordan.) Others have not received seven favorable votes because the United States and the United Kingdom have abstained or voted in the negative. These are the applicants whose admission the Soviet Union has seemed particularly to sponsor—Albania, Bulgaria, Hungary, the Mongolian People's Republic, and Romania.

The General Assembly has been dissatisfied with the actions of the Security Council. It has frequently asked the Security Council to reconsider the applications. It has passed resolutions to the effect that seven states vetoed by the Soviet Union are qualified for membership. It has noted in a resolution "the general sentiment in favor of the universality of the United Nations." It has approved a report of the Interim Committee that the veto should be foregone in questions of membership where the state concerned received seven favorable votes. It has not accepted the suggestion that it admit states not recommended by the Security Council by the special majority of Article 27.3. But the 1949 General Assembly, on the initiative of Argentina, referred to the International Court of Justice the question of whether or not a state can be admitted to membership in the United Nations by decision of the Assembly when the Security Council has made no recommendation.

Those states which have been admitted have been on the borderland between the Soviet Union and the Western powers, either ideologically or geographically. The others suffer from too strong sponsorship by one side or the other. When it became clear that political motives were responsible for the Security Council's failures to recommend, the General Assembly of 1947 sent to the International Court of Justice a request for an advisory opinion, first, as to whether tests of membership could be imposed other than those stated in the Charter and, second, as to whether a state's vote in the Security Council might be dependent on the admission of a group of states, since the Soviet Union had offered to approve the admission of all the ex-enemy states that signed the peace treaties in 1947 in one group. The Court, though not too clearly, seemed to decide against the Soviet policies, but its opinion has no coercive effect. Subsequently, the Soviet Union has proposed the bloc admission of all thirteen applicants, but its resolution to this effect received only two affirmative votes in the Security Council in September, 1949.

If the thirteen states were admitted, the United Nations would achieve as great universality as is possible at present. The only states properly so called that would remain outside would be Japan, Germany, Korea, Spain, and Switzerland. Japan and Germany are still under military occupation. "Franco Spain" was debarred by the General Assembly of 1946 from membership in the United Nations or in any specialized agency or any international conference. Switzerland holds its policy of neutrality to be inconsistent with the obligations of the Charter, though it has become a party to the Statute of the Court.

If the Security Council could agree to recommend all the thirteen applicants, it is probable that the General Assembly would admit them all. But the majority of the Security Council still insists that applications shall be voted on one by one. And the Western powers are reluctant to increase the size of either the Soviet or the anticolonial bloc in the Assembly.

Fortunately some states excluded from the United Nations belong to specialized agencies and thereby contribute to the performance of various functional tasks.

ATTEMPTS TO REFORM THE ORGANIZATION

The Interim Committee

By the autumn of 1947 the United Nations had been in existence long enough for one serious effort to be made to change its structure and to modify greatly the relative importance of its organs. The Security Council appeared impotent because of the veto, but there was no veto in the General Assembly. The United States therefore proposed a "Little Assembly" (as it was nicknamed) to supplement the work of the General Assembly itself in the field of peace and security, thus using the "untapped resources" of the United Nations. It proposed "a standing committee of the General Assembly, which might be known as the Interim Committee on Peace and Security" and which would serve while the General Assembly itself was not in session. It was not to "impinge on matters which are the primary responsibility of the Security Council or of special commissions." All members of the United Nations would be members of this Interim Committee.

The proposal was made in Secretary of State Marshall's speech of September 17, 1947 (from which the above quotations have been taken). The proposal was pressed by the United States and had wide backing from other states. It was bitterly opposed by the Soviet bloc, partly for the obvious political reasons, but partly on the stronger ground that the Interim Committee would be contrary to the Charter since it would deal with questions which belonged to the Security Council.

The constitutional argument had considerable appeal to many delegations. The General Assembly as a whole was clearly not willing to set up the proposed rival to the Security Council. But after the proposal had been redrawn in terms making it conscientiously consistent with the Charter, the Assembly supported the proposal with only six negative votes. The Committee was set up with a clear and limited authority, on a provisional basis until the 1948 Assembly should meet, and was continued by that Assembly for another year. The Soviet bloc, still insisting on the illegality of the whole proposal, has continued to refuse to take its seats in the Interim Committee.

Specified as being a subsidiary organ of the General Assembly in accordance with Article 22, the Interim Committee (as it is now named) is to assist the General Assembly, with the duties to:

Consider and report to the General Assembly on questions referred to it by the General Assembly;

Consider and report to the General Assembly on any dispute or situation proposed for the agenda of the General Assembly by a member, or by the Security Council, in the general field of pacific settlement (Articles 11.2, 14, and 35 are specified in the resolution), but in the first case only if the Committee votes to do so by a two-thirds majority;

Consider and report on methods for effecting Article 11.1, which deals with general cooperation in maintaining international peace and security, and Article 13.1a, which deals with promoting international cooperation in the political field.

Within its area of action it may advise the Secretary-General of the need of a special session of the General Assembly and may "conduct investigations and appoint commissions of inquiry" by a two-thirds vote. (If held elsewhere than at the Headquarters, the inquiry or investigation needs the approval of the state in whose territory it is to take place.)

Thus limited, the Committee has shown a usefulness in considering a small number of questions and has had a quiet and far from revolutionary career.   In the 1949 Assembly its life was extended indefinitely.

The Veto

The veto in the Security Council has also been the subject of discussion.   Various proposals to limit its use have been made. Secretary Marshall indicated the favorable attitude of the United States to a change which would eliminate the "unanimity requirement with respect to matters arising under Chapter VI of the Charter [peaceful settlement] and such matters as applications for membership."   The question of the veto was referred to the Interim Committee for study.   The Committee's report was discussed by the General Assembly in the spring of 1949, and the General Assembly approved its proposals for the limitation in the use of the veto, particularly in the fields of pacific settlement and recommendations of new members.

Since any change in the practices of the permanent members of the Security Council must depend on the attitude of these powers themselves, these proposals for reform of the veto power have been without result.

It is perhaps shortsighted to suppose that such fundamental changes as the limitation of the veto or the adoption of a new principle of membership can be made so early in the history of the Organization.   Most written constitutions resist amendment much longer than the five-year-old Charter of the United Nations.

Chapter 8. THE GENERAL ASSEMBLIES OF 1947 1948, AND 1949: SUBSTANTIVE PROBLEMS

Each session of the General Assembly has had its individual character. The world situation changes. National policies of member states change at least in emphasis. New problems emerge. Much of the character of a session depends on the political preoccupations of the moment. The questions attracting most attention are those coming within the province of the First Committee.

THE FIRST SPECIAL SESSION: APRIL 28 TO MAY 15, 1947

After the Second Part of the First Session was completed, just before Christmas, 1946, the wearied delegates and their advisers looked forward to a breathing space until the next autumn. Instead, the question of a special session arose.

The first Special Session was called on the initiative of the government of the United Kingdom. That government requested the Secretary-General to call the Special Session to constitute a special committee on Palestine. The Secretary-General consulted the other governments, and since a majority concurred in the request, the Special Session met at Lake Success in April, 1947. To call it proved simple, and its organization was simple also. Only its First (or Political) Committee functioned. To it were referred the British agenda item and other items proposed in relation to Palestine. The Special Session limited its business to the various aspects of this one question.

After lengthy argument the Special Session voted a committee as requested by the United Kingdom. (See the discussion of Palestine in Chapter 9.)

THE SECOND REGULAR SESSION: SEPTEMBER 16 TO NOVEMBER 29, 1947

The second regular session of the General Assembly was the first to be conspicuously overshadowed by Soviet-American disagreement. The United States Congress had voted military aid to Greece and Turkey, two states not previously in the direct American sphere of interest, and this aid was stated to be in accordance with a policy of resisting communism everywhere—the so-called Truman Doctrine. A little later the Marshall plan had been proposed to promote European recovery by American subsidy. It had been accepted by Western European nations, but was rejected and bitterly opposed by the Soviet Union. Furthermore, the occupying powers in Germany were in disagreement, and a deadlock was to be reached shortly after the General Assembly adjourned. There was unrest in many non-European areas—particularly in southeast Asia and in the Middle East. India and Pakistan had become separately independent and were in acute conflict. Palestine was the most conspicuous area of trouble.

American policy had stiffened and was conducted stiffly. In technical terms the United States had adopted a "positive" foreign policy. It was based on the theory of containment of the Soviet Union, politically and militarily, and the support politically as well as economically of Western European governments. For the first time since San Francisco the long-term policy of supporting a general international organization was sacrificed to the short-term policy of seeking allies. Though support of the United Nations continued to be stated as the basis of American foreign policy, and the statements were no doubt sincere, the immediate policy was to use the United Nations for American ends. This was no more than the British, the French, and the Russians had tried to do from the beginning, but it left the fate of the United Nations as a universalist organization at least temporarily in the hands of the smaller powers.

Soviet policy also stiffened. The Soviet Union not only insisted on full and positive support from its satellites but, feeling itself on the defensive, resisted American containment all along the line.

The 1947 session of the General Assembly, therefore, met in an atmosphere of acrimony and bad feeling. This was added to by the bad feeling which the problem of Palestine created. It is nevertheless possible that in the future the 1947 session will be best remembered for its contribution to the settlement of the problem of Palestine.

Palestine

The question of Palestine was discussed at unusual length on the basis of the report made by the United Nations Special Committee on Palestine, which had been created by the General Assembly in May. A decision was not reached until the very end of the session. In the politics of the Assembly the question was extremely significant because it did not follow a conventional pattern of East against West or established as against underprivileged nations. The Soviet Union and the United States both supported a solution based on the report of the majority of the Special Committee, and the necessary majority in the Assembly was secured—showing how powerful the two great powers are if they agree.

Greece

Another troubled area was Greece. Here the question was brought into the Assembly by the United States, and the Soviet Union was in strong and definite opposition. Since the Security Council had failed to proceed in the Greek situation because of the Soviet veto, the United States had the question removed from the Security Council agenda and placed on the agenda of the General Assembly.

There were border troubles for which Greece, and the majority of the Security Council's Committee of Investigation, blamed Albania, Bulgaria, and Yugoslavia because they supported guerrillas fighting against the Greek government. The General Assembly called on the three governments to do nothing to assist the guerrillas and on all four governments to settle their disputes by peaceful means. It also established an eleven-power special committee to observe and to assist in the implementation of its resolutions. The Soviet Union and Poland refused to take their places on the Special Committee—the Soviet Union having attempted to persuade the General Assembly to blame Greece for the disorders.

Korea

The question of "the independence of Korea" was also brought to the General Assembly by the United States. Korea was occupied in the north by the Soviet Union and in the south by the United States. It had been the subject of negotiations by the Soviet-American Joint Committee. These negotiations had broken down (not for the first time) in August. The United States persuaded the General Assembly to establish the United Nations Temporary Commission on Korea composed of nine members excluding the United States and the Soviet Union. This Commission was to go to Korea to arrange for elections to choose representatives to a national assembly which would then establish a national Korean government to administer the country and arrange for the withdrawal of the occupying forces.

The Temporary Commission was to consult, if necessary, with the Interim Committee, which it did. It was refused admission to the Soviet zone. In the American zone, it arranged and observed the elections, which were held on May 10, 1948. These elections were the essential step in establishing a Korean government in that zone.

Spain

Spain was the other great political problem. The partial diplomatic boycott proclaimed by the General Assembly in 1946 was not strong enough to suit some member states. The General Assembly refused to do more than it had already done, but voted its confidence that the Security Council (as requested in 1946) would take action in regard to Spain if necessary.

Economic and Social Questions

To the 1947 Assembly the major world economic problem seemed to be that of European reconstruction. The East-West split caused general discussions of this problem to be long and acrimonious. The Soviet bloc unsuccessfully urged the General Assembly to condemn the Organization for European Economic Cooperation and other Marshall-plan agencies which operated outside the United Nations machinery.

On the side of positive action a number of decisions were made. It was decided that the Economic and Social Council would be responsible for the production of an annual survey of world economic conditions. The General Assembly gave provisional approval to an Economic Commission for the Middle East similar to those for Europe, Asia, and Latin America. It approved agreements with further specialized agencies, such as the Bank, the Fund, the World Health Organization, the Universal Postal Union, and the International Telecommunications Union. It recommended closer cooperation between the Economic and Social Council, the specialized agencies, and the Secretariat. It urged member states to coordinate their policies in the United Nations and the specialized agencies.

The General Assembly also dealt with problems of relief, notably the International Children's Emergency Fund. It called the Conference on Freedom of Information.

Non-Self-Governing Territories

In the area of the Fourth Committee—Trusteeship and Information from Non-Self-Governing Territories—advances were made in developing both procedure and policy. The Trusteeship Council, it must be remembered, is responsible to the General Assembly.

Former Mandates. There were three former mandated territories not yet under trusteeship: Palestine, Nauru, and South-

West Africa. The Pacific Islands had become a strategic-area trusteeship by action of the Security Council in 1947. For the Trust Territory of the Pacific Islands so created, the General Assembly has no responsibility.

A trusteeship agreement for Nauru, which was to be administered by Australia for itself, the United Kingdom, and New Zealand, was approved by the General Assembly, with the Soviet bloc opposing.

The General Assembly took note of the opposition of the Union of South Africa to placing South-West Africa under trusteeship but continued its recommendation of 1946 that this action should be taken.

Palestine was, of course, the subject of special consideration.

Information. The problem of information from non-self-governing territories was the subject of lengthy consideration. In accordance with Article 73*e* of the Charter, administering authorities were giving information to the Secretary-General, and in accordance with a General Assembly resolution of 1946 the Secretary-General was summarizing the information. A resolution of 1946 had provided for an *ad hoc* committee to examine this summary. The *ad hoc* Committee was composed of the administering authorities and an equal number of other states, elected by the 1946 General Assembly, most of them anticolonial in attitude.

Two points of view had appeared. The colonial powers were reconciled to giving information relating to social, economic, and educational conditions in their dependencies. Sometimes the information was full, sometimes it was niggardly, but they gave it. But they objected to any very serious discussion resulting from this information. In particular, they objected to the proposals to try to force colonial powers to furnish political information. (The United States furnished it voluntarily.) India, China, and the Philippines, as well as the Soviet bloc, led what seemed to be an attempt to bring all colonies under effective United Nations supervision. In the General Assembly the colonial powers, on the whole, maintained their position effectively and resisted control. The resolutions passed on this subject continued the *ad hoc* Committee as a special committee for three years and encouraged the transmission of political information. In other words, the system of reporting and of examining reports was now well-established. Chapter XI had become more than a mere declaration of good intentions. It was beginning to be a basis for control.

Legal Matters

Legal matters included a recommendation for the greater use of the International Court of Justice and for the establishment of an international law commission. The commission would promote the progressive development and the codification of international law. It might draft multilateral conventions, select areas of international law for codification and begin to work on them, and act to make customary international law more generally known.

Conclusion

When the 1947 session adjourned, there was no feeling of jubilation over its results. One interesting manifestation of dissatisfaction was the decision of the General Assembly to hold its 1948 session in Europe. The plans for the construction of headquarters buildings in New York had lagged. Continuing inflation made New York increasingly expensive. Many governments still felt that Europe should have been the seat of the United Nations, and some governments felt that the United Nations was too easily dominated by the United States. Nevertheless, the vote to meet in Europe was far from unanimous (32 for, 17 against, and 5 abstentions).

SECOND SPECIAL SESSION: APRIL 16 TO MAY 14, 1948

Before the expected European session could be held, a second, suddenly called special session met in New York. The situation in Palestine had become so acute that the Security Council, on the initiative of the United States, called a special session of the General Assembly. This session limited its business strictly to the Palestine question, except for the admission of Burma as a member of the Organization. The sole practical result of the Special Session, and, as it proved, an important one, was the appointment of a United Nations mediator in Palestine.

Third Regular Session: September to December, 1948, and April to May, 1949

The third regular session of the General Assembly met in Paris on September 21, 1948. On December 12 it adjourned to resume its session in April, 1949, in New York.

Atmosphere of Bitterness

The Paris meeting took place during the height of Soviet-American tension, and the intransigence of both countries appeared to be intentional. There was bitterness even in the organization of the session. But for the rebukes of Dr. Evatt, the president, the majority might have chosen a general committee that had no representatives of the Soviet bloc. There was also bitterness over the agenda, from which the General Committee removed some Soviet-sponsored items.

The session, unlike the Special Session in the spring, was a full-dress affair. The American Secretary of State, Mr. George C. Marshall, the British Secretary of State for Foreign Affairs, Mr. Ernest Bevin, and the Soviet Under Secretary for Foreign Affairs, Mr. Andrei Vyshinsky, together with equivalent officials of many smaller states were present to lead their delegations. Whether governments were interested more in accomplishment or in propaganda might have been sometimes a question, but there was no doubt that national policies were to receive full expression.

No sooner was the Assembly organized and the general debate begun than violent, and often violently expressed, differences of opinion were proclaimed. Mr. Marshall put forward a full program of United States proposals for action in language which was moderate but which revealed American anger at Soviet opposition to American policies. Mr. Vyshinsky, using words that appeared to be intentionally undiplomatic, took the position that Western powers were warmongering against the Soviet Union under the leadership of the United States, whose new policy was one of imperialism and had nothing in common with a policy of peace. The one specific proposal which he put forward was that for a one-third reduction during one year of the armed forces of the Big Five.

Mr. Bevin, the third chief of a Big Five delegation to speak, appeared to take in his way as dismal a view of the future as did Mr. Vyshinsky and replied to the latter with an invective which was blunter, if less sharp. Mr. Robert Schuman, the French foreign minister, also condemned the Soviet policy unsparingly; and Mr. Spaak of Belgium, by saying that the policy of the small powers was based on fear of the Soviet Union, did not lend cheer to the discussion.

A different tone, unfortunately less effective, was taken by the foreign minister of China, Mr. Wang Shih-Chieh, who warned the disputants that there is no inevitable choice between capitalism and communism. Mr. Padilla Nervo, for Mexico, provided the one gleam of hope by expressing faith in the moral force that the Assembly possessed and proposing a resolution (later adopted) that the "great allied powers" should collaborate for peace in accordance with their avowals at Moscow and Yalta.

The session continued under a cloud that never lifted. Except for Palestine, all questions were argued in an atmosphere of East-West antagonism. The United States secured most of what it wanted. But many smaller powers, voting with the United States by conviction as well as by interest, hated to be obliged to take sides in a world which they did not believe needed to be divided. They objected also to the use of the General Assembly as a forum for sharpening the differences between great powers.

Their feeling was intensified by the Western powers' reference of the dispute over Berlin to the Security Council in the midst of the General Assembly session. Questions of peacemaking resulting from the Second World War were supposed to be outside the Charter, and there was no reason to refer to the Security Council an apparently hopeless problem for the purpose of showing that the Security Council was helpless to deal with it.

The assassination of Count Bernadotte, the United Nations mediator in Palestine, was another disheartening event. The one redeeming element in the whole situation was the effort of the six "neutral members" of the Security Council and of Dr. Evatt, as president of the Assembly, to work with the Secretary-General to produce some solution of the Berlin crisis. Any less devoted and powerful a president than Dr. Evatt might have accepted too readily the conclusion, stated by the United Kingdom's foreign secretary, that the United Nations had failed.

Specific Problems

The 1948 session produced greater accomplishments than could have been expected. Not an important question came before it which was not moved a little toward a solution.

Arms and Armaments

The problem of arms and armaments came back to the General Assembly for the first time since 1946. In December, 1946, the Assembly had passed a comprehensive resolution on armaments. During the two years that followed, the Atomic Energy Commission and the Commission on Conventional Armaments had worked on their respective problems under the control of the Security Council. In the Atomic Energy Commission a plan of international control, based on the United States proposals of the Acheson-Lilienthal Report, had been elaborated and adopted by the majority of the Commission; but owing to the Soviet veto, it was not adopted by the Security Council. Nevertheless, the Security Council (the Soviet delegate abstaining) had voted to transmit the three annual reports of the Atomic Energy Commission to the General Assembly. The third report included a statement to the effect that further work on the part of the

Atomic Energy Commission was useless in the existing political situation.

The Commission on Conventional Armaments, which was concerned with the old type of armaments, had likewise stated a program (though in outline form) which was acceptable to the majority but not to the Soviet Union.

The General Assembly in 1948, then, had before it two matters: first, the reports of the Atomic Energy Commission, which included what the majority of its members considered a practicable plan for the control of atomic energy, and, second, a resolution of the Commission on Conventional Armaments outlining a plan of control for nonatomic weapons. It had also the formal decision of the Western powers that further work was useless. All this came from the majority of the Security Council, led by the Western powers.

The Soviet Union in the General Assembly proposed two things: a proposal for immediate limitation of armaments and a counter-proposal on atomic energy. The first proposal, outlined in Mr. Vyshinsky's first speech, was that the Big Five should each reduce its armaments by one-third within one year. On the issue of atomic weapons the Soviet Union repeated, though in a modified form, its constant proposal before the Atomic Energy Commission that the first step in handling that problem should be a treaty outlawing atomic weapons.

The Western majority in the General Assembly had no difficulty in getting the reports of the Atomic Energy Commission approved by the General Assembly as an acceptable plan of atomic-weapon control. Furthermore, they easily persuaded the Assembly to reject the Soviet plan for the immediate reduction of great-power armaments. But when it came to their proposal that the work of the Atomic Energy Commission and the Commission on Conventional Armaments should stop, the smaller powers refused. They insisted that the consideration both of atomic weapons and of conventional armaments should continue. The General Assembly expressed its concern over the deadlock. It urged the six permanent members of the Atomic Energy Commission to consult together for possible agreement. It asked the Atomic Energy Commission to continue such studies as it could. As to the Commission on Conventional Armaments, it urged the continuance of its work and, in particular, a plan for the collection of information.

On the problem of armaments the position of the Western powers was weak. However much they might maintain that the Soviet proposal for immediate reduction of big-power armaments was made for propaganda only, their "dusty answer" that security must come before disarmament seemed peculiarly inept. From a practical point of view the Western powers (the United States in particular) were at a disadvantage, since they were engaged in a huge program of rearmament in the face of a Soviet Union which had not disarmed after the war so extensively as they had done. The smaller powers, by their action in the General Assembly, saved the principle that attempts should be made to break the deadlock.

Palestine, Greece, Korea

Palestine, Greece, and Korea were problems that had to be rediscussed.

On Palestine the General Assembly could do nothing, since the matter was in the hands of the Security Council and of the acting mediator, Dr. Ralph Bunche.

As to Greece, the United Nations Special Committee on the Balkans, appointed in 1947, had been unsuccessful in producing conciliation between Greece and its neighbors. The Assembly condemned the intervention of Greece's neighbors. It recommended the resumption of diplomatic relations between all the countries concerned, the making of agreements about frontiers, and the return to Greece of Greek children. It continued the life of the Special Committee. On the initiative of Australia, private talks for purposes of conciliation were held in Paris during the session of the General Assembly between representatives of the governments of Greece, Yugoslavia, Bulgaria, and Albania, Dr. Evatt, president of the General Assembly, the chairman and rapporteur of the First Committee, and Mr. Lie, the Secretary-General.

As to Korea, the United Nations Temporary Commission recorded the holding of elections in the southern zone, the establishment of a national assembly, and the creation of a national government on August 15, all under its supervision. It also reported the creation of the "People's Republic of Korea" in the northern or Soviet zone.

The Berlin Question

The question of the Soviet blockade of the Western zones of Berlin was constantly in the minds of delegates, because it so greatly increased the friction between East and West. It was never technically before the Assembly, but the fact that the Assembly was in session when the issue was brought before the Security Council gave opportunity for efforts toward conciliation which were far from useless.

Late in September the United Kingdom, the United States, and France brought the Berlin situation (blockade, divided administration, currency) before the Security Council as a threat to international peace and security. The Soviet delegate to the Security Council argued that the Council had no authority to consider the question since it was a question of relations with an enemy state (see Article 107). The six "neutral" members of the Council (Argentina, Belgium, Canada, China, Colombia, and Syria) made efforts at conciliation. They ventured to offer to the Security Council a resolution providing for the lifting of the blockade and the almost simultaneous settlement of the currency question. The resolution was vetoed by the Soviet Union.

At this point of deadlock the General Assembly entered the picture. It passed unanimously the Mexican resolution referred to above calling on the great powers to compose their differences and to establish a lasting peace. Dr. Evatt as president of the General Assembly and Mr. Lie as Secretary-General joined in a letter to the four great powers occupying Berlin asking them to lend active support to the mediatorial efforts of the president of the Security Council. The "neutrals," with the help of the Secretariat, started studies of the currency question. Eventually, Mr. Bramulgia of Argentina (the November president of the Security Council) made a final proposal for mediation which the four powers accepted. A committee of financial experts, composed of the six "neutrals" in the Security Council together with an expert (Mr. Gunnar Myrdal of Sweden, the secretary of the Economic Commission for Europe) who was chosen by the Secretary-General, was to discuss ways of establishing a single currency in Berlin.

Perhaps neither the Soviet Union nor the United States would have accepted a compromise arranged for them by others. In fact their delegates had already begun a *rapprochement* soon to bear fruit. But the mediatorial efforts of United Nations officials reminded them that there was an international opinion worth conciliating.

Economic Questions

In the economic field the great subject of discussion was European and general recovery. Harsh things were said by the Soviet bloc against the Marshall plan. Other delegations defended the plan and the Organization for European Economic Cooperation. The Marshall plan was characterized as American economic imperialism on the one hand and as unselfish and necessary on the other.

The discussions brought out the usefulness of the United Nations Organization as a leader in economic cooperation. In January, 1948, the United Nations had issued the first of a proposed series of annual reports entitled *Economic Report—Salient Features of the World Economic Situation 1945–1947*. The Economic Commission for Europe (ECE) had done unexpectedly useful work in uniting the activities of *all* European members of the United Nations and had issued a *Survey of the Economic Situation and Prospects of Europe*. The Economic Commissions for Asia and the Far East (ECAFE) and Latin America (ECLA) were at work, and the Commission for the Middle East (ECME) had been authorized. The General Assembly fixed upon the problem of technical assistance to undeveloped countries as the conspicuous economic need of the moment.

The specialized agencies (of which one, the International Refugee Organization, was formally established) were considered. Coordination among them and between them and the United Nations Organization was being established. Among the acts on particular issues was the unanimous approval in the General Assembly of a new and comprehensive convention on narcotic drugs.

Social Problems

In the social field attention was paid to the International Children's Emergency Fund and the United Nations Appeal for Children. A convention on genocide was unanimously approved. A Universal Declaration of Human Rights was approved by a large majority, only the Soviet bloc, South Africa, and Saudi Arabia abstaining.

Dependent Territories

The field of dependent territories received the usual close attention. As to South-West Africa, the General Assembly (with only the Union of South Africa opposing) repeated its recommendation for trusteeship and requested the Union to continue to supply information about the former mandate until agreement had been reached as to its future between the Union and the United Nations. The General Assembly resolved that the Trusteeship Council should pay particular attention to educational advancement in trust territories and that the administering authorities should accelerate the development of the trust territories toward self-government or independence. It also asked the Trusteeship Council to study the problems of administrative unions between the trust territories and the other dependent areas.

As to other non-self-governing territories, the General Assembly discussed the work of the Special Committee on Information under Article 73e, continued the Committee for 1949, and made suggestions for closer supervision by the Assembly. The extreme position, taken by the anticolonial bloc, that the Special Committee should be a supervisory body like the Trusteeship Council was not accepted, nor was the requirement for the transmission of political as well as social, economic, and educational information.

Legal Questions

Two legal questions were dealt with. The International Law Commission was constituted by the election of its fifteen members. Provoked by the assassination of Count Bernadotte, the General Assembly asked the International Court of Justice for an advisory opinion on the question of whether or not the United Nations could bring an international claim against a government responsible for damages caused to the United Nations and to one of its agents.

SECOND PART OF THEIR REGULAR SESSION: APRIL 5 TO MAY 18, 1949

The Political Atmosphere

Partly because of the large number of items on its agenda and partly because of its lengthy and bitter discussions, the Assembly decided to adjourn its session temporarily on December 12 and to continue in April, 1949, in New York.

The bitter feeling of December was intensified in April because the North Atlantic Treaty had just been signed. Though that treaty was drafted in professed accordance with the Charter, the Soviet bloc considered it an anti-Soviet military alliance. Some of the supporters of the treaty spoke of it as so important and so useful in itself as to make the Charter almost useless. Only Dr. Evatt of Australia, in his opening speech in the General Assembly, ventured to suggest to his noncommunist colleagues that they must be careful not to destroy the United Nations in the guise of strengthening it.

Feeling in the Assembly changed rapidly, however, as soon as it became known that Mr. Yakov A. Malik of the Soviet delegation and Mr. Philip C. Jessup of the United States delegation had engaged in conversations which looked toward the ending of the Berlin blockade. After the American-Russian *rapprochement* began, the work of the Assembly proceeded in harmony, though not always in agreement, and the Assembly was able to adjourn in the midst of general good feeling.

Voting in the Security Council

The problem of voting in the Security Council, which had been referred to the Interim Committee, was the major problem of organization discussed. On this question the East-West difference was sharp, but the West carried the Assembly on a series of recommendations whose effect would be to modify the use of the veto. A list of thirty-four types of decisions which should be treated as procedural was made. The permanent members were asked to consult and to try to limit their veto, and members were asked that, in making agreements giving functions to the Council, they make them to avoid as far as possible the need of unanimity. A number of member states, including China, Argentina, and New Zealand, had become convinced that the veto was in all ways bad. The Soviet Union insisted that it was properly used at present. Other members, including the United Kingdom and France, defended the veto but not its "abuse." Except to record a general dissatisfaction with the Soviet use of the veto, the action of the Assembly could not be considered productive.

Other Questions of Organization

The question of a United Nations guard, proposed by the Secretary-General, was referred for study to a special committee. A special committee was established also to study the question of speeding up the work of the Assembly. Both these questions might easily have been referred to the Interim Committee. Special committees were established, however, apparently with a view to securing the cooperation of the Soviet Union, which still refused to attend the Interim Committee.

Political Questions

The three greatest political arguments centered around Palestine, the Italian colonies, and Spain.

In relation to Palestine, the work of the United Nations acting mediator, Dr. Ralph Bunche, had been so effective that no general debate was needed. But the Security Council on March 4 had approved the application of Israel for membership in the United Nations, and a bitter discussion occurred in the General Assembly on this question. Admission was opposed by twelve Middle Eastern and Asiatic states. Nine other states, including the United Kingdom, abstained from voting. The necessary two-thirds was, however, secured.

The problem of the Italian colonies came to the Assembly in accordance with the treaty of peace with Italy, since the Big Four had not been able to agree on their disposition.

Many changes of opinion had occurred during the years since the Italian surrender. The British desire to strengthen the post-war position of Italy had produced proposals which were the basis of the resolution finally proposed by the First Committee. This Committee proposed that Libya should be granted independence in ten years. Meanwhile it should be under trusteeship in three divisions under three different administering authorities: Cyrenaica under the United Kingdom, the Fezzan under France, and Tripolitania under Italy. Italian Somaliland should be placed under trusteeship under Italy. Eritrea, except the western provinces, should be annexed to Ethiopia. These proposals were contrary to the Soviet proposal for United Nations trusteeship of all the colonies and to the Arab desire for independence for all Arab states. They were rejected by the Assembly, which deferred further consideration until its 1949 session.

The question of Indonesia came up briefly. Immediately after the adjournment of the Assembly in December, the Dutch government had terminated the truce agreement with the Republicans and had begun what it called "police action." The Security Council and its Committee on Good Offices had subsequently been active. The Australian and Indian delegations to the General Assembly, thinking a discussion in the General Assembly would promote settlement, offered the question for the agenda; but by the time the *ad hoc* Political Committee was ready to discuss it, a preliminary agreement had been reached between the Dutch and the Indonesian governments, and the question was dismissed until the next session.

On the continuing question of the treatment of Indians in South Africa, the General Assembly invited India, Pakistan, and South Africa to engage in a round-table conference.

In the field of human rights the General Assembly adopted the Convention on the International Transmission of News and the Right of Correction.

In bringing the session to the close, Dr. Evatt reminded the representatives of his statement that the United Nations is the only world instrument for peace with justice, and that any arrangements by member nations are necessarily ancillary and subordinate to the United Nations itself. "This Assembly," he said, "is emerging strongly as a parliament of the peace-loving nations of the world; indeed it is a mirror of the world in which we live . . . gradually the General Assembly is answering the role carved out for it at San Francisco."

FOURTH REGULAR SESSION: SEPTEMBER 20 TO DECEMBER 10, 1949

Coming so soon after the adjournment of the 1948 session in May, the 1949 session was largely concerned with registering opinions on matters already discussed. The political temper of the session was disturbed by three things: the announcement by President Truman that on September 12 there had been an "atomic explosion" in the Soviet Union; the disagreements between Yugoslavia and the Soviet Union, which caused the former to leave the Soviet bloc from time to time; and the attack of the Chinese representative on Soviet policy in China—an attack which began to make the Chinese government a political issue in the organs of the United Nations.

The 1949 session rivaled the meetings in Paris of the previous year in bitterness of invective, but at the same time business was done. There was unanimity on the proposals for technical aid to undeveloped areas. The Soviet bloc, with the aid of Arab and Latin-American governments, won a victory in requiring the internationalization of Jerusalem. The Soviet bloc and the other anticolonial states passed a series of resolutions intended to supervise the actions of colonial powers. There was the usual dead-lock on atomic weapons. The Western powers prevailed in regard to the continuation of the Interim Committee, in regard to Greece and Korea, and in securing the passage of a Western rather than a Soviet resolution on peace.

Political Issues

The outstanding political issues presented no extraordinary aspects.

The future of the Italian colonies was agreed upon. Libia was to be independent by 1952; meanwhile a United Nations commissioner would help in the transfer of authority from the occupying powers. Somaliland would be a trust territory in trust to Italy for ten years and then independent. Eritrea would be the subject of investigation by a commission which should report to the 1950 Assembly. Though the decisions were all of them political compromises, the final vote in the Assembly received a majority vote of 48, with only 1 negative vote, Ethiopia.

The Greek situation had improved because of Yugoslavia's quarrel with the Soviet Union. The Assembly continued its Committee on the Balkans.

For Korea, the General Assembly continued the United Nations Commission on Korea as a "watchdog" committee, with instructions "to assist in bringing about the unification of Korea."

Indonesia was on the agenda, and the Assembly was ready to discuss it if need arose. But the round-table conference at The Hague ended during the session of the General Assembly with agreement between Dutch and Indonesians. The Republic of Indonesia had secured its independence. Most of the credit went to the United Nations, and the General Assembly passed a resolution of mutual gratification.

Peace had come to Palestine, but no settlement as to Jerusalem, which was occupied in part by Israel and in part by Transjordan. Ever since 1947 the General Assembly had maintained that Jerusalem must be internationalized. Eventually on December 10, 1949, the General Assembly resolved that the city of Jerusalem should be a separate entity under United Nations control, administered by the Trusteeship Council, and it instructed the Trusteeship Council to put the resolution into effect. This dubious decision was adopted by 38 votes to 14. It was opposed by Israel, the United Kingdom, the United States, and, of course, by Transjordan, a nonmember.

The problem of Palestinian refugees was acted on according to a recommendation of the Economic Survey Mission for the Middle East. The Assembly established an agency to collaborate with local governments in carrying out relief and works programs for Palestinian refugees in the Middle East.

An ill-omened discussion was held on the accusation by the Chinese delegate that the Soviet government had violated the Charter and treaties by helping the advancing Chinese communists. The Assembly, after lengthy debate, called on all states to respect the political independence and territorial integrity of China.

In the same general area of conflict fell the question of whether or not the trials of ecclesiastics in Bulgaria, Hungary, and Romania were violations of the peace treaties signed by those countries. After bitter discussion, the General Assembly referred to the International Court of Justice a series of questions on the interpretation of the peace treaties and their guarantees of human rights and fundamental freedoms.

The Soviet-American Rivalry

The Soviet Union and the United States were in direct opposition to each other, as usual, in a number of ways.

The most conspicuous disagreement arose in the election to the Security Council. To replace the Ukraine, a member of the Eastern European or Soviet bloc, the official nominee was Czechoslovakia, supported by the United Kingdom among others. The United States supported Yugoslavia and won.

On the most important question of all—weapons of mass destruction—the conversations between the six permanent members of the Atomic Energy Commission had achieved no agreement; the Soviet Union now was said to have the atomic bomb; the smaller powers showed their deep concern, but the Assembly could not do more than urge the permanent members of the Commission to continue their consultation. The president of the Assembly appealed to the permanent members for a new approach to the problem, for compromise, and for the possibility of an atomic armistice during which there would be prohibition of the use of atomic weapons and a provisional inspection system. Both the Soviet Union and the United States seem to have been satisfied that neither of them had yielded sufficiently to make further discussions useful.

Over Soviet opposition the General Assembly requested further study of "conventional" armaments.

Two competing proposals, one by the Soviet Union, "Condemnation of the preparation for a new war and conclusion of a Five-Power pact for peace," and a British-American counterproposal on "Essentials of peace" were discussed, and the Assembly voted for the British-American proposal, which was little more than a statement of the fact that the Charter had laid down principles of an enduring peace and an exhortation to all member states to live by the Charter.

South Africa

As usual, the Union of South Africa and its attitude toward South-West Africa provided one of the points of keenest interest in the Assembly. The Union government, angered at criticism, had now refused even to send information on South-West Africa to the Trusteeship Council, as it had been doing, and continued to reject any claim on the part of the United Nations to consider the problem of South-West Africa in any way whatsoever. This attitude of the Union government probably represents the most specific refusal so far of any member state to respect the position of the General Assembly in a case where the General Assembly claims an interest. The situation is made more significant by the fact that feeling has been so divided. The old colonial powers have sympathized with South Africa, but to the majority of the Assembly the issue is freedom for subject peoples against the desire of Europeans to tyrannize over non-Europeans.

In the General Assembly of 1949 the focus of the conflict was the appearance at a meeting of the Fourth Committee of the Rev. Michael Scott, an Englishman, who spoke for groups of natives of South-West Africa. The delegates of the Union government refused to attend the hearings on the ground that they were illegal—a type of action for which the Soviet and Arab delegates had given precedents. The General Assembly in two resolutions reiterated its regret that the Union had failed to put South-West Africa under trusteeship, and referred to the International Court of Justice a number of questions:

(a) Does the Union of South Africa continue to have international obligations under the mandate for South-West Africa, and if so, what are those obligations?

(b) Are the provisions of Chapter XII of the Charter applicable, and, if so, in what manner, to the Territory of South-West Africa?

(c) Has the Union of South Africa the competence to modify the international status of the Territory of South-West Africa, or, in the event of a negative reply, where does competence rest to determine and modify the international status of the Territory?

A *Field Service*

After study by a committee, the Secretary-General's proposal of a United Nations field service was approved.   The Field Service will have a maximum strength of three hundred men and will provide technical services and security for United Nations missions.   It will be supplemented by a panel of field observers who may be called on.   The Soviet bloc opposed the project on the ground that the Field Service would be military, a contention denied by the Secretary-General.

Technical Assistance

In the field of economic activity the conspicuous act of the General Assembly of 1949 was to approve a plan for technical assistance to underdeveloped countries.   The program is to be administered by a board composed of the heads of the participating agencies, since not only the United Nations but a number of specialized agencies will be involved.   The project will be directed by a committee of the Economic and Social Council.

Refugees

In view of the prospective liquidation of the International Refugee Organization, the Assembly decided to establish as of 1951 a high commissioner's office for refugees.

Dependent Peoples

No less than ten resolutions were adopted relating to dependent areas.   The tenor of the debates in the Fourth Committee and the nature of the resolutions were distinctly unfriendly to the old colonial powers, who reacted by statements that they would not act in conformance with resolutions which they considered beyond the competence of the Assembly.

In regard to trust territories the General Assembly expressed itself in favor of hastening their advancement toward self-government or independence, supported proposals for their economic and educational advancement, and condemned practices contrary to the human rights provisions of the trusteeship system. The General Assembly also instructed the Trusteeship Council to study the administrative unions between trust territories and adjacent colonies—unions which are sometimes thought to interfere with the international status of the trust territories. The Assembly requested the Trusteeship Council to recommend that the United Nations flag be flown in all trust territories, side by side with any other flags that are flown.

In regard to non-self-governing territories generally, the Assembly continued for three years the Special Committee on Information under Article 73e. It recommended that the Committee give special attention to one field of advancement each year: for 1950, educational advancement. It touched on the definition of non-self-governing territories, came very close to asking for information on political advancement (a field carefully omitted from Article 73e), and in general gave the colonial powers the feeling that they were being harassed unjustly.

"The fourth session of the General Assembly," wrote the Secretary-General in the *Bulletin* of January 1, 1950, "took action on a greater number of important problems than any previous session . . . on balance [it] demonstrated more convincingly than before the capacity of the United Nations to do constructive work for the progress of peoples towards a better life even in the midst of the Great Power conflict."

Chapter 9. THE PROBLEM OF PALESTINE

NATURE OF THE PROBLEM

The United Nations must spend most of its time on routine matters. Its history, like that of any government, is made up of a succession of petty failures and successes, decisions and failures to decide. Sometimes, however, an issue of supreme importance arises, and a conspicuous and vital problem will come before the nations, requiring the United Nations to take responsibility.

In this class some persons have tried to put the issues of Germany and Japan, of European recovery, and perhaps even of the rivalries of capitalism and communism. But the makers of the United Nations tried to relieve the United Nations of any responsibility for peacemaking by Article 107 of the Charter, which puts all such matters up to the allied governments engaged in the war. Questions of national policy or organization seem to be precluded from United Nations action by Article 2.7, which reserves domestic matters to the jurisdiction of the member states.

Palestine, however, one of the greatest political problems of the postwar world, is a problem which for many reasons the United Nations could not have avoided. As a mandate under the League of Nations, Palestine had long been internationalized. Chapter XI of the Charter clearly applied to Palestine and so did articles in the chapters on the international trusteeship system. Palestine has been important also because it raised problems of international peace and security and, finally, because of the intense political interest in its status held by three members of the Big Five—the United Kingdom, the United States, and the Soviet Union—by all members of the Arab League, and by many other states as well.

137

Two sessions of the General Assembly, the only special sessions so far, have been held to consider the problem of Palestine. Much time of the regular session of 1947 was spent on it. It was discussed again in 1948 and 1949. The Trusteeship Council has considered it in regular and adjourned sessions. The Economic and Social Council has been involved. The Security Council has been seized of its problems for many months. It caused the creation of the first United Nations force by the Secretary-General. Much of the activity of the United Nations from the spring of 1947 was focused on it.

BACKGROUND AND EARLY HISTORY

The troubles of Palestine are of long standing. They were not created by the United Nations nor have they been increased by it. Indeed, the situation would have been incredibly more bitter had it been allowed to be a mere racial or religious war, or a struggle for military bases or for oil, without any arbiter pledged to a standard of decency.

What Is Palestine?

Palestine is an area about the size of Vermont or Wales. Its western boundary is the Mediterranean Sea. Its eastern boundary follows the lowest points of the below-sea-level dip in the desert which goes from Lake Hula at the north to Lake Tiberias (the Sea of Galilee), and along the Jordan River to the Dead Sea. South of the Dead Sea the boundary runs in an almost straight line along the Wadi el 'Araba south to the tip of the Gulf of 'Aqaba, an arm of the Red Sea. The boundary reaches the gulf just west of the Transjordan port of 'Aqaba.

On the north the boundary is a completely artificial one (agreed upon with the French in Lebanon and Syria while the British were in Palestine and Transjordan). On the south the border is with Egypt. It starts on the Mediterranean coast 15 miles south of the important city of Gaza and runs a little east of south until it hits the Gulf of 'Aqaba just east of the tiny

Egyptian port of Taba.   Palestine has a gulf coast of a few miles.

It is difficult for the American or the European to understand the physical contiguities and the political differences of this area. From Tel Aviv east to Jerusalem is 40 miles more or less.   From Jerusalem east across the Jordan River to Ammam the capital of Transjordan may be as much as 50 miles.

The rainfall of Palestine is low.   The soil has been put to hard use.   But Palestine is one of the crossroads of the world and has been swept again and again by tribes and peoples and armies. It has always been important to the nations.

The First World War

For centuries Palestine had been one of the more barren, desolate, and thinly populated parts of the Turkish empire.   It was revered by Jews as the historic homeland from which they had been twice, and it seemed irrevocably, cast forth.   It was revered by Christians as the scene of the birth and ministry of their Saviour.   To Moslems it was one of the lands containing holy places.   But the Turks had repressed outside religious interest in Palestine, as far as they could, and even its strategic importance between the Mediterranean and the Asiatic worlds had been minimized as long as the dead hand of the Turkish empire lay upon it.

Suddenly Palestine came into the center of modern world politics when, during the First World War, the British conquered it, not so much for itself as because it was a part of the Arab world which they were engaged in detaching from Turkey and its master, Germany.   What the British government may have promised to nearby Arab rulers as to the future of Palestine is still a subject for dispute.   But one cannot doubt that for wartime purposes they allowed Arab leaders to believe that Britain was freeing them from the Turks so that the Arabs might be free from any outside supervision or control.   The forces of nationalism had not reached their full strength in 1917, but they were strong in all parts of the semi-Europeanized world.

At the same time, for other reasons which formed a part of the great imperial design of the British empire, the rulers of Britain promised to the Jews a homeland in a Palestine that was to be redeemed from the Turks. This promise is less subject to doubt, since it is found in the Balfour Declaration, approved by the British Cabinet in November, 1917, which read as follows:

His Majesty's Government view with favour the establishment in Palestine of a national home for the Jewish people, and will use their best endeavours to facilitate the achievement of this object, it being clearly understood that nothing shall be done which may prejudice the civil and religious rights of existing non-Jewish communities in Palestine, or the rights and political status enjoyed by Jews in any other country.

Divided intentions, uncertainty of policy, even allegations of bad faith had, however, little to do with the problem of Palestine after the First World War was won. For the decision was made in the Peace Conference that the dependent parts of the Turkish empire should, like the German colonies, be placed under mandate in accordance with Article 22 of the Covenant of the League of Nations. Palestine, like Mesopotamia and the rest of Syria, was brought under international supervision in one of the decisions of the Paris Conference of 1919. From that moment it became an *international* problem.

THE MANDATE FOR PALESTINE

A decision of the Supreme Council of the Allied and Associated Powers, of April 25, 1920, assigned the mandate over Palestine to the United Kingdom. The terms of the mandate received the approval of the Council of the League of Nations on July 24, 1922. The United States was a member of the Supreme Council. All former Allied states (except the United States) and most neutrals were members of the League. The mandate was granted by such representatives of international right and justice as then existed. The mandate was intended to be liberating and not repressive. If there was any validity in the international arrangements made after that war, the arrangement made for Palestine seemed one of the most valid. From the establishment of the mandate, Palestine was no longer the property of the Turks, nor of the victorious Allies who took it from the Turks, nor even (as is the soil of a sovereign nation) the property of its inhabitants for the time being. It had become "affected with a public interest" in the international sense.

Palestine under Mandate

The terms of the mandate for Palestine are very definite and very distinctive. Palestine was what came to be called a class A mandate, one of "certain communities formerly belonging to the Turkish Empire [which] have reached a state of development when their existence as independent nations can be provisionally recognized subject to the rendering of administrative advice and assistance by a Mandatory until such time as they are able to stand alone." This statement in Article 22 of the League Covenant goes a long way, and the terms of the mandate did not go quite so far. Provisional independence was hardly recognized; though in considering the subsequent history of Palestine, it is important to note that all the rest of the class A mandates—former parts of the Turkish empire—had by 1945 become independent states, and if any Palestinian added lack of independence to his other grievances, he had some justification.

Since Palestine was soon to "stand alone," the mandate outlines an elaborate form of government taking into account the interests of the various parts of the population, giving the mandatory state (the United Kingdom) the necessary control, but establishing a local administration with a good deal of autonomy. One essential feature of the mandate was, of course, the provisions that implemented the Balfour Declaration about a Jewish national home. The precise words of the mandate on this point should be kept clearly before any person who attempts to comment on Palestinian affairs:

Whereas the Principal Allied Powers have also agreed that the Mandatory should be responsible for putting into effect the declaration originally made on November 2nd, 1917, by the Government of His Britannic Majesty, and adopted by the said Powers, in favour of the establishment in Palestine of a national home for the Jewish people, it being clearly understood that nothing should be done which might prejudice the civil and religious rights of existing non-Jewish communities in Palestine, or the rights and political status enjoyed by Jews in any other country. . . . [From the preamble.]

Article 2

The Mandatory shall be responsible for placing the country under such political, administrative and economic conditions as will secure the establishment of the Jewish national home, as laid down in the preamble, and the development of self-governing institutions, and also for safeguarding the civil and religious rights of all the inhabitants of Palestine, irrespective of race and religion.

In this way, in these precise terms, confirmed by the Allied Supreme Council and by the League of Nations, the Jewish people were given privileges which were specific, both in their wideness and in their limitations, and which were carefully prevented from being in conflict with the obvious and essential rights of other Palestinians and other peoples interested in Palestine.

A Palestinian government was set up under the mandate. In spite of the conflicting interests which the war had encouraged, and in spite of the difficulties of increased immigration into a barren, neglected, and wasted land, things went well. Only a minority of Jews throughout the world believed that Palestine should become the physical home of any considerable part of the Jewish people, but many outside the strict ranks of the Zionists were generous, and a considerable amount of Jewish immigration was subsidized from outside Palestine. (The extreme Zionists were the minority who believed that Palestine should be exclusively Jewish and that Jews should find their *only* home in Palestine.)

The movement toward Palestine may be compared with the planting of colonies like Virginia or New France in the seventeenth century, or New Zealand in the nineteenth. It meant an incursion of European, or Europeanized, persons into an economically undeveloped land and would have been impossible without capital supplied from abroad. The incoming Jews were well taken care of; the sections of Palestine where they settled began to flourish. A few Arabs also migrated into the land because the presence of the Jews and their money made it economically attractive, and the poor and barren land increased in fertility, in wealth, and in population. In 1922 and 1946 the population of Palestine by religions was as follows:

	Moslems	Jews	Christians	Others	Total
1922	486,177	83,790	71,464	7,617	649,048
1946	1,076,783	608,225	145,063	15,488	1,845,559

The increase in Arab population was almost entirely the result of an excess of births over deaths. The increase in Jewish population was due largely to immigration.[1]

Over the whole movement and settlement of the Jewish population the Jewish agency presided. For the mandate for Palestine provides:

Article 4

An appropriate Jewish agency shall be recognized as a public body for the purpose of advising and co-operating with the Administration of Palestine in such economic, social and other matters as may affect the establishment of the Jewish national home and the interests of the Jewish population in Palestine, and, subject always to the control of the Administration, to assist and take part in the development of the country.

The Zionist organization, so long as its organization and constitution are in the opinion of the Mandatory appropriate, shall be recognized as such agency. It shall take steps in consultation with His Britannic Majesty's Government to secure the co-operation of all Jews who are willing to assist in the establishment of the Jewish national home.

[1] United Nations Special Committee on Palestine, *Report*, Volume I, pages 11–12.

Early in the history of the mandate the United Kingdom separated the Transjordan administratively from Palestine, and the terms of the mandate applying to Jews were interpreted as being limited to the area between the Jordan River and the Mediterranean.

Up to 1933 the Jewish immigration into Palestine presented that country with an increasing group of residents who brought with them a European culture and considerable amounts of money. The Jews and the Arabs, two cultural groups differing more in their degree of Europeanization than in their racial background, lived together under the British administration without too much difficulty. After the intensive persecution of Jews began in Germany, the number of Jewish immigrants to Palestine increased. In 1936 disorders in Palestine grew into an Arab campaign of terrorism against both the Jews and the Administration (which was responsible to the British). At this time a Conservative British government, worried by Fascism and Nazism in Europe and by unrest in Asiatic possessions, seems to have given up the attempt (previously successful) to be impartial and to maintain a middle position between Zionism, or Jewish nationalism, on one hand and Arab nationalism on the other and to have decided that the Arabs must be conciliated, even at the expense of the Jews. Anti-Semitism throughout the world had been encouraged by Hitler's persecution of the Jews; for the first time in centuries there was anti-Semitism in England. Consequently the British government considered partitioning Palestine. Not being easily able to do this, it announced a new immigration policy in its White Paper of 1939. It is at this moment that the British government appears to have begun to abnegate its duty under the mandate. The new policy would permit only 75,000 more Jewish immigrants during the next five years. Subsequent Jewish immigration was to be permitted only with the acquiescence of the Arabs of Palestine. The Permanent Mandates Commission of the League held that the White Paper policy was not in accordance with the terms of the mandate.

During the war which began in 1939 the Jews fought on the

British side, which for the most part the Arabs did not. But the pro-Arab policy of the White Paper was directed toward the conciliation of Arab groups which might be important after the war.

THE ANGLO-AMERICAN COMMITTEE OF INQUIRY

When the First Part of the First Session of the General Assembly of the United Nations met in London early in 1946, the mandatory powers made statements of their intentions toward the mandated territories. The United Kingdom stated that steps would be taken so that Transjordan might be established as an independent state. A decision on Palestine must await the report of the Anglo-American Committee of Inquiry.

The Anglo-American Committee had been proposed by the British Foreign Secretary, Mr. Bevin, in the autumn of 1945. This committee was an attempt on the part of the Foreign Office to reconcile two things—President Truman's expressed interest in the reestablishment of unlimited immigration into Palestine and the British government's desire to continue the policy of the White Paper. The position of the British government was complicated by the fact that the Labour party when in opposition (and as recently as the spring of 1945) had always condemned the White Paper. It had supported the position that the terms of the mandate permitted unlimited Jewish immigration.

The Anglo-American Committee of Inquiry issued a unanimous report on May 1, 1946, proposing that Palestine be kept under mandate until a trusteeship agreement should be negotiated. The report included the stipulation that immediate entrance to Palestine should be permitted to 100,000 Jews.

The Committee had been composed half of Englishmen and half of Americans, none of them belonging to the two national groups immediately concerned and the majority of them being private citizens. They were chosen from the various political parties in the two countries. As requested, they had summarized the problem of the Jews in Europe as well as in the Middle East. They were stimulated to decide on a unanimous report by their understanding from Mr. Bevin that if their report were unanimous, the British government would put it into effect —the American President gave it his preliminary approval. The Arabs and the Arab League objected to it completely. Jews, except the extremists, were satisfied with it.

Instead of putting into effect the recommendations of the Anglo-American Committee, of which the most immediate was the lifting of the bars against immigration, the British government made another attempt to secure Anglo-American agreement on a policy more acceptable to the Foreign Office. A committee of English and American officials chosen on a subcabinet level met in London in the summer of 1946. Though the announced purpose of this group was to consider ways of implementing the report of the Anglo-American Committee of Inquiry, it accepted the so-called Grady-Morrison plan. This was a revival of an old prewar British plan providing for limited communal autonomy in a unitary Palestine. In this plan the possibility of future immigration was limited by the fact that Arabs as well as Jews must agree to it.

Meanwhile Arabs in Palestine, jubilant at the support of the British, were engaged in economic warfare against the Jews, and the Jews were engaged in smuggling their refugee coreligionists into Palestine. Physical conflict increased between the Jews and the Arabs and between the British and the Jews. The British administration in Palestine enforced the British restrictions on immigration as strongly as they could. Bitterness and disorder increased. The British troops in Palestine were many. The country was put under martial law. But the situation continued to deteriorate.

PALESTINE IN THE GENERAL ASSEMBLY

First Special Session of the General Assembly

So far, the question of Palestine had not been brought in to the United Nations, except in so far as the British had indicated that they intended to settle it themselves. Unexpectedly, in

April, 1947, the United Kingdom decided to ask the General
Assembly for advice, though without any suggestion that the advice, if given, would be taken. The government of the United
Kingdom was presumably moved by two considerations: the dis-
credit that the disorders in Palestine brought upon them as the
government responsible for the administration of the country
and the reluctant realization that in their extreme and suddenly
realized financial difficulties, they could not afford to keep sufficient forces in Palestine either to enforce their will or to maintain
order.

On April 2, 1947, the government of the United Kingdom requested that the question of Palestine be placed on the agenda
of the next regular session of the General Assembly. It requested
also that a special session of the General Assembly be called to
constitute and instruct a special committee to prepare for the consideration of the question. When circularized by the Acting
Secretary-General, the majority of the members of the United
Nations agreed to the summons of the Special Session. The
Special Session met at Flushing Meadow on April 28 and adjourned on May 15.

This first Special Session of the General Assembly decided to
admit to its agenda only one item, the proposal of the United
Kingdom for constituting a special committee, and to omit from
its agenda the item proposed by Egypt, Iraq, Lebanon, Saudi
Arabia, and Syria: "the termination of the mandate on Palestine
and the declaration of its independence." The committee work
of the session was done entirely in the First (Political and Security) Committee and that Committee's subcommittees. Yet the
discussions inevitably ranged over the entire question of the future
of Palestine. The First Committee gave hearings to two nongovernmental organizations, the Jewish Agency for Palestine and
the Arab Higher Committee. Throughout the discussions the
delegates of the Arab states acted as sponsors for the Arabs. The
Jews had no representation in the General Assembly.

The Special Session decided to constitute the special committee requested. Great differences of opinion showed themselves

as to the constitution of the special committee. Some govern-ments wanted the inclusion of the Big Five. Others wanted a committee composed only of representatives of lesser powers not directly concerned. The Big Five themselves were divided: China, the United Kingdom, and the United States opposed their inclusion; the Soviet Union wanted it; France specifically ab-stained from voting on this issue.

The resolutions finally passed by the General Assembly consti-tuted a special committee to be composed of representatives of eleven member states (Australia, Canada, Czechoslovakia, Guate-mala, India, Iran, the Netherlands, Peru, Sweden, Uruguay, and Yugoslavia) with wide powers to investigate and make recom-mendations in a report to the General Assembly—the report to be made by September 1, 1947. Further, the General Assembly called upon all governments and peoples, and particularly the inhabitants of Palestine, to refrain from the threat or use of force, pending the action of the General Assembly on the Committee's report.

No one could have expected the voting to be unanimous. On the essential paragraph of the resolution there were 40 votes in favor, 0 against, and 13 abstentions. The latter included the three Soviet republics, the five Arab League states, Afghanistan and Turkey, and two other Eastern European states, Czecho-slovakia and Yugoslavia.

The United Nations Special Committee on Palestine (UNSCOP)

The United Nations Special Committee on Palestine held its first meeting at Lake Success on May 26. It chose as chairman, Chief Justice Emil Sandström of Sweden, and as vice-chairman, Dr. Alberto Ulloa of Peru. After preliminary meetings in New York, the Committee went to Palestine, accompanied by members of the United Nations Secretariat.

The Report of the Special Committee on Palestine is a long document. Its first volume, of reasonable size, contains the report itself accompanied by the best historical analysis of the problem that exists. The rest is the supporting material. The actual substance of the report unfortunately approached in complexity the complexity of the problem.

The Committee agreed on a number of recommendations. Among them were the termination of the mandate and independence for Palestine at the earliest practicable date. During a "transitional period," preliminary to independence, the authority administering Palestine should be responsible to the United Nations. The report endorsed the principle of the preservation of the economic unity of Palestine. In relation to the Jewish problem in general it urged the General Assembly to undertake an international arrangement for the relief of the distressed European Jews.

As to the future government of Palestine, the Committee was divided. The majority proposed partition into an Arab state, a Jewish state, and the city of Jerusalem—but all within the framework of economic union of the entire country. The majority consisted of the representatives of Canada, Czechoslovakia, Guatemala, the Netherlands, Peru, Sweden, and Uruguay. The minority (India, Iran, and Yugoslavia) recommended one single state which should be a federation composed of a Jewish and an Arab state, each with powers of local government only. In the minority plan Jewish immigration into the Jewish state for three years was to be permitted up to the absorptive capacity of the state, the latter to be determined by three Arab, three Jewish, and three United Nations representatives. The Australian representative abstained from voting for either plan.

The minority plan was basically satisfactory to the Arabs because it gave them their essential demand, i.e., an independent sovereign nation in which they could outvote the Jews and from which they could exclude future Jewish immigrants. The majority plan was opposed by the Arabs. It was reluctantly accepted by most of the Jewish organizations, since it would give the Jewish state control over immigration into itself. But the plan did not include all of Palestine in the Jewish state and was, therefore, unsatisfactory to the extremists.

Palestine in the Second Regular Assembly

The General Assembly met for its second regular session in September, 1947. It set up an *ad hoc* committee to consider the report of the United Nations Special Committee on Palestine, the British agenda item of the future status of Palestine, and the Arab proposal for the recognition of the independence of Palestine. The *ad hoc* Committee was soon divided into two subcommittees, one of which consisted of states generally agreeable to the majority report of the UNSCOP, and the other consisting of those states agreeable to the minority report. The first subcommittee worked with the Jewish Agency and was refused help, except on boundaries, by the Arab Higher Committee. The second subcommittee consisted of states generally supporting the minority report and worked with the Arabs. Both subcommittees modified the plans greatly in detail. The full *ad hoc* Committee finally accepted the work of the first subcommittee and presented a partition plan to the General Assembly itself.

Eventually on November 29, 1947, the General Assembly, by the necessary two-thirds vote, adopted the report of the *ad hoc* Committee proposing partition with economic union. The vote was 33 in favor of the motion, 13 against, and 10 abstentions. Opposed were the six Arab League states (Egypt, Iraq, Lebanon, Saudi Arabia, Syria, and Yemen), five states with large Moslem populations (Afghanistan, India, Iran, Pakistan, and Turkey) and also Cuba and Greece. Abstaining were the United Kingdom—the mandatory—and China, Argentina, Chile, Colombia, El Salvador, Ethiopia, Honduras, Mexico, and Yugoslavia. But when the time for the decision came, the Soviet Union and the United States were strongly favorable, and the necessary majority went with them.

Certain aspects of the General Assembly decision need summary because of their political implications. In the first place, the basis of the decision—that Palestine should be partitioned into an Arab state, a Jewish state, and an internationalized Jerusalem, but with economic union for the whole area—was the decision of the majority of a United Nations committee, in which neither the United Nations member most closely concerned—the United Kingdom—nor any other nation of the Big Five had a seat. In the second place, the decision was unmistakably a compromise. It was not what either the Arabs or the Jews wanted, and both the United States and the Soviet Union, whose combined sponsorship had so much to do with its acceptance, expressed themselves as supporting it only as a practicable and workable solution. In the third place, it received a surprising measure of acceptance for the answer to so difficult and so divisive a question as the problem of Palestine.

For Americans it is important to realize what the American position had been. Though many plans for the future of Palestine had been seriously reviewed in Washington, partition had never been among those that commanded convinced support. But the problem had been duly referred to the United Nations, the United Nations *ad hoc* Committee's majority had proposed something not conspicuously impossible, and the United States, therefore, was prepared to back it. There is no question but that the combined support of the United States and the Soviet Union won many doubtful states to vote for the plan; however, the United States government itself did not use pressure to gain votes, though it used its influence.

THE GENERAL ASSEMBLY PLAN OF NOVEMBER, 1947

The Decision for Partition

The decision of the General Assembly on Palestine took the form of recommendations, since the General Assembly itself has no executive authority. These recommendations were made to the various organs of the United Nations which would be concerned with carrying out the decision and also to states which were members of the United Nations. The question of the constitutional competence of the General Assembly to make partition proposals had been raised by the Arab states, but the General Assembly's act in making recommendations would seem to be within the authority given it by the Charter. At any rate, the majority vote behind the resolution showed that the General Assembly believed itself to have the power. It is important to note that the Commission established in the resolution was made responsible to the Security Council if any question of a threat to peace should arise.

The Partition Plan

The plan as finally adopted had certain very peculiar geographical aspects. It established provisional boundaries for three entities, a Jewish state, an Arab state, and Jerusalem. The Arab state, which would occupy the greater part of the area, would include western Galilee, the central part of Palestine from the valley of Esdraelon down to Beersheba, and a strip of land along the Mediterranean coast (including Gaza) and along the Egyptian border about halfway from the Mediterranean to the Red Sea. It would also include Jaffa, which would be geographically an enclave in the Jewish state. Apart from Jaffa, the Arab state would consist of three areas, each touching other Arab areas at points where separate areas of the Jewish state would also meet. The Jewish state would also be composed of three separate areas, meeting at corners: eastern Galilee and the valley of Esdraelon, a coastal strip from Haifa to below Jaffa, and for the third area, that part of the Negeb not assigned to the Arabs. Jerusalem including Bethlehem and other suburbs (an area including some quarter of a million people, in which the Jewish population was slightly larger than that of the Arabs) would be a separate unit outside both states.

On the map, the partition looks fantastic. In terms of soil and population it was not unreasonable. The Jewish state would include most of the coastal strip, thickly populated with Jews and well developed economically. It would include another fertile and populous area, eastern Galilee. And it would include most of the Negeb, the sandy southern area of the country which is large and empty but intended by the Jews for future settlement whereby the desert would "blossom like a rose." (Unfortunately the Negeb was of strategic interest to the British, the Egyptians, and the Transjordanians.)

The important Arab areas were the southern part of the coastal strip and a strategic slice of the Negeb, running from the coast south along the Egyptian border, and most of the interior of Palestine going as far east as the border of Transjordan.

The great cities of Palestine were Jerusalem, Tel Aviv (originally a suburb of Jaffa), Haifa, Jaffa, and Gaza, in that order of size. Jerusalem, with a majority of Jewish population but with many Christians and Arabs, was to be internationalized. Tel Aviv was Jewish and to remain so. Haifa, with a majority of Jews, was in the Jewish coastal strip. Jaffa, mixed, but with a majority of Arabs, was to be an Arab enclave in the Jewish state. Gaza was Arab and would remain so.

The lack of geographical unity in both states was the greatest argument against the practicability of partition, but the boundaries followed the lines that had come to exist between predominantly Jewish and Arab areas as a result of British restrictions against Jewish purchase of Arab lands. A map of the partition plan of the United Nations looks very much like the maps of partitions proposed by British commissions in the late 1930's. The Arab state would be predominantly Arab in population. The Jewish state would include most of the Jews outside Jerusalem and also a substantial Arab minority—over 400,000 persons.

The Government of the States

Both states were to be sovereign and independent, with the expectation that they would soon be admitted as members of the United Nations. Their constitutions must have, however, guarantees of democratic government and against racial and religious discrimination and must include the protection of rights protected by the United Nations Charter. The complete independence of each state (which would permit the Jewish state to admit immigrants at its discretion) was an essential part of the plan. Economic union for the whole area—also an essential part of the plan —was to be established *pari passu* with the establishment of the two states.   It would be managed by a joint economic board, with three representatives chosen by each state and three foreigners chosen by the Economic and Social Council, and would have as its objective a customs union, a currency union, joint operation of all means of communication, including railways, highways, ports, and airports, joint economic development including immigration, and free access to water and power facilities for Jewish and Arab states and for the city of Jerusalem.   The drafters of the plan recognized as politically inevitable a political division of Palestine, but as economically essential a close economic union.

The City of Jerusalem

The city of Jerusalem, according to the final decision, was to have its own administration, responsible to the Trusteeship Council, though not as a trust territory under the international trusteeship system.   This separate administration would avoid racial, national, and religious struggles for control and would protect the interests of Moslems, Christians, and Jews.

Termination of the Mandate and Transitional Period

The United Kingdom government announced its intention of early withdrawal from Palestine, by August 1, 1948.   The General Assembly accepted the British warning and the consequent termination of the mandate at least as soon as August 1 and provided for the establishment of the two new states not later than October 1, 1948.   The period extending from the adoption of the resolution to the establishment of the new states "shall be a transitional period."   During this period British rule would be gradually replaced.   A United Nations commission, elected by the General Assembly, would progressively take over the administration of Palestine as the British withdrew their forces.   It would not only administer Palestine on behalf of the United Nations, but it would assist in the establishment of provisional councils, which under its authority would govern the two states, and it would assist in the making of constitutions and the establishment of the states themselves, which would be done by democratically elected constituent assemblies. The commission would also establish an economic committee to organize the economic union.

The commission was to report to the next session of the General Assembly.   It was to make periodic reports, at least monthly, to the Security Council and was to be guided by the recommendations of the General Assembly and by instructions from the Security Council.

The Security Council was requested to make the necessary plans for the implementation of the General Assembly resolution and in particular to take action if a threat to international peace and security should develop.

The Trusteeship Council was designated to discharge the duties of "administering authority" of the city of Jerusalem on behalf of the United Nations. Within five months it was to "elaborate and approve" a detailed statute for the city, in accordance with principles rather fully laid down in the General Assembly resolution.

Furthermore, the General Assembly in its resolution called upon the inhabitants of Palestine to do what was necessary to help implement the plan and appealed to all governments and peoples to do nothing to hamper or delay the carrying out of the recommendations.   It incidentally resolved that the mandatory power, the United Kingdom, should use its best endeavors to evacuate by February 1 a port and an area within the territory of the proposed Jewish state sufficient in size to provide facilities for substantial immigration.

Finally, the General Assembly resolution authorized the expenditure of money and the use of the staff of the Secretariat.

Implementing the Resolution

Having passed its Palestine resolution, the General Assembly elected Bolivia, Czechoslovakia, Denmark, Panama, and the Philippines as members of the Palestine Commission. The Commission chose Karel Lisicky of Czechoslovakia as chairman.

The Security Council on December 9 took cognizance of the

General Assembly's plan. The Trusteeship Council began work on a statute for Jerusalem. The Palestine Commission started work at Lake Success. The Arab Higher Committee refused to consult with it, but the Jewish Agency and the British government did so.

THE TRANSITIONAL PERIOD

The story of the first part of the transitional period can be learned from the reports which, in duty bound, the Commission made to the Security Council. It is a distressing story.

The situation in Palestine grew worse and worse. The Arabs and the Arab members of the United Nations (the Arab League) went so far as to inform the Secretary-General that they would refuse to recognize any action or decision deriving from the General Assembly resolution for partition and would resist by force any attempt to establish a Jewish state. Armed Arab forces entered Palestine, where armed conflicts between Jews and Arabs occurred. The position taken by the Jews was that they accepted partition, though as a compromise solution, and would defend themselves. But organizations of Jewish extremists took part in terroristic activity against Arabs and against the British administration of Palestine.

The British government had declared that it would do nothing to carry out the General Assembly decision since it was not satisfactory to both Jews and Arabs. In consequence, the British government refused to open a port to immigration by February 1 as the General Assembly had requested. Further, it maintained its old immigration policy, which meant that Jewish refugees attempting to enter Palestine were seized by force and deported to Cyprus, where the British government kept them in concentration camps at the expense of the administration of Palestine. The British government further insisted that it could not permit the United Nations Commission to enter Palestine sufficiently in advance of the termination of the mandate to permit the Commission to make the preliminary arrangements which the General

Assembly had entrusted to it or even to start making the final determinations of boundaries. Furthermore, the British government, while pointing out that disorder would increase after the mandate was terminated, insisted that the termination must take place by May 15, refused to agree to a progressive transfer of areas to the Commission, and refused to give countenance to the creation of security forces in the two prospective states. There were also difficulties in regard to food and finance, for the British government cut Palestine out of the sterling area, froze its balances, and even at one time refused to allow food to be imported beyond the amount that would be necessary up to May 15.

A small advance mission of members of the Secretariat only was sent to Palestine by the Commission early in March, but it resided there on sufferance, uncomfortably and dangerously.

The Security Council received reports from the Commission and discussed them. A special report of February 18 expressed the view that there must be an international armed force to keep order after the termination of the mandate. The Commission therefore referred to the Security Council the problem of providing the armed assistance "which alone would enable the Commission to discharge its responsibilities on the termination of the mandate."

All these difficult questions were discussed by the Security Council, which asked its five permanent members to consult and to report on the possibility of providing forces. The British government refused to consult except as the mandatory power.

United States Proposes Temporary Trusteeship

As the Security Council was beginning to consider what it might do, the pro-Arab forces, which had continued their fight to control the policy of the United States, temporarily succeeded, and in the Security Council on March 19 the United States representative proposed that, since partition had failed, a temporary trusteeship for Palestine should be instituted. To this end he proposed that a special session of the General Assembly should be called by the Security Council (as the Council has the authority to do under Article 20) and that the Security Council instruct the Palestine Commission to suspend its efforts to implement partition. The reaction of United States public opinion was so strongly opposed to this change of policy that the United States government began to retrace its steps. On April 1 the Security Council passed two resolutions, the first calling for the cessation of violence in Palestine and an immediate truce between Jews and Arabs and the second calling for a special meeting of the General Assembly.

Second Special Session of General Assembly

April 16, 1948, was set for the opening of the Special Session of the General Assembly. Attended by a comparatively small number of delegates and advisers, the Special Session met. It had before it a report of the Palestine Commission rehearsing the situation and pointing out that a *de facto* partition of Palestine was already taking place. At the same time that the General Assembly was meeting, the Security Council remained seized of the question of Palestine, and the Trusteeship Council met to refer its draft statute for the government of Jerusalem to the General Assembly, which the Assembly failed to adopt. In their appropriate ways all three of these "principal organs" of the United Nations were attempting to do their duty.

The Political Committee of the General Assembly entered on a long discussion of the agenda item, "further consideration of the question of the future government of Palestine." The United States proposed a temporary trusteeship, with the United Nations Organization itself as the administering authority and the Trusteeship Council to supervise the administration. It soon became plain that the proposal could not win the support of a two-thirds majority of the General Assembly. Force would be necessary to effect a trusteeship plan; would any less force be required than to effect partition? The most uncompromising position was taken by the Soviet Union, which maintained that the only legitimate activity of the United Nations would be to carry out the duly adopted partition resolution of the previous November. While the Political Committee continued its discussions, the Security Council established a truce commission consisting of the three consuls in Jerusalem of three members of the Security Council having career consuls there—the United States, Belgium, and France. (Syria refused membership.) And the Trusteeship Council was asked by the General Assembly to arrange a cease-fire order in Jerusalem by consultation with Jews and Arabs, a task which it succeeded in accomplishing.

While the total situation remained unresolved, the moment for the termination of the mandate approached. Eventually on May 14 the Political Commission of the General Assembly made a report, recommending (1) the appointment of a United Nations mediator to be chosen by the Big Five, (2) a United Nations commissioner for Jerusalem responsible to the Trusteeship Council, and (3) the suspension of the work of the Palestine Commission. The General Assembly agreed to points (1) and (3). Meanwhile important decisions had been made elsewhere. By decision of the United Kingdom the mandate was to end at midnight May 14 (which was 6 P.M. at Lake Success). Earlier in the day the Jewish state of Israel had been proclaimed. The delegates in the Assembly were startled by the announcement that the United States had given *de facto* recognition to the government of the new state. That evening the Special Session of the General Assembly, which had been called at the instance of the United States, adjourned.

PARTITION IN EFFECT

The immediate situation was left to the Security Council—and to the peoples of the Near East. Transjordanian and Egyptian forces immediately entered Palestine, and the government of Israel, soon recognized also by the Soviet Union, began to defend the frontiers recommended by the General Assembly on November 29. Count Folke Bernadotte of Sweden, vice-president of the International Red Cross, was chosen United Nations mediator on May 20 and began to act on the basis of a resolution of the

Security Council calling on governments to cease fire in Palestine. The mediator secured agreement of Arabs and Jews to a truce in Palestine for four weeks, beginning June 11, on terms which seemed to freeze the situation on a compromise basis. He established his headquarters on the island of Rhodes and proceeded to perform his vital functions.

The abandonment of the mandate by the government of the United Kingdom on May 14, 1948, resulted in an intensification of the fighting in various parts of Palestine. This fighting involved Israeli forces on the one side and, on the other, forces of Egypt, Transjordan, Syria, Lebanon, and Iraq. The Security Council called for a four-week cease-fire period which eventually became effective by means of the truce of June 11 and which was supervised by Count Bernadotte with the aid of military observers from the United States, Belgium, and France and with the assistance of ships, aircraft, and transportation and communication facilities loaned by the United States, France, and the United Kingdom.

When the four-week truce ended, fighting began again on some fronts, and the Israeli forces demonstrated superiority over Arab arms. Before a second truce began, Israel controlled not only most of the area assigned to it in the partition plan of November, 1947, but also Beersheba and a corridor to Jerusalem.

An additional truce resolution was adopted by the Security Council on July 15 and became effective on July 18. The previous truce, that of June 11, had been negotiated. That of July 18 was imposed by the Security Council. The Security Council went so far as to hold that the situation in Palestine was a threat to peace within the meaning of Article 39 of the Charter and ordered the governments and authorities concerned to stop further military action. In case the order was not complied with, the Council would immediately consider further action under Chapter VII, the chapter authorizing action provoked by breaches of the peace. In particular an immediate and unconditional cease-fire order was issued for the city of Jerusalem. The cessation of fighting, begun in Jerusalem, was quickly extended to the other areas of conflict. The truce was promptly complied with by the

Arabs and was reasonably well observed by both sides until fighting began again in October in the Negeb.

In preparing his report for the regular 1948 session of the General Assembly, the mediator decided to recommend boundaries different from those which had been established in the November, 1947, resolutions. All of Galilee should be Jewish, but the Negeb, or most of it, should be Arab. The proposed boundaries would give population to the Jews and area to the Arabs. Most of the Arabs had (early in 1948) left territory occupied by the Jews. The Jews, however, wished further land for colonization and were unimpressed by the argument that the vast stretches of the Negeb were valueless, though they were at the moment arid. The Jews knew, as did everyone else, that the British still dreamed of strategic control of the Middle East, which required a route across a Negeb in presumably friendly Arab hands.

Bernadotte proposed also that some sort of special control over Jerusalem be exercised by the United Nations. The state of Israel, which already existed, should continue to exist. The Arab areas should be disposed of by the governments of the Arab states in consultation with the Arabs of Palestine, but they might best be united to Transjordan. He recommended a conciliation commission to effect these recommendations and to bring about a permanent armistice, definite boundaries, and peace.

The mediator's report was dated September 16. The next day, while driving through a section of Jerusalem under Jewish military control, he was shot by men in Israeli uniform. The Security Council appointed Dr. Ralph J. Bunche, an American citizen, the personal representative of the Secretary-General to the mediator, as acting mediator.

Before the Political Committee of the General Assembly had reached the question of Palestine on its agenda, fighting broke out again, this time between Israeli and Egyptian forces in the Negeb. The Egyptians were driven back. The Security Council, in a succession of meetings, called on the two governments to cease fighting and to withdraw behind the lines which they had previously held. The success of the Jewish forces in gaining territory which they claimed by virtue of the resolution of November, 1947, made them refuse to carry out the order of the Council completely. A later resolution of the Security Council of December 29, ordering an immediate cease-fire period and armistice negotiations, was complied with.

The Bernadotte plan for Palestine did not win the support of the General Assembly. The Assembly, on December 11 just before its adjournment, adopted a comprehensive resolution on Palestine, the essence of which was the appointment of a conciliation commission to try to aid the conflicting governments to achieve a final settlement of all outstanding problems. This commission was eventually to take over the functions given by the General Assembly to the mediator and, at the request of the Security Council, any or all of the functions of the mediator or of the Truce Commission. Jerusalem was to be accorded special treatment and to be under United Nations control. The commission was also to concern itself with arrangements for the economic development of Palestine and for the care of refugees. France, Turkey, and the United States were to be its members.

By the beginning of 1949 the Israeli forces had been sufficiently successful in the field so that Israel's claim to existence and to most, if not all, of the territory it occupied could not be challenged by its Arab neighbors. The General Assembly had refused to revise its November, 1947, resolution. But it had given up any attempt to insist on boundaries or on political or economic arrangements. The acting mediator (whose functions were not yet terminated) and the conciliation commission were to act on the spot, dealing on behalf of the United Nations with the conflicting interests and governments and to work out the details of the future one by one. The Security Council had not been completely successful in suppressing violence, but acting through Count Bernadotte and Dr. Bunche and their truce observers, it had minimized both the area and the intensity of armed conflicts.

The Acting Mediator Arranges Armistices

The Conciliation Commission met and organized in Geneva on January 24, 1949, and subsequently established its headquarters in

Jerusalem. But the acting mediator presided over the armistice discussions on the island of Rhodes, which had begun before the Conciliation Commission was organized. There ensued a succession of negotiations, astonishingly successful, to which the patience and skill of the acting mediator made an impressive contribution.

The first, and perhaps greatest, obstacle was overcome when the representatives of Egypt met with those of Israel under the presidency of Dr. Bunche. On January 25 a formal and general cease-fire period was agreed upon between the representatives of Egypt and Israel, and on February 24 the two governments signed an armistice. Talks between Israel and Transjordan and Lebanon resulted in armistices with Lebanon on March 23 and with Transjordan on April 3. The latter armistice included Iraq as well. Only one armistice was left to be signed—with Syria, and this was finally signed on July 24. The acting mediator, in the meantime, had returned to Lake Success and, his mission concluded, was relieved of further responsibility. The Conciliation Commission carried on.

Meanwhile the problem of the refugees, most of them Arabs, was in charge of a director of United Nations Relief for Palestinian Refugees, Stanton Griffis, United States ambassador to Egypt. Under his direction the various specialized agencies and many nongovernmental organizations like the Red Cross co-operated.

SINCE THE ARMISTICES

Early in 1949 the Security Council gave its approval to the application by Israel for membership in the United Nations. After a widely ranging and bitter debate the General Assembly in May approved the admission by the necessary two-thirds majority, and Israel took its place as the fifty-ninth member of the Organization.

Those parts of Palestine not occupied by the state of Israel remained without a government of their own. Most of the

Arab area was occupied by Transjordan. The strip in the south-west was occupied by Egypt.

The General Assembly of 1949 further considered two Palestinian questions—refugees and the status of Jerusalem. An Economic Survey Mission for the Middle East, headed by Mr. Gordon Clapp of the United States, had made recommendations on the refugee problem. The General Assembly established the United Nations Relief and Works Agency for Palestine Refugees in the Near East. This agency will work with local governments.

Reaffirming its previous decisions about Jerusalem, the General Assembly continued to maintain (contrary to the wishes of both Israel and Transjordan) that the city of Jerusalem should be placed under a separate international regime administered by the Trusteeship Council, and the General Assembly asked the Trusteeship Council to complete and implement the statute of Jerusalem which had been drafted in 1948.

At the End of 1949

The year 1949 saw the coming of peace to Palestine, though it was not in every way peace with justice. The fighting seemed unlikely to be resumed. The state of Israel was established as an active member of the United Nations and faced its domestic problems confidently. Israel occupied more territory than the General Assembly assigned to it in 1947. Transjordan (or Jordan, as it renamed itself) had gained prestige by its occupation of most of non-Jewish Palestine. Israel and Transjordan were on friendly terms and seemed agreed to keep Jerusalem divided between them rather than to let it be internationalized. The other Arab states had lost prestige, and the Arab League had been weakened by dissension.

The general feeling had come to be one of satisfaction that the problem of Palestine was no longer great and urgent. No one could maintain that the settlement was a triumph for the United Nations alone. But in the settlement the United Nations and its officers and agents played the major and effective part.

PART THREE

The United Nations at Work

Chapter 10. THE SECURITY COUNCIL

ORIGINS OF THE SECURITY COUNCIL

From one point of view the Security Council is the essential organ of the United Nations. From another it is a disappointingly ineffective agency, failing to perform duties laid upon it and seriously in need of reform.

The form, power, and procedure of the Security Council are what they are because of the nature of the Council of the League of Nations and its history.

We have referred to the problem of creating an executive authority for the United Nations. The general experience of modern governments has been that a single, individual man as chief executive is the normal pattern—one to which governments and peoples adjust themselves, and one which can be either autocratic or democratic depending on circumstances. This pattern is not, however, universal nor is it essential. Some contemporary governments, the Swiss and the Soviet for instance, are headed by executive councils rather than by one chief executive. Though they have persons called presidents, it is the council as a whole rather than one man who has the executive authority.

In any government as loosely organized as the League of Nations or the United Nations Organization, much directive authority remains in the member states, and such executive powers as exist are distributed among the various organs of the League or the Organization. There can be no single person at the head. There can be no president of the United Nations, no president of the world. Consequently, in each case a council was established, not as chief executive, but to exercise directive powers.

The Council of the League of Nations was originally a small

body. It included as permanent members the representatives of the Principal Allied and Associated Powers which were five, the United Kingdom, France, Italy, the United States, and Japan. And it included "Representatives of four other Members of the League . . . selected by the Assembly from time to time at its discretion." At the figure of nine members, as first constituted, the Council was small. The great powers possessed a majority in it. And (as always in the League) it acted by unanimity, though in a dispute involving a member of the Council, that member's vote need not be taken into consideration. The Council could "deal . . . with any matter within the sphere of action of the League or affecting the peace of the world."

The Council was intended to be a sort of steering committee for the League, if not quite an executive. From the first its character and its actions were different from what had been intended and expected. Since the United States never took its seat, the Council consisted at first of the representatives of Great Britain, France, Italy, and Japan with those of smaller nations (at first, Belgium, Brazil, Greece, and Spain). No sooner had the Assembly of the League started meeting annually and (like the Council) attempting to deal with "any matter within the sphere of action of the League or affecting the peace of the world" than the Assembly began to be the more important body. Japan was remote; Italy was not too powerful. In the Council (as in the Assembly) Great Britain and France gave leadership to the small nations, but the small nations made contributions of their own. The Principal Allied and Associated Powers did not dominate the Council; they certainly did not dominate the Assembly. In recognition of this situation, the Assembly increased the number of positions on the Council to be held by representatives of small powers so that the majority on the Council became a small-power majority, and toward the end of the life of the League the Council was a large representative committee mostly elected by the Assembly. Furthermore, though the United States never took its seat, Germany, when admitted to the League, was made a permanent member of the Council, and so was the Soviet Union, thus increasing the number of permanent members; and when Germany, Japan, and Italy left the League, their defection decreased it again. A Council so shifting in membership and so lacking in firm direction was not what the planners of the Covenant intended—it was much more an executive committee of a dominant assembly. Furthermore, it met regularly only three times a year.

The United Nations was planned to work very differently. The functions of *its* council and *its* assembly were to be differentiated. The assembly might continue to be a general forum, which had its uses, but it was *not* to exercise authority over the council. The council was to have real independent and indefeasible authority of its own. And since the United Nations in its original Dumbarton Oaks form was the creation of the big powers, the big powers were not merely to dominate the council but to control it effectively and completely.

THE ORGANIZATION AND PROCEDURE OF THE SECURITY COUNCIL

Membership

The Security Council of the United Nations is definite and unchangeable in size and in nature of membership—subject, of course, to amendment of the Charter, which is so difficult as to be almost out of the question. The Security Council consists of eleven members of the United Nations. China, France, the Soviet Union, the United Kingdom, and the United States "shall be permanent members." Nothing is said about possible additions to their number. The Security Council has also six nonpermanent members, elected by the General Assembly for a term of two years and ineligible for immediate reelection. No provision is made for increasing this number. In election of the nonpermanent members (apparently to ensure their quasi-representative capacity) regard shall be specially paid to their contribution to international peace and security and the other purposes of the Organization and to geographical distribution.

The membership, then, is fixed as to size and method of choice.

At the first election for the Security Council in January, 1946, Australia, Brazil, Egypt, Mexico, the Netherlands, and Poland were elected to the Security Council as nonpermanent members.

Since it was decided to elect three nonpermanent members each year, at the end of 1946 the General Assembly elected Belgium, Colombia, and Syria to take the places of Egypt, Mexico, and the Netherlands and to serve until January 1, 1949. At the end of 1947 the General Assembly elected Argentina, Canada, and the Ukraine to replace Australia, Brazil, and Poland and to serve until January 1, 1950. In 1948 Cuba, Norway, and Egypt were chosen to replace Belgium, Colombia, and Syria and to serve until January 1, 1951. In 1949 Ecuador, India, and Yugoslavia were chosen to replace Argentina, Canada, and the Ukraine and to serve until 1952.

Organization

The intention to create a central executive committee of the United Nations (at least for the maintenance of international peace and security) is shown in the Charter provision stating that the "Security Council shall be so organized as to be able to function continuously," that each "member of the Security Council shall for this purpose be represented at all times at the seat of the Organization," and that it may meet at other places at its discretion (Article 28).

The Security Council is the heart of the United Nations Organization. Whether in time of crisis or of calm, regardless of other organs of the United Nations or of time of year or of weather, the Security Council goes on. It meets so often that the representatives to it must be constantly present, themselves or by deputy, and seldom until the end of one meeting can one tell when the next meeting will occur. It has met on an average of five times in every fortnight since it was first organized. The agenda is never free of business. Some items on the agenda are immediate and some are almost forgotten. Often it assembles under the tensions of an emergency, but the very next time it sits, it may carry out matters of mere routine.

As the heart of the Organization it beats irregularly. Sometimes its cardiac spasms have seemed to signalize the dissolution
of the Organization in the pains and rigor of death—but like all
hearts it is tougher than you think.

In its conveniently arranged chamber the Security Council has
settled down. The curved table bears placards, each with the
name of a member state, and behind these placards familiar
faces appear. In order that it may be able to function continuously, "each member of the Security Council . . . shall be represented at all times at the seat of the Organization." Each member
state, therefore, has designated one particular person as its representative, and to an increasing extent the Security Council becomes a council of human beings and not merely of states. This
situation is particularly noticeable in the case of the permanent
members. Sir Alexander Cadogan for the United Kingdom,
Senator Austin for the United States, Mr. Gromyko for the Soviet
Union, Mr. Parodi for France, and indeed hardly less intensely
such representatives of nonpermanent members as Lange for
Poland, el-Khouri for Syria, Hodgson for Australia, and McNaugh-
ton for Canada—these men who served for long periods of time
seemed almost to be the Security Council itself.

The position of representative to the Security Council is one
that requires the highest intelligence and greatest devotion to
duty in addition to a background of infinite political and diplomatic experience. Constant and sometimes even daily meetings,
the preparation for meetings, the consultations with the home
government, and the essential informal contacts with other members make the position the fullest of full-time jobs. In theory
no representative speaks without the full concurrence of his government, and statements and sometimes sessions are postponed
because a government has not made up its mind. In fact the
ingenuity and diplomatic address of the representative are half
the thing that counts.

Behind the representatives sit their advisers. In front of them
sit the observers from the specialized agencies. They face the
public—and their words go to the ends of the earth, over the

microphone or in the written accounts of their listeners in the press gallery.

Procedure

Representatives of sovereign states, meeting in a Council concerned with international peace and security and meeting in public, are peculiarly difficult to unite into a coherent group. The Security Council is quite different from the General Assembly, where a large number of persons from many nations easily and inevitably absorb characteristics of a representative and legislative assembly. The Security Council is very small, and its members are very self-conscious. From the beginning the Council has had difficulty over its rules of procedure—for it must be both a solemn conclave of sovereign states and (if it is to do business at all) a compactly organized group. The inevitable instinct for cohesion has struggled against the individual pride of the member state. The Committee of Experts, created at the first meeting of the Security Council, advises the Council on matters of procedure which include quasi-constitutional matters.

In accordance with the precedent of rotation established in the Council of the League of Nations and in order to avoid the possibility of dominance by one nation or by one personality, the Security Council decided that its president should change monthly and that members should rotate in that office in accordance with the names of the states they represent, following alphabetical order in the English language. The first meeting of each month, therefore, will see a different, and perhaps an untried, man producing such cohesion as may exist—but at the same time using his office to help the position which his government takes in the business before the Council. (Each other principal organ of the United Nations has a president chosen by vote, therefore possessing a representative capacity and presumably expected to lead, though not to domineer). In the arrangement of business, in the decisions as to time of meetings, in the conduct of discussions, and in the ruling on points of order, he decides—subject, however, to the ability (quite firmly exercised) of seven members of the Council to overrule him on procedural matters. He possesses far more influence over debates than does the British Lord Chancellor as speaker of the House of Lords but far less than the elected speakers of the House of Commons, the American House of Representatives, the French National Assembly, or the Swiss Councils.

The initiative of the president of the Security Council is always exercised provisionally. For example, according to the Provisional Rules of Procedure of the Security Council, he calls the meetings, but he must call a meeting at the request of any member of the Council, or when a matter is brought before the Security Council in accordance with the Charter. He determines the provisional agenda, but the first business of any meeting of the Security Council is to determine the agenda on which they will actually act. On points of order his decision stands, unless immediately challenged, when the Security Council itself decides.

Until the General Assembly moved temporarily to Paris in 1948 and was followed by the Security Council, the Security Council had never met elsewhere than at the seat of the Organization. The presence of the representatives at the seat of the Organization, where the Secretariat is located, makes it easiest for them to meet there, whatever the difficulty may be which they attempt to solve. Indeed, they may discuss Korea, Indonesia, Palestine, or the proposed membership of Ceylon in rapid succession, but they do it most easily at the Headquarters.

The definite and exclusive quality of meetings of the Security Council is broken, not infrequently, by two Charter provisions. When a matter is before the Security Council in which a member of the United Nations not on the Security Council is interested, the member may have a representative present, *if the Security Council agrees.* And even a nonmember of the United Nations may be represented if it is a party to a dispute before the Security Council, again if the Security Council agrees. These representatives take their places at the table; they may speak and even enter into the discussion, but they have no vote.   This privilege of being heard by the Security Council is valuable, and the Security Council has been generous in granting it.

Power and Authority

The power and authority of the Security Council are intended to be great.   It may make decisions, and may enforce them, in the field of international peace and security—a field as wide as the world.   But its *authority* is greater than any *power* which it possesses, for the Charter (following Dumbarton Oaks) clearly states that "In order to ensure prompt and effective action by the United Nations, its Members confer on the Security Council primary responsibility for the maintenance of international peace and security, and agree that in carrying out its duties under this responsibility the Security Council acts on their behalf" (Article 24.1).   Furthermore, "The Members of the United Nations agree to accept and carry out the decisions of the Security Council in accordance with the present Charter" (Article 25).

PERMANENT MEMBERS AND THE VETO

The position of the permanent members of the Security Council is unique.   It is the clue to the political problems of the Security Council.   For the method of voting in the Security Council is its most astonishing characteristic.   And the problem of the veto, as Americans call it, is the most difficult question in the United Nations, both as a problem of organization and as a problem of policy.

The Charter provides (Article 27) that "Each member of the Security Council shall have one vote."   Thereafter it provides for as ingenious a system of unequal voting as the world has ever seen.

On *procedural* matters each member of the Council has one vote, seven is a majority, and all votes count equally.   In other words, any seven members have power to place a matter on the agenda, to advance or defer it, to suspend a meeting, to invite the attendance of nonmembers, to create subsidiary organizations, and to do other similar things.

On *all other matters* decisions shall be made "by an affirmative vote of seven members including the concurring votes of the permanent members." Here, the necessary majority for a decision is still seven votes, but in these seven must be included the votes of all the permanent members.

There are two classes of substantive decisions where the special majority is not required: "decisions under Chapter VI" which deals with the pacific settlement of disputes "and under paragraph 3 of Article 52" which provides for the pacific settlement of local disputes through regional arrangements. In these two cases "a party to a dispute shall abstain from voting."

History of the Veto

The problem of the veto cannot be understood without a reference to its history. It goes back to the League of Nations where, as we have seen, all decisions had to be by a unanimous vote of all members, *i.e.*, all members present and voting, for the practice of abstention as the sign of willingness to go along, though without specific approval, had become accepted. To modify the rigors of the requirement of unanimous consent which it inherited from the conference system, the League had developed a number of practices. One was to proceed by recommendations or *voeux* which could be voted by a majority only. Another was to allow a majority vote in committees and to establish the practice of not bringing matters to a final assembly vote unless there was agreement. Decisions in the full sense, however, continued to require unanimity, and any member, large or small, could exercise a free or *liberum* veto.

This precedent seemed intolerable to those who planned the United Nations and wanted an organization that could be effective and reasonably quick in accomplishing things. The requirement of a two-thirds vote in the General Assembly was not difficult to secure agreement on. The Economic and Social Council and Trusteeship Council could be allowed to make decisions by a majority vote because they had above them and controlling them the General Assembly. In other words a minority might have to accept General Assembly decisions made against them— though in the case of Palestine the Arab states, the British, and Israel have all refused to do so.

The position of the big powers—who planned the Charter—was a little different. None of them would submit to domination by the other big powers or by any organ. They seemed to be safe-guarded in the General Assembly in three ways: First, the General Assembly has no power except to recommend. Second, if the great powers should work together and should control the votes of most of the states naturally dependent on them, they would have a two-thirds majority. Third, the great powers could at least prevent adverse General Assembly decisions if they could control one-third of the votes plus one.

The Security Council was different. It has to have coercive power, and its functions might touch any state intimately. The basis of voting, *i.e.*, making decisions which may involve coercion, in the Security Council is twofold. The small powers *may* be decided against and thereafter coerced. For if the Big Five *agree*, they can (almost) always have their way, since they can usually get two nonpermanent members to vote with them. As it has been written, the Charter gives the great powers the legal right to coerce the small powers. But the Big Five may neither be decided against nor coerced.

The discussions which resulted in these arrangements have not yet been made public. It would seem, however, that the four powers which engaged in the Dumbarton Oaks Conversations were not originally in agreement. The original plan of the United States appears to have been drafted so as to make it impossible for the general international organization, as proposed, to exercise any authority over the United States without the consent of the latter. In other words, the United States insisted that it should have a veto in the Security Council—and *pari passu* the other great powers must be allowed to have it also. The Soviet Union, thinking of the general international organization as a

security organization, and determined to protect the position of
the Soviet Union, took a stand for what it calls the "principle of
unanimity," *i.e.*, that no action of *any* sort should be taken unless
all the big powers were agreed. The British and the Chinese
appear to have been less insistent on these principles.

At Dumbarton Oaks no agreement was reached as to the principles of voting in the Security Council—and, indeed, no effective
decision was reached for the establishment of the United Nations.
This decision was made only at Yalta.   There, at the same time
that the United Kingdom, the United States, and the Soviet Union
decided to call the San Francisco Conference, they agreed upon
the formula for voting in the Security Council, which they proposed at San Francisco and which is incorporated without change
in the Charter.

At San Francisco, it may be recalled, the relative position of
the small powers as against the big powers was the greatest point
of difference in the Conference—and in nothing was this difference more clearly shown than in regard to voting in the Security
Council. The small powers, wanting to establish an effective
general international organization and conscious that in any such
organization they would inevitably be liable to coercion, in the
interest of international peace and security, were unwilling to
agree that the Big Five should be exempt from any possibility
of coercion at all. They did not assume that it would often be
desirable or ever be easy to coerce even the weakest of the Big
Five. But they did desire the possibility in a case where the
maintenance of world peace would be at stake.

As soon as the Conference began to discuss the proposed provisions for voting in the Security Council, the smaller powers
tried to amend the Yalta formula in order to modify the privileged position which the great powers were proposing for themselves.

The discussions were conducted in the appropriate technical
committees, and particularly in Committee III/1. Since the
committees made their decisions and drafted their text by a two-
thirds vote, there was a real possibility that the small powers

could secure a two-thirds support for their amendments. At first the great powers insisted that the formula should be accepted without clarification or explanation. A subcommittee of Committee III/1 drew up a questionnaire for submission to the Big Four, hoping to learn from the answers the way in which the voting formula might be applied in specific cases. For the distinction between "procedural matters" and "all other matters" seemed far from clear.

It required over two weeks for the sponsoring powers to come to an agreement on their answer to the questionnaire. Eventually they did so. Their *Statement . . . of the Four Sponsoring Powers on Voting Procedure in the Security Council* is an ingenious document which, in essence, states merely that the powers claimed for the big powers in the Yalta formula were still claimed by them. In the committee discussions the delegates of the big powers made clear to the delegates of the smaller powers, first, their unwillingness to be coerced (or even decided against) under the Charter and, second, their belief that if any situation arose in which the coercion of a big power was necessary, the result would be another world war and the incidental breakup of the United Nations Organization.

The practical decision that the smaller powers faced was that of agreeing to provisions of which they disapproved or of going home without any Charter at all. The small powers yielded, and the Yalta formula, unamended, received the necessary two-thirds vote.

The Yalta Voting Formula

What Does the Formula Mean? The *Statement* of the sponsoring powers does illuminate the voting formula to some extent. In procedural matters, as explained above, the permanent members of the Security Council exercise no veto, which means that the Security Council may have on its agenda and may in a preliminary way discuss matters over the objection of a permanent member. It means also that when the Security Council contemplates any action, even the calling for reports, the hearing of witnesses, or the appointment of a commission of investigation, the veto will apply. And, further still, if an actual question arises as to whether a particular matter is procedural or not, the decision on this point is in itself a decision on a substantive matter and can be made only with the concurrence of all the permanent members of the Council.

An interesting, and perhaps significant, discussion of the veto was held in the Security Council itself on May 24, 1948. The Council had before it a proposal to set up a three-member subcommittee to hear testimony on the case of Czechoslovakia. When the proposed resolution came to a vote, Mr. Parodi of France, the Council's president, outlined the procedure to be followed. According to his suggestion, the Council would first decide whether the proposal was procedural or substantive and then would vote on the proposal itself. This ruling of the president raised the question of what is called the "double veto." According to the San Francisco *Statement* any decision as to what is procedural is itself a substantive decision and is, therefore, subject to the veto. To follow Mr. Parodi's procedure would be to allow opponents of the resolution (of which the Soviet Union was naturally the chief) to veto a motion to consider the resolution merely procedural, and then, when the resolution itself came to a vote, to veto it.

There was nothing novel in the possibility of the double veto, for it had been used twice before—in the Spanish and in the Greek questions. The Council discussed the validity of the San Francisco *Statement*. The Soviet Union insisted that the *Statement* was binding on the five permanent members and also that the decision to make an investigation was substantive. Mr. Parodi for France agreed. Sir Alexander Cadogan for the United Kingdom expressed support of the *Statement*, but interpreted it to mean that the proposal before the Security Council was procedural. Mr. Austin for the United States said that the *Statement* was not legally binding but that the United States still adhered to it; he, too, interpreted it to mean that the proposal before the Council was procedural only. China also expressed adherence to the view that the proposed action was procedural. The non-permanent members of the Council, except the Ukraine, were agreed that the proposal was procedural and also that the San Francisco *Statement* was not binding on them.

A vote of the Council on Mr. Parodi's procedural ruling received only 6 votes to overrule him (the United States, France, and the United Kingdom here abstained), and therefore his ruling held. A vote on the question of interpretation was taken, and a Soviet veto caused a proposal that the resolution was procedural to fail. The president then held that the resolution was substantive, and when it was put to the vote, the Soviet Union vetoed it.

The justification for their position given by the Big Five is what is known as the "chain-of-events" theory. In their *Statement* they say that "consideration and discussion" of a dispute or situation cannot be vetoed. But:

Beyond this point, decisions and actions by the Security Council may well have major political consequences and may even initiate a chain of events which might, in the end, require the Council under its responsibilities to invoke measures of enforcement under Section B, chapter VIII [of the Dumbarton Oaks Proposals, *i.e.*, Chapter VII of the Charter]. It is to such decisions and actions that unanimity of the permanent members applies.

How Has the Formula Worked? In practice the voting formula has meant that disputes and situations have been freely—indeed, sometimes frivolously—brought to the Security Council. They have been discussed with great frankness, often hurting the pride of one of the permanent members and sometimes effecting a change in its policy. But whenever even the least approach to a decision, even a preliminary decision, has been made, the veto is available and has sometimes been exercised. This has been done on most occasions by the Soviet Union, since its policy or that of its satellites has usually been the policy complained of.

In a single, but important, respect the voting formula has been modified by interpretation. The formula and Charter state that the vote must include "the concurring votes of the permanent members." This seems to mean that no nonprocedural decision can be made by the Security Council unless each permanent member votes positively for it—and that the absence or abstention of any permanent member would cause the vote to be lost. Absence is not often a problem. But the practice has grown up by which permanent members sometimes abstain from voting, allowing their abstention not to count as a veto. The decision is thereby made by seven affirmative votes in which theirs need not be counted. For example, in the decision that the Corfu Channel dispute should be referred to the International Court of Justice, the Soviet Union abstained but did not indicate abstention as a veto. This was true also in the useful decision to send the Committee of Good Offices to Indonesia.

The validity of the practice of abstention was raised in the Security Council on January 23, 1948, by Dr. José Arce of Argentina, with his customary emphasis. He pointed out that the Council's resolution of January 20 establishing a commission of mediation for the Kashmir dispute had been considered validly passed, though the Soviet delegate had abstained. Dr. Arce considered the decision legally invalid, though Argentina had voted in the affirmative. And Dr. Arce suggested that if the permanent members of the Security Council were to renounce their privilege, they should do so publicly. The British representative, Mr. Noel Baker, pointed out that every written constitution is developed by practice and that hitherto abstention has not been considered a negative vote; he hoped the practice would be continued. Further discussion was discouraged by the president of the Council, Mr. van Langenhove of Belgium. The particular occasion taken by Dr. Arce to make his point is an interesting one. When the Soviet representative, Mr. Gromyko, abstained from voting, he made it clear that he approved the general purpose of the resolution and indeed wished the Commission all success.

On the legal point that Dr. Arce raised, he would seem to be quite correct: the Charter requires the concurrent vote of every permanent member on every substantive issue, and abstention is not a concurrent vote. This is one of the two important respects in which the Charter has been specifically changed by interpretation.

As part of their justification for their position, the Big Four in San Francisco stated: "It is not to be assumed, however, that the permanent members, any more than the nonpermanent members, would use their 'veto' power willfully to obstruct the operation of the Council." This guarded negative was in no sense a pledge, and no government would accept an accusation of willful obstruction.

The Veto in Practice

The basis of organization of the Security Council was the assumption that the Big Four (or Five), having fought the war together would then, together, establish postwar policies and carry them out in the Security Council. Agreed as to what should be done or not done, they would have to submit their decisions to the nonpermanent members and secure the concurring votes of at least two of the latter. Unfortunately, the establishment of the Security Council occurred at a moment when many resultant problems of the war had not become subject to Big Five agreement and, indeed, when a fundamental difference of policy was establishing itself, with some permanent members on one side and some on the other. The working agreement—so useful during the war—by which the spheres of influence of the Soviet Union, the United Kingdom, and the United States were pretty well established and mutually accepted fell into the discard. The Soviet Union, stronger than it expected to be, pursued its inevitable policy of expansion more purposefully, since it met with less opposition. The United Kingdom, weaker than was expected, found itself on the defensive. The United States found itself not only more powerful but more relied upon by states and forces previously outside its area of interest, and more in opposition to Soviet expansionism. China, more troubled at home, was unwilling to take even a minimum of responsibility. France found itself on the defensive.

It must be remembered that the delegates at San Francisco

sincerely believed that the major international problem of the future would be the repression of Germany and Japan and not the postwar rivalry between the victors. Consequently, when the postwar problems which went to the Security Council were problems involving the special interests of individual members of the Big Five, the Security Council was called upon not to carry out a policy of unanimity, but to moderate or decide between the interests of its permanent members. The first issue (the Iranian question) was a question of Soviet expansion. The second issue (the first presentation of the Greek situation) arose from the weakness of the United Kingdom in one corner of its accepted area of influence; if the United Kingdom had retained its strength and had used it, the question would not have been raised. The third issue (Syria and Lebanon) was one in which the French and British were under attack.

Still more unfortunately for the smooth working of the Security Council, the postwar difference of policy usually put the Soviet Union on one side and the United Kingdom and the United States on the other and brought most of the elected members of the Security Council on the side of the United Kingdom and the United States. Consequently, the Western powers together commanded a majority of the Security Council and did not need to exercise a veto to have their way, while the Soviet Union with only one collaborator in the Council (Poland and later the Ukraine) could safeguard its policy only by the veto. From the "Western" point of view the Soviet Union obstructed. From the "Eastern" point of view the Western powers took advantage of a numerical majority, whereas the Charter assumed big-power unanimity. It is significant that France also has used the veto when it has believed itself under attack.

Amending the Veto Power

The result of the Soviet use of the veto has been a demand for its modification. The government of the United States has tended to rethink its attitude on the veto. As insistent as anyone at San Francisco that it must not be coerced, it has come to wish to use the Security Council as an instrument of coercion—or, if not quite coercion, as an instrument of its own policy. Consequently, American thinking tends to draw a line between the veto as used to prevent the use of physical force against a permanent member, and the veto as used to prevent various procedures for the peaceful settlement of disputes. The United States still insists on the veto in the first situation, but would let an ordinary majority make decisions in the area of "pacific settlement."

The Security Council was expected by its planners to be the center of possible conflicts of policy. It has been so.

DIRECTIVE FUNCTIONS OF THE SECURITY COUNCIL

It would be unrealistic, however, to think of the Security Council as merely a body concerned with international peace and security. By careful and intended Charter arrangements it is also an organ of the United Nations exercising a special influence on many areas of the Organization's work. These may be summed up as directive, or "organizational."

Admission of Members

The Security Council has come to control the admission of members to the United Nations. The Charter in Article 4 says that:

1. Membership in the United Nations is open to all other peace-loving states which accept the obligations contained in the present Charter and, in the judgment of the Organization, are able and willing to carry out these obligations.

2. The admission of any such state to membership in the United Nations will be effected by a decision of the General Assembly upon the recommendation of the Security Council.

The relative positions of the General Assembly and the Security Council in this matter have been the subject of continued dispute. According to the rules of procedure of the Security Council, an application for membership is made to the Secretary-General who transmits it to the Security Council. The Security Council, advised by its Committee on the Admission of New Members, decides whether in its judgment the applicant meets the qualifications and, if satisfied, makes a recommendation to the General Assembly. In making its recommendations, the Security Council has been highly selective, and most applicants have not received the necessary vote, which requires the concurrence of all the permanent members.

The position of the General Assembly has thus been one of receiving a limited number of recommendations—all of which it has approved. The General Assembly would almost certainly be more liberal in regard to new admissions than the Security Council. It has annually requested a reexamination of the rejected applications. But the Security Council still remains as a body which winnows out applications, and the General Assembly does not act without its recommendation.

Election of the Secretary-General

The Secretary-General is appointed by the General Assembly on recommendation of the Security Council. When the first Secretary-General was to be chosen, the General Assembly waited for the Security Council to take the initiative. The Security Council waited for a decision by its permanent members. When they agreed upon Mr. Trygve Lie, the Council and the Assembly immediately accepted their decision.

Elections to the International Court of Justice

The fifteen members or judges of the Court are chosen by concurrent vote of the Security Council and the General Assembly. In this case, according to Article 10 of the Statute of the Court, the Security Council as well as the General Assembly act by an absolute majority, and in the Security Council no distinction in voting is made between permanent and nonpermanent members. Since no more than one judge may be chosen from any member state, each of the permanent members of the Council is certain to be able to designate a judge of its own nationality.

Membership in the Trusteeship Council

By a decision reached by the Big Five at San Francisco, each of them, as a permanent member of the Security Council, is also always a member of the Trusteeship Council.

The peculiar constitution of the Trusteeship Council, according to which it must have equality of members as between administering and nonadministering powers, makes it impossible for the Big Five to dominate it numerically. And in the Trusteeship Council decisions are made by vote of a simple majority of any members, without any special privileges for the Big Five.

Amendment to the Charter

The veto exists in regard to amendments to the Charter. Here again the smaller powers at San Francisco tried, but only with limited success, to democratize the process. In the arrangement finally adopted, amendments may be proposed by a two-thirds vote of the General Assembly or by a general conference called by a two-thirds vote of the General Assembly and any seven members of the Security Council. The final approval of amendments, however, occurs only when they are ratified by two-thirds of all members of the United Nations, including *all* permanent members of the Security Council.

Subsidiary Groups

Not only does the Security Council establish committees to facilitate its work, but it has created committees and commissions which serve as its agents for special or continuing jobs. The Charter gives it the power in Article 29 to establish subsidiary organs; none of its existing agencies have been formally established under this authority; they all come under its general powers (Article 24) or its specific powers found elsewhere than in Article 29. The Charter gives it the Military Staff Committee, and the General Assembly gave it the Atomic Energy Commission. It has established the Commission on Conventional Armaments (under Article 26). These are its major functional subordinate organs. It has also created lesser committees and commissions, some for staff purposes, such as its Committee of Experts, and others to handle special problems, like its Committee of Good Offices on the Indonesian Question. It consequently receives reports and gives directions to an increasing variety of subsidiary groups.

Special Supervisory Functions

Though the functions of the Security Council are either organizational or related to international peace and security, it has (like any other governmental body) the possibility of adding additional substantive functions. Two of these have already been approved—cases in which the Security Council in fact exercises, or is prepared to exercise, supervisory, if not actually administrative, functions.

Japanese Mandated Islands. The first of these is in relation to the Trust Territory of the Pacific Islands. This area, offered by the United States in 1947 as a trust territory of the sort called in the Charter "a strategic area," comes to some extent under the supervision of the Security Council. The proposed trusteeship agreement establishing this trust territory was submitted, in accordance with Article 83.1, to the Security Council for approval, and approved. Any alteration or amendment to the agreement must likewise be submitted to the Security Council. Furthermore, the Security Council, under Article 83.3, is to avail itself of the assistance of the Trusteeship Council in relation to political, economic, social, and educational matters in this area.

Trieste. Another area brought indirectly under Security Council supervision is the Free Territory of Trieste. The establishment of this territory was agreed upon in the Italian treaty of peace, with the proviso that its independence and integrity would be ensured by the Security Council. The Security Council accepted the responsibility in January, 1947, under its general authority, as given in Article 24, and approved the three instruments which established the Free Territory and its government. The Security Council is to appoint the governor of Trieste and is to be responsible for the maintenance of its statute and of order and security. So far, the Security Council has been unable to agree upon the choice of a governor. In 1949 the United States stated that it no longer approved the arrangement voted in 1947, but the Security Council has taken no further action on the matter. The territory remains under occupation by forces of the United Kingdom, the United States, and Yugoslavia.

SITUATIONS AND DISPUTES BEFORE THE SECURITY COUNCIL

The major work of the Security Council is presumed to be to deal with particular situations and disputes which raise questions of international peace and security. From the moment of its organization it has had to deal with such questions. A few of them have been on the agenda briefly; others require recurrent attention over the years. Some have proved insoluble. Others have been settled in one way or another. The record of the Security Council is a spotty one. Persons desiring to see quick and spectacular action will usually be disappointed with the Security Council. And since it had not yet proceeded to the organization of the forces which it is supposed to have available to enforce its decisions, it had not up to the end of 1949 caused a single shot to be fired.

The cases analyzed below are the major ones that have gone to the Council as "situations" or "disputes" involving international peace and security—those which the Security Council took upon itself to attempt to settle, or at least to discuss purposefully.[1] They are analyzed here as continuing problems, and not year by year. The annual reports of the Security Council to the General Assembly summarize them fully, but without comment. In his annual reports on the work of the organization the Secretary-General also summarizes the cases objectively.

[1] This account goes up to the lull in Security Council action in the latter part of 1949. For the Korean question in 1950, see the Preface.

The Iranian Question

On June 19, 1946, only two days after the Security Council had held its first meeting, it had to face its first and one of its most peculiar problems. The head of the Iranian delegation to the United Nations wrote the Secretary-General that owing to the interference of the Soviet Union's officials and armed forces in the internal affairs of Iran, a situation had arisen which must lead to international friction. He therefore asked the Executive Secretary (for there was as yet no Secretary-General) to bring the matter to the attention of the Security Council.

The Council considered the matter. In view of the fact that both parties had affirmed their readiness to settle the matter by direct negotiation, it asked the parties to keep it informed.

A little later (in March) the Iranian government brought the matter forward as a dispute: it said that the Soviet government was marching troops into Iran contrary to treaty. The representative of the Soviet Union withdrew from the Security Council for a month, but his government indicated that they were withdrawing troops from Iran. The Council waited to see what would happen. The Iranian government first withdrew its complaint to the Security Council and later expressed itself as satisfied that Soviet troops had been withdrawn within the time indicated as proper. The Council was not entirely satisfied that the difficulties were over and decided to keep the question as one of which the Council was still seized. In other words, the question remained on the nonactive agenda of the Council.

Whether or not the withdrawal of the Soviet troops ended external interference in Iranian affairs, the outcome has been considered a success for the Security Council, since the troops complained of were withdrawn.

The Greek Question

On January 21, 1946, the Soviet delegation requested a discussion of the situation in Greece on the ground that the presence of British troops in the area after the war was over constituted interference in Greece's internal affairs. (Certain suggestions were made that this case was brought as a countercharge to the complaint of Soviet troops in Iran.) After hearing all nations concerned, the Council voted that the question should be considered closed.

A few months later the Ukrainian government complained to the Security Council of incidents along the Greek-Albanian frontier and ascribed the difficulties primarily to the presence of British troops in Greece. After lengthy discussion which centered around the responsibility of persons on both sides of the border (Albanians, Yugoslavs, and Bulgarians as well as Greeks), an American resolution for a commission of investigation was agreed to by eight members, but lost by the negative vote of the Soviet Union.

On December 3, 1946, the Greek government brought the question of guerrilla warfare on the Greek border to the attention of the Security Council. This time the Security Council did appoint a commission to investigate alleged border violations; the Commission was composed of a representative of each of the 1947 members of the Council. It was to conduct its investigations in Greece, Albania, Bulgaria, and Yugoslavia where necessary.

The Commission went to the area of the disputes and made investigations. When the investigating Commission was about to return to make its report, the United States proposed that it should leave behind it representatives in Greece who could report border violations. This creation of a subsidiary group was voted by the Security Council. The Subsidiary Group had difficulties arising out of lack of cooperation by Yugoslavia, Albania, and Bulgaria and was attacked, ineffectively, in the Security Council by the Soviet Union.

The investigating Commission itself made a report to the Security Council on May 23, 1947, in which eight of the eleven members found that Yugoslavia and, to a lesser extent, Bulgaria and Albania had supported the guerrilla warfare in Greece. The representatives of the Soviet Union and Poland considered the "monarcho-fascist" government of Greece wholly responsible for all border difficulties. The representative of France abstained from expressing an opinion. The entire Commission, except the Soviet and Polish members, proposed a new commission to deal with border difficulties and to report. When the question was discussed in the Security Council, all members of the Security Council, except the Soviet Union and Poland, took the border difficulties very seriously and wanted to call upon the border countries to desist from helping the Greek guerrillas. Since Council action was blocked by Soviet Union veto, the United States had the question removed from the Security Council agenda (an action which requires only a procedural vote) so that it might be discussed by the General Assembly. From that point on, the problems of Greek border warfare passed from the Security Council to the General Assembly.

The problem was, of course, complicated politically by the announcement in March, 1947, by President Truman that the United States must give aid to Greece to prevent the spread of communism.

The Indonesian Question

The great Indonesian question, second only in importance to the question of Palestine, came before the Security Council quietly and early. On January 21, 1946, the Ukrainian government alleged that British and even Japanese troops were being used against the population of Indonesia and asked the Security Council to investigate. In its first decision, made in response to this suggestion, the Security Council refused to interfere.

The situation in the Netherlands Indies had been made difficult by the war. Hitherto peaceful colonies, enormous in size and population, great sources of wealth to the European Kingdom of the Netherlands, had been occupied by the Japanese. The already emerging nationalism of the Indonesians had been encouraged by the conquerors. When the war was over, Dutch rule was not easy to reestablish. A Republic of Indonesia proclaimed its existence and demanded the recognition of its independence. If the Dutch had been able to regain their authority, the Western world would no doubt have been satisfied. As it proved, the Dutch could not restore their control over Indonesia and yet they were not willing to let it go.

The easiest answer was to allow the parties concerned to settle the question among themselves. For almost two years after the Japanese surrender, negotiations went on between the Dutch and the Indonesians. An agreement was made at Linggadjati. The Dutch government recognized the *de facto* authority of the Republic over Java, Sumatra, and Madura. An Indonesian Republic existed. But there was friction between it and the Dutch, and the Dutch engaged in what they called "police action" directed against the Republic.

On July 30, 1947, the representatives of India and Australia in the Security Council complained of the hostilities resulting from the "police action," calling them a threat to international peace and security. The sympathy of the Indians (newly free from their European masters) might be presupposed. The sympathy of the Australians arose from the danger that an imperialist war in the Far East might cause to Australia itself, which was already fearful both of the attempts to repress nationalistic feeling and the opportunity such attempts would give to communist agitation.

The Security Council's majority could not seem to deny legitimate nationalist aspirations. On the accusation of hostilities amounting to war, it called on both the Dutch and the Indonesians to suspend hostilities and to report to the Council. Both of the contestants issued cease-fire orders, but hostilities continued.

The United States proposed good offices. The Security Council created the three-member Committee of Good Offices, one to be chosen by each of the parties and the third by the two so selected. Belgium was chosen by the Netherlands; Australia by Indonesia; the United States was the third.

The Committee went at once into action. It arranged for negotiations, which since no land area was available took place on the U.S.S. *Renville* at Batavia. A truce was agreed upon. Political questions were redetermined. The Republic of Indonesia was to be created within a sovereign federal United States of Indonesia. The United States of Indonesia was to remain under the Dutch crown. The Committee reported from time to time to the Security Council, which gave it wide discretion. During most of 1948 it seemed as if a tremendous but inevitable reassignment of authority was taking place in the Netherlands Indies.

The Dutch, however, continuing to resent what they considered interference in their domestic affairs, and feeling stronger, signalized the breakup of the General Assembly session in December, 1948, by renewed "police action." By this time the good repute of other nations was involved, and the Security Council met at once at the instance of the United States. A series of Security Council resolutions demanded cessation of hostilities and the yielding of positions which the Dutch had illegally taken. The Committee of Good Offices was reconstituted as the Commission for Indonesia to advise the two governments. After six months the Dutch government yielded completely, and the kidnapped government of the Indonesian Republic was returned to its capital.

In the summer of 1949 a conference was held at The Hague between the Dutch and the Indonesians, and a new constitution was drawn up which gives to the Indonesians the independence they have been seeking, though Indonesia will still remain legally under the Dutch crown.

In advancing the cause of peoples struggling for independence, in moderating local hostilities, and in preventing a major war originating in the Far East, the work of the Security Council in the Indonesian question has been a striking success.

The Syrian-Lebanese Question

On February 4, 1946, the heads of the Syrian and Lebanese delegations to the United Nations brought to the attention of the Security Council the presence of French and British troops in their countries. After the situation had been thoroughly discussed, the United States submitted a resolution expressing confidence that the foreign troops would "be withdrawn as soon as practicable" and requested the parties to keep the Security Council informed. This resolution was lost because it did not receive the affirmative vote of the Soviet Union. The French and British representatives, however, stated that their governments would give effect to the decision of the majority of the Security Council. The troops were withdrawn.

Spanish Question

The Polish representative, on April 8, 1946, brought forward the existence of the Franco regime in Spain as a danger to international peace and security and proposed that all members of the United Nations maintaining relations with the Franco government should sever them. A subcommittee of the Security Council was appointed to investigate. This subcommittee found that the Franco regime was not an existing threat to the peace, as Poland suggested, but a potential menace. It, therefore, proposed that the General Assembly be asked to recommend that diplomatic relations with the Franco regime be terminated by members of the United Nations. This proposal failed to receive the support of the Security Council, which merely decided to remain seized of the question but later dropped the matter so that the General Assembly could consider it.

The Corfu Channel Question

On January 10, 1947, the British representative brought before the Security Council the dispute between his government and that of Albania over the presence of mines in the North Corfu Channel, an international waterway between Corfu which is a Greek island and the mainland which is Albania. After discussion, and further discussion by a subcommittee, the Council voted that the mine field could not have been laid without the knowledge of the Albanian government and urged the British and Albanians to settle the dispute on this basis. The resolution failed because of the Soviet veto.

Later the Council decided to refer the dispute to the International Court of Justice.

The Dispute between Egypt and the United Kingdom

On July 8, 1947, the Egyptian government said a dispute had arisen between Egypt and the United Kingdom which might endanger international peace and security. The question was twofold: the presence of British troops in Egypt and the policy of the United Kingdom in regard to the Anglo-Egyptian Sudan. This question was discussed for over two months by the Security Council. It was one in which the United Kingdom, as a party to the dispute, had no vote. The Security Council was plainly in favor of action which would further free Egypt and the Sudan from British control, but it could not agree on a resolution. The Council remained seized of the question.

The Palestine Question

The question of Palestine, which is discussed fully in Chapter 9, was first brought to the General Assembly and handled there. When the Assembly, on November 29, 1947, resolved the partition of Palestine with economic union, it referred to the Security Council questions of international peace and security in relation to the country. From that time on the Council was frequently concerned with the Palestinian problem.

The India-Pakistan Question

Early in 1948 India protested that Pakistan was pursuing aggressive activities in Kashmir, a separate state whose government had chosen to accede to the Indian dominion, though a large part of its population was Moslem. In response to the Indian complaint, the representative of Pakistan replied by broadening the issue to quarrels between the two dominions over other native states. The general question of relations between India and Pakistan was raised. This question, involving hundreds of millions of persons, was faced squarely by the Security Council, which appointed a commission to investigate the facts and to exercise a mediatory influence in the area. The Security Council persuaded the two disputant states to accept a plebiscite for Kashmir under United Nations auspices. Later on, the Security Council increased the commission to five members to go at once to the Indian subcontinent. The two disputants both disliked the terms of references of the commission but did not refuse to cooperate with it. It was sent off by the Security Council with instructions to deal first with Kashmir and then to make other recommendations.

When the question first arose, both Indians and Pakistani were engaged in the use of force, and the danger of war (which might easily have become a general war) was great. Though the commission found itself unable to make progress on the problem of Kashmir during 1949, the danger of war seemed to have receded.

The Czechoslovakian Situation

In February, 1948, a new government under Communist domination came into power in Czechoslovakia. The Czech representative to the United Nations, appointed by the previous government, requested that the Czechoslovak situation be brought to the Security Council as endangering international peace and security. On March 12 the Chilean representative gave the backing of his government to this request.

A thoroughly fruitless discussion occupied nine Council meetings. All parties that professed an interest were heard, except the new Czechoslovakian representative, who declined to take part in the discussion. The Chilean government proposed a subcommittee to obtain information for the Council's use. But on the proposal to consider the appointment of this commission a procedural matter, the Soviet Union voted in the negative, thereby making the issue a substantive one, according to the Four Power *Statement*. And on the substantive question the Soviet Union again voted "No," thus causing the proposal to be lost.

This issue before the Security Council is the best example so far of a question which could have been raised only for propaganda purposes. Had the Security Council decided against the new government of Czechoslovakia, or against the Soviet Union which had created it, the Security Council neither could nor would have taken action.

The Hyderabad Question

Hyderabad, one of the largest of the Indian native states, did not join either India or Pakistan when the two latter states succeeded to British power in India. Its ruler is a Moslem, inclined toward Pakistan. A majority of its people are Hindus. It is surrounded by India, which desired its accession to that state.

The Nizam of Hyderabad made a one-year agreement of temporary and partial association with India. Permanent agreement was prevented by action which Hyderabad called a threat to the peace and which caused its government to complain to the Security Council against India. Pakistan intervened in the situation. A slight show of force by the Indian government persuaded the Hyderabad government to decide to leave the question of accession to India to popular vote and to withdraw its complaint from the Security Council. The situation was hardly suited to decision by the Security Council, since the general feeling must inevitably be that because of its geographical location Hyderabad must work closely with India. The Security Council attempted no decision.

The Berlin Blockade

"Identic notifications dated September 29, 1948," were received by the Secretary-General from the French, British, and American governments complaining that the Soviet restrictions on transport between Berlin and the Western zones of occupation in Germany were a threat to the peace. They asked the Security Council to consider the question at its earliest opportunity.

The Council decided to admit the question to its agenda, in spite of a Soviet argument that according to Article 107 of the Charter the matter must be settled directly by the countries concerned. After lengthy discussion the six "neutral" states on the Council proposed a resolution for the lifting of the blockade on terms considered friendly to both sides, but the Soviet Union vetoed the resolution.

Mediatorial efforts of the presidents of the Council and of the Assembly (which was meeting) were continued. (They are referred to in Chapter 8 above.) Eventually discussions begun between Soviet and American delegates resulted in a lifting of the blockade.   In May, 1949, the complaining governments wrote to the Secretary-General that they had come to an agreement with the Soviet government on the Berlin question.

Without doubt the Council may discuss *any* matter which in its judgment affects international peace and security.   Undoubtedly it discussed the Berlin blockade with good will and ingenuity, and its discussions may have been useful.   But the three complaining governments received much adverse criticism for bringing· to the Security Council a dispute between four permanent members of the Council which the four had been unable to settle for themselves.

THE SECURITY COUNCIL AS CONCILIATOR

When the Security Council began its sessions in January, 1946, it seemed as if its agenda was to be crowded with questions brought to it for political reasons or simply to test its endurance. No doubt attempts are still made to use the Council for propaganda purposes or to strengthen the position of international political factions.   It has come to spend most of its time, however, on substantive issues which its members actually want to solve, though they may disagree as to details of procedure or ultimate solution.

In his report to the General Assembly in 1948, the Secretary-General says that "The Security Council has not yet been able to act as an agency for the enforcement of peace, but it is achieving increasing success as a mediator and conciliator."   And he instances the Indonesian and India-Pakistan questions as "the two outstanding cases of this kind, apart from Palestine."

Had the Security Council the forces at its disposal which according to the Charter it should have, perhaps it would be less patient as a conciliator and perhaps it would be listened to less willingly.   In the Indonesian question (where trouble broke out again after the Secretary-General wrote his 1948 report) the members of the Security Council were sufficiently divided as to the solution desired (though agreed that strife in Indonesia was a bad thing) so that the Security Council would never have been able to decide to use force against either the Dutch or the Indonesians. In the India-Pakistan dispute, forces (if they had been available) could undoubtedly have policed Kashmir, but it is doubtful if they could have kept Indian and Pakistani forces from moving. "Police" efforts by British troops in Palestine or by French troops in Indochina have been conspicuously ineffective. There is no guarantee that troops of these and other states would be more effective merely because they were under the direction of the Security Council. Nor can one be sure that the causes backed by the Security Council with force would appear to be more just and more irresistible than the same causes backed by separate states with force. Would the Security Council be more efficient in maintaining international peace and security if it had forces at its disposal?

There are clearly two kinds of situations. In some, force seems inapplicable or useless. In others, it might be useful. Of the first Indonesia and Kashmir are examples. In Indonesia the struggle was between independence and colonialism. Whatever the Dutch may say, it was never a mere question of keeping order in the Indies. From the United Nations point of view the only answer was a slow approach to a new equilibrium, pursued through compromise. No United Nations forces (if they had existed) could justly have been used either to free or to reenslave the Indonesians. Again, in the India-Pakistan question it would have been very undesirable for the United Nations to fight either state, even if either one of them were more unequally responsible for the troubles than it was; and clearly it would be undesirable for the United Nations to fight them both. The British were considered oppressors because they kept down Hindus and Moslems by force, and the United Nations might easily be considered merely another oppressor.

In other cases, however, small forces at the disposal of the Security Council, not attempting to win a victory for one side or another, might be useful. In Palestine there would have been no Arab-Jewish war if a small United Nations force had been able to step in to keep order while the British were withdrawing, and the United Nations forces could not have been accused of working for the selfish ends of a nation as the British were. A small United Nations force along the Greek border four or five years ago when the trouble began might have kept Albanians, Yugoslavs, and Bulgarians on their own side and Greeks on theirs.[1]

To sum up the work of the Security Council as an agency dealing with substantive questions, one can suggest certain conclusions. Cases which the Security Council tries to handle usually follow a definite pattern. Though any member of the United Nations may bring a complaint, and though many members may be *indirectly* interested in a case, the case (whether classifiable as a "situation" or a "dispute") always has two sides and definite parties on the two sides. Most often the parties are states: Egypt vs. Great Britain in regard to the Sudan; United Kingdom vs. Albania in regard to the Corfu Channel; India vs. Pakistan. Sometimes they are a state against a revolutionary government, as the Netherlands against the Indonesian Republic. And the tendency will always be to crystallize a situation as an issue between two parties: Palestine becomes an issue between the member states of the Arab League and the Jewish state of Israel.

In every case force has been used by one or both sides to a greater or lesser degree. Every case can be made to seem between oppressed and oppressor—though the manifold and varying sympathies of members of the United Nations and the Security Council will cause them to take different views as to which side is which. There are always claims of oppression. And in every case there has been at least *some* claim of right on the side of the oppressor.

No complaint brought to the Council has been frivolous in substance; in every case (however minor) there has been a serious issue between at least two governments which *might* be a threat

[1] The question of forces used to repel the aggression in Korea is discussed in the Preface.

to international peace and security. Sometimes, it is true, complaints are brought to gain political ends rather than with any serious belief that the Security Council will take action—but in all free countries people are familiar with the use of the legislature for political propaganda or for attempting to change the political balance of power. It is a sign of the health of the United Nations if nations are anxious to use the Security Council as well as the General Assembly as a forum for international education. And no one can see the Council at work without realizing that the representatives there—however bound by their instructions—are influenced by what goes on and, in turn, influence their own governments.

REGIONAL ARRANGEMENTS

Chapter VIII, one of the shortest chapters in the Charter, is entitled "Regional Arrangements." Since it is concerned with international peace and security, it is in a sense a footnote to Chapter VII on breaches of the peace.

The heart of Chapter VIII is the statement:

Nothing in the present Charter precludes the existence of regional arrangements or agencies for dealing with such matters relating to the maintenance of international peace and security as are appropriate for regional action, provided that such arrangements or agencies and their activities are consistent with the Purposes and Principles of the United Nations (Article 52.1).

and the later provision that

. . . no enforcement action shall be taken under regional arrangements or by regional agencies without the authorization of the Security Council . . . (Article 53.1).

These provisions of the Charter are usually read with Article 51, the last article in Chapter VII, which was originally drafted by Committee III/4 on Regional Arrangements. Article 51 states:

Nothing in the present Charter shall impair the inherent right of individual or collective self-defense if an armed attack occurs against a Member of the United Nations, until the Security Council has taken the measures necessary to maintain international peace and security. Measures taken by Members in the exercise of this right of self-defense shall be immediately reported to the Security Council and shall not in any way affect the authority and responsibility of the Security Council under the present Charter to take at any time such action as it deems necessary in order to maintain or restore international peace and security.

Origins of Chapter VIII

When the Charter was drawn up, there was already in existence an Inter-American system, which had recently held a conference in Mexico City and had agreed upon the Pact of Chapultepec and whose members intended to maintain peace in the Americas by collective action and believed themselves able to do so. The American republics were unwilling to give up the machinery of consultation which they had long used. They had been making serious efforts to organize themselves not merely for consultation but for collective action. If they were to be satisfied with the Charter, the *international* security system of the United Nations, so far untried, must not supplant their *regional* security system, at least until it had proved itself efficient.

On the other hand, if the United Nations Organization was to be effective as a security organization, the Security Council must not find itself interfered with or hampered by any local system.

The compromise of Chapter VIII was, therefore, agreed upon. The Inter-American system—or any similar system—could continue, but when it was to take action, it must obtain the consent of the Security Council. Furthermore, the Security Council might find it useful to let regional agencies deal with regional problems. Article 52.3 encourages it to do so in the following words:

The Security Council shall encourage the development of pacific settlement of local disputes through such regional arrangements or by such regional agencies either on the initiative of the states concerned or by reference from the Security Council.

In this way the Security Council is given an over-all control, but the work of regional agencies is not necessarily interfered with. Regional arrangements like the Locarno pacts had been established under the League of Nations and had proved useful. They might be useful under the United Nations Charter. At any rate one of them existed and could hardly be abolished.

The Inter-American system may be a good example of a regional arrangement, but what other system could also have been contemplated? The Arab states had formed the Arab League during the war. Though it was in its formative stages and hardly as yet more than a propaganda organization, its members believed that it also fell within the provisions of Chapter VIII. This belief was not altogether acceptable to the great powers. Regional arrangements in other parts of the world had been talked about; they had not yet been created.

Other Regional Security Arrangements

In 1947 and 1948, partly under the stimulus of the Truman Doctrine and the Marshall plan, the nations of Western Europe began to consider not only cooperation for recovery but also possible cooperation for defense, actually though not ostensibly against the Soviet Union. It seemed possible to plan cooperative defense arrangements under Chapter VIII. An agreement between the United Kingdom, France, Belgium, Luxembourg, and the Netherlands came into existence in 1948. A North Atlantic agreement to include nations of Western and Northern Europe together with the United States and Canada was planned by the United States in the same year, and the North Atlantic Treaty was signed by twelve states on April 4, 1949.

Regional Security Treaties and the Charter

The legal relationship of regional security treaties to the Charter of the United Nations is difficult to determine. As suggested above, regional arrangements under Chapter VIII are intended to be related to international peace and security and, therefore, subject to a superior control by the Security Council.

Can a regional security arrangment be made, however, which will be beyond the control of the Security Council and yet consistent with the Charter? The question has to be squarely faced in connection with the North Atlantic Treaty. That treaty in its Preamble reaffirms the parties' "faith in the purposes and principles of the Charter of the United Nations," and in Article 5 the parties agree that in case of "an armed attack against one or more of them" each of them will exercise the "right of individual or collective self-defense recognized by Article 51 of the Charter of the United Nations" to assist the parties attacked. So far, there seems to be no difficulty in reconciling the treaty with the Charter. The treaty provides further, however, for collective defense machinery and for the development of "individual and collective capacity to resist armed attack," and the effective force of the treaty lies not in the treaty itself but in the Military Assistance Program of the United States which, if successful, will bind the signatories into one unified military organization—a regional security council, so to speak, which *will* have forces at its command. Article 7 of the treaty states that:

This Treaty does not affect, and shall not be interpreted as affecting, in any way the rights and obligations under the Charter of the Parties which are members of the United Nations, or the primary responsibility of the Security Council for the maintenance of international peace and security.

But since the security arrangements under the treaty will be impaired in efficiency if they are made a matter of common information, it would seem that they will in practice conflict with Article 54 of the Charter which states that:

The Security Council shall at all times be kept fully informed of activities undertaken or in contemplation under regional arrangements or by regional agencies for the maintenance of international peace and security.

So far, no situation has arisen which has had to be dealt with by any organ of the United Nations under Articles 51 or 52, 53, and 54. But problems may arise in the future.

Chapter 11. REGULATING THE USE OF FORCE

The Problem of Enforcement

The United Nations was intended to be superior to the League of Nations in that, unlike the League, it would be able to enforce its decisions. The United Nations, then, must have forces at its disposal, that is, at the disposal of the Security Council. Arrangements are provided in the Charter by which such forces are to be brought into existence.

But the granting of forces to the Security Council is only one side of the picture. If the United Nations itself is to use force, it is almost equally essential that the United Nations shall try to limit, if not to abolish, other existing forces. Just as in the League of Nations, it was necessary for the United Nations to provide not for complete national disarmament, but at least for the limitation, and even reduction, of national armaments and armed forces.

The Charter, therefore, provides that the Security Council shall have forces at its disposal with which to enforce its decisions. It also includes provisions, somewhat less emphatic than those of the League Covenant, looking toward reduction of armaments. The Charter includes provisions in relation to disarmament, it is true, but they are minimized.

The Security Council is not directly given any specific authority in relation to limitation of armaments. The Charter provides, however, that "The General Assembly may consider the general principles of cooperation in the maintenance of international peace and security, including the principles governing disarmament and the regulation of armaments, and may make recommendations with regard to such principles to the Members or to the

Security Council or to both" (Article 11.1). A reasonable division of activity seems to indicate that the General Assembly may deal with principles and broad policies and that the Security Council will make specific studies and recommendations. It is on this basis that the organs of the United Nations have proceeded. As a result, the General Assembly has developed into an over-all policy body in relation to most questions regarding the existence and use of force, except in specific cases of United Nations enforcement.

In approaching this whole difficult but vital problem, therefore, we must first look at the discussions and recommendations of the General Assembly and then at the specific work of the Security Council, the Military Staff Committee, and those other bodies, the Atomic Energy Commission and the Commission on Conventional Armaments, which were created subsequent to the Charter to deal with specific aspects of the question of armaments and armed forces.

The Part Played by the General Assembly

During the First Part of its First Session the General Assembly by resolution created an Atomic Energy Commission to make proposals "for the elimination from national armaments of atomic weapons and of all other major weapons adaptable to mass destruction."

During the Second Part of the First Session the General Assembly passed a comprehensive resolution on the principles governing the regulation and reduction of armaments. Arising out of a Soviet proposal that the General Assembly consider necessary a general reduction of armaments, as well as the prohibition of the use of atomic energy for military purposes, the resolution as adopted was considered by the United States "an outstanding achievement" and was agreed to unanimously by the General Assembly. The resolution as finally passed covered many aspects of the broad question.

It recommended that the Security Council formulate practical measures for the general regulation and reduction of armaments and armed forces and for the assurance that such regulations would be generally observed.

It urged the Atomic Energy Commission to work expeditiously under its terms of reference, including the drafting of conventions for the creation of an international system of control and inspection.

It recommended that the Security Council work out proposals for the "early general regulation and reduction of armaments and armed forces."

It recommended that the Security Council accelerate the placing at its disposal of the armed forces mentioned in Article 43.

It recommended the withdrawal of armed forces of members from ex-enemy and member states.

And it recommended a corresponding reduction of national armed forces and a "general progressive and balanced reduction of national armed forces."

In accordance with these resolutions, and also in accordance with the authority granted to the Security Council by the Charter, consideration of these manifold problems began in the Security Council, the Military Staff Committee, the Atomic Energy Commission, and the Commission on Conventional Armaments. The United States was the only great power which had a program as well as a policy and consequently pressed insistently for decisions in all the areas concerned. It met with general support from most of the small powers but less cooperation than it expected from the other great powers, none of which saw quite the same degree of urgency in reaching decisions in a matter which was so complicated and which had so little of an emergency aspect. Even in the matter of atomic energy the other powers sharing the responsibility for the bomb left the initiative to the United States.

The only other effective program making seems to have been done by the Soviet Union, which proceeded slowly and, as usual, even more slowly when under pressure from other countries. Eventually the Soviet Union developed a counterprogram in all the areas relating to national and international forces, and put forward this counterprogram with increasing firmness. However unrealistic and sophistic it may have seemed to most of the members of the Security Council, it took form as a program of firm resistance to every suggestion made by the United States.

As a result, the discussions in the Security Council and its subordinate bodies eventually resulted in an apparently insoluble difference of opinion as to the proper program by which to carry out an agreed end, although it continued to be agreed that the Security Council should have forces at its disposal, that national armaments should be limited, and that methods of warfare involving weapons of mass destruction should be abolished.

By the middle of 1948 a deadlock had been reached all along the line. In the introduction to his 1948 report to the General Assembly the Secretary-General stated that "One of the most discouraging aspects of United Nations work during the year under review has been the failure of the Atomic Energy Commission, the Commission on Conventional Armaments, and the Military Staff Committee to make any real progress."

When the general debate in the Third Session of the General Assembly began in Paris in September, 1948, great disappointment was expressed by many speakers, particularly at the failure to control atomic energy. The United States took the position that the present situation could be remedied only by a restoration of political confidence. The representative of the Soviet Union, Mr. Andrei Y. Vyshinsky attacked the United States and its policy with peculiar violence and lack of restraint. At the same time he proposed a resolution recommending that the five permanent members of the Security Council should each during one year reduce by one-third all its present land, naval, and air forces. Though this resolution had no chance of acceptance, it did force the Assembly toward an attempt to break the existing deadlock.

Lengthy discussions of disarmament and atomic energy were held in committee and on the floor of the Assembly. Eventually the Assembly, on November 4, passed a resolution on atomic energy by a large majority with only the Soviet bloc in opposition. This resolution gave general approval to the reports of the Atomic

Energy Commission, asked the six permanent members of the Commission to consult together in an attempt to find a basis of agreement, and called on the Commission to continue its work. On November 13 the Assembly asked the Security Council to continue the study of reduction of conventional armaments through the Commission on Conventional Armaments and suggested, as an approach to the problem, the collection of information.

These two resolutions showed the unwillingness of the smaller powers to allow the deadlock between the United States and the Soviet Union to turn into a stalemate. The small powers accepted the general position of the United States, but they insisted that the appropriate organs of the United Nations should keep on trying to do their duty.

In the 1949 Assembly the deadlock continued with the attitude of the small powers unchanged.

FORCES FOR THE SECURITY COUNCIL: THE MILITARY STAFF COMMITTEE

How Can Forces Be Provided?

The Security Council of the United Nations was intended to be in a position to enforce peace. This was to be one of the great advantages of the United Nations over the League of Nations, which was considered to have been weakened in making decisions by the fact that it would not be able to enforce them when made. The United Nations was to be like the League of Nations—it could hardly be otherwise—in that it would try persuasion in case of a dispute and next might try economic sanctions, but it was to have both the authority and the power to use military sanctions—force in the most conventional sense. We have discussed its *authority* to coerce in the preceding chapter. Here we discuss its *power*.

In the days when the League of Nations was faced with problems of enforcement, a good deal of attention was given to the suggestion that the League should have at its disposal an international police force which would carry out its decisions and judgments. This force, as usually envisaged, would have uniform organization and command (under the League of Nations) and would be relatively small, well-equipped, and modern. It would, of course, be military in organization and equipment—in other words, an army. As the airplane began to have greater military use, it seemed as if an international police force might perhaps be an air force—particularly if limitation of national armaments affected first, and most of all, the new weapon—the airplane. Finally, an international force might best be stationed permanently at certain strategically located places throughout the world which might be made over by the nations that owned them to the League of Nations. Such plans, reasonable as they might seem (for the principle is that on which national police forces are organized in difficult countries) were too radical to be adopted by the League and, in fact, received serious support only from such minority groups as the British Labour party.

In the early planning for a better organized postwar world, the suggestion of international bases with an international force to preserve law and order was recurrently made, and in 1941 and 1942 was not unpopular, even among conservative planners. Long before the Dumbarton Oaks Conversations, however, the idea of an international force had been laid aside, because no strong state would agree to the consequent restriction on its national sovereignty. To give the United Nations its own army, navy, or air force would, indeed, make it a superstate.

The plan for providing force to enforce peace, as proposed at Dumbarton Oaks and accepted at San Francisco, is simple in principle and complicated in detail. There is to be no United Nations force. The only armies will still be national armies. But the Security Council is to have the authority to call upon member states to provide at any time contingents whom it may direct for enforcement purposes.

The details are complicated. They are outlined at length in the Charter and have been the subject of elaboration since San Francisco.

The Machinery of Enforcement

The Charter authorizes the Security Council to "take such action by air, sea, or land forces as may be necessary to maintain or restore international peace and security" (Article 42). Where are the forces to come from? Articles 43, 44, and 45 explain. "All Members of the United Nations . . . undertake to make available to the Security Council, on its call and in accordance with a special agreement or agreements, armed forces, assistance, and facilities, including rights of passage . . ." (Article 43.1). Furthermore, "In order to enable the United Nations to take urgent military measures, Members shall hold immediately available national air-force contingents for combined enforcement action" (Article 45). (This provision, as limited by the rest of the article, would seem to be legally redundant, though from a practical point of view it seems to suggest that air contingents should be the first type considered for use by the Security Council.)

The national forces available to the Security Council are to be arranged for in special agreements made "as soon as possible on the initiative of the Security Council" with each member or with groups of members of the United Nations.

These agreements "shall govern the numbers and types of forces, their degree of readiness and general location, and the nature of the facilities and assistance to be provided."

Thus, in a highly complicated way, the Security Council by a series of treaties with the members of the United Nations would get the specific authority to use specific numbers of troops, ships, planes, etc., and also "assistance, and facilities, including rights of passage." Presumably the Security Council has to decide on what it wants from any particular member state and specify its requirements; but then when the agreement has been made, the forces, etc., are constantly available to it—available "on its call." The use of the agreement is a way of refraining from infringing upon national sovereignty. The terms "assistance, and facilities, including rights of passage" are very vague terms, subject (as we shall see later) to various possible interpretations, but potentially covering other things besides troops, *e.g.*, food, munitions, or harbor facilities. "Rights of passage" might be interpreted broadly to mean any use of the territory of a member state.

Creating the Military Staff Committee

A special organ was created to have immediate charge of all these matters. "Plans for the application of armed force shall be made by the Security Council with the assistance of the Military Staff Committee" (Article 46). The latter is an expert body composed of strategic and military experts, like the Combined Chiefs of Staff of the Second World War. The Military Staff Committee is to advise and assist the Security Council in all questions relating to (1) its military requirements, which includes the special agreements and their content; (2) the use of forces by the Security Council; and (3) "the regulation of armaments, and possible disarmament."

How is the Military Staff Committee composed? "The Military Staff Committee shall consist of the Chiefs of Staff of the permanent members of the Security Council or their representatives" (Article 47.2). Here the reality behind the façade is revealed. The Security Council, as a political organ, is composed of permanent members and nonpermanent members. The former dominate, but they do not exclude the representatives of the latter. Any decisions which the permanent members make must have some support from the nonpermanent members. On the other hand, the Military Staff Committee which will plan enforcement action is composed of representatives of the Big Five alone— though it is provided that "when the efficient discharge of the Committee's responsibilities" requires it, the Committee shall invite the participation of any other member of the United Nations.

History of the Military Staff Committee

The Security Council, at its second meeting, on January 25, 1946, issued the directive proposed by the Preparatory Commission in its report (page 25), asking its permanent members to direct their Chiefs of Staff to meet, constituting this assemblage as the Military Staff Committee, and asking it to formulate proposals for its organization and procedure and submit them to the Security Council. The Military Staff Committee met on February 4, 1946, in London.

The Committee adjourned on February 14 and met again in New York on March 25 and has been functioning ever since. It meets in secret.

On February 16, 1946, the Security Council directed the Military Staff Committee as its first task to examine from a military point of view the provisions of Article 43. The Military Staff Committee decided first to formulate recommendations to the Security Council concerning basic principles to govern the organization of United Nations forces. Two subcommittees worked, one to formulate recommendations and the other to prepare a standard form of agreement between the Security Council and member nations.

The Military Staff Committee made little progress until the General Assembly, in a resolution on regulation of armaments, recommended that the Security Council "accelerate as much as possible the placing at its disposal of the armed forces mentioned in Article 43 of the Charter."

On February 13, 1947, a resolution of the Security Council (which also set up the Commission on Conventional Armaments) requested the Military Staff Committee to submit to the Security Council "as soon as possible and as a matter of urgency" the recommendations for which it was asked by the Security Council on February 16, 1946, in pursuance of Article 43, and as a first step to submit to the Security Council not later than April 30, 1947, its recommendations as to "basic principles which should govern the organization of the United Nations Armed Force." Long discussions before the passage of this resolution (by 10 votes, the Soviet Union abstaining) concerned the question of whether the Atomic Energy Commission and the Commission on Conventional Armaments should work on parallel lines or whether the Commission on Conventional Armaments would interfere with the Atomic Energy Commission.

In accordance with the resolution, recommendations were submitted by the Military Staff Committee to the Security Council on April 30, 1947. The report of the Military Staff Committee included recommendations agreed upon by all delegations and also the proposals of individual delegations on points where agreement was not reached.

The 1947 report of the Military Staff Committee, which is the largest measure of agreement and accomplishment of which the Military Staff Committee can as yet boast, contained forty-one articles on twenty-five of which there was unanimous agreement. The report was discussed in general by the Security Council in four meetings, and then the Security Council decided on June 16, 1947, to treat it as a working paper and to discuss the articles one by one in the Security Council.

Perhaps in this report, and in the divergent opinions on which its disagreements are based, will be found the heart of the disagreements between permanent members of the Security Council.

During the course of a discussion, first of the report in general and then of specific articles, the Security Council adopted provisionally twenty-five articles. The discussion was dropped in the middle in July, 1947.

Apart from some general statements difficult to disagree with, the report dealt with two subjects. On the first, the question of making special agreements, the Military Staff Committee and the Security Council seem to be in substantial agreement. On the second, the armed forces to be made available, seriously felt differences were evidenced.

As soon as the Security Council has agreed on the general principles which should govern the whole matter, the Security Council, with the help of the Military Staff Committee, will estimate the over-all strength of the armed forces which the Security Council will need. The individual agreements will then be negotiated in view of the over-all requirements. They will include the size and composition of the contributions of the member nations, each of which will be determined in the process of negotiation. The agreement will presumably state the degree of readiness, general location, etc., of contingents. Member states in their agreements will not necessarily contribute armed forces, but may contribute "facilities and other assistance." It is made clear that when not called by the Security Council the contingents are a part of the national forces of the member states, under the command of the member states.

When the agreement has been negotiated, it must be approved by the Security Council and by the member state. It can then be supplemented or changed by a similar process.

As to the nature of the armed forces and the facilities, there was a large amount of agreement, yet very marked disagreement on certain points. It was agreed that the armed forces available "should be limited to a strength sufficient to enable the Security Council to take prompt action . . ." and that the permanent members "shall contribute initially the major portion of these forces." It seems to be implied that the first agreements will be made with the permanent members. A great difference arose as to their prospective contributions. All the permanent members appeared to agree that their contributions should be equivalent to those of each other. The Soviet Union took the extreme position that there must be equality among them as to the contributions—apparently man for man, gun for gun, plane for plane (though the Security Council might make exceptions). The United States took an almost equally extreme view that, though the contributions should be "comparable," they could hardly in any sense be equal, i.e., that some states might furnish planes, some men, etc. The other permanent members found equality impracticable, but feeling it substantially desirable, differed as to the extent to which contributions might match each other. Almost equal emphasis was placed on this issue by the United States and by the Soviet Union; unfortunately the Security Council interrupted its discussion before the subject had been talked out. The Soviet Union was insistent that the forces made available should be small. If disarmament proceeded according to the Charter, small United Nations forces would be enough; and if small, then equality was possible. In the very informal estimates as to the size of small forces needed which entered into the discussions, the United States suggested far greater strength of forces than did any of the other powers.

Granted the principle that the forces remained part of the national forces of the member state until called by the Security Council, the question of their general location then arises and gave ground for disagreement. The Soviet Union insisted that they be stationed only on the land and in the waters of their own state, lest if stationed abroad they exercise a political influence on the area in which they were located. The United States, the United Kingdom, and China wished them stationed in any territories or waters to which they had legal access—for efficiency of possible action. The Soviet Union insisted (contrary to the other four powers) that "facilities" did not, and must not, include bases. All agreed that when called by the Security Council the forces will be "based . . . in areas designated by the Security Council," but the four powers wished them more flexible when not under call. The Soviet Union insisted also that transportation of forces must be national. A final and somewhat substantial disagreement was as to whether they must return to their home territory within a specified time after the end of their mission or whether they would return only when the Security Council recalled them. (The veto enters here.)

The disagreements were important, since their basis was essentially political and apparently ran through all the discussions, both in the secret ones of the Military Staff Committee and the public ones of the Security Council. They have at any rate been considered serious enough to prevent further progress. From the American point of view they have prevented the great necessity—the establishment of a large, well-trained force available to the Security Council, mobilized, stationed all over the world, and ready to act. The Soviet counterposition seems clear—small forces, perhaps contributed only by the Big Five, stationed at home and so exactly equal that no political implications (as between the Big Five) would be involved in their existence or use. Whether or not the Soviet Union would have gone further toward the actual establishment of the system had the other states agreed with its proposals as to basic principles, it is impossible to tell; many Americans came to doubt it. If, however, the Security Council needs forces at its disposal, perhaps limited forces, not too efficient in themselves and in their general location, are better than none, and the plan agreed to in Article 43 of the Charter might be put into effect on a minimized basis instead of the maximized basis which seems (to most Americans) most reasonable.

One important question was discussed. The Big Five and some other members of the Security Council seemed reasonably agreed that the Charter did not envisage a possible use of force against any permanent member. Some members of the Security Council wished to retain this as a possibility, particularly since the Charter did not outlaw it.

The Further Program of the Committee

Pending a decision by the Security Council as to the general principles which should govern the organization of the armed forces of the United Nations, the Military Staff Committee has been much limited in its work. On May 16, 1947, it agreed on a program of work which is still before it. This program includes a study of:

1. The preliminary estimates of the over-all strength and composition of the armed forces to be made available

2. The preliminary estimates of the forces to be made available by the five permanent members of the Security Council

3. The preliminary estimates of the forces to be made available by other member nations

4. The preparation of a draft standard form of special agreement

So far, the Military Staff Committee has released only the varying suggestions of the powers concerning the first item.

THE ATOMIC ENERGY COMMISSION

The Atomic Bomb

The second chief concern of the Security Council (and of the United Nations) in relation to armaments consists of the Atomic Energy Commission.

The work of the Security Council and the Military Staff Committee in regard to a United Nations was deliberately planned as part of the United Nations machinery. So was the consideration of the limitation of armaments and disarmament as centered, so far, in the Commission on Conventional Armaments. On the other hand, "When the United Nations met at San Francisco to draw up the Charter of the United Nations, atomic energy as a deadly weapon was as yet unknown to the world" (*United States and United Nations, 1947*, page 44).

But the bombing of Hiroshima by United States forces was officially interpreted as having brought the war with Japan to a quick close, economical in time and in loss of life, and certain members of the United Nations were seen to possess a weapon of such extreme potency, so unpredictable in its political results, that a new and imperative problem for the United Nations existed.

The United States government, having been primarily responsible for the development of the atomic bomb and entirely responsible for its deadly use, decided to propose arrangements by which atomic energy should henceforth be eliminated as a deadly weapon and devoted only to peaceful uses. On the invitation of the President, Congress recommended domestic legislation for its control. The President also met (in November, 1945) with Mr. Attlee, the prime minister of the United Kingdom, and Mr. King, the prime minister of Canada, to concert international proposals. These two men represented the other two governments which had been actively concerned with the development of the bomb. The heads of the three governments issued an Agreed Declaration. At the Moscow Conference of December, 1945, the foreign ministers of the United States, United Kingdom, and Soviet Union drafted proposals to be made to the General Assembly, and the governments of France and China joined them in introducing the proposals into the General Assembly at its First Session in London. On January 24, 1946, a resolution was passed by the General Assembly to establish an Atomic Energy Commission.

The Atomic Energy Commission was to consist of the members of the Security Council plus Canada when Canada was not a member of the Council. The Commission was to submit its reports and recommendations to the Security Council, and the Security Council "in appropriate cases" should transmit these reports to the General Assembly, to other organs of the United Nations, and to the members of the United Nations. Since the Security Council has "primary responsibility under the Charter of the United Nations for the maintenance of international peace and security," the Council should issue directives to the Atomic Energy Commission "in matters affecting security," and on these matters the Atomic Energy Commission should be accountable to the Security Council. The Commission should present recommendations to the various organs of the United Nations. The Atomic Energy Commission thus became a special and separate agency of the United Nations. The constitutional question of its precise place in the United Nations organization under the Charter was raised in the General Assembly discussions. It was pointed out that, though the General Assembly was creating the Commission, it was yielding control over it to the Security Council, and yet the Commission is not a creation of the Security Council. It seems to have been created out of an implied power possessed by the General Assembly, for it was not ticketed as a subsidiary organ of the General Assembly under Article 22 or of the Security Council under Article 29. Its anomalous position has presented difficulties.

The terms of reference of the Atomic Energy Commission are broad and important. It is to make specific proposals for:

(a) The exchange of basic scientific information for peaceful ends

(b) The "control of atomic energy to the extent necessary to ensure its use only for peaceful purposes"

(c) "The elimination from national armaments of atomic weapons and of all other major weapons adaptable to mass destruction"

(d) "Effective safeguards" by "inspection and other means" to protect complying states against violations and evasions

The work of the Commission was to proceed by stages, yet with the "utmost dispatch to inquire into all phases of the problem."

History of the Atomic Energy Commission

The designated members (the members of the Security Council and Canada) chose their representatives on the Atomic Energy Commission, who for the most part have been the same persons as their representatives to the Security Council but have acted by deputy. The Atomic Energy Commission held its first meeting on the call of the Secretary-General in New York on June 14, 1946. (Mr. Bernard Baruch served as first United States representative and as chairman at the first meeting, after which the chairmanship rotated among the members.)

In the meantime the United States government had explored the basis of a policy and had issued the Acheson-Lilienthal Report (known officially as A Report on the International Control of Atomic Energy and published by the Department of State). This report was written by a group of expert consultants. It analyzed the nature, development, and possibilities of atomic energy, pointing out the enormous possibilities of its use for harm or for peaceful, constructive purposes. It discussed the question of control—to prevent harmful, and to promote constructive, use. It made almost inevitable the acceptance of its conclusions that only by government control within any country and by strict international control in the world at large could atomic energy be neutralized in its harmful, and promoted in its constructive, aspects. A great public corporation of an international sort was proposed as the means of development and control. The thinking of the United States government and of most American citizens on the subject of atomic energy has subsequently been largely determined by this report, which is one of the great state papers of the century. Somewhat earlier (in 1945) the War Department had released a report by H. D. Smyth on *Atomic Energy for Military Purposes* which divulged sufficient technical information to drive home the danger of the uncontrolled development of atomic energy.

When the Atomic Energy Commission met in June, 1946, it heard statements of national policy from its members. The first was made for the United States by Mr. Baruch. The United States proposed the creation of an international atomic development authority, "to which should be entrusted all phases of the development and use of atomic energy, starting with the raw material." Its functions should include:

. . . managerial control or ownership of all atomic-energy activities potentially dangerous to world security;

. . . power to control, inspect, and license all other atomic activities;

. . . the duty of fostering the beneficial uses of atomic energy;

. . . the responsibility for "research and development" so as to make it the leading authority in the field.

When the system of control has been established, and the bomb has been renounced as a weapon, the United States proposals further said,

Manufacture of atomic bombs shall stop;

Existing bombs shall be disposed of pursuant to the terms of the treaty;

The Authority shall be in possession of full information as to the know-how for the production of atomic energy.

The United States representative went on to point out how essential would be the punishment of any misuse or diversion of materials or plants concerned with atomic energy. "The matter of punishment lies at the very heart of our present security system." And he went on to say that "there must be no veto to protect those who violate their solemn agreements not to develop or use atomic energy for destructive purposes." He went on to specify in some detail the way in which the authority would work and the powers which it must necessarily possess, including the powers of inspection and control in any place that seemed to it necessary.

From these basic proposals the United States has never receded. From the point of view of the United States the proposals were extremely generous. The United States alone possessed atomic bombs, the knowledge and equipment with which to make them, and the wealth to develop atomic energy unilaterally in any way it saw fit. The United States was willing to yield its monopoly of knowledge and to destroy its bombs. But it insisted, as a prior requirement, that, before it yielded either its knowledge or its bombs, no other nation should have the right or the power to produce them. It would yield its peculiarly privileged position, but only in return for a previous agreement that the bomb should never be used for national ends. This agreement must be completely enforceable by entrusting to an atomic energy authority such powers that the United States would be safeguarded. From the American point of view the creation of the all-powerful, international authority came first; then would follow the United States relinquishment of its supreme weapon.

The second statement of policy was that of the representative of the Soviet Union. His proposal was that the first step should be the conclusion of an international agreement to prohibit the production and use of atomic weapons, and to provide that within three months after the agreement went into effect all atomic weapons should be destroyed. The agreement would be effective when ratified by the permanent members of the Security Council and should be obligatory on all states.

Other states who were members of the Atomic Energy Commission expressed varying views, most of them generally supporting the American proposals; most of them wishing further discussions of the subject. The Atomic Energy Commission appointed committees which discussed political and technical points, in particular explaining the implications of the American proposals. In the fall of 1946 the General Assembly showed an interest in the question of atomic as well as other armaments, and the Atomic Energy Commission decided to submit a report to the Security Council before December 31. In the discussions on this report, in the Atomic Energy Commission and in the Security Council, the different positions on the basic issues became clearer. Two points of view were potent. The United States (which possessed atomic bombs) insisted on the establishment of an international authority with comprehensive power and authority and was then willing to yield its bombs and its power to make them. The Soviet Union (which possessed no bombs) insisted on the agreement to destroy bombs and after their destruction was willing to establish a system of international control. The other member states (except Poland) had reached a general acceptance of the United States point of view because they were convinced by the expert information which came to them through the work of the Scientific and Technical Committee of the Commission that only by complete international control could the danger of diversion of atomic energy from peaceful uses be prevented. The report itself—the First Report of the Atomic Energy Commission— in its elaborate popularization of information as to atomic energy processes would seem to make clear that any development of atomic energy may so easily be diverted to the manufacture of weapons that no control except the most complete and comprehensive would be effective. If there is *any* control of atomic energy at all, it must be single-handed, comprehensive, and complete.

At the same time the position of the Soviet Union was clarified, notably in a speech by Mr. Gromyko in the Security Council on March 5, 1947. Assuming the destruction of existing bombs (which it puts first), it will accept international regulation including inspection and punishment of violations. But the question of the veto, raised first by the United States, was countered by the Soviet Union on two grounds. One was legalistic—that the General Assembly had resolved, in its resolution of December 14, 1946, that the establishment of "an international system" of control and inspection, including prohibition of atomic weapons, should be "within the framework of the Security Council," which includes the veto. The second was practical—that any authority acting by majority vote, without the veto, "may take one-sided decisions" and that the majority would be one "on whose benevolent attitude towards the Soviet Union the Soviet people cannot count." Consequently the Soviet Union "cannot allow the fate of its national economy [to] be handed over to this organ." The representative of the Soviet Union went even further. "In reality," he said, "to grant to the control organ unlimited rights and possession and management of the atomic establishments, cannot be looked upon as anything but an attempt by the United States to secure for itself world monopoly in the field of atomic energy."

In an attempt to explain the Soviet attitude, Prof. James T. Shotwell wrote that "the Soviet government's distrust of the motives of the outside world is rooted deep in the attempts made for its overthrow by force of arms in its early years and the long diplomatic boycott that followed. In particular, international machinery devised in the West is suspect" (*International Conciliation*, April, 1947, page 171).

Soviet amendments to the proposals of the first report were made and discussed. Finally the matter was reported back to the Commission, which should formulate specific proposals and report again before the next General Assembly in September, 1947. With many formal and informal committee sessions much elaboration occurred, largely on the problems of technical control. In June, 1947, the Soviet Union offered specific proposals—in a sense a counterplan to that of the majority. But the majority were still not satisfied that the Soviet plan would provide effective controls.

A Second Report of the Atomic Energy Commission was essentially an interim report. It summarized its activities from January 1 to September 11, 1947. It gives fuller and further conclusions of the majority as to the details of control. It shows also an intensification of the differences between the majority and the minority.   The Second Report was approved with 1 negative vote, the Soviet Union, and 1 abstention, Poland.

Subsequent to the making of this report, further discussion in the Atomic Energy Commission and its committees became largely wrangles on political matters, even during a discussion of the Soviet's proposals on June 11, 1947.   The Soviet Union became more intransigent in insisting on its proposal for the abolition of atomic weapons before anything further could be discussed, and in its attacks on the United States as responsible for the failure of the whole disarmament program.   Eventually, on May 17, 1948, the Atomic Energy Commission issued a Third Report (voted by 9 members, with the Soviet Union and the Ukraine in the negative) stating that the Commission "has reached an impasse" and its belief that the deadlock cannot be broken at the Commission level.   The Commission, in submitting this report to the Security Council, asked that it be transmitted to the next regular session of the General Assembly, along with the two previous reports of the Commission, "as a matter of special concern."   In its resolution the Commission recommended that the "negotiations in the Atomic Energy Commission" be suspended until the General Assembly should find that the (political) situation hampering the work of the Commission no longer existed.

When the report was received by the Security Council, the United States proposed that the Council approve the general findings of the three reports and send them to the General Assembly with a record of the Council's approval.   This proposal was lost as a result of the veto of the Soviet Union.   A Canadian resolution was then proposed to transmit the reports to the General Assembly and the members of the United Nations "as a matter of special concern."   The Soviet representative expressed his disapproval but ostentatiously refused to veto this resolution, which therefore passed.

Many hours were spent by the General Assembly of 1948 discussing the reports of the Atomic Energy Commission and in airing the differences between the majority and minority positions. Since the small powers were unwilling to have the work of the

Commission stop, the Assembly eventually passed a comprehensive resolution on November 3, 1948. This resolution first gave approval to the findings and recommendations of the Commission. Second, it asked the six permanent members of the Commission (the Big Five and Canada) to consult together to determine whether a basis for agreement on international control exists and to report to the Assembly not later than the next regular session. Finally, it called on the Commission to resume its sessions and to continue its work.

During most of 1949 no advance toward agreement was made in the Commission or in the consultations among the six members. The announcement by President Truman on September 12, 1949, that an "atomic explosion" had occurred in the Soviet Union, followed by Mr. Vyshinsky's claims of the development of atomic weapons and energy in the Soviet Union, brought home the urgency of the problem to the General Assembly. The United States and the Soviet Union both remained firm in their sponsorship of their proposals, still essentially unchanged. The smaller powers, who now felt that they would suffer most from an atomic war, tried to improvise some plan of temporary control of atomic weapons.

COMMISSION ON CONVENTIONAL ARMAMENTS

Creation of the Commission

The latest, and so far the least fruitful, of the Security Council's efforts to deal with the question of armed force was the establishment of the Commission on Conventional Armaments. This Commission owes its establishment to the General Assembly resolution of December 14, 1946, which among other things asked the Security Council to "give prompt consideration to formulating the practical measures . . . which are essential to provide for the general regulation and reduction of armaments and armed forces."

In accordance with this request, the Security Council on February 13, 1947, established the Commission on Conventional Armaments composed of representatives of the members of the Security

Council. It instructed the new Commission to submit to the Security Council within three months proposals for the general regulation and reduction of armaments and armed forces and for "practical and effective safeguards." The Security Council excluded from the competence of this new Commission all matters falling within the competence of the Atomic Energy Commission. The Soviet Union did not veto the establishment of the Commission on Conventional Armaments, but tried to have the Commission consider armaments as a whole, including atomic weapons. As elsewhere in the United Nations, the Soviet Union continued to maintain the position that the first step to be taken was an immediate reduction of armaments. The United States kept insisting that reduction of armaments was subsidiary and secondary to the "establishment of essential conditions of international peace and security."

Discussion in the Commission

The Commission on Conventional Armaments met first on March 24, 1947. It succeeded in preparing an extremely general "plan of work," which the Security Council approved. The Commission further managed to define those "atomic weapons and weapons of mass destruction" which fell outside its province. During the ensuing months, the Commission met as a "working committee" of the whole and considered proposals made by various delegations.

In preparation for the third regular (1948) session of the General Assembly the Commission in August, 1948, adopted a resolution stating that it considered that its jurisdiction covered all armaments and armed forces except weapons of mass destruction, the latter including atomic weapons. It further drew up a resolution on general principles which stated that "a system of regulation and reduction of armaments and armed forces can only be put into effect in an atmosphere of international confidence and security" and mentioned certain conditions necessary to that security, some of them political. The resolution further stated that, under an effective system of regulation, national armaments should not exceed those necessary to carry out a member's rights and duties under the Charter. The representatives of the Soviet Union and the Ukraine opposed these resolutions and sponsored counterresolutions which were voted down. On August 17 the Commission finished drawing up its second report, which included the ideas of the majority, and agreed that it would be considered approved if not brought up again before September 15.

In spite of the resolution just mentioned which appeared to show that the majority of the Commission thought its discussions were useless, the 1948 session of the General Assembly did not allow the Commission to stop its work. On November 19 the General Assembly declared that the aim of the reduction of armaments and armed forces can be attained only "in an atmosphere of real and lasting improvements in international relations." But it went on to recommend that the Security Council pursue the study of such reduction through the Commission on Conventional Armaments "in order to obtain concrete results as soon as possible." It also recommended that the Commission formulate proposals according to which an international organ of control, within the framework of the Security Council, would obtain and publish information from member states on their armed forces and armaments.

Chapter 12. GENERAL WELFARE:
THE ECONOMIC AND
SOCIAL COUNCIL

THE SECOND PURPOSE OF THE UNITED NATIONS: ECONOMIC
AND SOCIAL COOPERATION

Though the first purpose of the United Nations, in the eyes of the powers that planned it, is the maintenance of international peace and security, the Organization has a second purpose equally important to most of the peoples of the world. This second purpose is the promotion of economic and social well-being.

The Dumbarton Oaks conferees were interested in establishing an "international security organization." Their Proposals include only the most rudimentary machinery for economic and social cooperation. At San Francisco the emphasis was different. The lesser governments in particular, most of whose domestic activity was directed to the promotion of domestic well-being, wished to carry over this type of governmental activity into the international organization. The San Francisco Conference, acting through Committee II/3, drew up two lengthy chapters of the Charter. These chapters lay down the policy and state the purposes of economic and social cooperation. They also establish as a "principal organ" of the United Nations an Economic and Social Council which (under the General Assembly) is responsible for policy in this broad field.

The shift of emphasis from a "security organization"—essentially negative and punitive—to a general international organization positively promoting the general welfare was evident in the San Francisco Conference, is clear in the Charter, and becomes more and more conspicuous in the work of the United Nations since its foundation. If it ever seems that the United Nations as a police organization is ineffective, one may usefully look at its many accomplishments as a welfare organization.   Yet a warning is necessary.   No field of activity of the United Nations is so broadly defined as the economic and social field.   In no field are the structural arrangements so complicated.   No field is so difficult to survey, either broadly or in detail.   In no field is most activity so inconspicuous, so unromantic.   The Security Council, the Trusteeship Council, or even the Court are concerned with immediate events and problems, and the conspicuous issues of international politics heighten the tension.   In the field of general welfare many months and much routine work are needed to accomplish results.

With a sound instinct for the ways in which governments help peoples, earnest and competent leadership in this field has organized the day-by-day work of hundreds of people.   In the long run the United Nations will probably be judged by the effect that it has (directly itself, or indirectly through member governments and specialized agencies) in raising standards of nutrition and health, making the seas safer to travel, protecting all men and all nations against harmful drugs, furnishing statistical information and expert advice, and planning (regionally or universally) a freer, more prosperous, better educated, and more highly integrated world.

The Charter Scheme

The provisions of the Charter dealing with international, economic, and social cooperation include statements of principle and purpose; arrangements for the relationship between the United Nations and "the various specialized agencies . . . established by intergovernmental agreement and having wide international responsibilities"; and the creation of an Economic and Social Council which, under the authority of the General Assembly, has the responsibility for carrying out the principles and arrangements outlined.

The United Nations is to promote:

a.   higher standards of living, full employment, and conditions of economic and social progress and development;

b. solutions of international economic, social, health, and related problems; and international cultural and educational cooperation; and

c. universal respect for, and observance of, human rights and fundamental freedoms for all without distinction as to race, sex, language, or religion (Article 55).

This extremely comprehensive set of objectives was intentionally expanded to its present detail at San Francisco. The emphasis on "health" and "education" (words written into the Charter at almost every point where "economic and social" appear) reflects the concern of the less developed members of the United Nations with the sort of problems which they, rather than the richer nations, face. The mention of "full employment" indicates the attitude of nations in which the government must take the initiative and do most of the work. The mention of "human rights and fundamental freedoms" specifically related to nondiscrimination as to "race, sex, language, or religion" reminds the Western European that the United Nations contains peoples of all colors and languages, that it is not Christian or Moslem, Hindu or Buddhist, but all of them. Indeed Field Marshal Smuts, as prime minister of the Union of South Africa, when the Union had been criticized in the General Assembly of 1946 for its discriminatory race policies, once reminded his parliament that the majority of the peoples whose governments were members of the United Nations were nonwhite.

Machinery

All members of the United Nations pledge themselves, in Article 56, "to take joint and separate action in cooperation with the Organization" to achieve the purposes mentioned. Policy, in the broadest and most general sense, is the affair of the General Assembly and of the Economic and Social Council. The carrying out of the policy is decentralized.

The precedents were clear. In the ordinary national government, the legislature determines the policy in all fields—whether agriculture, trade, or health—and the administrative departments carry out the policies and give their accounting to the legislature. The United Nations could have attempted to set up such a ma-

chinery, but such an attempt would have failed, being unsuited
to what is essentially a loose confederation of governments with
no coercive authority, except in the most limited field. The
League of Nations, which had economic and social objectives
similar to those of the United Nations and considerable accomplishments in these fields, operated in quite a different way. Under the vaguest and most general directions of the Council of the
League and in accordance with the feeling of the international
community as reflected in the League Assembly, a miscellaneous
collection of commissions and committees applied themselves to
a large variety of problems. Besides these, and legally and administratively quite separate, were the International Labour Organisation and many other "public international unions," such as
the Universal Postal Union, the Pan-American Sanitary Organization, or the Institute for Intellectual Cooperation. The planners
of the United Nations decided to continue the same basic pattern
of administration. Part of the work of administration would be
done by commissions directly responsible to the Economic and
Social Council. Part would be done by inter-governmental organizations, functional in character, called in the Charter "specialized agencies." But the latter—this was a change—should be
incorporated into the United Nations system.

The existing machinery, planned in San Francisco, therefore,
includes three things: the Economic and Social Council as a great
directive and policy-formulating organ, the Commissions of the
Economic and Social Council, and the various specialized agencies.

The Economic and Social Council

Membership and Organization

The Economic and Social Council (as planned in Chapter X
of the Charter) consists of eighteen states, which are members
of the United Nations, elected by the General Assembly. They
are elected for overlapping terms, six each year for a three-year
term. Members are eligible for reelection. In meetings of the

Economic and Social Council (just as in meetings of the Security Council and the Trusteeship Council) each member has one representative.

There is no provision in the Charter which states that members of the Big Five must hold places in the Economic and Social Council. In fact, however, they have always been elected to it and probably always will be. But this is because the Assembly wants them there. The other thirteen members are broadly representative of the regions, blocs, and special interests that influence United Nations politics and determine the membership in all the organs of the United Nations.

Since the work of the Economic and Social Council is basically nonpolitical, it is only rarely that states are represented by the same persons as those which represent them in the more political organs of the United Nations. The United States, for example, was first represented by Mr. John G. Winant, former director of the International Labour Organisation, and is now represented by Mr. Willard Thorp, Under Secretary of State for Economic Affairs. India, represented in the General Assembly by the most political of delegates, was long represented in the Economic and Social Council by Sir A. Ramaswami Mudaliar who, as chairman of Committee III/1 at San Francisco and as first president of the Economic and Social Council, had so much to do with the effective organization of the Council.

Each member of the Economic and Social Council has one vote, and all decisions are made by a majority of members present and voting. This provision—like a similar provision for voting in the Trusteeship Council—promotes cooperation in the Council itself. Matters brought by a vote of the Economic and Social Council to the General Assembly may presumably then also be determined by a simple majority (cf. Article 18). But the Economic and Social Council and the General Assembly acting on economic and social matters have no coercive authority and, in general, cannot create any specific obligations for member states.

The Economic and Social Council chooses its own president, who according to its rules of procedure is elected for one year.

So far, Sir Ramaswami Mudaliar has served for two years (though his duties as prime minister of Mysore kept him from the summer session of 1947). He was replaced in 1948 by Mr. Charles Malik of Lebanon. In 1949 Mr. James Thorn of New Zealand was elected president. The Council met three times in 1946 and after that settled down to a program of meetings twice yearly, beginning in February and July. It meets ordinarily at the seat of the United Nations. The July, 1948, session was held in Geneva, since the United Nations was to meet in Paris that autumn. The Geneva session proved so satisfactory to the representatives that the Council scheduled its July, 1949, and July, 1950, sessions for the same place.

The Council is to be assisted in its work by commissions which it may set up in any field that its work requires. (It must set up a commission on human rights.) It is to invite members of the United Nations to participate in its deliberations on any matters of particular concern to that member. It is to send and receive representatives to meetings of specialized agencies on a reciprocal basis. It may arrange for consultation with nongovernmental organizations on matters which it has in common with them (Articles 68 to 71). It is to help the Security Council (Article 65) and the Trusteeship Council (Article 91). One may think of the Economic and Social Council as a group consulted by and consulting all the other groups that exist, on any and all questions, not strictly political, that are of common concern to the world.

The commissions of the Economic and Social Council report to it. The specialized agencies are coordinated by it, without coercion. It reports to the General Assembly, receives instructions from the General Assembly, helps carry out the recommendations of the General Assembly.

As expressed formally in Article 62 of the Charter, the forms which the activities of the Council may take are as follows:

It makes studies and reports on "international economic, social, cultural, educational, health, and related matters."

It makes recommendations on such matters (and in regard to human rights and fundamental freedoms) to the General Assembly, to members of the United Nations, or to the specialized agencies.

It calls international conferences on the matters within its area of competence.

Commissions versus Specialized Agencies

The field of competence given to the Economic and Social Council is extraordinarily broad. One might say that it covers all areas of international government except questions directly relating to international peace and security (for which the Security Council has primary responsibility) or to the trusteeship system and non-self-governing peoples (the province mostly of the Trusteeship Council and of the General Assembly) or to judicial matters brought to the International Court of Justice. It was realized as early as the Preparatory Commission that the many and diverse fields with which the Economic and Social Council would be concerned would each need a group of specially competent persons to deal with it. In some of the fields there would be a specialized agency, a separately constituted inter-governmental organization. In other fields the Economic and Social Council would act itself through its commissions. Consequently, the Preparatory Commission proposed, and the Economic and Social Council followed, an admittedly arbitrary classification of subjects according to which certain fields would go to specialized agencies and certain others remain for commissions of the Economic and Social Council.

The subjects assumed in the Report of the Preparatory Commission to be the province of specialized agencies were the following:

(*a*)   relief and rehabilitation [UNRRA. But UNRRA was terminated, and the field became one of the most important areas directly under the Economic and Social Council. The International Refugee Organization, a temporary specialized agency, occupies part of the field.]

(*b*)   monetary cooperation and international investment [the Bank and the Fund]

(c)   trade policies [International Trade Organization]

(d)   food and agricultural policies [Food and Agriculture Organization]

(e)   labour standards, labour welfares and related social questions [the already long-existent International Labour Organisation]

(f)   educational and cultural cooperation [UNESCO]

(g)   health [World Health Organization]

(h)   some aspects of transport [International Civil Aviation Organization, Inter-Governmental Maritime Consultative Organization]

(i)   some aspects of communication [Universal Postal Union, International Telecommunications Union]

They forgot to include the weather, the province of the World Meteorological Organization.

THE COMMISSION STRUCTURE UNDER THE ECONOMIC AND SOCIAL COUNCIL

The Functional Commissions

For the other areas of its responsibility, the Economic and Social Council would do its work directly through commissions established by it and responsible to it. The commissions initially proposed by the Preparatory Commission and established by the Economic and Social Council were, therefore, to deal with matters *not* presumptively assigned to a specialized agency. They included the area—in some respects of first importance—of activities "nonpolitical in character" which had been performed by the League of Nations and were to be taken over by the United Nations. The control of the manufacture and use of narcotic drugs is the best example of these activities, one in which the League had achieved great effectiveness.

The Preparatory Commission, therefore, recommended that the Economic and Social Council should establish at its first session the following commissions:

Commission on Human Rights

Economic and Employment Commission

Temporary Social Commission

Statistical Commission

Commission on Narcotic Drugs

It recommended also the early establishment of the following commissions:

Demographic (Population) Commission

Temporary Transport and Communications Commission

Fiscal Commission

At its first session in London in January and February, 1946, the Economic and Social Council, concerned almost entirely with matters of organization, created one full commission, the Commission on Narcotic Drugs. It created five "nuclear commissions," each a group of nine experts to plan for a permanent commission, as follows:

Commission on Human Rights with a Subcommission on the Status of Women

Economic and Employment Commission

Statistical Commission

Temporary Social Commission

Temporary Transport and Communications Commission

After reports from the nuclear commissions, the Economic and Social Council at its second session at Hunter College in the spring of 1946 determined the composition and terms of reference of permanent commissions other than the already established Narcotics Commission. As a compromise between the Soviet view that commissions should have states as members and be composed of government representatives or they would be "mere discussion clubs," and the opposite view (not clearly put forward by any government, even that of the United States) that a technical commission should be composed of technicians regardless of politics, it was decided that commissions should be composed of representatives of the governments of members of the United Nations, chosen by the Economic and Social Council. But the governments should consult with the Secretary-General before nominating their individual representatives. The latter must subsequently be confirmed by the Council.

This elaborate rigmarole of appointment does not conceal the fact that the members of the commissions are entirely subject to the control of their own governments and that few governments expect them to use their expert knowledge for strictly international ends. At the same time, even the most governmentally controlled of commissioners must seem to be an expert, as many of them are. Since the commissions have definite tasks and definite membership and meet under their own officers, they take on some sense of corporate unity and individuality. Subcommissions are elected by the commissions, and their members are chosen in their individual capacities and not as representatives of states.

These commissions have come to be referred to as "functional" commissions, as a distinction from the "regional" commissions later established. They consist of twelve to eighteen members, chosen for three years. By 1948 they had been able to meet, some of them more than once, and to report to the Council. Unless otherwise instructed, they hold meetings once a year.

The functional commissions vary astonishingly as to the sort of work they do and the way in which they do it. Some—for instance, the Statistical Commission and the Population Commission—are only in a minimum sense concerned with political questions and have no operational responsibilities at all. Their work is staff work; its results will be useful to the United Nations and to member governments, but the commissions themselves merely collect, organize, and publish information and then are finished.

At the other extreme is the Narcotics Commission which has important operational responsibilities under narcotics conventions. A middle ground is occupied by such commissions as the Commission on Human Rights, which has drafted a convention, and the Social Commission, which not only makes studies and develops policies but has been given administrative responsibilities in the care of refugees and funds with which to operate.

As of September, 1949, there were nine functional commissions, as follows:

The Economic and Employment Commission, which has been concerned largely with economic recovery in the postwar period and with problems of unemployment. It has two subcommissions, one on *Employment and Economic Stability* and the other on *Economic Development.*

The Transport and Communications Commission, which took over League responsibilities in its field. It has been concerned largely with questions of international transport organization in the various regions of the world. It has recommended reduction of passport and frontier formalities.

The *Fiscal Commission,* which is concerned primarily with research in problems of government finance and in taxation.

The *Statistical Commission,* which is concerned with statistical sampling and classification, coordination of statistical activity, and statistical education. It has a subcommission on *Statistical Sampling.*

The *Commission on Population,* which is concerned with the development of population reporting, analysis, and forecasting. It is immediately concerned with the national censuses that will be taken in 1950 and 1951.

The *Social Commission,* which has a very broad area of reference. It has made recommendations in the field of health and of refugees and is also concerned with social welfare, planning, crime, migration, and the white-slave traffic. It has inherited various important League functions. It has initiated the United Nations International Children's Emergency Fund, which has a separate administrative organization under the Economic and Social Council.

The *Commission on Narcotic Drugs,* which is concerned with policy and with control over opium and other narcotic drugs, including synthetic drugs recently developed.

The *Commission on Human Rights,* which has been chiefly concerned with drafting the Declaration on Human Rights. Its draft Declaration was approved by the General Assembly in December, 1948. It has two subcommissions, one on *Freedom of Information and of the Press* and the other on *Prevention of Discrimination and Protection of Minorities.*

The *Commission on the Status of Women,* which has explored the rights of women.

The Regional Commissions

The regional commissions were unforeseen when the United Nations were planned. They developed from the work of the Temporary Subcommission (of the Economic and Employment Commission) on the Economic Reconstruction of Devastated Areas. This latter has given way to the regional commissions because the immediate problems of reconstruction seem most easily approached on a regional basis. The regional commissions differ from the functional commissions in that they are intended to be primarily operational, their membership is determined on a geographical basis, and though they report to the Economic and Social Council, they may make recommendations directly to specialized agencies and to member governments.

The *Economic Commission for Europe*, the first regional commission, has been extremely active and effective. Its job was to preside over the reconstruction of Europe, replacing wartime and temporary agencies, and encouraging and working with newer agencies. Established in Geneva, with the Swedish economist-statesman Gunnar Myrdal as executive secretary, and a staff from the United Nations Secretariat, it has bridged the gap between East and West and has made conspicuous accomplishments. It took over the work of the temporary wartime organizations, the Emergency Economic Commission for Europe, the European Central Inland Transport Organization, and the European Coal Organization, and with some success has managed allocations of materials, especially fuel. It has kept within its area of co-operators the Eastern European nations whose economic assumptions are opposed to those of the majority of its members. It has been hindered somewhat by the ill-feeling produced by the Marshall plan and has suffered from ideological wrangles. The United States is a member, presumably as an occupying power in Germany. The other seventeen members are the European states that are members of the United Nations Organization.

The *Economic Commission for Asia and the Far East*, dealing with a more primitive area, has been concerned chiefly with the questions of food, population, and the development of industries and flood control in the Far East. Its members are the Big Five, the Netherlands, and the other members of the United Nations Organization that lie in the area from Pakistan on the west to the Philippines and New Zealand on the east. Representatives of non-self-governing territories within the area are admitted as associate members, at the discretion of the Commission.

The *Economic Commission for Latin America* has been created to promote cooperation for economic advancement in an unevenly developed continent which had suffered greatly from dislocations resulting from the war. Its members are the Latin-American states, France, the Netherlands, the United Kingdom, and the United States.

An *Economic Commission for the Middle East* has been proposed and has been discussed in the Council.

What the Economic and Social Council Itself Does

As Mr. John G. Winant, the first United States representative to the Economic and Social Council, pointed out in his first report: "Essentially, the Council constitutes a means of coordination, consultation, and recommendation. Operative functions generally are to be detailed to specialized inter-governmental agencies closely related to the United Nations Organization."[1] Apart from operative responsibilities resting in the commissions as explained above, this remains true.

The Economic and Social Council met first in January, 1946. It now meets twice a year. Each session lasts several weeks, and its business is to discuss at greater or lesser length the many items on its agenda and to declare itself on matters of policy when such declarations would seem to be useful.

To be more specific, the Economic and Social Council:

Creates commissions, gives them their terms of reference, and receives their reports. Most of the time of recent Council meetings has been devoted to this activity.

[1] United States and United Nations, Economic and Social Council, *Report to the Secretary of State* . . . , *July 15, 1946*, p. 3.

Sponsors the establishment of specialized agencies (the World Health Organization, the International Refugee Organization, and the International Trade Organization all were initiated in the Economic and Social Council), watches over them in their provisional form, and makes the agreements by which (after their establishment) they are brought into relationship with the United Nations. Then it works with them, "coordinating" them according to provisions of the Charter.

Works with the other organs of the United Nations.

Makes arrangements for consultation with nongovernmental organizations and puts their suggestions on its agenda.

Considers major economic and social questions which are brought before it, by bodies or member states, and may send them to commissions or special committees for consideration.

The Council and Nongovernmental Organizations

According to the Charter the Council is to consult with nongovernmental organizations, some of which are of great importance. In the early days of the United Nations Organization a long and unsuccessful fight was waged by the Soviet Union, with support from some noncommunist governments, to secure for the World Federation of Trades Unions a position of special privilege in the meetings of the Economic and Social Council. Eventually a pattern of consultation was established for all nongovernmental organizations whose activities and whose proposals may be of value to the Economic and Social Council but which are not integral parts of the United Nations structure.

Nongovernmental organizations are classed in three categories, depending on their degree of universality of membership and of relationship to the general functions of the Economic and Social Council. Those nongovernmental organizations put in the first class—World Federation of Trades Unions, American Federation of Labor, International Cooperative Alliance, etc.—may offer items for the agenda of the Economic and Social Council, may attend its meetings, as well as meetings of its commissions, and may be invited to speak. Other nongovernmental organizations have lesser privileges.

A conference of nongovernmental organizations was held in Geneva in May, 1948. It set up an Interim Committee of Consultative Non-Governmental Organizations, proposing future conferences of accredited organizations and an internationalization of their status.

The Council, the Assembly, and the Secretariat

The Economic and Social Departments of the Secretariat, into which have been recruited a large number of experts, have furnished the greater part of the working staff for the activities of the Economic and Social Council and its commissions. Not only in doing such work as that planned by the Statistical Commission but in publishing a series of studies on economic conditions, the Secretariat has integrated its work with that of the Economic and Social Council. The *Economic Report—Salient Features of the World Economic Situation 1945–1947*, the *World Economic Report* for 1948, the studies of economic conditions in selected countries and in Europe, the study of inflationary and deflationary tendencies are all studies which integrate with the work of the Economic and Social Council.

Many subjects within the area of the Economic and Social Council have been discussed and acted upon by the General Assembly, to which the Economic and Social Council is responsible. The Economic and Social Council has fitted into its position as the principal organ of the United Nations making preliminary decisions on economic and social policy—leaving final determinations to the General Assembly and allowing its commissions and the specialized agencies to do the work of administration.

The Accomplishments of the Council

Most of the time in the earlier sessions of the Economic and Social Council was devoted to organization. Most of the time in recent sessions has been devoted to reports from subordinate and related bodies.

Apart from its routine work—which is probably, in the long run, its greatest contribution—the Economic and Social Council has considered questions either urgent or vital or politically striking which have attracted more than usual attention.

Its first sessions were particularly concerned with problems of refugees and of economic reconstruction. UNRRA (the United Nations Relief and Rehabilitation Administration) was being brought to an end. But the resettlement of refugees and displaced persons was still an urgent problem. Eventually an International Refugee Organization was created to handle this problem.

In its second session (in the summer of 1946) the Council established the Temporary Subcommission on the Economic Reconstruction of Devastated Areas. As a result of its work, the Economic Commission for Europe was created and the precedent for the other regional economic commissions was established.

In the fields of international trade and of health the Council called conferences out of which began the International Trade Organization and the World Health Organization.

In the field of social problems the dissolution of UNRRA also left a gap. The International Children's Emergency Fund, to which the United States is the chief contributor, was established, and also the United Nations Appeal for Children.

In the field of human rights, intense and varied activity in the Commission on Human Rights and discussions in the Council have been directed toward the drafting of the Declaration of Human Rights which was approved by the third regular session of the General Assembly in 1948. The Conference on Freedom of Information met in Geneva in the spring of 1948.

The draft Convention on Genocide was prepared by an Ad Hoc Committee on Genocide and approved unanimously by the 1948 General Assembly.

The basic decision that "nonpolitical" functions of the League of Nations might be taken over by the United Nations Organization has been implemented largely through the Economic and

Social Council. With the help of its commissions it assumes former League responsibilities in regard to such matters as child welfare and traffic in women and children, obscene publications, and narcotic drugs.

The major problem which has concerned the Economic and Social Council in its most recent sessions has been that of economic assistance to undeveloped areas. The summer session of 1949 eventually worked out a program for such assistance. This program will bring together activities of the United Nations and of the specialized agencies. It involves questions of financing, of technical assistance, and of direction. The control is to be in the hands of a Technical Assistance Committee composed of members of the Economic and Social Council, concerned with policy, and a Technical Assistance Board, concerned with administration and composed of representatives of participating organizations.

In all the areas covered by the work of the Economic and Social Council differences of opinion are expressed, which sometimes penetrate the details of small matters. Its deliberations are therefore conducted in as much of a political atmosphere as those of national legislatures. But as Dr. Jan Papanek (who was acting president of the 1947 summer session) said in his closing speech, the purpose of the Council "is not to prove that any economic theory or practice is the only acceptable one, but to find the common denominator of all our economic and social systems to achieve the aims of the United Nations—to provide a better fuller life for all people in a peaceful world."

Chapter 13. THE SPECIALIZED AGENCIES

The United Nations is the "general" international organization, but it is not the only international organization nor is it the only one whose members are members of the United Nations. There exist also a number of other international organizations of wide membership which are associated with the United Nations but perform special and limited functions. They are the so-called "specialized agencies."

AGENCIES BORN IN WARTIME

Four large conferences of members of the United Nations were held before San Francisco. Each of the four established one or more organizations to perform specific jobs which needed to be taken in hand. In that way began the creation of that confusing and important group of bodies which the San Francisco Charter calls the "specialized agencies."

At Hot Springs, Virginia, in May and June, 1943, representatives of forty-four governments met to discuss the problem of food and the implementation of the concept "freedom from want." The Hot Springs Conference issued a declaration and established the Interim Commission on Food and Agriculture. This Commission maintained its headquarters in Washington. It proceeded to draft a constitution which was ratified by a sufficient number of participating states so that the first session of the Conference of the Food and Agriculture Organization of the United Nations could meet in Quebec in October, 1945.

A conference on relief—another matter rendered important by the war—met in Atlantic City on November 10, 1944, after the representatives of forty-four nations had signed the Agreement for the United Nations Relief and Rehabilitation Administration. UNRRA, as this organization was always called, was established as an immediately going concern. Long before the end of the war UNRRA began to move into devastated countries.

A conference on financial and monetary questions was held at Bretton Woods, New Hampshire, in July, 1944. Representatives of forty-four nations attended the Bretton Woods Conference and drafted two agreements, the first to set up the International Monetary Fund to create stability in national currencies, and the second to create the International Bank for Reconstruction and Development to make and sponsor loans for reconstruction.

At Chicago, in November, 1944, fifty-two nations, including some not numbered among the United Nations, met to make rules to govern civil aviation. The conference was concerned partly with technical questions and partly with questions of international cooperation to regulate traffic in the air. Its deliberations led to the eventual formation of the International Civil Aviation Organization.

These four conferences, and the provisional preliminary or temporary organizations that resulted from them, were concerned with international cooperation and international organization on a functional basis.

There already existed a great functional agency, the International Labour Organisation, with a well-defined sphere of activity of its own, most of whose members were members of the United Nations. This organization, established in the peace treaties of 1919, was the great prototype of the inter-governmental organization established to perform international functions of a specialized economic and social character. A large number of lesser inter-governmental organizations also existed to perform international functions in special fields. Some of these, like the Universal Postal Union, were long established and conspicuously useful.

The San Francisco Conference considered it important that all major inter-governmental organizations should be included in the United Nations system by being brought into close relationship with the great central political organization, the United Nations itself. Consequently, provisions were inserted in the Charter to bring about such a relationship. Furthermore, it was expected that other special organizations would be created and would likewise need to be tied to the United Nations Organization.

These functional organizations, each with its special purpose, are called, in the language of the Charter, "specialized agencies."

WHAT IS A SPECIALIZED AGENCY?

Since a number of specialized agencies already existed when the Charter of the United Nations was drafted, the Charter assumes their existence and does not define them clearly.

The specialized agencies are referred to in Article 57 of the Charter as "established by intergovernmental agreement and having wide international responsibilities, as defined in their basic instruments, in economic, social, cultural, educational, health, and related fields."

The first characteristic mentioned here is the fact that a specialized agency owes its legal existence to a special agreement or treaty made between the states which thereby become its members. A second characteristic is that the specialized agency must be general, that is, not confined to any one geographical region and not otherwise limited to a small group of members. Presumably its membership is open to all states (except, at present, Spain) and should be as nearly universal as possible.

The specialized agency referred to in the Charter is to be distinguished from the ordinary "public international union." The latter, though based on an international agreement or treaty, may have limited functions and responsibilities. A very large number of such organizations exist.

The specialized agency is to be distinguished also from the nongovernmental organizations, referred to in Article 71 of the Charter, which may be concerned with the same sort of things as the specialized agencies, but whose members are not governments but private persons or organizations. The World Federation of Trades Unions served as an excellent example of the non-governmental organization during the formative period of the United Nations. It worked in the same field as the International Labour Organisation. Both the International Labour Organisation and the World Federation of Trades Unions were concerned with problems of the status and conditions of labor. But the members of the International Labour Organisation are governments, and the International Labour Organisation was created by a convention or treaty between governments. The World Federation of Trades Unions, on the other hand, was composed of trade unions, which in most countries are purely private organizations and which even where they are treated as agencies of the government (as they were in fascist Italy and as they appear to be in Soviet countries) are nevertheless not the government itself. The World Federation of Trades Unions was created by an agreement which legally has the status not of a treaty but of a private contract.

The specialized agencies are found in many and varied fields of activity. Presumably the specialized agency exists because of a need for joint action in its special field. It is an organization of some sort, though how simple or complicated is not important. In practice, the typical specialized agency is a body which has a periodic conference or assembly of all its members, a smaller elected council, and some sort of an executive, as, for example, a director with a staff.

THE SPECIALIZED AGENCY AND THE UNITED NATIONS

The specialized agency is an institution of great importance, but its place in the international scheme of things had not been sufficiently thought out at San Francisco for it to be the beneficiary of a distinct section of the Charter. Consequently, the references to the specialized agencies occur at various places in the Charter and are not coordinated. But the Charter does assume that all specialized agencies worthy of the name will become part of a coordinated United Nations system by being "brought into relationship" with the United Nations Organization (Article 57.2).

Relationship between a specialized agency and the United Nations Organization is established by an agreement. This agreement is made by the agency with the Economic and Social Council. It states in detail the terms of the relationship. The agreement becomes effective when approved by the General Assembly (Article 63.1).

After the agency has been "brought into relationship" with the United Nations, the Economic and Social Council exercises a limited supervision over it. To be specific, the Economic and Social Council "may coordinate the activities of the specialized agencies through consultation with and recommendations to such agencies and through recommendations to the General Assembly and to the Members of the United Nations" (Article 63.2). In fact, the reports, and sometimes the work, of the specialized agencies are discussed in the Economic and Social Council and in the General Assembly.

The United Nations Organization may make arrangements for mutual representation of the organs of the United Nations and of the specialized agencies in each others' deliberations.

One very important relationship between the United Nations Organization and the specialized agencies is that the agreements between them may include financial and budgetary arrangements. The Charter says that the General Assembly "shall examine the administrative budgets of such specialized agencies with a view to making recommendations to the agencies concerned" (Article 17.3).

The specialized agency is not part of the United Nations Organization; it is a separate organization. But it will be related closely or distantly to the General Assembly and the Economic and Social Council as determined in each case by an agreement.

THE INDIVIDUAL AGENCIES

By the end of the Third Session of the General Assembly nine specialized agencies had been formally "brought into relationship" with the United Nations Organization. Two more, the International Trade Organization and the Inter-Governmental Maritime Consultative Organization, exist in provisional form. Still another, the World Meteorological Organization, is undergoing the preliminaries of organization. Another, the International Refugee Organization, had been created as a temporary agency. Two others lived unexpectedly short lives, illustrating some of the dangers such agencies run. These agencies were the United Nations Relief and Rehabilitation Administration (UNRRA) and the European Central Inland Transport Organization (ECITO).

The International Labour Organisation (ILO)

The International Labour Organisation is much the oldest and most important of the specialized agencies. It was established by Part XIII of the Treaty of Versailles in 1919. It was part of the League of Nations system, though actually related to the League itself only in that its budget was part of the League budget. It was established with the particular purpose of improving labor conditions and living standards by international action and has already had a long history of making recommendations and preparing draft conventions or treaties for acceptance by its member governments. Its success in getting its draft conventions ratified by large numbers of governments illustrates the effectiveness with which a specialized agency can operate in a controversial field.

The International Labour Organisation has always managed its own affairs. Indeed, it even drew up its own budget (though the money was appropriated by the League). Its policy is made by the International Labor Conference which meets annually. The Conference is composed of national delegations, each of which comprises two delegates representing the government, one delegate representing the employers, and one delegate representing the workers. The governing body is composed of representatives of sixteen governments, half from employers and half from workers. The International Labour Organisation possesses a large central staff, the International Labor Office, with headquarters in Geneva.

The first Director-General of the International Labour Organisation was Mr. Albert Thomas of France, whose energy and vitality were responsible for much of its effectiveness. Mr. Thomas organized it, he talked and worked for it, he maintained it in healthy rivalry with the League of Nations, he got governments to appropriate money for it gladly. He was succeeded in 1932 by Mr. Harold B. Butler of the United Kingdom. Mr. Butler was succeeded in 1938 by Mr. John G. Winant, an American conspicuous for his public spirit, who left the International Labour Organisation only to become American ambassador to the United Kingdom in 1941. Mr. Winant was succeeded as Acting Director (Director from 1946) by Mr. Edward Phelan of the United Kingdom. Mr. Phelan had been appointed to the staff of the International Labour Organisation in 1920 when his country, Ireland, was still part of the United Kingdom. He served for many years as Assistant Director and became perhaps the most experienced, as well as the ablest, international civil servant of his time. He managed the affairs of the International Labour Organisation during the difficult years of wartime and of reconstruction. On his retirement from the directorship in 1948 he was succeeded by Mr. David A. Morse, who had been Under Secretary of Labor in the United States.

When the war of 1939 isolated Geneva, the International Labor Office established its working headquarters in Montreal.

On November 5, 1945, the International Labor Conference drew up an instrument for the amendment of the constitution of the International Labour Organisation permitting the International Labour Organisation to sever its relations with the League of Nations and to become completely autonomous. In the Second Part of the First Session of the General Assembly of the United

Nations an agreement was approved by which the International Labour Organisation entered into formal relationship with the United Nations.

At the end of 1948 the International Labour Organisation had sixty members. Some of its members are not members of the United Nations Organization; some members of the United Nations Organization (including the Soviet Union) are not members of the International Labour Organisation. The United States joined the International Labour Organisation in 1934.

The Food and Agriculture Organization (FAO)

The Food and Agriculture Organization was the eventual product of the Hot Springs Conference of 1943. This conference of forty-four nations provided for the creation of the Interim Commission on Food and Agriculture, which had its headquarters in Washington and which drew up a constitution for the permanent organization. The permanent organization was created at the first session of the Conference of the Food and Agriculture Organization of the United Nations which met in Quebec in October, 1945. Thirty nations signed the constitution at that meeting, and the membership (as of November, 1949) was sixty-three. The Soviet Union was a member of the Interim Commission and an observer at Quebec but is not a member of the permanent organization.

The Food and Agriculture Organization was created in order to raise standards of nutrition throughout the world and to improve the production and distribution of food and agricultural products. It is to concern itself not only with agricultural questions but also with forestry, fisheries, and marketing, and with problems of nutrition. In no sense was it intended to be a relief organization; it was to deal with questions of permanent importance in its field, since UNRRA existed for United Nations relief.

The Food and Agriculture Organization is governed by a conference of representatives of the member states, which meets in annual sessions—at Quebec in 1945, Copenhagen in 1946, Geneva in 1947, Washington in 1948 and 1949. The conference elects a council of eighteen states. It has a Director-General with a central staff. The temporary seat of the Organization is in Washington. In 1949 it voted to establish its permanent seat in Rome. Sir John Boyd Orr of the United Kingdom, a well-known expert in nutrition and an effective propagandist, was the first Director-General. He was succeeded in 1948 by Mr. Norris E. Dodd, who had been at the time of his appointment Under Secretary of Agriculture in the United States.

The Food and Agriculture Organization was created at the time when it was expected that the wartime and postwar scarcities of food would be temporary and that its great permanent problem would be not only to stimulate more efficient agricultural production but also to prevent surpluses. Its Conference of May, 1946, on Urgent Food Problems centered, however, on the continuing gap between production and need and initiated the establishment of the International Emergency Food Council as an allocating agency to replace the wartime Combined Food Board. The International Emergency Food Council was composed of representatives of some thirty-five nations and was staffed by the Food and Agriculture Organization.

The chief subject for consideration at the Copenhagen session of the conference of the Food and Agriculture Organization was the establishment of a World Food Board. This Board was planned to be a long-term agency for stabilizing agricultural prices, establishing a world food reserve, and distributing surpluses to countries where the need is urgent. Further study of the question resulted in the decision not to create a special agency but to establish an International Emergency Food Council as a part of the Food and Agricultural Organization.

The 1949 conference rejected a proposed international commodity clearinghouse whose purpose would have been to transfer surplus stocks to countries undersupplied with food.

An agreement which brought the Food and Agriculture Organization into relationship with the United Nations as a specialized agency was approved by the General Assembly on December 15, 1946.

The United Nations Relief and Rehabilitation Administration (UNRRA)

UNRRA, the United Nations Relief and Rehabilitation Administration, was a wartime creation whose initial policies were laid down by the Atlantic City Conference of November, 1943. It was a relief agency, giving aid, mostly in the form of food and supplies for immediate consumption, to members of the United Nations which were devastated by the war.

UNRRA was one of the most spectacular of the agencies. Its reason for existence was the tremendous need for relief, which became so widespread in Europe and Asia in the later days of the war and the early postsurrender period. It was concerned with procurement, transportation, and even production of vast quantities of goods. To finance its work, it had its own budget (to which the United States was the greatest contributor) of 1 per cent of the annual income of its members for two successive years. (In no case was the second year's contribution fully paid.) Its field of activity was limited in ways unappreciated by those who criticized it, since it provided help only for members of the United Nations and only for countries which asked its aid. Because of the location and the political disorganization of many of the aided countries, most of the aid of UNRRA went to places where the danger of misuse of supplies was greatest. A number of devastated and liberated countries, such as France, preferred to obtain the necessary supplies in other ways. Only one belligerent on the enemy side—Italy—was voted relief by UNRRA. Relief for other enemy areas occupied by the United States was administered by the United States Army with funds appropriated by Congress.

UNRRA prevented an enormous amount of suffering and gave a great deal of temporary help pending reconstruction, but its operations were inevitably interfered with by local politics and sometimes by the incompetence and corruption of local governments. UNRRA faced the further difficulty that it could secure no supplies unless they were allocated by the Combined Food and

Raw Materials Board, a wartime agency, and that its requirements were usually met only after all military requirements had been satisfied.

In its original plan UNRRA was also to be an agency for rehabilitation of countries which had been devastated—a tremendous long-term enterprise which could not be managed by any nation acting alone. In this capacity it had no fair chance. The nations that were to receive help were politically suspicious; the donors felt that their aid was unwanted or wasted.

In its day UNRRA was a huge project, employing a large staff. It was directed by a council (representing all the member states), a central committee, and a Director-General. The first Director-General was Mr. Herbert Lehman, former governor of the State of New York, the second Director-General was Mr. Fiorello La Guardia, former mayor of New York City. The staff, whose operations were world-wide, was recruited under the conditions inevitable in a temporary agency. It reached a peak of over twelve thousand persons.

The American people, the chief support of UNRRA, were also its chief critics. It was originally an American conception. Seventy-two per cent of its operating expenses came from the United States Treasury. Ninety per cent of its supplies came from the United States. Its successive Directors-General were Americans. Its headquarters were in Washington.

Its activity, which started slowly and which was really under way in Europe only by the middle of 1945, was hampered by the food crisis which became pronounced early in 1946. The need of continuing the agency and giving it increased help in doing its work was obvious. But the UNRRA council meeting in London in August, 1945, had decided to end UNRRA activity in Europe in December, 1946, and in China, the following spring. And in view of the dissatisfaction that UNRRA had incurred, the government of the United States decided that any further relief should be unilateral. The United States had brought about the creation of UNRRA; the United States brought about its termination.

The International Monetary Fund

The International Monetary Fund was the first of two specialized agencies planned at the United Nations Monetary and Financial Conference at Bretton Woods, New Hampshire, in July, 1944.

Both the Fund and its twin agency, the Bank, were the outgrowth of American initiative planning for increased freedom of international trade, to be developed after the end of the war, and, as particular means to that end, machinery for stabilizing currencies (to be the concern of the Fund) and for providing loans for long-term reconstruction and development (the concern of the Bank).

The Bretton Woods Conference was held at a time when it was expected that the chief members of the United Nations would find themselves, as soon as the war was over, in a position to expand rapidly and perhaps irrationally their individual national economies. The chief conflict of policy in the Conference arose between the British and the Americans. The British delegation thought in terms of a postwar prosperity promoted by abundant government credit. Lord Keynes was the head of the delegation. The American delegation, whose chief expert was Mr. Harry D. White, wished to maintain a gold standard which should be as nearly universal as possible. The United States had the gold; the United Kingdom had Keynesian economics; and it has been a question ever since whether money or a revolution in economic theory will carry a nation farthest.

Delegates of all nations recognized the value of an international stabilization fund to deal with short-term problems of international exchange and to discourage nations from attempting to gain temporary advantages over their competitors by manipulation of the values of their currencies.

The problem which the Fund was created to alleviate was an extremely technical problem but one related to national and international well-being in the highest degree. Every state represented at Bretton Woods remembered the monetary confusion and economic dislocation caused by the devaluations of currencies which had accompanied, and perhaps had magnified, the financial crisis of the early 1930's.

The International Monetary Fund was to be a fund subscribed to by the member states in proportion to the importance of their currencies. It was to be used as a channel through which member states desiring currency of another state might secure it by depositing the equivalent in gold or in its own currency. The control, for purposes of stabilization, would come from the fact that each member state had to make an initial determination of the par value of its currency and would be unable to change that par value by more than 10 per cent without a possible review by the officials administering the Fund. In other words, a slight depreciation or appreciation of a currency could officially be made, but any change in value that might have serious international consequences became an affair of all the members of the Fund.

The Articles of Agreement of the International Monetary Fund (Annex A of the Final Article of the Bretton Woods Conference) provided for national subscriptions to the Fund in accordance with individual quotas. As machinery, the Agreement created three organs—the Board of Governors (on which all members of the Fund are equally represented); the executive directors, twelve (later fourteen) in number, nine chosen from the member states and the other five the representatives of the five member states with the highest quotas, and the managing director, who is chosen by the executive directors and who administers the affairs of the agency.

The Agreement was drawn up at Bretton Woods. It went into force on December 27, 1945, when signed by thirty countries. The inaugural meeting of the Board of Governors was held at Wilmington Island (Savannah), Georgia, in March, 1946. The first annual meeting of the Board of Governors was held in Washington in September and October, 1946. Mr. Camille Gutt, formerly Minister of Finance and Economic Affairs of Belgium, was chosen by the executive directors as first Director-General of the Fund.

The Soviet Union, a signatory of the Final Act of the Bretton Woods Conference, did not ratify the Fund Agreement. Consequently, it did not become an executive director of the Fund. The five executive directors representing the members with the largest quotas were therefore the United States (2,750 million dollars), the United Kingdom (1,300 million dollars), China (550 million dollars), France (450 million dollars), and India (400 million dollars). The quota of the Soviet Union, which it accepted at the time of Bretton Woods, would have been 1,200 million dollars. As of May, 1949, the Fund had forty-eight members, including Italy.

An agreement negotiated between the Fund and the Economic and Social Council was approved by the General Assembly of the United Nations in 1947 and defines the relations between the Fund and the United Nations. It differs from other agreements with specialized agencies in that the relationship is not close. The policies and actions of the Fund (and the same thing is true of the Bank) will not be under any effective control or supervision by the General Assembly or the Economic and Social Council, nor will the United Nations consider the administrative budget of the Fund. The officials of the Fund were insistent that the Fund should not seem to be under political control, since such a situation might hamper it in floating loans. As for the budget, since the Fund is financed by its own operations and not by national contributions, its budget concerns only itself. Approval of the agreement was opposed by the Soviet Union because of these unusual characteristics and also on the ground that the voting power of the United States, which controls one-third of the votes, makes the Fund and Bank agencies of the United States. The agreement was also criticized by Australia on the ground that relations between the Fund and the United Nations could be closer without interfering with the special nature of the activities of the Fund. The agreement was approved by the General Assembly on November 15, 1947. The vote was unanimous, the Soviet Union abstaining.

In accordance with the agreement, which provides that the

principal office of the Fund shall be in the country with the largest quota, that office is established in Washington, D.C.

Owing to the great monetary confusion which followed the war, the Fund was slow in beginning its work. Its first year was devoted to administrative organization. Exchange transactions through the Fund began as of March 1, 1947.

When the Fund was created, it was assumed that the postwar world would be characterized by relatively free multilateral trade and by relative freedom of exchange. But currency restrictions are even greater than they were, and the economic policies of most nations have been planned for nationalistic and political purposes. International exchange of goods (and the payments therefor) have been controlled by governments instead of being conducted in a free market.

Consequently, the Fund has found difficulty in supervising and regulating the value of national currencies, and there has not been the flow of currencies through the Fund that was expected. It has been necessary to assume that a "transitional period" exists which must continue for the first five years of the operation of the Fund, and during which its operations will not be normal.

By the end of 1948 the Fund had succeeded in taking the first necessary steps—the establishment of par values for the currencies of most of its members. By September, 1949, two countries, Colombia and Mexico, had established new parities with the Fund's consent, and France without its consent. In September the British pound was devalued with the consent of the Fund, and a large number of other consequent devaluations were approved. In the transitional period the Fund will look favorably on most readjustments, though even so it dislikes multiple or flexible exchange rates.

Lending from the Fund has been hampered by the instability of the transitional period. Up to the end of June, 1949, the Fund extended credits to seventeen of its members, mostly to countries whose disequilibrium appeared only temporary.

When the present imbalances disappear, the Fund will be able to serve its original purposes more fully.

The International Bank for Reconstruction and Development

The other specialized agency provided for in the Final Act of Bretton Woods was an International Bank. This Bank is to assist in the long-term reconstruction of countries damaged by the war and in the development of underdeveloped countries. It is to perform these functions by making loans, participating in loans, and guaranteeing loans.

The organization of the Bank resembles that of the Fund, and the history of the Bank has paralleled that of the Fund. Their members are the same. The Bank is capitalized at 10 billion dollars, the shares to be subscribed by the member states in proportions similar to, though not identical with, the Fund quotas. It possesses the Board of Governors composed of all its members, a group of fourteen executive directors chosen as are those of the Fund, and a president who directs its administrative staff. It has also an advisory council, international in character, representing varied economic interests.

Like the Fund, the Bank came into existence on December 27, 1945. It has held the meetings of its Board of Governors along with those of the Fund, and like the Fund its principal office is in Washington, D.C. Its first president was Mr. Eugene Meyer of the United States, replaced in 1947 by Mr. John J. McCloy and in 1949 by Mr. Eugene R. Black.

After a period devoted to organization, the Bank was ready to consider the granting of loans. It made its first loan on May 9, 1947, to the Crédit National of France, to the amount of 250 million dollars. It made its first bond issue (in the United States market) of 225 million dollars on July 15, 1947.

An agreement with the United Nations, similar to that of the Fund, was approved at the same time as the one made by the Fund.

The purpose of the Bank is to lend money or to guarantee loans to governments, or to organizations guaranteed by governments, for the purposes of reconstruction and development. The loans are not to replace private foreign investment, but are to supplement it.   They are to be loans which will pay interest and whose capital will be secure.   Ordinarily the loans are for specific projects.   The Bank can lend or guarantee only within the limits of its capital reserves and surplus.

Since the Marshall plan began, the Bank has tended to direct its loans to "undeveloped" countries.

The total amount of its loans (about 700 million dollars up to October, 1949) is small compared with the desires of possible borrowers.

Almost as important as loans is the financial advice given to member governments by missions sent by the Bank.

The United Nations Educational Scientific and Cultural Organization (UNESCO)

The ambit of the specialized agency, like that of the Economic and Social Council itself, is by no means limited to the material or even to the economic. . The "social" field is included, and the content of the social field is extended by a number of words, among them "cultural" and "educational."   In the cultural and educational fields the United Nations Educational Scientific and Cultural Organization has been created, as an operating agency, to do in its wide area what such agencies as the Food and Agriculture Organization and the International Civil Aviation Organization do in perhaps more easily defined compartments of international activity.

UNESCO arose from a feeling, most strongly manifested in England, that an agency should be created for cultural reconstruction and rehabilitation and for the incidental promulgation of the best modern Western culture throughout the world.   The call for the preliminary conference for UNESCO was issued by the governments of the United Kingdom and of France.   The United States government, which was then engaged in a wholehearted attempt to sell Western ideas to the world, through the Public Information Office of the Department of State, joined warmly in the project.   The French government, conscious of France's *mission civilisatrice*, claimed a conspicuous share in the enterprise.

A conference of forty-four states, held in London in November, 1945, did three things. It adopted a constitution for UNESCO, decided on Paris as its headquarters, and established the Preparatory Commission to make the arrangements to establish the final organization. Sir Alfred Zimmern, a distinguished English professor of international relations, was the first executive secretary of the Preparatory Commission. When he resigned for reasons of health, he was succeeded by Mr. Julian Huxley, a widely known English biologist.

The machinery of government of UNESCO is simple. Membership is open to members of the United Nations and to other states by a two-thirds vote of the General Conference (unless the applicant is disapproved by the Economic and Social Council of the United Nations). At the end of October, 1949, the membership of UNESCO comprised fifty states. The organization of UNESCO follows the conventional pattern. There is a General Conference consisting of representatives of all member states and meeting annually. There is an executive board consisting of eighteen persons elected by the Conference from among the delegates. The executive board is responsible for the execution of the program adopted by the Conference. There is also a secretariat consisting of the Director-General and staff. The first Director-General, Mr. Julian Huxley, was chosen to serve for two years, during 1947 and 1948. He was succeeded by Mr. Jaime Torres Bodet of Mexico.

It is suggested that each member state shall form a national commission, representative of its government and of educational, scientific, and cultural bodies, to promote liason with UNESCO. Such a national commission exists in the United States with a distinguished educator as chairman and a large and distinguished membership.

The first General Conference of UNESCO met in Paris from November 19 to December 10, 1946, and was attended by twenty-eight delegations from members which had ratified the Charter. The second General Conference was held in Mexico City in 1947, the third in Beirut in the republic of Lebanon in 1948, and the fourth in Paris in 1949.

UNESCO was brought into relationship with the United Nations as a specialized agency through an agreement approved by the General Assembly of the United Nations on December 15, 1946. Its first year's budget, for 1947, was voted as 6 million dollars with a revolving fund of 3 million dollars. The proposed budget for 1950 was almost 9 million dollars. The contributions from members follow the scale of contributions for the United Nations budget, with modifications resulting from the smaller membership of UNESCO.

The reason for UNESCO is made clear in the Preamble to its Charter. "Since wars begin in the minds of men, it is in the minds of men that the defenses of peace must be constructed." Peace must be "founded, if it is not to fail, upon the intellectual and moral solidarity of mankind."

The purpose of UNESCO is difficult to state in summary fashion. It is "to contribute to peace and security by promoting collaboration among nations through education, science and culture in order to further universal respect for justice, for the rule of law and for the human rights and fundamental freedoms . . . affirmed . . . by the Charter of the United Nations."

Not even the Charter of UNESCO can state its field of activity simply, for the reason that this activity may cover so many specific matters and may range from exhortation of individuals to sponsorship of scientific expeditions. UNESCO has one peculiarity, however, in that it can attempt to reach individual persons with its information and propaganda. As Mr. Clement Attlee said at the first Conference, UNESCO's field of activity "can be described broadly as the life of the mind."

An organization concerned with men's minds, with education, and with the flow of information must rest on certain assumptions as to the nature of knowledge and even of truth. The assumptions underlying UNESCO can be seen, by a reading of its Charter, to be the ordinary assumptions of nineteenth-century liberalism. The Marxist views, which are the basis of Soviet culture, are quite different. It is natural, therefore, that, after some pronounced and public disagreements as to the ideology proper to UNESCO, the Slavic states (except Czechoslovakia and Poland) should decide not to become members of the organization. The situation was complicated by a proposal that "scientific humanism" should be considered the basic philosophy of UNESCO. This proposal seemed tactless, since "scientific humanism" is not only non-Marxist but also non-Christian. But UNESCO by the nature of its activity is perhaps bound to arouse great enthusiasm in some persons and lack of interest in others.

The immediate program that UNESCO should attempt to carry out has been a difficult question because of the vast extent of its possible activity and the large expenditures that would be involved. A program was adopted in the Paris Conference in 1946. As applied to the work of the year 1947, the program included, first, a project for rehabilitation and reconstruction in the general field of education; second, an "international understanding project" concerned with such subjects as textbook revision and international study centers; third, a project dealing with "fundamental education" involving education for adults, for health, and for economic development, as well as for international understanding.

In addition a set of specific projects have been determined on in each of the six areas under which the work of UNESCO has administratively been classified. These six areas are reconstruction, communications, education, cultural interchange, human and social relations, and the natural sciences. In the natural science field, for example, there is a project for the survey of the resources of the Amazon Valley.

Furthermore, UNESCO engages in continuing activities such as collaboration with other organizations, and it attempts to serve as a general clearinghouse in the whole field of educational and intellectual activity.

The International Civil Aviation Organization (ICAO)

No field of commercial activity would seem to be more suited to international supervision than civil aviation. If aircraft are to serve their many purposes as means of transportation, there must be broad international agreement both on technical aspects of the regulation of aviation and on the politicoeconomic problem of the use of national air space by foreign planes.

On the invitation of the United States government the International Civil Aviation Conference was held in Chicago in November and December, 1944. This conference drew up the Convention on International Civil Aviation which included a constitution for a permanent International Civil Aviation Organization. It also established the Provisional International Civil Aviation Organization.

The Provisional International Civil Aviation Organization, with its headquarters in Montreal, began an active supervision of the problems of civil aviation through its technical committees and did the preparatory work of organizing the permanent International Civil Aviation Organization. The ICAO came into legal existence on April 4, 1947, when the convention creating it had been ratified by twenty-six states. The first assembly of the International Civil Aviation Organization was held in Montreal in May, 1947.

The membership of ICAO numbers fifty-four states, most of them members of the United Nations. It does not include the Soviet Union. Spain was an original member, but the assembly of ICAO voted to expel Spain, in accordance with the decision of the General Assembly of the United Nations.

The organs of ICAO are an assembly, a council, various committees, and a secretariat. The assembly is composed of representatives of all members. The council is elected by the assembly and is composed of twenty-one states. The president of the council, who is elected for three years, and the secretary-general, are the two most important administrative officials. Mr. Edward Warner of the United States is the president of the council and Mr. Albert Roper of France the secretary-general. Both these men held corresponding administrative positions in the provisional organization.

ICAO entered into an agreement by which it becomes a specialized agency related to the United Nations. This agreement was approved by the General Assembly of the United Nations on December 4, 1946, to go into effect when the expulsion of Franco Spain from the ICAO has occurred.

The budget of ICAO for 1948 is $2,600,000. Contributions are made on a sliding scale related to the size of the members' airline operations. ICAO seems permanently located in Montreal.

In addition to work directed from the Montreal headquarters, ICAO holds regional conferences in all parts of the world and has established four regional offices. Most of its work is definitely technical. It has not yet succeeded in drafting a generally acceptable multilateral civil aviation agreement. Such a convention was discussed at Geneva in November, 1947. The chief point of disagreement concerned the provisions for the authorization of international air routes.

The "five freedoms" which are the maximum amount of internationalization of the air space that seems to be contemplated are (1) the right of innocent passage, (2) the right to land for non-traffic purposes (such as refueling), (3) the right to carry traffic from the country whose nationality the aircraft possesses to other countries, (4) the right to carry traffic from other countries back to the country whose nationality the aircraft possesses, (5) the right to carry traffic between intermediate countries.

Universal Postal Union (UPU)

The Universal Postal Union, one of the best known and oldest of inter-governmental organizations, became associated with the United Nations as a specialized agency by agreement accepted by the General Assembly of the United Nations in 1947. The Union is an organization composed of practically all postal administrations. It came into existence in 1874 and has its headquarters in Bern. An international bureau, in Bern, serves as its secretariat. The Congress of the Union, which ordinarily meets every five years, reviews the International Postal Convention which is the basis of action by the Union.

The Twelfth Congress of the Union met in Paris in 1947 to make arrangements for the Union to become a specialized agency of the United Nations. It provided for the addition to the simple machinery of the Union of a permanent executive and of a liaison commission.

The Universal Postal Union makes possible the international postal service by coordinating the actions of the eighty-eight postal administrations that belong to it. It has long been considered a model inter-governmental organization in a nonpolitical field.

International Telecommunications Union (ITU)

The International Telecommunications Union is an organization which parallels the Universal Postal Union. It exists to organize and regulate communication by telegraph, telephone, and radio between its member countries.

The legal basis of the International Telecommunications Union is the International Telecommunications Convention. The Union dates from 1932. In that year it replaced the International Telegraph Union, which had been established in 1865. The International Telecommunications Union has eighty-one members.

A conference of the International Telecommunications Union held in Atlantic City in July, 1947, amended the International Telecommunications Convention and drafted an agreement which was approved by the General Assembly of the United Nations in 1947 and which made the International Telecommunications Union a specialized agency in relationship with the United Nations.

For revision of its constitution, the members of the Union may meet in plenary conference, as they did in 1932 and 1947. Administrative conferences in the various fields of activity are held more frequently. The International Telecommunications Conference of 1947 established an administrative council of eighteen members, to meet once a year. The bureau of the Union was located in Bern under the supervision of the Swiss government.

The budget of the Union is to be kept below a ceiling of 3 million Swiss francs. Its most difficult problem has been the assignment of international radio frequencies.

The World Health Organization (WHO)

The World Health Organization occupies perhaps the least contentious ground of any of the specialized agencies. No social problem is less political than that of health, and in no area of human life are peoples associated so irrevocably.

The World Health Organization is one of the specialized agencies whose creation was stimulated by the United Nations Organization. The Economic and Social Council in its first session, on February 15, 1946, established the technical Preparatory Commission to prepare for an international health conference. The Commission drafted a constitution for a specialized agency in the field of health. The International Health Conference met in New York City from June 19 to July 22, 1946. This Conference agreed upon the constitution of the World Health Organization and created the Interim Commission which served from 1946 to 1948. The constitution of the World Health Organization went into effect, and the Organization was in full formal existence on April 7, 1948, with ratification of its constitution by the twenty-sixth member state. The original ratifying members included, among others, Albania, Italy, Switzerland, and Transjordan, for the Conference was attended by many "observers" which were not members of the United Nations Organization itself, and the observers were allowed to sign its Final Act. The World Health Organization is the only one of the specialized agencies to which the Soviet Union has belonged. It announced its withdrawal in 1949.

The objective of the World Health Organization is "the attainment by all people of the highest possible level of health." The functions which are assumed by the World Health Organization to implement this objective are manifold, for the World Health Organization is both an educational and an executive organization. But perhaps its most significant characteristic is the fact that it has inherited the successful health activities of the League of Nations Health Organization, of the Office international d'hygiène publique, and of UNRRA. No interest of the League of

Nations was perhaps more impressively cared for than health; and in the prevention of epidemics and the training of governments in advanced hygienic procedures, the League made some of its conspicuous accomplishments.

According to the terms of its establishment, the Interim Commission of the World Health Organization was to arrange to assume the functions of the League of Nations Health Organization and the other agencies just mentioned, and this it promptly did. It was to negotiate an agreement, as a specialized agency, with the United Nations; and the agreement, drawn on conventional lines, was approved by the General Assembly of the United Nations in 1947. It was to call the first meeting of the World Health Assembly (the governing body of the World Health Organization), and this meeting was held in Geneva in the summer of 1948.

Meanwhile, meeting every four months, the Interim Commission proceeded to act in the field of health. It took over the well-known Singapore Epidemiological Institute, which the League of Nations had administered until 1942. Its expert committees deal with everything from statistics of death to the evaluation of new serums.

The constitution of the World Health Organization provides for an organization which is conventional in type, with a few significant modifications of the specialized-agency pattern. The governing body is a World Health Assembly, composed of delegates representing all the members. An executive board is composed of eighteen persons designated by eighteen states elected by the Assembly for three years. The persons chosen are to be technically qualified in the field of health. The board serves as the executive of the Organization. A secretariat is provided for, composed of a Director-General and staff. In November, 1949, the World Health Organization had sixty-seven members.

The chief distinguishing characteristics of the World Health Organization are its associate members and its regional arrangements. In view of the importance to health of full cooperation by all governments, the membership of the Organization is open to all states, and associate membership is open to "territories or groups of territories which are not responsible for the conduct of their international relations." Applications for the admission of such associate members must be made by the member having responsibility for their international relations. The rights and obligations of associate members will be determined by the Health Assembly.

The constitution provides that the Health Assembly may establish a regional health organization in any defined area, with the approval of a majority of the members within the area. Regional offices, committees, and directors will serve the areas.

In providing for associate members and for regional organization, the Organization appears to have made provision for intensive activity in less favored parts of the world.

The budget of the World Health Organization is, like that of other specialized agencies, eventually its own problem. For the period of organization, however, the World Health Organization was financed by loans from the United Nations and grants from UNRRA residual funds. Its budget for 1949 amounted to 5 million dollars.

The World Health Organization had its headquarters provisionally in New York City but decided in 1948 to establish itself in Geneva. Dr. Andrija Stampar of Yugoslavia was the chairman of the Interim Commission. Dr. Brock Chisholm of Canada was executive secretary of the Interim Commission and is the Director-General of the Organization.

Inter-Governmental Maritime Consultative Organization (IMCO)

Need for an international shipping organization was felt, and the customary steps for bringing such an organization into existence are being taken.

The Temporary Transport and Communications Commission of the Economic and Social Council recommended to that body that a shipping organization should be established as a specialized agency. The Economic and Social Council in June, 1947, requested the United Maritime Consultative Council (a temporary organization) to prepare a draft convention establishing such an agency. A United Nations Maritime Conference (attended by representatives of thirty-two states) met in Geneva on February 19, 1948, and on March 6 signed a convention which, when ratified, will bring into existence the Inter-Governmental Maritime Consultative Organization. Meantime a preparatory committee, created by the Geneva Conference, will arrange for the first session of the assembly of the Inter-Governmental Maritime Consultative Organization as soon as the necessary ratifications to its charter are obtained. A draft agreement has been prepared by which the Inter-Governmental Maritime Consultative Organization can be brought into relationship with the United Nations as a specialized agency.

The IMCO is to be essentially consultative, with a broad competence, though with a particular interest in settling technical questions. It will deal with international agreements concerned with safety at sea, of which there are already many. It may also encourage the removal of discriminatory action by governments affecting shipping and unfair restrictive practice on the part of the shipping concerns.

The council, which will be the directing body of the Organization, will be composed of sixteen members, eight representing countries providing international shipping services, and eight whose particular interest is in the use of such services. The Organization will also have an assembly, a secretariat, and a maritime safety committee.

The IMCO will come into existence when the convention establishing it is ratified by twenty-one states, of which seven will each have shipping of not less than 1 million gross tons.

International Refugee Organization (IRO)

The initiative in creating the International Refugee Organization was taken by the Special Committee on Refugee and Displaced Persons of the Economic and Social Council. It is a temporary organization, superseding UNRRA and the Inter-Governmental Committee on Refugees in their work with refugees and displaced persons. Its purposes are to give care and assistance to refugees and displaced persons and to repatriate and resettle them.

The General Assembly of the United Nations on December 16, 1946, approved a constitution for the International Refugee Organization and provided it with a temporary budget. It also authorized the Preparatory Commission to carry out the purposes of the proposed organization.

The International Refugee Organization was to come into existence when fifteen states, whose required contributions to the operational budget will amount to 75 per cent of the total, have become parties to it. This occurred only in the summer of 1948, after the Preparatory Commission had been active for fourteen months.

The principal organs of the International Refugee Organization are the General Council (which met first in September, 1948), an executive committee, and a secretariat headed by a Director-General.

When the Preparatory Commission began operations on July 1, 1947, it assumed responsibility for the care of over 700,000 persons in its camps. Since then nearly 400,000 have been returned to their own countries or resettled elsewhere. But new refugees have been added to the rolls, and it still takes responsibility for about 450,000 persons.

The General Council of the International Refugee Organization decided in its meeting in Geneva in April, 1949, that IRO should be liquidated as soon as possible after July 1, 1949. In October, 1949, the effective life of the IRO was extended until not later than October, 1950. The terminal date was later postponed to March 31, 1951.

Mr. William Hallam Tuck of the United States was first Director-General of the IRO. He was succeeded by Mr. J. Donald Kingsley. Its headquarters are in Geneva.

World Meteorological Organization (WMO)

A specialized agency is being planned to promote the exchange of meteorological information and to standardize world meteorological activities.

It will come into existence when thirty states have ratified a convention adopted on October 11, 1947, by the International Meteorological Organization (a semiofficial organization existing since 1878). Its organization will be similar to that of other specialized agencies primarily technical in function. Its interim headquarters are in Lausanne, Switzerland.

International Trade Organization (ITO)

After two years of planning in which the United States took the lead, a United Nations Conference on Trade and Employment was held in Havana in 1947 to draft the charter of an International Trade Organization. Its purpose is to promote international trade. It must do this by freeing international trade from the handicaps of tariffs, preferences, and quotas, without at the same time interfering with a reasonable domestic development of industry in undeveloped countries.

The Havana charter will come into effect sixty days after twenty nations have ratified it. In the meantime an Interim Commission has been created, of which Mr. Eric Wyndham White of the United Kingdom is executive secretary. Its headquarters are in Geneva.

The General Agreement on Tariffs and Trade (GATT) was sponsored by the Geneva Conference of 1947 (one of the conferences preparatory to the Havana meeting). Signed by twenty-three nations, GATT provides for mutual lowering of tariffs on specialized articles. Negotiations under GATT continued in 1948 and 1949 and resulted in many tariff reductions.

PROBLEMS OF DEVELOPMENT AND COORDINATION

Development

"International institutions are not made by written constitutions. They must grow like gardens, and, like gardens, they must be watered and tended." This remark of Mr. Phelan, based on his long experience of the International Labour Organisation, would seem to bear on the whole situation of the specialized agencies today. The United Nations Organization itself we need not worry so much about, for though it may go through periods of lack of support or of effectiveness, it serves so many imperative needs that it must continue to exist and to function, if there is any international cohesion at all. The world of the specialized agencies, however, appears different. A casual glance at it is like glancing at the desert where uncalculated rains have fallen and strange desert flowers have sprung up—whether to bloom or to wither, who can tell? In the fertile soil of the postwar period, with the fructifying rains of a contribution from the United Nations budget or the assurance of support by nations who can pay the bill, new specialized agencies have sprung up and some of them have grown sufficiently to become formally associated with the United Nations. The period of testing, to see whether they will survive drought, disease, and attack, is just beginning.

The United Nations Organization itself was planned as monolithic in structure, though not in powers. The specialized agencies were apparently to be allowed to grow by themselves with whatever attention the great gardener, the United Nations Organization, or the lesser gardeners, the member states, would choose to give.

Already it is clear that some agencies have been too ambitious—UNESCO suffers most often from this accusation, but the Food and Agriculture Organization also, perhaps, has tried to do too much. Still others, organized to give both political and technical services, have not served as impressively in their fields as they were intended to do. The Fund and the Bank have been disappointing (though certainly not through faults of their own) because they were planned for international financial conditions which are the very reverse of those which actually exist. It is easy to say that if an agency sticks to a technical job (as, on the whole, the International Civil Aviation Organization does), it will succeed, but then what about international policy in its field? Perhaps the International Labour Organisation, the great example that illustrates Mr. Phelan's text, offers from its experience the best answer. If well intended, well planned, and well administered for a number of years, an agency can serve its purpose better and better as time goes on and will have a survival power (illustrated by the International Labour Organisation) in spite of world wars and revolutions.

Coordination

Meanwhile, serious problems of coordination and cooperation arise. How can the agencies, which are juridically separate, be made to work with each other and with, or even under, the direction of the United Nations? How can the overlapping of functions be avoided? How can such funds as are available for international organizations be properly distributed between the separate agencies and the United Nations itself? How can competent staffs and competent direction be provided? The difficulties are many.

In the first place, each specialized agency owes its origin to a conference of states (varying in number but usually large) who draw up a constitution which was then submitted for signature and ratification. Even agencies like the World Health Organization or the International Maritime Consultative Organization, whose establishment was encouraged by the Economic and Social Council, have constitutions drawn up in special conferences. Though the grants of powers and obligations and machinery of the specialized agencies resemble each other, nevertheless there are at least minor differences.

Again, a relationship between the specialized agency and the United Nations must be made. A basic draft agreement exists to which all agreements conform to a large extent. Even so, some of the agreements differ because of special situations. For example, the agreements made with the Fund and the Bank free those agencies of most of the checks that other agencies have accepted.

Again, each agency has its governing organs, never identical with the governing organs of the other agencies. Sometimes the director-general is an executive officer, sometimes he takes the orders of an executive council, and his differing powers are given to many different men for different lengths of time. Even apart from the differences in purpose which inevitably differentiate the agencies, their peculiar structure will lend them an individuality. In some cases the council is elected at its discretion by the conference or assembly; in others, voting is weighted or there are special qualifications for council membership.

The difference in membership also produces a lack of uniformity. The Universal Postal Union and the International Telecommunications Union are almost universal in membership. The other specialized agencies are much less universal, though their membership has grown in 1948 and 1949. The Soviet Union, Byelorussia, and the Ukraine belong only to the Universal Postal Union and the International Telecommunications Union. Other members of the Soviet bloc are sporadic in membership. The International Trade Organization still waits for its twenty initial members.

Difference in membership and function results in a budgetary difference. The Bank and the Fund pay their own expenses from profits on the business they do. The Universal Postal Union and the International Telecommunications Union cost almost nothing, for their expenses are almost purely administrative and are light. At the other extreme lies the IRO, which as a relief organization could spend many millions, or UNESCO which could spend almost infinite sums. The amount of money an agency receives will determine what it does and how it does it, and an agency (like anything else) may get less money for quiet work of permanent value than if it can boast spectacular accomplishments or grandiose plans. Again, differences between the agencies result partly from differences between secretariats located in different places. Some secretariats are notoriously more efficient than others.

Finally, the varying locations of the headquarters of the different agencies have made coordination difficult. For purposes of easy cooperation all specialized agencies should have their headquarters at the seat of the United Nations. All the secretariats should be side by side, and council meetings should normally be in the same place, though assembly meetings may properly move from place to place.

In fact, the International Labour Organisation has central headquarters in Geneva, where the World Health Organization and the International Refugee Organization are located and the International Trade Organization is also to be. The Postal and Telecommunications Unions have always been in Bern. The Fund and the Bank are situated in Washington. The International Civil Aviation Organization has settled in Montreal. UNESCO is in Paris. The Food and Agricultural Organization, after long discussion, has chosen Rome. It may be well enough to have Geneva a European subcapital of the United Nations if the capital is to be New York City, but it is certainly undesirable that the staffs of the specialized agencies should be as widely scattered as they are.

How Is Coordination Secured?

Under the Charter, coordination between United Nations and specialized agencies and between agency and agency is voluntary. Even the provision for bringing the agency into relationship with the United Nations is in itself optional—an agency may quite correctly decide to remain aloof. And even when the agreement has been made by the Economic and Social Council and approved by the specialized agencies and by the General Assembly, the only supervision which the Economic and Social Council can exercise is that it may coordinate the activities of the specialized agencies through consultation with and recommendations to the agencies and through recommendations to the General Assembly and to the members of the United Nations (Article 63.2). If this means what it says, coordination will be persuasive, not coercive.

There are two things which the Economic and Social Council or General Assembly may do if the agreement permits. One is to exercise a veto on the election of new members by the specialized agencies. Another is to consult with the agency in regard to its budget. These two things are provided for in most agreements. Agreements also sometimes provide that the agency budget might be included within a general United Nations budget, if a separate agreement were made to this effect. Many other permissive arrangements concerning cooperation are written into many agreements.

Some of the agreements provide for the reference of legal questions to the International Court of Justice, and the General Assembly has authorized this, but again there is no compulsory reference.

How are these permissive and optional arrangements actually implemented? Largely in five ways:

First, there is the part played by the Economic and Social Council (or the General Assembly) in the establishment of agencies. The earlier agencies existed more or less provisionally before San Francisco. But UNESCO was arranged for by a resolution of the General Assembly, and the World Health Organization, International Refugee Organization, International Maritime Consultative Organization, and the International Trade Organization were planned in conferences called by the Economic and Social Council.

Second, there is the making and approving of agreements by which the agency is brought into relationship with the United Nations Organization. This function has been more formal than had been intended. In practice the agency makes its agreement, and the Economic and Social Council and General Assembly accept it. A basic reasonableness, however, is secured.

Third, there is the Coordination Committee established by the Economic and Social Council "for the purpose of taking all appropriate steps, under the Secretary-General, to insure the fullest and most effective implementation of the agreements entered into between the United Nations and the specialized agencies." This Committee consists of the Secretary-General of the United Nations and the Directors-General of the specialized agencies. Slow to get under way, this Committee shows progress.

Fourth, there are subdivisions of the United Nations Secretariat, either specifically or generally working along parallel lines.

Specifically, subdivisions of the Social Welfare Department work with the World Health Organization, the International Refugee Organization, and with the International Children's Emergency Fund.

Fifth, there is the normal relationship of persons engaged in the same general task and therefore having the same general interests. Just as in any profession, fellow members of the profession of international government not only work together but tend to be together in their hours of ease. They lunch together, sit together in the delegates' lounge, drink orange juice or whisky together. The large number of meetings brings many persons into constant association, though unfortunately the pressure of business caused by the enormous number of meetings makes the possibility of full, friendly, and relaxed contacts difficult, especially for the more important international officials. Much of the most effective business of all government is done off the record. There is still need for more leisure and for more friendliness, leading to greater cooperation.

Sixth, there is coordination through the programs of the member governments. To a large extent the membership of the United Nations and of the specialized agencies is the same. Presumably any delegate to any of these organizations goes instructed by his government. It is quite possible, therefore, for the member governments to implement their policies by giving identical instructions to all their representatives, who will therefore pursue everywhere a national policy. If, for example, a government should desire to see the work of UNESCO expanded and that of the Food and Agriculture Organization limited, it could easily instruct its delegates to UNESCO to vote for large and expensive programs and to the Food and Agriculture Organization to vote against expenditure. And this national policy might go so far as to involve a vote against one budget and for another. Only a few governments, however, are sufficiently well-coordinated and consistent to force their representatives to pursue one firm and steady international policy. Most governments which are at all democratic and individualistic are represented in different international meetings by different persons, whose ideas vary and whose instructions may be vague. Furthermore, the specialized agencies are the area within which technicians and experts work and play, while the United Nations is the field of the politicians. The United States, for example, will send the Secretary of State to the United Nations Assembly and the Secretary of Agriculture to the Food and Agriculture Organization; and the Secretary of State will be accompanied by political advisers from the Departments and from Congress, whereas the Secretary of Agriculture will be accompanied mostly by experts in crops, nutrition, forestry, and marketing. To the World Health Assembly will go the Surgeon General, to the International Trade Organization will go an assistant secretary of state for economic affairs. The Department of State is supposed to coordinate, but Congress may overrule. There is always a professional interest in the subject matter and in the organization to which one belongs oneself. Consequently, many governments, influenced by their technicians and experts, contribute to the establishment and expansion of almost all organizations for international well-being, regardless of the proportionate importance of the work that they do.

The Residual Problems

Budgets. The problem of the budgets is the greatest problem of the specialized agencies. In any case where it belongs to a specialized agency, the United States pays roughly two-fifths of the expense. It is able to do so; a few millions of dollars distributed here and there are not worth bothering about when one examines the American budget as a whole. At the other extreme are member states whose contributions, though measured in the few thousands, can be paid only after the conquest of real political and economic difficulties. Lying between are states like the United Kingdom and the Soviet Union who want the advantages of international organization but also want to economize. The United Nations has an annual budget of 40 million dollars. The most enterprising of the specialized agencies have budgets of 5 to 8 million dollars. With these budgets—inadequate and stingy if the project of international government is worth while and if such a project should reduce the expense of a great war by even one day—they must run the central office and they must produce obvious and effective international results. While they are under attack as extravagant, they are also under attack for ineffectiveness.

It has been suggested that there should be one administrative budget for central and overhead expenditures of all international organizations, to be contributed to on the basis of ability by all member states. Then the special work of the special agencies might be the subject of contributions scaled to some other criterion. In all probability, however, the multiplicity of organizations, each with its own separate budget, has encouraged the contribution of more funds to international organization purposes than if there were a consolidated budget.

Coordination of staff should be counted on in international agencies, especially in view of the world shortage of competent persons. The separateness of organizations has made this difficult. To a very limited extent it has occurred. Exchange of experience on the conference level goes on—representatives of the International Labour Organisation attend meetings of the Food and Agriculture Organization and the Trusteeship Council, and so on—but that is not quite the same thing.

Programs. With independent and autonomous agencies, there is an inevitable overlapping of programs. Limited budgets would indicate limited programs, but each agency (like all human organizations) is expansive and even imperialistic if it is at all vital. There are inevitable possibilities of overlapping, as between the FAO and the ILO on questions of agricultural labor, and much of such overlapping is bad. On the other hand, planned cooperation on programs far too large for any individual agency is highly desirable. Of this cooperation, the 1949 project for the development of backward areas is to be an example.

Already, for the most part, the specialized agencies are learning that to interpret their terms of reference narrowly gives them power. But it is a principle of life, in whatever social unit, that the unit will try to grow and expand. And it should. The garden of international organizations must be a large garden full of flowering plants. Each year a larger area must be reclaimed from the wilderness. Each year more of the hillside must be brought under cultivation.

Chapter 14. TRUSTEESHIP AND THE TRUSTEESHIP COUNCIL

It is sometimes complained that the United Nations is not a world government. It is not, nor was it intended to be. But it most nearly performs governmental functions, perhaps, in the trust territories—those dependent areas which it does not administer, but whose administration it supervises.

THE PROBLEM OF DEPENDENT AREAS

The problem of territories whose inhabitants are not fully self-governing is one of the great problems of world government. To this problem the United Nations devotes a good deal of attention by Chapters XI, XII, and XIII of the Charter and in the work of the Trusteeship Council. Over *all* dependent territories and peoples the United Nations, through Chapter XI and the procedures which have grown up for its implementation, exercises an influence which begins to approach control. For a certain special and significant group of dependent territories, "trust territories," the United Nations has taken special responsibility.

What Is a Dependent Area?

When the national state system of Europe had reached its full maturity at the end of the nineteenth century, most of the land surface of the world was claimed and was administered by sovereign states. All sovereign states possess a definite territory, a people, and a government. Ordinarily the territory is one contiguous unit. As a result of the centuries of exploration and colonization, due to the expansion of Europe overseas, all the larger and more powerful states and some of the lesser ones had come to control territories and people outside their original borders. These territories and people under the rule of a state but not part of it (and not sharing in its government) were called "colonies." The modern euphemism for "colonies" is "dependent areas," or "non-self-governing territories." The "mother country," or dominant state, has come to be called the metropolitan state or, in some instances, deriving from the French expression, the "metropole."

Dependencies were usually remote from the metropolitan state, often on another continent. Their people were ordinarily less advanced, economically, socially, and politically according to European standards. When colonial empires began, the Spanish empire in the new world, and even the British and French empires, were used for exploitation by the metropolitan governments and peoples. These earlier empires shrank or disappeared when the colonies (as for example, those of the American mainland) secured their independence and were accepted into the European state system. But later on other dependent areas came within European control—vast areas in Asia, the greater part of Africa, and the islands of the Pacific. At times, as with the British empire, which was extended to all parts of the world, or the vast Netherlands East Indies, or the Belgian Congo, the nonmetropolitan areas were larger and were actually or potentially richer and more populous than the metropolitan power which owned and governed them.

Should one people, who order their own government as they see fit, govern another people who must submit, willy-nilly? The rule of one nation or one people by another, even if exploitatory, was not held wrong until the American Declaration of Independence stated the right of peoples to rebel against external dominance and to choose for themselves a government they considered more acceptable. (The argument that dependencies are incapable of taking proper care of themselves was a favorite argument with the ministers of George III, as it has been with ministers since.)

The right to self-government, proclaimed in 1776 and so ably defended by the colonists and their descendants, was a political right. The political right of independence was reinforced by the humanitarian principles of the nineteenth century which taught that men should rule each other kindly, if at all. Rivalries between colonial powers attracted the attention of the world to the anomaly of dependent peoples dominated by nations that (at home) professed to believe in self-government and the equal rights of man.

Fragmentary and incomplete efforts were made two generations ago to secure for the dependent peoples of Africa a kind of treatment which would exploit them less and help their own development more. In the Berlin Conference of 1885 and the Brussels Conference of 1890 the European powers concerned in Africa agreed upon regulations for the occupation of the continent and tried specifically to provide for the abolition of slavery, the slave trade, and other conditions harmful to the natives. But the first serious attempt to defend dependent peoples against misrule was the mandates system of the League of Nations.

The League of Nations Mandates

When the war of 1914 ended with an Allied victory, the colonies of Germany and the outlying parts of the Turkish empire lay at the disposal of the Allies. They might have been annexed in full sovereignty by the victors. Instead, largely owing to the insistence of President Wilson, they were placed under the supervision of the League of Nations, on whose behalf they were administered by individual members of the community of nations known as "mandatory powers." The territories themselves were known as "mandated territories" or "mandates." The Permanent Mandates Commission, composed of experts and reporting to the Council of the League, received annual reports from the mandatory power and exercised a measure of supervision over the acts of the mandatory power. Article 22 of the League Covenant, which establishes the mandatory system, states that the principle to be applied to the people of the mandated territories is that "the well being and development of such peoples form a sacred trust of civilization."

The Supreme Council of the Principal Allied and Associated Powers (of which the United States was a member) assigned the mandated territories to states which were to act as mandatories. There were three classes of mandates, depending on the degree of advancement of the territories concerned. The first class, informally known as "class A," included "certain communities formerly belonging to the Turkish Empire [which] have reached a stage of development where their existence as independent nations can be provisionally recognized subject to the rendering of administrative advice and assistance by a Mandatory until such time as they are able to stand alone" (Article 22). France was given a class A mandate over Syria (soon divided into Syria and Lebanon); Great Britain, class A mandates over Iraq and Palestine (administered in two units as Palestine and Transjordan).

Class B mandates, former German colonies in Africa, were safeguarded as to native rights and freedom of international trade and assigned to mandatories. Belgium received Ruanda–Urundi, Great Britain received Tanganyika (formerly German East Africa) and parts of the Cameroons and Togoland, and France received the other parts of the Cameroons and Togoland.

Very thinly populated areas, which were to be administered as "integral parts" of the mandatory power, i.e., as class C mandates, were assigned as follows: South-West Africa to the Union of South Africa, the German islands in the Pacific north of the equator to Japan, Western Samoa to New Zealand, New Guinea to Australia, and Nauru to "His Britannic Majesty" on behalf of the governments of the United Kingdom, Australia, and New Zealand. By agreement, it was administered by Australia.

Iraq was recognized as independent in 1932 and Syria and Lebanon by 1945, the time of their admission as members of the San Francisco Conference. The United Kingdom entered into treaty relationships with Transjordan in the autumn of 1945 in such a way that its independence was virtually established. The other mandated territories, however, were still completely under tutelage, both during the San Francisco Conference and when the United Nations began to function. The Japanese Mandated Islands had remained under Japanese administration, even when Japan withdrew from the League of Nations, and had been occupied by the United States in the course of the Second World War.

PLANNING FOR TRUSTEESHIP

As part of the transition from a world in which the League of Nations was the international authority to a world in which the United Nations was to be a newer and better world authority, it was necessary to make new arrangements to replace the mandates system and perhaps to take care of other territories for which international supervision might be a desirable arrangement.

The issue of dependent peoples had grown more acute for many reasons. Nationalist feeling had increased among dependent peoples, greatly stimulated by pan-Arab nationalism, by the efforts of India to secure its independence, and by the anti-European and antiwhite propaganda of the Japanese.

The feeling that colonial peoples were entitled to independence —or at least to a degree of self-government that amounted to independence—had grown in the West. The British dominions were unquestionably independent after the enactment of the Statute of Westminster in 1931. Not only India but a number of British colonies were apparently headed in the same direction. The United States had determined to free the Commonwealth of the Philippines, which was admitted as a member of the San Francisco Conference and whose independence was to be formally proclaimed on July 4, 1946. To Alaska, Hawaii, Puerto Rico, and the Virgin Islands of the United States American policy had granted almost complete self-government. There was a general impression that "colonialism" had failed; and the easy Japanese conquests in 1941 and 1942 gave evidence thereof.

There were logically only four possible destinations for colonies which were to cease to be colonies: independence, incorporation into existing sovereign states, incorporation into groupings similar to the British Commonwealth, or some form of international administration or supervision. In 1943 Secretary Hull and President Roosevelt agreed upon proposals looking toward independence for all dependent peoples who desired it and who seemed ready for it, and suggesting a sort of "colonial timetable" to be made by each colonial power indicating the date at which the independence of each colony should be granted; in the meantime there should be an international trusteeship system for colonies detached from their previous owners. At one moment during the war President Roosevelt went so far as to suggest that French Indochina should never be returned to France. The Soviet Union, which had boasted that even its least developed areas were equal and constituent parts of the Union, was uncompromising in its insistence that colonies must cease to exist. Proposals were advanced during the war for a French Union and a Dutch Commonwealth in which all French and Dutch colonies should be incorporated into a greater France and a greater Netherlands. Dependents would thereby be raised to the status of citizens, and yet at the same time the metropolitan power might be strengthened.

Many changes were bound to occur. At the same time there would remain, from a practical point of view, many territories not ready and able to maintain a fully sovereign status in a difficult postwar world. Some of these, like the former mandates, were already the beneficiaries of existing international agreement and obligation. Other areas were going to be detached from the vanquished powers in the Second World War. By the Cairo Declaration of 1943 Japan was to lose all of its empire and to be reduced basically to the four main Japanese islands. The Italian colonies in Africa were to be taken away from Italy. Yet, just as in 1919, these areas were not to be annexed by the victor states because international opinion would not permit it.

This was the situation, or the prospective situation, when plans for the San Francisco Conference were made. The powers that were to dominate that Conference began each with its separate point of view. The Soviet position has been referred to above. The British position assumed a continuance of colonial empires but accepted the possibility of regional grouping of colonies under some regionally organized international supervision. The American planners drew up proposals for an international trusteeship system which should replace the League mandates system and which should be more widespread and more effective as a kind of international government. They were also thinking in terms of a "colonial charter" or statement of principles that would be binding on all metropolitan powers in relation to such colonies as they might continue to keep. And their thinking paralleled that of the British and the Australians and New Zealanders in envisaging the possibility of regional associations in largely colonial areas. The Anglo-American Caribbean Commission was already in existence, and the Australian–New Zealand Agreement of January, 1944, proposed a South Seas regional commission. One thing was clear—immediate independence for all dependent areas was, at the moment, impracticable.

In the Dumbarton Oaks Proposals not a single reference appears concerning colonies or dependent peoples, because the British supported the principle of colonial rule, the Russians opposed any proposal for subordination as between peoples, and the Americans wanted an extension of the mandatory system or international "trusteeship." At the Yalta Conference, however, American pressure secured three-power agreement to its recommendation that an international trusteeship system might be established as part of the proposed Charter of the United Nations.

At San Francisco

No question at San Francisco was more influenced by fundamental political factors than that of trusteeship and non-self-governing territories, though it was dealt with more inconspicuously than such other major problems as the veto. The range of what was considered desirable ran all the way from a dogmatism in favor of independence shown by the Soviet Union, the Philippines, and the Arab states, to the old-fashioned imperialist assumptions made by the conservative representatives of the United Kingdom, France, and the Netherlands. A middle ground, that some sort of trusteeship and/or international supervision of colonies should be established, was held by such empire-possessing states as the United States, Australia, and New Zealand.

Eventually compromise produced two things: first, an international trusteeship system for such territories as might be subsequently placed thereunder, very likely a limited and definite number of dependent areas (Chapters XII and XIII of the Charter); and, second, the Declaration Regarding Non-Self-Governing Territories with a bearing on *all* dependent territories and peoples (Chapter XI).

The International Trusteeship System

The international trusteeship system is a method of administration, under United Nations supervision, of selected territories. The San Francisco Conference formulated the system, but did not apply it to any particular territories; that was left to future determination under procedures specified in the Charter.

Which Territories?

According to Article 77 of the Charter the system may apply to three classes of territories:

a. territories now held under mandate, [These have been enumerated above.]

b. territories which may be detached from enemy states as a result of the Second World War, [These were presumably the Japanese and Italian territories already referred to.]

c. territories voluntarily placed under the system by states responsible for their administration.

The third category was intentionally wide. In the planning for the trusteeship system, it had been thought that states might upon occasion wish to relieve themselves of the ultimate responsibility for a dependent area, whether for reasons of convenience or economy, or to promote good will. In fact no territory in category *c* has been made a trust territory, nor has any administering state apparently thus far seriously considered detaching a dependency from itself, though the unhappy postwar experiences of certain metropolitan powers with their dependencies, notably in Malaya, Indonesia, and Indochina, suggest that they might well have taken advantage of this provision.

Article 77 goes on to say, very specifically, that "It will be a matter for subsequent agreement as to which territories in the foregoing categories will be brought under the trusteeship system and upon what terms." In other words, it was clearly understood in San Francisco, and the Charter clearly specifies, that nothing in the Charter itself requires the placing of any territory under trusteeship.

No territories which are *members* of the United Nations can be under trusteeship, for they are treated as sovereign states (Article 78). This proviso laid to rest any fears on the part of mandates like Syria and Lebanon that they might have international controls reimposed on them. Syria and Lebanon, not yet formally freed from France, were members of the United Nations. This proviso also furnishes the only suggestion given in the Charter as to when a trusteeship must terminate.

How a Trust Territory Is Established

The determination to place a territory under trusteeship is taken outside the United Nations machinery. The "states directly concerned" draw up a trusteeship agreement, which includes the "terms of trusteeship." This trusteeship agreement is in essence a charter or constitution in accordance with which the territory will be governed. The "terms of trusteeship" embodied in the "agreement" will then be submitted to the appropriate organ of the United Nations—to the General Assembly in the case of most trusteeship territories, to the Security Council in the case of strategic areas. When the General Assembly or the Security Council has approved the agreement, it goes into effect and the trust territory is established.

"States Directly Concerned"

Among the questions intentionally left unanswered in the Charter was the question of which were the "states directly concerned" who must agree to the trusteeship agreement in the case of any given territory. The Charter does say that in the case of a mandate the mandatory power shall be a state "directly concerned." Further than this, the Charter does not specify the "states directly concerned."

The great powers differed in their interpretation of the phrase. The position of the American Department of State ever since the institution of the mandates system had been that since the ex-German and ex-Turkish territories had been surrendered to the Principal Allied and Associated Powers (the United States, Great Britain, France, Italy, and Japan) and since the mandates had been granted by the Supreme Council of these powers, the legal title to the mandated territories rested in these powers, subject to whatever authority over them had been given (by Article 22 of the Covenant) to the Council of the League. If "states directly concerned" was a legal concept, those "states" must be those Principal Allied and Associated Powers which were members of the United Nations (*i.e.*, the United Kingdom, the United States, and France). The other two (Japan and Italy) must in their surrenders have yielded their share of the title to the three. This admirable, if rather legalistic, argument was never effectively put forward by the United States.

Other states adopted other interpretations of the vital phrase. The governments of the United Kingdom and of France, when they took a position in relation to their African mandates, acted as if the "states directly concerned" were those having geographical propinquity to the proposed trust territory. The Soviet Union maintained that all permanent members of the Trusteeship Council, the Big Five, were by reason of this permanent membership "states directly concerned."

When the decision had to be made as to the meaning of "states directly concerned," after trusteeship agreements had been drafted in 1946, all states except the Soviet bloc accepted a new American interpretation that the "states directly concerned" need not be defined or enumerated. As a practical consequence, the "states directly concerned" thereby became one state only, the mandatory power in the case of a former mandate, and in other cases the state having actual administration over the territory in question. In order to avoid the consequent sterile concept that this state should agree upon terms of trusteeship with itself (Article 79), the provisions of the Charter were further strained by the interpretation that the "agreement" becomes an agreement between the one state directly concerned and the General Assembly or Security Council, as the case may be. And when Article 79 says the terms of trusteeship shall be "approved," it really means they shall be accepted by a partner practically precluded from refusal to accept.

Presumably the "approval" of a trusteeship agreement by the General Assembly or the Security Council makes it valid and connotes approval of the preceding steps, and the General Assembly and the Security Council have in every case "approved" the appropriate agreements.

The "Administering Authority"

Each trust territory is administered by an "administering authority." In the proposals originally discussed at San Francisco, it was assumed that the "administering authority" would be one state, a member of the United Nations. An amendment proposed by the Chinese delegation and firmly opposed by the colonial powers was accepted, and the Charter consequently reads that the administering authority "may be one or more states or the Organization itself" (Article 81).

In fact, all trust territories so far have one state as administering authority except Nauru which (just as when it was a mandate) is nominally in trust to three states, though it is administered by one, Australia. The possibilities of administration by more than one state have been contemplated nevertheless. Korea, by the Moscow decision of 1945, was to be under four-power

trusteeship.   The Italian colonies were proposed in 1945 by the
United States and in 1949 by the Soviet Union for administration
by the Organization itself.   The Trusteeship Council itself is to
administer Jerusalem, according to a decision of the General
Assembly late in 1949, although not as a trust territory.

Terms of Trusteeship

The "terms of trusteeship" or "trusteeship agreement" constitute
a charter or constitution for the trust territory.   In each case they
have been written as such, though in no case are they the sort of
constitution which a free people would write for themselves.

The terms of trusteeship name the administering authority.
Once approved, they cannot be altered without the consent of "the
states directly concerned, including the mandatory power . . ."
and of the organ of the United Nations which originally approved
them.

Military Activity and "Strategic Areas"

One intended difference between the mandates and the trust
territories was in regard to their use as focuses of military activity.
The class B and C mandates were to be placed outside the areas
of international military activity, and in practice the same principle was applied to class A mandates.   But the United Nations
originated as a league to enforce peace.   Its planners, therefore,
believed that trust territories, like other territories, must be incorporated into the system of "international peace and security."
The old League principle of demilitarization of mandates must
be replaced by the new United Nations principle that trust territories might be centers of military activity.   (As a matter of
fact, the Japanese Mandated Islands had been fortified by the
Japanese and formed an important outpost of Japanese power,
and some of the most important concentrations of allied military
power had centered in the Australian mandate of New Guinea,
which included the Admiralty Islands.)

Conflicting proposals were made at San Francisco to deal with
the problem of making trust territories useful in the maintenance

of "international peace and security." The British approached the problem functionally and made suggestions which are incorporated in Article 84 of the Charter. This article provides that the administering authority shall ensure that "the trust territory shall play its part in the maintenance of international peace and security" and "to this end . . . may make use of volunteer forces, facilities, and assistance from the trust territory in carrying out the obligation towards the Security Council undertaken in this regard by the administering authority." This provision applies to *all* trust territories.

Naval and military advisers of the United States were not satisfied with this. They did not think that it would sufficiently militarize the places they considered dangerous. They therefore insisted that the problem should be treated geographically. They had in mind particularly the Japanese Mandated Islands which they intended to keep, in future, under their control, but which they were willing to see incorporated into a system of "international peace and security" as long as the national defense of the United States should be the first consideration. Consequently, the Charter provides that a special kind of trust territory can be created by a special trusteeship agreement. This special kind of trust territory is designated as a "strategic area." The trusteeship agreement for the strategic area is subject to the approval of the Security Council and not of the General Assembly. Any part (or all) of a trust territory may be designated as a strategic area (Article 82). The advantage, from the military point of view, of creating a strategic area is that neither the General Assembly nor the Trusteeship Council has any rights therein. No civilians can interfere. The Charter does not give any definition of strategic areas.

Supervision

Having created a trust territory, and having entrusted it to an administering authority in accordance with the terms of a trusteeship agreement, what further responsibilities does the United Nations assume? Under what sort of international supervision or control does the administering authority find itself?   The General Assembly, which has the authority to approve trusteeship agreements, has also an authority to supervise the administration of trust territories, except strategic areas.   To assist the General Assembly in this function a Trusteeship Council was established.

Basic Objectives

Equally as important as the creation of trust territories are the basic objectives which the trusteeship system is to carry out.   As stated in Article 76, they are:

a. to further international peace and security; [This is stated as a sort of preliminary objective, since the Charter exists for that purpose.]

b. to promote the political, economic, social, and educational advancement of the inhabitants of the trust territories, and their progressive development towards self-government or independence as may be appropriate to the particular circumstances of each territory and its peoples and the freely expressed wishes of the peoples concerned, and as may be provided by the terms of each trusteeship agreement;

c. to encourage respect for human rights and for fundamental freedoms for all without distinction as to race, sex, language, or religion, and to encourage recognition of the interdependence of the peoples of the world; and

d.   to ensure equal treatment in social, economic, and commercial matters for all Members of the United Nations and their nationals, and also equal treatment for the latter in the administration of justice, without prejudice to the attainment of the foregoing objectives and subject to the provisions of Article 80.

This condensed and careful language is the result of long and careful deliberation at San Francisco.   It is all to be taken seriously.   In the political context of the postwar world, however, the emphasis is on the promotion of the advancement of the inhabitants of the trust territories.   These territories, in other words, are not areas for exploitation by the administering powers, they are areas where the development of backward peoples have been made an international concern.   In particular, the attention of the world is fixed on "their progressive development towards self-government or independence."

The Trusteeship Council

Finally, in its general plan of the trusteeship system, the Charter establishes a Trusteeship Council, to be one of the six principal organs of the United Nations and to assist the General Assembly in carrying out the functions of the United Nations Organization with regard to ordinary or nonstrategic trust territories (Article 85). Chapter XIII of the Charter is devoted to the composition, functions, and procedure of the Trusteeship Council.

THE FIRST TRUSTEESHIP AGREEMENTS AND THE ESTABLISHMENT OF THE TRUSTEESHIP COUNCIL

The Trusteeship Council was the latest of the organs of the United Nations to come into actual existence. By Article 86 it must be composed half of states which administer trust territories and half of states which do not. Before there could be a council, there had to be trust territories; before there could be trust territories, trusteeship agreements had to be made and had to be approved by the General Assembly. Consequently, the Trusteeship Council could not be established during the London meetings of the First Part of the First Session of the General Assembly in 1946.

Should the Former Mandates Be Placed under Trusteeship?

In the London meetings representatives of most of the mandatory powers made statements declaring their intention to place their mandates under trusteeship. The exceptions were: Palestine and Transjordan, in regard to which the United Kingdom expressed its intention of establishing the independence of Transjordan and of studying the problem of Palestine; South-West Africa, in regard to which the Union of South Africa expressed the intention of consulting the natives as to the future status of the territory; and the Japanese Mandated Islands then under occupation by the United States. The General Assembly consequently passed a resolution welcoming these declarations and inviting all states administering mandated territories "to undertake practical steps" to conclude trusteeship agreements for their mandated territories in order that these agreements might be submitted for approval "preferably not later than during the second part of the first session of the General Assembly."

The nominal part still played by the League of Nations in relation to the mandates was ended in the final session of the League Assembly on April 18, 1946. The League Assembly recognized that on the termination of the League its functions in relation to the mandates would disappear but that Chapters XI, XII, and XIII of the Charter embodied principles similar to those of Article 22 and took note of the expressed intentions of members of the League to continue to administer their mandates in accordance with the preexisting obligations, until other arrangements for them should be made between the United Nations and the mandatory powers.

The Original Trusteeship Agreements

The most complicated and detailed work toward the establishment of the trusteeship system was the drawing up of the trusteeship agreements for the trust territories. The mandatory powers which were to become administering authorities under the new system were willing to accept most of the responsibilities which they accepted under the mandates, but wished somewhat greater freedom. The general interest in closer and more complete supervision had to be satisfied by only partial modification of the terms of the mandates. An infinite amount of consultation went on.

Eventually trusteeship agreements were submitted to the General Assembly on the formal initiative of each individual mandatory power alone, and after considerable discussion and some modification they were approved by the General Assembly in December, 1946. There were eight separate agreements, for New Guinea (Australia), Ruanda-Urundi (Belgium), Togoland (France), Togoland (United Kingdom), Cameroons (France),

Cameroons (United Kingdom), Western Samoa (New Zealand), and Tanganyika (United Kingdom).

In essence, each trusteeship agreement is a brief charter or constitution for the trust territory, designating the administering authority and giving it large powers of government, paraphrasing the Charter obligations which the administering authority has undertaken, and elaborating somewhat the obligations of the administering authority to promote special aspects of the political, social, and educational advancement of the inhabitants.

No existing trusteeship agreement makes any provision for the termination of the trust status of the territory. Such termination could presumably occur only with the consent of the administering authority or if the trust territory should be admitted as a member of the United Nations.

The eight trusteeship agreements were approved in a resolution of the General Assembly of December 13, 1946. On the following day a further resolution of the General Assembly stated that the conditions for the completion of the Trusteeship Council had been met, elected Mexico and Iraq as members of the Trusteeship Council, and directed the Secretary-General to convoke its first meeting. The Soviet Union had objected to the approval of the trusteeship agreements, partly on the ground that the Soviet Union should have been treated as a "state directly concerned," did not participate in the elections to the Trusteeship Council, and for over a year did not take its own seat in the Council.

Nauru, South-West Africa, and Palestine

Consideration was given by the same session of the General Assembly to the cases of South-West Africa and Nauru. The Australian representative declared his government's intention of submitting a trusteeship agreement for Nauru. Such an agreement was approved by the General Assembly on November 1. 1947.

In regard to South-West Africa, the delegate of the Union of South Africa submitted a proposal calling for the General Assembly's approval of the annexation of South-West Africa by the

Union. After much discussion in committee the General Assembly (the majority of whose members strongly opposed the suggested annexation) refused to approve annexation and passed a resolution inviting the Union to propose a trusteeship agreement for the territory.

The important question of Palestine was allowed to wait, pending proposals which the United Kingdom government might make after the Anglo-American Palestine Committee had finished its investigations.

The Pacific Islands

The former German islands north of the equator, which had been under Japanese mandate, had been occupied by the United States during the Second World War. They presented a very complicated and very special problem of trusteeship.

Because these islands had proved so valuable to Japan in its war in the western Pacific, the Joint Chiefs of Staff of the United States had decided that it was necessary for the islands to remain permanently under the control of the armed forces of the United States. The conquest of the islands by the United States and their administration by the American Navy put the United States in a dominant position in determining the future of these islands. In the period before the disposition of the islands was determined, a good deal of effort was made to try to persuade the American people to demand annexation, on the ground that only in this way could the American expenditure of lives in their conquest be paid for. Most departments of the United States government, however, led by the Department of State, were convinced that the islands should be placed under trusteeship. They took this position for three reasons. The first was the Atlantic Charter pledge against the annexation of territory. The second was the United States pledge to support the United Nations and consequently the trusteeship system. The third was the fact that the islands had become a matter of international concern when they had been made a League mandate twenty-five years earlier. On November 6, 1946, President Truman issued a statement in which he said that "the United States is prepared to place under trustee-ship, with the United States as the administering authority, the Japanese Mandated Islands and any Japanese islands for which it assumes responsibilities as a result of the Second World War." His statement went on to say that a draft trusteeship agreement was presently to be submitted to the Security Council for its approval.

If the Japanese islands must be made a trust territory rather than annexed, the elements in the United States government which would have preferred annexation were, nevertheless, in a position to insist on a form of trusteeship which would avoid most of what they considered to be the dangerously international aspects of the system. The United States delegation at the San Francisco Con-ference had insisted on what finally appeared in the Charter as the "strategic area"—a special form of trusteeship in which neither the General Assembly nor the Trusteeship Council had any au-thority, but in which the Security Council should exercise "All functions of the United Nations relating to strategic areas" (Article 83).

Since the only authority granted by the Charter to the Security Council in relation to strategic areas is that of approving the terms of the trusteeship agreements and of their alteration and amendment (Article 83) and since the United States possessed the veto in the Security Council, this fully guaranteed to the United States government its exclusive control of the islands with-out any possible interference at any time by anyone. It is true that Article 83 goes on to say that the basic objectives of the trusteeship system "shall be applicable to the people of each strategic area" and that the Security Council shall (subject to the terms of trusteeship and of security considerations) avail itself of the assistance of the Trusteeship Council to perform the func-tions under the trusteeship system "relating to political, economic, social, and educational matters in the strategic areas." But this requirement is also subject to the fact that the Security Council can take no action contrary to the principle of the unanimity of the great powers.

Safeguarded from any possible interference by outside authority, the United States drafted a trusteeship agreement for the islands. This agreement includes excellent statements of principle in regard to the treatment of the natives of the trust territory and indicates a willingness to permit that the inspectional and supervisory activities of the Trusteeship Council be exercised in the islands, except in so far as the United States reserves the right to declare any area therein as a closed area in which such activities are forbidden.

A trusteeship agreement for what was to be known as the Trust Territory of the Pacific Islands was submitted by the United States to all members of the Security Council, and to other Pacific neighbors of the United States, and was formally proposed for Security Council approval in February, 1947. After thorough discussion and after three amendments had been accepted by the United States, it was approved by the Security Council. Upon subsequent approval by Congress, given on July 18, 1947, it went into effect on that date.

THE TRUSTEESHIP COUNCIL

The Trusteeship Council met for the first time on March 26, 1947, at Lake Success. The meeting was attended by five representatives of administering powers, Australia, Belgium, France, New Zealand, and the United Kingdom, and four nonadministering states, China, the United States, Iraq (member till December 31, 1949), and Mexico (member till December 31, 1949). The Soviet Union designated no representative and was absent until April 27, 1948.

Members and Organization

The Trusteeship Council is constituted in a peculiar way. All states which are permanent members of the Security Council are permanent members of the Trusteeship Council. And all states which are administering authorities of trust territories are also members. But there must be a numerical balance in the Council between "administering" and "nonadministering" states. Consequently the General Assembly is authorized to elect (for terms of three years) enough nonadministering states as members of the Council in order to make an exact balance between the two groups.

When it first met, the Trusteeship Council consisted of the following states:

Administering members:
    Australia, administering New Guinea
    Belgium, administering Ruanda-Urundi
    France, administering French Cameroons and French Togoland
    New Zealand, administering Western Samoa
    United Kingdom, administering British Cameroons, British Togoland, and Tanganyika
Nonadministering members:
    China, a permanent member
    United States, a permanent member
    Soviet Union, a permanent member
    Iraq, elected
    Mexico, elected

After the Trust Territory of the Pacific Islands was created in 1947, the United States became an administering member; and to keep the numerical balance, two other nonadministering members were elected by the General Assembly, Costa Rica and the Philippines. The Council was then composed as follows:

Administering members:
    Australia
    Belgium
    France
    New Zealand
    United Kingdom
    United States
Nonadministering members:
    China
    Soviet Union

Iraq, elected 1946

Mexico, elected 1946

Costa Rica, elected 1947

Philippines, elected 1947

In 1949 Argentina was elected for a three-year term to take the place of Mexico, Iraq was reelected for three years, and the Dominican Republic was elected to fill the remainder of the term of Costa Rica, which had resigned.

The approval of a trusteeship agreement for Nauru, submitted jointly by Australia, New Zealand, and the United Kingdom, did not change the membership of the Council.

Though the members of the Council are states, it was hoped that their representatives in the Council might be men of technical experience. Consequently the Charter provides that "each member of the Trusteeship Council shall designate one specially qualified person to represent it therein."

Procedure

The procedure of the Trusteeship Council is simple. The Charter gives each member one vote and provides that decisions may be made by a majority of members present and voting. As in the General Assembly and Economic and Social Council, there is no veto. And like the Economic and Social Council, the Trusteeship Council makes its decisions by a simple majority (Article 89).

The Trusteeship Council adopts its own rules of procedure (Article 90). It has decided to meet regularly twice a year, in January and in June. Each year, in June, it elects a president and vice-president for the year. The first president, elected in 1947, was Mr. Francis B. Sayre of the United States, a former Assistant Secretary of State. The president for 1948–1949 was Mr. Liu Chieh of China, and for 1949–1950 Mr. Roger Garreau of France.

The Charter provides that on appropriate matters the Trusteeship Council shall avail itself of the assistance of the Economic and Social Council and of the specialized agencies.

The Functions of the Trusteeship Council

The general purpose of the Trusteeship Council is to supervise the administration of trust territories. Strong objection at San Francisco on the part of the existing mandatory powers prevented any statement to this effect from appearing on the Charter. Instead, the Council was given authority to do a number of specific things. Governments or persons anxious that the trusteeship system should be a real system of international supervision had to be satisfied with a very narrow letter of the law. They could hope that when the system started operating the Trusteeship Council would interpret its responsibilities broadly. It has done so. Even the representatives of administering authorities sometimes refer to the Trusteeship Council's "control."

The specific functions granted to the Trusteeship Council relate to questionnaires, reports from trust territories, petitions, and visits to trust territories.

The Trusteeship Council, according to the Charter, is to formulate a questionnaire for each trust territory "on the political, economic, social, and educational advancement of the inhabitants." On the basis of the questionnaire "the administering authority for each trust territory within the competence of the General Assembly shall make an annual report to the General Assembly."

The Trusteeship Council may consider reports submitted by the administering authority. It may also accept petitions and examine them and provide for periodic visits to the trust territories. These three powers—to consider reports, to accept and examine petitions, and to visit—are subject to the authority of the General Assembly. And Article 87, which grants these powers, also permits the Trusteeship Council to "take these and other actions in conformity with the terms of the trusteeship agreements."

The reports on trust territories supply information on which the Trusteeship Council, the General Assembly, and the world at large, judge the performance of the administering authority in carrying out the objectives of the trusteeship system. At each meeting the Trusteeship Council examines a group of reports, discussing each report with a special representative of the administering authority.

Petitions "may be accepted and examined by the Trusteeship Council if they concern the affairs of one or more Trust Territories or the operation of the International Trusteeship System" (*Rules of Procedure*, Rule 76). Petitions may be written or oral; they need not come from inhabitants of a trust territory; they need not be transmitted through the administering authority. The examination of petitions takes an appreciable amount of the Council's time and provides opportunity for rather detailed discussion of affairs within the trust territories.

Visits to the trust territories are made by representatives of the Trusteeship Council for the purpose of firsthand observation and report. For purposes of the periodic visits the trust territories have been arranged in three groups—East Africa, West Africa, and the Pacific. One group will be visited each year, East Africa in 1948, West Africa in 1949, the Pacific in 1950, and so on.

The specific functions granted to the Trusteeship Council, taken together, have given the Council power to exercise a real supervision over the government of the trust territories. The higher authority of the General Assembly, which also receives an annual report from the Council, permits the General Assembly to discuss the same questions and to make recommendations in regard to them.

THE HISTORY OF THE TRUSTEESHIP COUNCIL

At its first session, in March and April, 1947, the Council organized itself by adopting rules of procedure and choosing a president and vice-president. It drew up a draft questionnaire on the administration of trust territories, made provision for visits to trust territories, and discussed arrangements for cooperation with the Security Council, the Economic and Social Council, and the specialized agencies.

The substantive work of the Council began at this meeting with the consideration of petitions, which had already begun to come in. Of these the most important was a petition from the native authorities in Western Samoa, which is under New Zealand administration. At the request of the New Zealand representative, the Council decided to establish a special committee to visit Western Samoa during the summer.

The committee to visit Western Samoa was composed of Mr. Sayre of the United States, Mr. Pierre Ryckmans of Belgium, and Dr. Eduardo Cruz-Coke of Chile. These three men, accompanied by members of the Secretariat, visited the islands during July and August.

The second session of the Trusteeship Council convened at Lake Success on November 20, 1947. The Council received a report from its mission to Western Samoa proposing a new plan of government for that area which would give more authority to representatives of the native population. The Council approved the recommendations of the mission and the intention of the New Zealand government to proceed along lines suggested in the report.

South-West Africa was also before the Council. The Union of South Africa had refused to place the territory under trusteeship, but had stated its intention to transmit annual reports on the territory to the United Nations. At the request of the General Assembly the Trusteeship Council examined the 1946 report on South-West Africa, transmitted questions on it to the Union government, and received replies. In its third session the Council, as the Assembly had requested, transmitted observations on the report to the Assembly.

What may be considered the regular routine work of the Council continued with the examination of petitions relating to trust territories. In particular, petitions on behalf of the Ewe people in Togoland proposed the unification of the administrations of the two parts into which Togoland is divided. The Trusteeship Council decided to consider this problem further after its mission had visited the area. Petitions in regard to Tanganyika were also considered.

Further routine work consisted of an examination of Australia's report on New Guinea.

The Council decided that the first periodic visit to trust territories should be made during 1948 to the East Africa trust territories, Ruanda-Urundi and Tanganyika.

The Council also appointed a special committee to confer with a committee of the Security Council on the way in which the Security Council might avail itself of the assistance of the Trusteeship Council, under Article 83 of the Charter, in relation to the strategic Trust Territory of the Pacific Islands.

Like other organs of the United Nations the Trusteeship Council found itself (beginning at its second session) involved in the question of Palestine. The resolution on Palestine, passed by the General Assembly on November 29, 1947, included the establishment of a special regime for the city of Jerusalem and designated the Trusteeship Council "to discharge the responsibilities of the Administering Authority on behalf of the United Nations." It further requested the Trusteeship Council to draw up a detailed statute for the government of the city and outlined the form which this government was to take.

Accordingly the Trusteeship Council appointed a working committee to draft such a statute. To examine this draft, the Trusteeship Council met in adjourned session from February 18 to March 10, 1948. With some changes the draft was accepted. The Council met again on April 21, 1948, and referred the draft statute to the General Assembly (then meeting in special session) for further instructions. The General Assembly considered the statute but deferred and finally (on May 14) failed to adopt it.

Meantime on April 26 the General Assembly requested the Trusteeship Council to take steps to protect Jerusalem. The Trusteeship Council, therefore, met again from April 27 to May 4. On April 27 it was attended for the first time by a representative of the Soviet Union. After consultation with the Arab Higher Committee and the Jewish agency, it arranged a cease-fire order and made recommendations for turning the cease-fire order into a truce. It further suggested that the mandatory power should choose a special municipal commissioner to serve after the termination of the mandate. Its report including these two items was agreed to by the General Assembly on May 6. A United States proposal to the Trusteeship Council for establishing a temporary trusteeship for Jerusalem failed in the Trusteeship Council.

The third regular session of the Trusteeship Council met at Lake Success on June 16, 1948. Freed for the time being from its concern with Jerusalem, it returned to the work of examining reports and considering petitions.

At this session the Council began a full and regular examination of the annual reports in a pattern which still continues. Most of the representatives of administering states feel on the defensive: what touches one touches all; a complaint against one will be a complaint against all. Only the United States, which administers the Trust Territory of the Pacific Islands with the determination and the resources to do the best possible job, has received praise from all representatives on the Council except that of the Soviet Union. The United States is therefore in a unique position—not uncritical itself but free from any criticism that it respects. The Soviet Union's representative, ever since he took his seat in 1948, has been universally critical, even of what everybody else looked upon as advances in the right direction. The representatives of nonadministering powers have been severely critical of trust-territory administration. The elected members of the Trusteeship Council represent an anticolonial majority in the General Assembly and usually come from states conscious of a long, and sometimes recent, history of oppression. The feeling of the majority of the Trusteeship Council is bound therefore to be critical, but except for the Soviet representative the critics are friendly.

The discussion of the largest of the trust territories, Tanganyika, was perhaps the most important, since the discussion on the annual report in 1948 was supplemented by a report from the first Visiting Mission and by a series of discussions in 1949. Having great possibilities for development, Tanganyika has been united since 1947 in an "administrative union" with Kenya and Uganda, both of which are British colonies. Such a union is permitted in the trusteeship agreement, though it must be consistent with the basic objectives of the trusteeship system. Tanganyika served, however, as the first conspicuous warning that an administrative union might mean the absorption of a trust territory into an empire. Furthermore, the economic development of Tanganyika seemed to some representatives on the Council directed more toward the welfare of the white man than that of the native. The "groundnuts" scheme was criticized in the Trusteeship Council long before it was criticized in the Parliament of the United Kingdom. And education for the natives has been conspicuously inadequate.

Criticism of other reports has tended to center on the same things. Administrative unions colonialize territories, whereas according to the Charter the goal is self-government or independence. Education, economic welfare, and health are inadequately taken care of. The goal of political development is too often forgotten.

In writing its report to the General Assembly, the Trusteeship Council decided in this session that the report should include not only the views of the Council, agreed upon formally, but also minority views of any representative who wished to express them.

At this session the Council drafted for report to the General Assembly comments on the administration of South-West Africa which were uniformly unfriendly to the Union of South Africa.

The General Assembly session of 1948, discussing the report of the Trusteeship Council, engaged in a sharp debate which reflected the intensity of feeling on the problem of dependencies. The Assembly agreed to ask the Trusteeship Council to study two things: the expansion of education in trust territories and the problem of administrative unions.

The fourth session of the Trusteeship Council assembled on January 24, 1949, at Lake Success. This session had before it the reports of its Visiting Mission on Ruanda-Urundi and on Tanganyika. The subjects referred to it by the General Assembly were handled by the appointment of two committees, one on administrative unions and one on higher education in trust territories. As usual, the major work of the session was the examination of reports and the consideration of petitions.

Since the Security Council had finally decided to ask the Trusteeship Council to act for it in performing functions relating to "political, economic, social, and educational matters in the strategic areas," the Trusteeship Council sent its questionnaire to the United States government as administering authority of the Trust Territory of the Pacific Islands.

The fifth session of the Trusteeship Council began on June 15, 1949. Among the reports it examined was one from the United States, which was generally congratulated on its good administration in the Pacific Islands.

In regard to administrative unions the Council decided to keep a watch over the effects of such unions and to request separate records, statistics, and information from all trust territories. On education it made recommendations in regard to specific territories.

Since the government of the Union of South Africa had informed the Secretary-General that South Africa would no longer report on South-West Africa and had given information of a legal change bringing South-West Africa into closer association with the Union, the Trusteeship Council decided to report its dissatisfaction with these acts to the General Assembly.

OTHER PROBLEMS OF TRUSTEESHIP

So far, the only territories placed under trusteeship are territories which are included in category *a* of Article 77—those formerly under mandate. There has been much discussion but only one decision about territories under category *b*—"territories which may be detached from enemy states as a result of the Second World War."

The Italian Colonies

Libya, Eritrea, and Italian Somaliland, three Italian possessions in Africa, were yielded by Italy and were at the disposal of the

Council of Ministers when they were drawing up the Italian peace treaty. The natural disposition of these colonies, under the Charter, would have been trusteeship, since none of them seemed viable alone. Indeed, at the first meeting of the Council of Foreign Ministers in 1946 the United States made the proposal that they should all be placed under trusteeship and administered by the United Nations Organization itself. Other proposals were made for individual trusteeship under one or more of the victors or even Italy. The foreign ministers were unable to agree, the peace treaty was made, and under the treaty the disposition of the colonies was finally to be made by the General Assembly of the United Nations.

When the General Assembly came to a final decision on the matter in the fall of 1949, the Western powers were unable to dominate the situation. A combination of states—Latin states favorable to Italy and Arab states favorable to independence for what they considered parts of the Arab world—determined the decision. It was decided that Libya should be independent by January 1, 1952. Somaliland should be independent, its independence effective after ten years. In the meantime it should be under trusteeship with Italy as the administering authority. The future status of Eritrea was to be inquired into by a commission reporting by June 15, 1950.

Trieste and the Ruhr

Trieste, not an Italian colony but a part of the Italian metropole, was considered for possible trusteeship by the Foreign Ministers. Their final decision was against bringing it under the international trusteeship system. Instead the Italian peace treaty placed it under a special administration under the Security Council.

The Ruhr, part of the German metropole, was suggested for trusteeship informally, from time to time, immediately after the end of the war.

The Charter does not explicitly limit the application of the trusteeship system to colonies or dependent territories. The objectives of the system, however, seem suited for dependent peoples and areas and not for areas like Trieste or the Ruhr which have been integral parts of sovereign states.

Korea

Korea has been a special problem. The Council of Foreign Ministers, meeting at Moscow in December, 1945, decided that Korea should be independent, but that pending its organization for independence it should be placed for not more than five years under a joint trusteeship of the United States, the United Kingdom, the Soviet Union, and China. This decision was not carried out because of disagreement between the United States and the Soviet Union, who were to arrange for it.

Jerusalem

The problem of Jerusalem was unexpectedly brought back to the Trusteeship Council in December, 1949. In April, 1948, it will be recalled, the General Assembly had refused to take action on the statute of Jerusalem, which had been drawn up at its request by the Trusteeship Council. Meanwhile the city had been divided in fact between Israel and Transjordan. The General Assembly of 1949 adopted a resolution calling on the Trusteeship Council to complete the preparation of the statute and to implement it. The intent of the Assembly's resolutions of November, 1947, and December, 1949, seems to be that the "City of Jerusalem" shall not be a "trust territory" in the sense of Chapter XII of the Charter, but that it shall be administered by the Trusteeship Council for the United Nations Organization.

CONCLUSIONS ON TRUSTEESHIP

The development of the international trusteeship system has been quite different from what the drafters of the Charter anticipated. The system has been more limited in its area of application than had been expected. But the degree of influence of the General Assembly and the Trusteeship Council in the affairs of the trust territories has been greater than was foreseen.

In both the General Assembly and the Trusteeship Council the strong anticolonialism of many of the member states causes them to be unfair to the states that are the administering authorities. Most of the latter, on the other hand, are angered because the Council tries to hold them to a higher degree of care for the peoples of the trust territories than is given to the inhabitants of many areas in many member states. The administering authorities do not like to be expected to create new gardens of Eden for "lesser breeds without the law." They are not unselfish willingly.

Nevertheless, the supervision of the Trusteeship Council encourages the administering authorities to try to demonstrate what some of the planners of the trusteeship system believed—that honest, unselfish, and skilled administration of backward areas will improve the lot of the inhabitants rapidly and without undue expense and that a wise paternalism can make men out of children. If the administering authorities will go further and insulate the trust territories from the political and economic stresses of the outside world, as they are supposed to do, they may find themselves creating areas where life is kinder than it is in metropolitan territories. We may find ourselves wishing to reside in trust territories, or at least to vacation in them.

The General Assembly of 1949 proposed that the flag of the United Nations be flown in trust territories side by side with the flag of the administering authority, since the flag of the United Nations symbolizes the ideals and aspirations proclaimed in the Charter. The resolution is intended to remind us, as the sight of the flag will do, that under the Charter the territory belongs less to those who rule it than to those who live there.

Chapter 15. NON–SELF–GOVERNING TERRITORIES

The establishment of the trusteeship system and the Trusteeship Council by no means exhausts the concern of the United Nations Organization for dependent peoples. The trusteeship system is limited in the areas it covers and the people it concerns. What about the rest of the people scattered all over the world, but mostly in its remote and less developed regions, who do not govern themselves?

When the Charter was drawn up, about one-fourth of the population of the world had not attained the status of full self-government. Now that India, Pakistan, Burma, and other smaller areas have become independent and sovereign states, large numbers of recently subject peoples do completely manage their own affairs. It is still true, however, that 300 million people, about one-eighth of the world's population, continue to live in a dependent status.

Has the United Nations a responsibility for these people? In Chapter XI of the Charter, entitled "Declaration Regarding Non-Self-Governing Territories," it accepts that responsibility.

THE BACKGROUND OF CHAPTER XI

In Chapter 14 on trusteeship it was pointed out that some of the governments making plans for San Francisco took a middle ground on colonial questions. They rejected the concept that immediate independence for all dependent peoples was desirable. But they rejected also the idea that colonial empires should remain areas for unsupervised exploitation by the colonial powers that happened to possess them. The governments most conscious in their thinking on this subject were perhaps those of the United States, Australia, and New Zealand. The government of the United Kingdom, though at that time very conservative, was aware of all aspects of the problem.   Only two public statements dealing with the colonial problem as such had been made.   One was the declaration of March 9, 1942, establishing the Anglo-American Caribbean Commission.   The other was the Australian–New Zealand Agreement (the "Canberra Pact") of January, 1944.

Thought concerning what would be desirable in the general colonial field came to stress three possibilities.   The first was an internationally approved statement of principles which should be followed by metropolitan powers in the administration of their dependencies.   The second was a trusteeship system.   The third was another practical instrument of cooperative action in the colonial field, the regional advisory commission.   The Charter establishes a trusteeship system in Chapters XII and XIII.   It includes a declaration of colonial policy in Chapter XI and incidentally opens the door to very limited United Nations supervision of colonial administration.   And in Chapter XI it also indicates the possibilities of cooperative action in colonial areas, where the regional advisory commission has already in two instances come into existence.

The Declaration Regarding Non-Self-Governing Territories is unique in three ways.   It is the first general statement of policy toward colonies ever made.   It specifically recognizes the principle "that the interests of the inhabitants of these territories are paramount."   And in the obligation to transmit information, it gives the United Nations a lever for some, if only a very limited, supervision over colonial areas.

THE DECLARATION

The Declaration itself (Article 73) consists of one sentence of many words.   It is incapable of accurate paraphrase, and any adequate analysis of it would be far longer than itself.   It must be read, but along with the reading the following summary of its provisions may be useful.

In the Declaration, "members of the United Nations which

have or assume responsibilities for the administration of territories whose peoples have not yet attained a full measure of self-government recognize the principle that the interests of the inhabitants of these territories are paramount" and accept the obligation to promote the well-being of the inhabitants.   To that end they accept the obligation to:

ensure the advancement of those peoples (political, economic, social, and educational)

"develop self-government"; to assist the peoples "in the progressive development of their free political institutions"

"further international peace and security"

"promote constructive measures of development," research, and cooperation for social, economic, and scientific purposes

"transmit regularly to the Secretary-General . . . [information] relating to economic, social, and educational conditions" in the territory.

Apart from the ingenious, comprehensive, and high-minded language of this Declaration, certain specific things stand out.

It is a unilateral and not a joint declaration. This was intentional. Some colonial powers at San Francisco were willing to make such a declaration but unwilling that they should seem to be bound by each other in so doing.

It stresses advancement of all sorts.

It states "self-government" as an objective for all dependent peoples. It does *not* say "self-government or independence" as the comparable objective of the trusteeship system does (Article 76b), for the simple reason that colonial powers led by the United Kingdom refused to approve the Declaration if it mentioned "independence" as a possible objective.

The Declaration makes a vague reference to constructive measures, etc. This vagueness was intended to cover such cooperative activity as those of regional advisory commissions.

The Declaration requires one act—the regular transmission of information to the Secretary-General. But, clearly, if information is transmitted, it will at least become public; it may be discussed by the General Assembly (Article 10); and the General Assembly may make recommendations in relation to it (Article 10). If the General Assembly cannot *control* governments, it is able to bring their activities to public attention.

Danger of Confusion

In the machinery of the United Nations there are thus two separate ways of dealing with dependent territories. One, the trusteeship system, is a specific and clearly defined system of international supervision, but it applies only to a limited and definite set of territories. The other is a system of the mildest sort of supervision, but one which applies to *all* the colonial territories and particularly to those which do not come under the trusteeship system. The trusteeship system is given in Chapters XII and XIII; the other system, in Chapter XI. Since the basic purpose of each is the same, though the machinery is different, and since both emerged from the Trusteeship Committee at San Francisco, the practice of the General Assembly has often been to include the whole colonial area in its discussions and its resolutions. All matters relating to Chapter XI as well as to the trusteeship system are considered in Committee 4 (which is called the Trusteeship Committee). The Secretariat has one department, though divided into two parts, to deal with Chapters XI, XII, and XIII, known as the Department of Trusteeship and Information from Non-Self-Governing Territories. The public and even the official representatives of governments confuse the two systems. It is important, however, to see that they are separate, though closely parallel.

THE GENERAL ASSEMBLY AND THE TRANSMISSION OF INFORMATION

At the First Session of the General Assembly in London an omnibus resolution was passed dealing with trusteeship and also with all non-self-governing territories. As to the latter, it called attention to the fact that Chapter XI of the Charter was in effect and requested the Secretary-General to include in his annual report a summary of information submitted to him under Article 73.

At the Second Part of the First Session in the autumn of 1946, the General Assembly went farther in regard to information from non-self-governing territories. It invited member states transmitting information to send each year by June 30 the most recent information at their disposal and instructed the Secretary-General to summarize and analyze the information transmitted by members, to communicate it to the specialized agencies, and to convene an *ad hoc* committee to examine the information transmitted with a view to making recommendations to the General Assembly.

This machinery in regard to information got fully under way for the 1947 Assembly. Already in 1946 some members had voluntarily transmitted information about their nonmetropolitan territories, and the United States in doing so had ventured to say that Chapter XI would "appear to apply to any territories administered by a Member of the United Nations which do not enjoy the same measure of self-government as the metropolitan area of that Member." Eight members in all (the United States, the United Kingdom, France, Belgium, the Netherlands, Australia, New Zealand, and Denmark) had transmitted information in time to be summarized in 1947. These eight, together with eight members elected by the General Assembly, composed the *ad hoc* Committee, to which were also invited representatives of the Food and Agriculture Organization, International Labour Organisation, UNESCO, the World Health Organization, and the International Trade Organization, in an advisory capacity. The *ad hoc* Committee, like the Trusteeship Council, is balanced between "administering and nonadministering" states.

The *ad hoc* Committee met at Lake Success before the 1947 meeting of the General Assembly and examined the information from the eight members.

The *ad hoc* Committee proposed to the General Assembly five resolutions relating to its work. These resolutions were the subject of much discussion in the Fourth Committee and in the

General Assembly itself. They were all concerned with methods of eliciting full information and with ways in which information transmitted to the Secretary-General should be used. Controversy arose from a difference of opinion as to the speed at which dependent territories should receive full self-government or even independence and the extent to which machinery under the Charter could be used to hold administering powers accountable for their actions in colonial territories. Some powers insisted that Chapter XI, being part of the Charter, was to be implemented by specific machinery and specific requirements on the administering powers. They wanted to create a permanent "colonial committee," an organ for non-self-governing territories fully equal to the Trusteeship Council for trust territories. Some of the far eastern powers—notably China, the Philippines, and India—took this position, as did the Soviet Union and other states under communist direction. At the other extreme were colonial powers who insisted on a restrictive interpretation of Chapter XI and extolled the virtues of colonial systems. They wished to refuse authority to review the information which, according to Article 73e, they had agreed to submit. The United States took a middle position, attempting to liberalize the attitudes of the colonial powers but to ensure that progress should be definitely within the framework of the Charter. The independence of the Philippine Republic and of India, Pakistan, Ceylon, and Burma and the struggles in the Dutch and French areas in Indochina and Indonesia were conspicuous examples of the changes that have come since Chapter XI was written and offered at least some justification for changes in emphasis in interpreting the Charter.

A compromise series of resolutions was adopted by the General Assembly of 1947. The Assembly agreed that there should be a standard form or questionnaire in which information should be transmitted, so that it might be as complete and up to date as possible, and that the Secretary-General should follow this form in his summaries and "should include summaries of such information as may be transmitted on the participation by local populations in local organs of government." It was recommended that the Secretary-General should be authorized to use official publications of members furnishing information, if the publications are transmitted to him, and documents of inter-governmental and scientific bodies, and that he might for purposes of comparison use official statistical information so long as the member state agrees. From the beginning the United States has transmitted information on governmental institutions.

Taking a long step forward—since Article 73e carefully omitted "political" as one of the types of information to be transmitted—the General Assembly voted that, since some member states have transmitted political information, it "considers that the voluntary transmission of such information and its summarizing by the Secretary-General are entirely in conformity with the spirit of Article 73 of the Charter, and should be therefore duly noted and encouraged."

The General Assembly approved the collaboration of the specialized agencies in bringing to the attention of the General Assembly their conclusions as to conditions which are within their respective fields of interest. Finally the General Assembly continued the *ad hoc* Committee by approving for another year a Special Committee of the Fourth Committee to study the information and to make reports and substantive recommendations in functional fields, though not in relation to specific territories. This Committee, like the *ad hoc* Committee, is composed half of administering powers and half of elected members. It met for the first time in Geneva in August, 1948, preliminary to the meeting of the 1948 Assembly.

The Present System

It can be seen that the pledge to transmit information placed in Article 73e of the Charter has found a degree of implementation certainly not contemplated when the Charter was drafted. But conditions have changed. Even a modernized colonialism is hard to maintain. Many members of the United Nations were dependent peoples not long ago. Few members of the United Nations possess empires. Those who do are on the defensive. This is true even of the United States, which has granted so much autonomy to its overseas possessions.

The Reporting Powers

Eight members of the United Nations have reported on non-self-governing territories under their administration: Australia, Belgium, Denmark, France, the Netherlands, New Zealand, the United Kingdom, and the United States. They have reported on a maximum of seventy-four territories; in 1949 the number was only sixty-two. The Canal Zone, reported on in 1946 by the United States, has been excluded in subsequent years owing to the protest of Panama and pending consultations between the two governments. France has ceased to report on nine territories which have come to participate in the French Union. (This grand exemption has seemed difficult to justify, since membership in the French Union has not changed the status of the areas in any important respect. They are neither effectively self-governing nor effectively a part of metropolitan France.) The United Kingdom has ceased to report on Malta, which it admits is not fully self-governing but which it contends is self-governing in all respects in which, if it were not so, it would be reported on under Article 73e.

A number of territories probably not fully self-governing have never been reported on: Newfoundland and Labrador before their incorporation into Canada, Spitzbergen, the Sudan, South-West Africa, and no doubt many others. The point to note, however, is that the Declaration in the Charter puts the obligation of reporting on the member state which administers the area. In 1949 the General Assembly resolved that the United Nations should be informed of any change in the status of a non-self-governing area and that it had power to express its opinion on the principles governing the classification of non-self-governing territories. Undoubtedly reporting states should interpret their obligations broadly, but it is difficult to see how they can be forced to do so.

It has to be noted also that nonmembers of the United Nations, such as Spain and Portugal, do not report on their colonies.

The Information Reported

The "Standard Form for the Guidance of Members in the Preparation of Information to Be Transmitted . . ." begins with an optional category called "general information" which covers political matters. The rest of the Form is strictly social, educational, and economic. The United States and Denmark offer information on governmental institutions freely. The other reporting states with various degrees of stubbornness refuse to do so. Repeated anticolonial efforts to try to force states to report on political development have so far failed. There is no doubt that political information cannot be required under the Charter.

The Special Committee

The United States together with the other reporting states objected to the establishment of the *ad hoc* Committee in 1947. This Committee, now called the Special Committee, was constituted annually until 1949 when it was given a three-year lease of life. The United States, which has tried to mediate between the anticolonial bloc and the small bloc of old colonial powers, proposed this extension of its life, lest the alternative be to make it permanent. The United States also got the Assembly to approve the paying of special attention each year to the information in one field, and for 1950 that field is education. It is perhaps natural that the United States has incurred the resentment of the colonial powers for its efforts to follow a middle path.

The problem for the future is the extent to which colonial powers will continue to follow not merely the letter of the Declaration, narrowly interpreted, but the resolutions of the General Assembly as well. The ability of colonial powers to shore up temporarily the pillars of the imperialist temple must command our admiration if not always our approval.

Other Agencies and Non-Self-Governing Territories

Non-self-governing territories are not the concern of the General Assembly and its Special Committee alone. They are important for the specialized agencies and in the work of the Economic and Social Council and its committees. For many years the International Labour Organisation has concerned itself with social policy for nonmetropolitan territories and in its meeting on July 11, 1947, adopted five conventions on that subject. Dependent territories may become associate members of the World Health Organization. They may also be associate members of the Economic Commission for Asia and the Far East and the Economic Commission for Latin America. Other organs and agencies find in them an important area of action.

REGIONAL ADVISORY COMMISSIONS

Any slight study of the map shows that regionalism, a problem in all international affairs, is a particular consideration in the problem of non-self-governing territories. Such territories exist in all parts of the world. But they are most numerous in certain specific areas, and in these same areas they are most conspicuously divided between different colonial powers. The Caribbean, the Pacific, Southeast Asia, and eastern and western Africa are the particular areas in which constellations of non-self-governing territories glow in semidarkness.

Regional cooperation between colonial powers (occasionally even shared by representatives of the dependent peoples themselves) has seemed a useful aid to progressive policies in the colonial field. In Article 73d the member states pledge themselves "to cooperate with one another and, when and where appropriate, with specialized international bodies with a view to the practical achievement of the social, economic, and scientific purposes set forth in this Article." The only action taken by any organ of the United Nations looking toward regional cooperation in the field of non-self-governing territories was a resolution recommending administering powers to call conferences of non-self-governing peoples. This was passed by the General Assembly on December 14, 1946, but has not been carried into effect.

Two organizations for regional cooperation exist in the field of dependent areas—brought into existence partly out of practical need and partly from the conviction that they would establish a useful pattern.

The Caribbean Commission

The Caribbean Commission is a peacetime expansion of the Anglo-American Caribbean Commission which was one of the brilliant improvisations of the war. On March 9, 1942, the British and American governments created a commission to give aid and assistance to the various islands of the Caribbean which were under either British or American rule. The purpose was the improvement of economic and social conditions in that area, which the war had rendered almost desolate.

The Caribbean, which for a century had become more and more a depressed area, and in some respects almost an international slum, was cut off by the war from its ordinary channels of economic life. And yet, in view of the submarine warfare, it was an area of extreme military importance. Furthermore, the low standard of living in so many of the islands and the general colonial unrest had produced increased agitation for political rights. The Anglo-American Caribbean Commission was carefully excluded from political and military action. But it created a shipping pool for the islands, made possible the importation of food, maintained a radio program, and in the West Indies Conference and the Caribbean Research Council it brought together representatives of the governing and governed communities to consider long-term problems of the area. Under the brilliant leadership of its cochairmen, Sir Frank Stockdale for the United Kingdom and Mr. Charles W. Taussig for the United States—the latter with the assistance of Governor Rexford G. Tugwell of Puerto Rico—it made more than a beginning in social and economic improvement.

The experiment seemed worth continuing and broadening when the war was over, and an expanded Caribbean Commission was created in December, 1945, by including the Dutch and French governments, each of which possessed small but not unimportant islands in the region. An agreement signed by the four governments on October 30, 1946, establishes the Commission to encourage "cooperation among themselves and their territories with a view towards improving the economic and social well-being of the peoples of those territories," and "to promote scientific, technological, and economic development in the Caribbean area"— all this provided that the objectives are "in accord with the principles of the Charter of the United Nations."

The Commission has four national groups of commissioners, and there are four cochairmen. It meets twice a year, and under its auspices a West Indies Conference meets every two years. It has a research council. The Commission itself is, of course, an instrument of the metropolitan powers (though some of the commissioners are members of the dependent peoples), but the Conference has been widely attended by citizens of the islands themselves. The Commission has a central secretariat established on the island of Trinidad. The Commission is "a consultative and advisory body."

The South Pacific Commission

A second regional advisory commission was established in 1947 by the four governments which are members of the Caribbean Commission plus the governments of Australia and New Zealand. It is known as the South Pacific Commission. Its area begins in the west with Netherlands New Guinea and includes the dependent areas in the Pacific east from Netherlands New Guinea and south of the equator. The only United States possession of any importance included is American Samoa.

The area covered by the South Pacific Commission contains many small islands and only one large area (the island of New Guinea) with a numerous population. The islands and groups of islands are scattered over almost limitless spaces of ocean.

Intercommunication in peacetime is largely nonexistent. Life for the natives is relatively easy in a warm though not healthful climate. Disease is widespread, and wealth, except in agriculture and mineral resources, is almost nonexistent. If this area is to participate in the benefits of civilization, as the Western world knows it, cooperative activity is necessary.

The South Pacific Commission owes its existence in part to the proposals of the Australian–New Zealand Agreement of 1944 and in part to the interest of the United States government in regional commissions. Its organization is similar to that of the Caribbean Commission. Its secretariat has been established in Nouméa in (French) New Caledonia. It has a research council. It plans to hold periodic South Pacific conferences in accordance with the resolution recommending such conferences adopted by the General Assembly on December 14, 1946. The first South Pacific Conference will be held in Suva (Fiji) in April, 1950.

The islands of the South Pacific seem admirably suited for the work of such a commission. Difficult political and military problems are few. The islands are scattered, their population is small, and social services and economic aid of various kinds are almost impossible to maintain on a strictly national basis. It is a superb area for inter-governmental cooperation.

These two commissions are not direct agencies of the United Nations. But they illustrate the value of cooperation by member states on a voluntary basis for the general purposes of the Charter and in particular for the well-being of dependent peoples.

THE FUTURE OF CHAPTER XI

When the Charter was being drafted, the trusteeship system and the Trusteeship Council were the focus of the attention given to problems of dependent peoples, and the Declaration on Non-Self-Governing Territories seemed almost an afterthought. Since then, the trusteeship system and the Trusteeship Council have proved extremely important as part of the United Nations system; but however much attention they attract, their area of incidence is small.   The trust territories include areas that are important strategically, politically, and economically, but except for Italian Somaliland, which is to be added to their number by decision of the General Assembly in 1949, they are unlikely to be increased in number.   And they contain a total population of only 17 million.

On the other hand the particular non-self-governing territories on which information is transmitted under Article 73e have a total population of 85 million, are much more important and widely scattered than the trust territories, and their importance relative to the importance of Chapter XI in the United Nations system is clearly increasing.   The problem of "colonialism" is one of the most divisive problems in the United Nations and it focuses most strongly on the Special Committee and on the Fourth Committee of the General Assembly.   Furthermore, the need to raise to a higher economic and educational level the underprivileged people of dependent areas is one which is felt strongly by many colonial powers and was one of the bases of the Point Four program for the undeveloped areas.

The capacity for the growth of the United Nations system in uncontroversial fields is shown nowhere better than in the creation and development of these two regional commissions, that in the Caribbean and that in the South Pacific.

Chapter 16. THE HEADQUARTERS, THE
SECRETARY–GENERAL, THE
SECRETARIAT, AND THE
BUDGET

THE HEADQUARTERS

In the center of any organization, public or private, are people sitting at desks in offices, working with papers which transmit, put into effect, or record the decisions taken loudly and conspicuously in council chambers and in committee rooms. The central offices of all organizations look alike, for they consist merely of men and women sitting at desks covered with papers and telephones. This is true whether the office is that of an army divisional headquarters, a farmers' cooperative, or the government of a sovereign state. The headquarters is the quiet center of such human hurricanes as blow. It is the center of the nervous system of the organization, of its brain.

In the center of the United Nations is a physical headquarters, at present the buildings at Lake Success; a staff, the Secretariat; and a general manager, the Secretary-General. In this place and by these people the United Nations is serviced. And within the Secretariat, because nowhere else can it be done, are handled certain problems of a central sort (like that of the budget) which touch all parts of the Organization but do not fall within the special province of any other organ.

At one time the English king wore his crown each year in three places—Westminster, Winchester, and Gloucester. More recently the elected assemblies of Connecticut met alternately in Hartford and New Haven. Today governments must have definite headquarters, at least to house their records and their central staffs.

330

The United Nations—a government in embryo, or perhaps an awkward colt which is not yet a stallion—must have a headquarters for its records and its staff and for most of its meetings, though it will continue till the end of time to hold conferences in all sorts of places all over the world.

Finding a Headquarters

Where should the headquarters be? The problem is even greater than that of finding the correct site for a national capital. London and Paris, Rome and Lisbon, all are natural capitals. The United States, Canada, and Australia have located their capitals in places chosen for political reasons. Washington, Canberra, and Ottawa lie near the frontiers of rivalry and possible conflict.

An international capital should be neutral, convenient of access, pleasant, comfortable, orderly, and properly related to the centers of power.

The United Nations was fortunate in its origin in San Francisco. It has since been unfortunate in the local habitations in which it has had to develop. Furthermore, the Secretariat was obliged from the beginning to grow beyond its strength and to expand its cradle into an office building.

Successive commissions and committees were formed to find a home for the United Nations. The obvious place was the Palais des Nations on the outskirts of Geneva in Switzerland, which had been built for the League of Nations and was the only set of buildings in the world both suitable and available. Most sensible people and many delegations favored Geneva. But in 1946 Geneva was impossible. Switzerland, a neutral and a neutralized state which had been barely hospitable to the League, would probably not even join the United Nations. (It has not done so.) The Soviet Union was engaged in a political quarrel with Switzerland. And Geneva lay in the midst of a ruined Europe, too far from the new world of America and the Pacific and much too far from the United States which was to be the chief support of the United Nations.

If the United Nations could not meet in Geneva, as nearly neutral ground as could be found, there was perhaps no other reasonable home for it in Europe. The General Assembly, therefore, voted by a small majority that the seat of the United Nations should be in the United States, that its headquarters should be established near New York City, and that the interim Headquarters should be in New York City.

An apparently unending discussion in the General Assembly as to which United States site would be best was concluded in December, 1946, when Mr. John D. Rockefeller, Jr., offered to pay for a site on the East Side of Manhattan Island between 42d and 48th Streets. This site was accepted by the General Assembly. Plans were drawn up, and the only obstacle was finance. It was finally suggested, with the approval of the President of the United States, that the United States should loan the United Nations 65 million dollars for the construction of the necessary buildings on the approved site. The United States Congress put off approving the loan until its special session in 1948.

The huge skyscraper that will house the Secretariat is now under construction. Its cornerstone was laid on October 24, 1949, United Nations Day. The building should be fully occupied before the General Assembly meets in 1951.

Interim Headquarters

Meanwhile the United Nations had to have a temporary home— an "interim Headquarters" in New York City. For the first few months after migration from London, the Secretary-General was able to rent buildings from Hunter College in the Bronx. This interim Headquarters was temporary and inconvenient. And where would the General Assembly meet in the fall of 1946? New York City offered the City Building at Flushing Meadow on Long Island. Part of the Sperry Gyroscope Plant at Lake Success (8 miles from Flushing Meadow) was available for the Secretariat. On August 15, 1946, the Secretariat and the Councils established themselves at Lake Success on the basis of a lease expiring on July 1, 1949, and renewable for two years.

In October the adjourned 1946 Assembly met at Flushing Meadow, as did the First Special Session in the spring of 1947, the Second Annual Session in the fall of 1947, the Special Session in the spring of 1948, and the sessions in 1949.

Dissatisfaction with the inconvenience of the accommodations at Lake Success and Flushing Meadow, the expense, and the slowness of the United States Congress in approving a loan for the construction of the Headquarters buildings encouraged certain European states, which had never liked the United States as headquarters, to make an effort to reverse the 1946 decision. As a preliminary move, they persuaded the General Assembly of 1947 to vote to meet in 1948 in Europe. The choice of the city was left to the Secretary-General advised by a committee. The Secretary-General chose Paris. Because the General Assembly was to meet in Europe, the Economic and Social Council decided to hold its summer 1948 meeting in Geneva, and at that meeting decided to hold its summer meeting of 1949 in the same place. Other agencies of the United Nations met in Europe in 1948. The Security Council followed the General Assembly to Geneva and then returned to New York.

The Headquarters Today

The plenary meetings of the General Assembly are held at the City Building in Flushing Meadow. Its committees meet at Lake Success, where the Councils and the Secretariat are established.

Lake Success presents special difficulties to members of the Secretariat, to delegates, and to the public. Members of the Secretariat, who work a standard day and week and must be in their offices at nine o'clock, have found housing and transportation difficult. Lake Success lies at that point where Long Island becomes thoroughly suburban, after the outskirts of the City of New York have been passed. Officials and employees must live either in an expensive part of the suburbs of a great city, far from its center, or they must commute, with distance and inconvenience as handicaps.

The delegates of the member states are only a little more fortunate. Most of them reside, more or less temporarily, at hotels in midtown Manhattan. Such delegations as have office headquarters maintain them in Manhattan. From their hotels or headquarters a fifty-minute drive takes them to Lake Success. Flushing Meadow is a little nearer. Two hours a day are spent by the delegate in going to and from his work, whether he be the chief representative of his government at the General Assembly or a minor member of his nation's staff. In Manhattan and at Lake Success he can do his work adequately, but he wastes time between.

For members of the public the approach to the United Nations is a serious excursion. If the headquarters were near other New York City attractions, the visitor might stroll in and out, as do the visitors to the congresses and parliaments of the world. In Washington the tourist can reach the Capitol easily and can stand in line for the Senate or House galleries. And he does. In London the Houses of Parliament, in Paris the National Assembly and Council of the Republic are convenient and accessible. A short bus or train ride, or a taxi for the rich, and you are there. A trip to Lake Success, however, must be planned and is likely to take a whole day.

The determined visitor benefits by an excellent system which the Secretariat has worked out. He can telephone and can have a seat held at the reservation desk. And the General Assembly and Council chambers can accommodate a reasonable number of visitors.

Then the visitor goes—in his own car, if he wishes freedom and convenience, otherwise by public transport. Trains from the Pennsylvania Station in New York reach Great Neck in half an hour (and run half hourly), and busses to the Headquarters take another ten minutes. The reverse journey is the same.

Within the Headquarters itself, things are made convenient in spite of the crowding. Well-trained United Nations guards and considerate members of the Secretariat do what they can to help the stranger, and he is surprisingly free to roam.

Meetings in Public

The pattern adopted by the United Nations for its principal organs is essentially democratic. Their meetings are open—except special meetings for special purposes. The General Assembly is a great gathering of the representatives of the member nations and has all the lengths of boredom and moments of interest with which spectators of national legislatures are so familiar. The Councils are smaller, more informal, more directly purposive, and they show international cooperation or rivalry on an easily comprehensible scale.

Since the public meetings of the United Nations are held in the suburbs of New York City, most of the visitors are Americans. The press of the world, however, is well-represented. Every meeting place of the principal organs is provided with a large press gallery, and reporters and delegates mingle freely. As a result the United Nations is well-reported, and information about its activities is full and far-flung. In the United States *The New York Times* and *New York Herald Tribune* furnish the best accounts of its doings, day by day.

Languages and Interpretation

The problem of languages invariably troubles an international assembly. English, as the language of two of the principal members of the Security Council, is the native language of more of the persons concerned, as delegates, members of the Secretariat, and visitors, than any other. French, as the traditional language of diplomacy and the language of that one of the principal powers which all the others desire to conciliate, has been given an equally privileged position. These two have been "working languages" of the United Nations since San Francisco. From the beginning, attendants at meetings could follow discussions directly if they knew either English or French. Members of the Secretariat were to be able to use one; they should be able to use both. Three other languages are also "official languages," by custom dating from San Francisco, and Russian, Chinese, and

Spanish, as well as English and French, are the languages in which official documents eventually appear. At the 1948 General Assembly the Spanish-speaking countries, with the aid of the Arab bloc, got a resolution passed adding Spanish to the list of working languages—a convenience, but also an expense, to the Organization.

At first the traditional practice was followed, and speeches were interpreted by oral interpreters directly after they had been made. A considerable waste of time resulted. The method of simultaneous interpretation has now been adopted. Each delegate to the General Assembly or to one of the Councils has before him on his desk a small microphone which picks up his voice and sends it throughout the chamber and also to the interpreters, who are shut off but not concealed by a glass front to the gallery in which they sit. As the speaker talks, interpreters in all the official languages, other than that which he may be using, make an oral translation sentence by sentence or sometimes phrase by phrase. The delegates and their advisers, the members of the Secretariat who are present, and the persons in the galleries all find on their chairs small machines through which they can hear the speech or its interpretation in any one of the five languages. The instrument is a small radio receiving set, provided with earphones. Most delegates listen to the discussions directly or use the machine only for purposes of amplification. During speeches in a language which they do not understand, they can use the earphones entirely, switching the dial to that language which is most intelligible to them. In many cases, however, the delegates will use one earphone for the interpretation and will keep the other ear free for direct sounds from the chamber.

It is possible, for instance, that a question-and-answer discussion may be conducted between a French speaker and an English speaker, neither of them knowing the other's language. The questions in French are heard in interpretation by the English speaker over his earphone. He replies immediately in English, and his interlocutor receives the reply in French from the interpreters' gallery over his own earphone. A further convenient

subtlety is the fact that a speech in indifferent and badly pronounced English may sometimes be better understood by one
who listens to the interpretation in another language.

For reasons of national or cultural pride, the representatives
of French-speaking and Russian-speaking nations ordinarily use
French and Russian for their public utterances, however good
their English may be. Members of the Arab League states and
Orientals are likely to make their speeches in English. If the
headquarters of the United Nations remains in the United States,
English will become more and more the working language in
actual practice.

The Secretariat Is Everywhere

Here and there, sometimes numerous, sometimes few, but everywhere in the corridors and chambers of Lake Success are the members of the Secretariat. They have prepared the agenda which
lies on the tables before the delegates, and the documents which
are distributed to the delegates by one of their number over in the
corner. They fill the interpreters' gallery. They take steno-
graphic notes of what is said (and also record it by machine)
and will prepare and process the records. They chat in the
lounge with the delegates because they must be up to date in
the substance of what goes on. They are represented by an
assistant secretary (or his deputy) in each council meeting—a
man who probably knows more about the business of the council
than its chairman, and certainly surpasses in knowledge most of
its members. When an important subject is up for debate, they
will slip into chairs in the corner of the council chamber. Usually,
however, they are to be found in their offices, to which most of
the space at Lake Success is devoted.

The multitudes of miscellaneous people at Lake Success—
guards and delegates, chauffeurs, ambassadors, typists and trans-
lators, economists and radio experts—private citizens, delegates,
advisers, members of the United Nations staff—circle around in
ordered confusion. Coordination is the work of the Secretariat.
The Secretariat is the responsibility of the Secretary-General.

THE SECRETARY-GENERAL

The Secretary-General is the spider in the center of the web. He is the most important person in the United Nations Organization. He is present personally or by deputy at all its meetings. He chooses and directs the entire Secretariat and manages the headquarters and the business affairs of the Organization. He has large authority to propose and many opportunities to suggest. He is not a "chief executive" (like the President of the United States) or even a chief minister, but he has powers unusual in a secretary or even a secretary-general. The Charter intends him to exercise an initiative of his own and to coordinate the work of the other organs of the United Nations. Mr. Trygve Lie has not yet shown those qualities which made Sir Eric Drummond, the first Secretary-General of the League of Nations, the fulcrum of all its activities. But he is an admirable official, and the possibility is there. The Charter does not prevent—indeed it invites— the Secretary-General to be the "boss" of the General Assembly, the *Éminence Grise* of the Security Council, the elder statesman of the Economic and Social Council and Trusteeship Council, and the great white father of the member states—as well as the benevolent despot of Lake Success.

The Secretary-General as Executive

No doubt the experience of the League of Nations had something to do with the granting of a certain amount of what is usually called "executive authority" to the Secretary-General. The League had been headless in theory and in practice. The Assembly of the League, in the long run its most important organ, had elected a president for each of its annual sessions, but he lacked any authority except when the Assembly was actually gathered together. The Council of the League, which came to meet regularly three times a year, had a president for each session, and after the session for which he was chosen and until the choice of his successor, he possessed the power to recall the Council to a further session. But he was merely a chairman of the Council for the time being. The League had a Secretary-General who was the head of the Secretariat, the only part of the League in permanent and continuing existence, but he had no authority except as the head of the Secretariat. Sir Eric Drummond, who served as Secretary-General of the League from its organization until 1933, was a man of tact and initiative, and during his tenure of his position, he was both the fulcrum on which the organization turned and an effective part of the force that moved it. This position of his was, however, personal. His successor, less gifted and much more timid, allowed the League to become merely a congerie of disconnected units, uncoordinated and unactivated.

The United Nations, being also essentially a league of sovereign states, can hardly have a chief executive with large authority in initiative and in policy formation. Its Security Council was perhaps intended to be an executive council. According to the Charter, it "shall be so organized as to be able to function continuously"; it is so organized and it does so function. It is more nearly an executive council than was the Council of the League. But it has so established its own procedure that its chairmanship rotates monthly. And though some chairmen are energetic, just as some are lethargic, no one of them is in office long enough to secure a firm hold. Furthermore, though very nearly supreme in its field of activity relating to international peace and security, the Security Council has no authority in many fields of United Nations activity—unlike the League Council, which was competent in all fields of League activity.

The General Assembly of the United Nations chooses a president for each session. Spaak (Belgium) Aranha (Brazil), Arce (Argentina), Evatt (Australia), and Rómulo (Philippines), who have held this position have had great influence, but only so long as the General Assembly was actually meeting. They have no interim authority. The Economic and Social Council and the Trusteeship Council both elect presidents annually, but both these organs have specialized duties.

The Secretary-General of the United Nations Organization,

then, has been so instituted as to fill a part, if only a small part, of the gap which exists when no other person can exercise initiative or can cause the Organization's machinery to function. The Dumbarton Oaks Proposals went so far as to give the Secretary-General the right to bring to the attention of the Security Council any matter which "in his opinion" threatened international peace and security. The Charter goes much further. Not only is the Secretary-General the head and the director of the entire staff of the Secretariat, not only does he act as Secretary-General in all meetings of the General Assembly and the Councils (and thereby possess every opportunity to exercise personal influence), but he is also empowered to exercise such other functions as are entrusted to him by any of these organs. He makes an annual report to the General Assembly on the entire work of the Organization and he has the special and clearly political function of bringing to the attention of the Security Council any matter which "in his opinion" may threaten the maintenance of international peace and security. His influence is intended to be great, but, more than that, he may take a certain public initiative of his own.

The Rules of Procedure of the General Assembly give him a modified form of initiative in relation to that body. Rule 62 reads that "The Secretary-General or a member of the Secretariat designated by him as his representative, may at any time make to the General Assembly either oral or written statements concerning any question under consideration by it."

The position of the Secretary-General is enhanced by the fact that the Charter lists the Secretariat as one of the six principal organs of the United Nations.

A very self-confident and strong-minded Secretary-General may therefore exercise a large amount of initiative which would be no less strong by being implied rather than stated in the Charter. The first Secretary-General of the United Nations, Mr. Lie, has from time to time made statements which indicated his desire to intervene actively in matters of United Nations policy. These statements have always been received with approval by those member governments whom they seemed to favor and have been disapproved by opposing governments. His statements made on policy in 1946 were complained of as being pro-Soviet; in 1948 the Soviet representative in the General Assembly complained that the Secretary-General's annual report was anti-Soviet.

At times the Secretary-General has taken a useful initiative, as when he had prepared a legal opinion that after India and Pakistan became independent, India would still be a member of the United Nations but Pakistan would need separate admission. In 1948 he recruited fifty members of the Secretariat as a small Palestinian guard force, in view of the fact that the United Nations had so far created no armed forces at all.

Mr. Lie has shown a clear desire to keep the exercise of his public initiative within narrow bounds and not to attempt the role of a great international policy maker. A rasher man might ruin the position of the entire Secretariat by intervention when intervention was indiscreet. A more ingenious man, who proved able to find the passage between the Scylla of the Soviet Union and the Charybdis of the United States, might lead the wanderers more quickly home. On the whole, however, the United Nations has been singularly fortunate in its first Secretary-General.

THE SECRETARIAT

The Secretariat at present consists of about four thousand persons. They are chosen, organized, and directed by the Secretary-General under regulations made by the General Assembly.

Charter Provisions

The Charter expresses itself briefly in regard to the Secretariat. There is to be a Secretary-General and "such staff as the Organization may require." The Secretary-General is "chief administrative officer of the Organization." (All this is contained in Article 97.) He himself, or by deputy, acts as secretary of all the meetings of the General Assembly and the councils (Article 98). He and his staff "shall not seek or receive instructions from any government or from any other authority external to the

Organization" nor shall they behave other than as international officials responsible to the Organization alone (Article 100).

"The staff shall be appointed by the Secretary-General under regulations established by the General Assembly" (Article 101.1). Appropriate staffs are assigned to the various organs of the United Nations, but these staffs are all part of one Secretariat (Article 101.2). "The paramount consideration in the employment of the staff and in the determination of the conditions of service shall be the necessity of securing the highest standards of efficiency, competence, and integrity." But, as the very next sentence goes on to say, "Due regard shall be paid to the importance of recruiting the staff on as wide a geographical basis as possible" (Article 101.3).

The precedents which the delegates at San Francisco had in mind were two. The first was the Secretariat of the League of Nations, which had been a small, efficient, and, on the whole, non-political body, not too highly influenced by pressures from the member governments. The second was the example of the national civil services of the more mature and well-organized national states which were to be members of the United Nations. A competent international secretariat can exist, just as a competent national secretariat or civil service can exist, though there are manifold difficulties in its way.

What was, and must be, assumed is that the Secretariat shall be one body, organized on hierarchical principles, whose members are responsible to the Secretary-General and to him alone. The important part to be played by the General Assembly, as representing the great international constituency, is to lay down rules by which the Secretary-General must be guided and then annually, by its control over the budget and the activities of the United Nations, to make the broad decisions within the ambit of which the Secretariat will work.

The Executive Committee and the Preparatory Commission, working in London, went thoroughly into questions of the Secretariat (with the help of the Advisory Group of Experts), and their decisions, as modified and adopted by the First Part of the First

Session of the General Assembly, are the basis on which the Secretariat has been established. The Advisory Committee on Administrative and Budgetary Questions continues scrutiny over the Secretariat on behalf of the General Assembly, and reports to the Fifth Committee of that body.

The Organization of the Secretariat

The Secretariat, as at present organized, is managed by one Secretary-General, eight Assistant Secretaries-General, some fifty directors or persons of similar rank, and an appropriate number of chiefs of section. Under these are about four thousand other employees. The classified service, which includes all under the rank of director, is organized in nineteen grades.

The Assistant Secretaries-General

Each Assistant Secretary-General presides over a department and is chosen from a different member state:

Security Council Affairs. Arcady A. Sobolev, Soviet Union, replaced on April 28, 1949, by Konstantin E. Zinchenko, Soviet Union.

Economic Affairs. David Owen, United Kingdom.

Social Affairs. Henri Laugier, France.

Trusteeship and Information from Non-Self-Governing Territories. Victor Chi-Tsai Hoo, China.

Public Information. Benjamin Cohen, Chile.

Legal. Ivan Kerno, Czechoslovakia.

Conference and General Services. Adrian Pelt, the Netherlands.

Administrative and Financial Services. Byron Price, the United States.

A ninth Assistant Secretary-General was appointed in December, 1947, as Assistant Secretary-General for the Executive Office of the Secretary-General and for General Coordination. The position was given to Mr. R. G. A. Jackson of Australia, who had been senior Deputy Director-General of UNRRA. The position was abolished by the Secretary-General as of September 1, 1948.

Of the Assistant Secretaries-General, three had been closely connected in one way or another with the League of Nations, five had been in the diplomatic service of their countries, and four had been on their countries' delegations to the San Francisco Conference. In the absence of the Secretary-General an Assistant Secretary-General becomes Acting Secretary-General.

Subdivisions of the Secretariat

The size of the staff subordinate to any particular Assistant Secretary-General depends on the functions which his department must perform. The Department of Security Council Affairs serves the Security Council in its manifold activities and its subordinate agencies and also serves as Secretariat to the First (Political and Security) Committee of the General Assembly. The Department of Economic Affairs serves the Second (Economic and Financial) Committee of the General Assembly, the Economic and Social Council in its economic functions, and various subsidiary organs of the Economic and Social Council, of which the regional economic commissions are among the most important. The Department of Social Affairs serves the Economic and Social Council, the Third Committee (Social, Humanitarian, and Cultural) of the General Assembly, and many commissions. The Department of Trusteeship and Information from Non-Self-Governing Territories serves the Trusteeship Council and the Fourth (Trusteeship) Committee of the General Assembly. Through these departments are served not only the General Assembly but also the three councils. The four other departments of the Secretariat are more specifically staff departments but service also the Fifth (Administrative and Budgetary) and Sixth (Legal) Committees of the General Assembly. But all the Departments are advisory to the Secretary-General, and though their staffs may be generally assigned to particular duties, they are all available for any work which the Secretariat may be called upon to perform.

Regulations

The members of the Secretariat live under a comprehensive set of staff regulations which follow the best civil service practices.

Salaries were originally not considered a problem. The Secretary-General and Assistant Secretaries-General have adequate salaries and allowances for their important representative functions. The Secretary-General receives a net (*i.e.*, without taxes) salary of $20,000, allowance of $20,000, and a residence. The Assistant Secretaries-General receive $13,500 and an allowance which may be $11,500. The directors and the other high-ranking officials are also well-compensated. Other ranks have found their compensation rendered none too adequate by the expense of working at Lake Success, living within commuting distance, and by the rising cost of living in the United States. From the point of view of the members of the Secretariat, the salaries are seldom more than adequate. But since salaries are paid in dollars, the Secretariat is expensive from the point of view of most member states of the United Nations.

As to hours and conditions of work, leave, pensions, insurance, and so on, the rules laid down by the General Assembly follow the best practices of the best civil services of the member states.

Choice of Personnel

The problem of choice of personnel has been a serious one, and most of the difficulties are incapable of quick resolution. The Charter requires two things: competence and geographical distribution. In practice the two criteria have been reversed in importance. The United Nations is an organization of sovereign states. Each member contributes to the budget of the Organization and has its own special interests in the work of the Organization. As a result each member can insist on placing some of its nationals in the Secretariat, and in as high places as possible, partly for the influence that they may exert on the work of the Organization and partly because good jobs are political plums. The higher positions in the Secretariat have been allocated informally to the member states capable of exercising enough pressure to secure them. Furthermore, it is inconceivable that an important post in the Secretariat should be filled by a person who is not in good standing with his government. In practice, therefore, the most important posts have been filled on national nomination, and no post could be filled against national protest. The important appointments have gone to members of the government service of the countries concerned. In other words, "geographical distribution" has been the first criterion to be met. At the same time, it has been noted that the national of a member state, however conformative to his country's point of view he may have been when in its service, will often become internationally minded when he takes a United Nations post, fortified by a five-year or indefinite contract and by his obligation to take instructions only from the United Nations itself.

One of the curious results of the situation is that, though the United States pays a considerable share of the United Nations budget and though Americans are readily available since the headquarters is in the United States, Americans are numerous in the lesser ranks of the Secretariat and rare in its higher ranks.

Efficiency

Men experienced in international conferences and in the work of the League of Nations predicted at San Francisco that about one-third of the members of the Secretariat which the United Nations would establish would be useless for any practical purpose: they would be there as "political" or national appointments, for political reasons they would be uncontrollable and unreasonable, and the organization would have to accept them as deadwood. At the start the United Nations Secretariat, because it had to be built up so quickly, probably contained more than this proportion of deadwood. Certain member states with claims to appointments do not normally produce qualified persons in many fields of United Nations activity, and yet it is unwise to choose only from the trained, for their training may be one-sided. For example, powers without colonies do not usually produce colonial experts, and on the other hand most colonial experts are found in the service of the imperial powers and hold the point of view of the metropolitan governments rather than the point of view adopted in Chapter XI of the Charter. Or again, few nations have adequate statistical services, few nations have scientific control of narcotic drugs or of deficiency diseases, and when they possess competent experts in these fields, they wish to keep them at home.

The Western European standards of efficiency in the conduct of professional and semiprofessional jobs are only beginning to be imitated by other nations. The person skilled enough to occupy a professional post in the United Nations Secretariat must, if the organization is to function, be in his office most of the time during the working day. And yet, according to the standards of many countries, if he is sufficiently educated and important to occupy such a position, he is too important to be held down to any administrative requirements whatsoever.

An organization regulated physically by clocks and timetables and administratively by rule rather than by administrative discretion is still rare in the world. In the interests of the United Nations as a genuinely international organization, the Secretariat must carry this burden of inefficiency, and it may be hoped that good examples will improve bad manners. Meantime, officials from such countries as the Netherlands and New Zealand will help the representatives of the great powers in establishing an organization not too lacking in efficiency.

Technical Competence

Individual competence in specialized jobs is difficult to discover easily, and the problem of choosing personnel, even when political considerations are not overruling, has been, and will continue to be, a difficult job. If the Secretariat is well-directed, however, its officers will become better fitted for their jobs. They already show a service-mindedness which indicates that the Secretariat will grow more and more to be a group with a feeling of unity.

Members of the Secretariat, like those of the civil service of any democratic country, must be accessible, at least to delegates, and agreeable and self-sacrificing to a high degree. At the same time, they must perform tasks which can best be done under protection of time and of professional study. The Secretariat has already been able to enjoy the service of many persons whose role is essentially research, or at least the accumulation and interpretation of information. It may in time become a body learned in all international problems as well as a group of technicians serving an elaborate conference system.

The actual functions of the Secretariat are, of course, advisory. Only when they assist the Secretary-General to make policy decisions are they more than servants of the General Assembly, the councils, and the other agencies of the United Nations. In particular they prepare for meetings of the various organs, assist their officers in the conduct of the meetings, report the meetings, and produce the vast quantity of printed material which is needed by the organs of the United Nations, by the member governments, and even by the public. As a means of doing these things well, they must become learned in the subject matter and skilled in the techniques of the substantive business whose progress they assist. They must never try to formulate policy, but they must always facilitate the work of the policy makers. Each part of the United Nations Organization must have in the Secretariat persons who devote themselves to the easy working of that organ.

The Future of the Secretariat

The Secretariat of the United Nations, like its other organs, is in a formative stage. It has come to perform its routine work with more than routine efficiency. In other respects it varies in competence.

To Americans the Secretariat seems foreign, to foreigners it seems strongly Americanized. The provisional basis on which much of it was hastily recruited in 1946 and 1947 will be modified as new recruitment occurs and particularly as the five-year contracts given originally to many of the higher officials expire and as the officials in the higher grades attain indeterminate appointments. A proposal to intensify the "geographical" distribution of its members, made in the General Assembly of 1948, was a movement to increase the amount of political patronage—one of the greatest dangers the Secretariat faces. But the Secretary-General was able to report in 1949 that forty-six of the member states had adequate representation of their nationals in the Secretariat.

The Budget

The control of the finances of the United Nations is one of the chief functions of the Secretariat, though the decision as to the size of the budget, the purposes for which it is used, and the scale of contributions are political questions left to the General Assembly.

Charter Provisions

What the Charter says about finance is simple and clear.
Article 17:

1. The General Assembly shall consider and approve the budget of the Organization.
2. The expenses of the Organization shall be borne by the Members as apportioned by the General Assembly.
3. The General Assembly shall consider and approve any financial and budgetary arrangements with specialized agencies referred to in Article 57 and shall examine the administrative budgets of such specialized agencies with a view to making recommendations to the agencies concerned.

The first two of these paragraphs deal with the finances of the United Nations Organization itself. They follow League precedent, which was good in the sense that it worked. They put the authority in the General Assembly—the only possible place, since it is composed of all members, and all members will be called upon to contribute.

The General Assembly decides when and where to spend

money. It also levies contributions on the member states. Contributions levied on sovereign states which cannot be forced to pay them are an unsatisfactory way of raising money, as the United States discovered in its early years. But there is no alternative, for the United Nations Organization has no dealings but with governments; it cannot tax individuals. Indeed, a basic weakness of any inter-governmental organization, even so great a one as the United Nations, is seen in its inability to finance itself except through contributions. Yet even the most extreme American proponent of "world government" would probably hesitate to establish a system by which a United Nations tax inspector would be authorized to look over his books.

A member state two years in arrears in payment of contributions may be deprived of its vote in the General Assembly (Article 19). Presumably continual refusal to pay might eventually be interpreted as persistent violation of the Charter and ground for the expulsion of the state from the Organization (Article 6).

Like any governmental budget voted by a parliament, the budget of the United Nations is in the final essence political. Its preparatory stages, however, have been entrusted to the hands of experts.

Drawing Up the United Nations Budget

The Advisory Group of Experts, chosen by the Executive Secretary of the Preparatory Commission, made a report which was the basis of the Preparatory Commission's comprehensive, and generally acceptable, outline of financial organization for the United Nations. The Secretary-General, when appointed, continued this Advisory Group to advise him. The first budget of the United Nations, which was the provisional budget for the year ending December 31, 1946, was drawn up with their help.

The General Assembly, as soon as it organized, set up a main committee (Fifth Committee) on Administrative and Budgetary Questions. This Committee (which, of course, consists of representatives of all member states) is aided in its work by a standing committee of the General Assembly composed of nine experts selected as individuals. This committee of experts, called the Advisory Committee on Administrative and Budgetary Questions, examines the budget as prepared by the Secretary-General and makes recommendations to the Assembly. There is also the Committee on Contributions, composed of ten experts serving as individuals.

The budgetary procedure of the United Nations is, then, as follows.

The Department of Administrative and Fiscal Services of the Secretariat draws up the annual budget for the Secretary-General. It is examined and commented on by the Standing Committee on Administrative and Budgetary Questions. (The budget and the comments are published as parts of the Secretary-General's annual financial report.) When the General Assembly meets in the autumn, its Fifth Committee reviews the budget and sends it to the General Assembly in plenary meeting. The final decision is made there.

The Secretary-General (or, in other words, the appropriate division of the Secretariat) collects the contributions, pays out the money, and keeps the accounts. The fiscal year of the United Nations coincides with the calendar year. The budget and the contributions are stated in United States dollars.

The Budget for 1946

The first budget of the United Nations was a provisional budget for 1946 voted by the General Assembly on February 13, 1946. It was necessarily very tentative, since 1946 was the year in which the organs of the United Nations were being established and the staff of the Secretariat recruited. The provisional budget was summarized as follows:

For the General Assembly and Councils	$ 1,500,000
Secretariat	16,510,750
International Court of Justice	617,250
Unforeseen expenses	2,000,000
Expenses of the Preparatory Commission and General Assembly to January 31, 1946	872,000
Total	$21,500,000

The final budget for 1946 was lower than the provisional budget
—$19,390,000 in all.

At the same time it voted this budget, the General Assembly
set up the Working Capital Fund of 25 million dollars from which
advances could be made to the budget. Contributions to this
fund were made on the basis of the average of the first and second
years' scales of contributions to the Food and Agriculture Organization. As soon as the General Assembly in the Second Part of
its First Session decided on a basis of contributions, contributions
to the capital fund were made according to that scale, and each
state's previous contributions were a credit against its new obligations.

The Committee on Contributions, meeting during the summer
of 1946, made estimates of the ability to pay of member states.
They used as evidence total national income, corrected for wartime dislocations and for availability of foreign exchange, and as
related to per capita national incomes. The Fifth Committee,
not unexpectedly, modified the resulting scale of contributions.
The chief point at issue was the placing of floors and ceilings on
contributions. The United States protested against its apportionment of 49.89 per cent of the total contribution. Their representative warned that disproportionate assessment threatened to
impair the sovereign equality of nations, but they accepted an
apportionment of 39.89 per cent. The next largest apportionment
for 1946 was that of the United Kingdom, 11.98 per cent. That
of the Soviet Union, the third in size, was 6.62 per cent. The ap-
portionments as made in 1946 have remained substantially unchanged.

Later Budgets

The budget for 1947, as finally voted in November of that
year, was $28,616,568. The great increase over 1946 was in ex-
penses of personnel and common services, since the Secretariat
was expanding and the headquarters were in full use. The capital
fund for 1947 was reduced to 20 million dollars and the Secretary-
General was authorized to draw on it for unforeseen or for extraor-

dinary expenses—the prior consent of the Advisory Committee being necessary beyond 3 million dollars for these two categories. He was also authorized to lend from the fund to certain specialized agencies to help them to get started.

The budget for 1948 as finally passed by the General Assembly in November, 1948, was $34,825,195. The scale of contributions remained the same as in 1947, except for minor adjustments. The Working Capital Fund was maintained at 20 million dollars for two reasons: first, because some members do not ordinarily make their annual contributions until late in the fiscal year (the United States, for instance, has a fiscal year beginning July 1 and therefore cannot normally pay until after that time); and, second, to facilitate advances toward unexpected expenses incurred during the year. For such things as these, national governments borrow. The United Nations does not borrow to meet current expenses. It can spend only what it has.

The budget for 1949, approved in December, 1948, fixed a total gross amount of $43,487,128. The net assessment was expected to be $41,650,814. According to the estimates for 1950, the total expenditure for that year was to have been under the expenditure for 1949. In fact, the General Assembly in December, 1949, approved a budget of $49,641,773, but this amount included 8 million dollars for the international regime of Jerusalem.

Of the 40 million dollars which seem now to be established as a budgetary norm, the largest allocations for 1949 and 1950 are roughly as follows:

Sessions of Assembly, Councils, Commissions, and Committees	$ 2,000,000
Special conferences and investigations	5,000,000
New York headquarters	27,000,000
European office	4,000,000
Regional economic commissions outside Europe	1,000,000

The cost of the Court is about $650,000.

The Working Capital Fund has been kept at 20 million dollars and is now fully paid up. Assets of the League of Nations to the amount of about 10 million dollars have been transferred to the United Nations.

In the General Assemblies of 1947 and 1948 some states demanded economy and objected even to the modest totals that were proposed—totals of which they would pay only a small proportion. Conspicuous among them were two great powers, the United Kingdom and the Soviet Union. The contributions assessed on these members are exceedingly small for such large and wealthy nations. The problem of dollar exchange is not serious, taking into consideration their total national budgets and their total foreign trade. Their reasons for demanding economy must, therefore, be political. In the case of the Soviet Union the motives are clear: it opposes, or at least lacks enthusiasm for, many of the miscellaneous activities of the United Nations Organization, each of which costs money. The position of the United Kingdom, one of the chief beneficiaries of the United Nations, is less logical. A similar disposition toward economy appears from time to time on the part of lesser governments. The attitude sometimes felt by the taxpayer toward his government is reproduced in the attitude of his government toward the United Nations —he does not want to support a host of lazy bureaucrats living in luxury on Long Island, whose only relation to him is to interfere with what he wants to do. The desire for economy which so badly damaged the League of Nations may become a serious problem for the United Nations.

Administrative versus Program (or Operational) Budgets

The United Nations budget we have been discussing is for the most part what is called an administrative budget. That is, it is spent to provide physical headquarters space, salaries, traveling expenses, telephone calls, paper, printing, and other overhead expenses. Only a limited part of it has gone even to the expense of United Nations commissions and their staffs operating in the Balkans, in Indonesia, in Korea, in Palestine, and elsewhere. No money as yet has been appropriated or spent to do the sort of things that all governments do today, and not least the government of the United States: to subsidize agriculture, to prevent disease, to map deserts, to enforce law and order. The basic concept of the United Nations is that it should be primarily directive and that the work should be done and paid for elsewhere. The expense of enforcing law and order, when the United Nations gets around to doing it, will be paid for by the states who furnish the armed forces on the call of the Security Council. The carrying out of specific policies will be largely left to the specialized agencies. It will be the Food and Agriculture Organization that will spend money on agriculture, the World Health Organization on health, UNESCO on education. Each of these specialized agencies has its own budget; the resultant problem will be discussed later in this chapter. At the same time there begin to be other than administrative or staff purposes that the United Nations itself must serve. It accepted the administration of Trieste, and there for the first time provided for an operational or program budget which might be assessed on a basis of contributions different from that of the ordinary budget of the United Nations. It has assumed obligations for relief of refugees through the Social Commission of the Economic and Social Council and has appropriated some hundreds of thousands of dollars for that purpose. If the United Nations Organization should become responsible for other expensive and large-scale operations not equally useful to all members, how would the expenses be paid? The problem will arise.

The expense of a permanent headquarters for the United Nations is the one immense financial problem which the Organization has had to face. The League of Nations for many years inhabited an old hotel and held its assembly meetings in a municipal hall. So doing, it saved money with which it eventually built a headquarters building both convenient and magnificent. The United Nations, condemned to establish its headquarters in the most crowded and expensive city in the world and to find large accommodations at once, accepted the gift of a site but must pay for its own building. Consequently as a special and extra expense, the United Nations will borrow 65 million dollars from the United States government to construct headquarters buildings. It is not clear from what funds the loan will be repaid.

Budgets of the Specialized Agencies

Each specialized agency has its own budget, drawn up by its executive officer or council, voted by its annual assembly. Its receipts, like those of the United Nations, come from contributions from the members, which are assessed on scales similar to that used by the United Nations. The only exceptions are the Fund and the Bank, whose administrative expenses are a charge on the business done and are not paid from members' contributions. The expenses of the International Trade Union and the Universal Postal Union are so small that they hardly matter. The World Health Organization was started by temporary subsidy from the United Nations and from residual UNRRA funds. After it came into full existence, its first Assembly, which met in June, 1948, approved a budget of 5 million dollars. The International Trade Organization can be hardly less expensive. The figure of 5 million dollars (or somewhat more) seems at present a standard specialized-agency figure. Such an amount will pay for headquarters, staff, meetings, and enough of a program to keep going. For the more technical agencies which, like International Civil Aviation Organization, can work by cooperation with national governments, this suffices. UNESCO, on the other hand, has from the beginning found that it will never command money enough to do even the minimum that it plans.

The budgets of the specialized agencies bear unequally on the members of the United Nations, since membership in the specialized agencies is variable. The total burden, however, for states that belong to all or most of them, is a burden even greater than that of the United Nations budget itself. For 1948 the administrative budgets of the specialized agencies then in existence totaled about 30 million dollars—almost as much as the budget of the United Nations Organization itself.

Coordination of Budgets. The existence of a variety of specialized agencies with somewhat varying membership inevitably increases the total amount of the budgets taken all together.   The need of separate headquarters and separate staffs and the inevitable overlapping of programs are administrative reasons for the greater expense.   Another important factor enters in.   Just as in national governments, some special field of activity, be it agriculture or aviation, may be a favorite with the government or with the people and therefore may be able to obtain money when other areas of government cannot.   So the specialized agencies are pushed forward by the zealots and the successful money-getters.   This is proper and desirable, for it is the way progress is made in a free world.   But it is also expensive.

Could not all the budgets of all the international organizations be combined into one budget, with resultant economies and a smaller total?   Such a joint and combined budget, prepared under the supervision of the United Nations Organization, would be legitimate under the Charter provisions providing for the General Assembly's examination of administrative budgets and making of recommendations.   But it could be carried out only if, in their agreements with the United Nations Organization, the specialized agencies had accepted an effective supervision.   They have not done so.   As a result, any coordination is of a loose sort, worked out by the Coordination Committee of the Economic and Social Council.   The Preparatory Commission saw the problem and recommended collaboration of staffs and budgets, but the tendency has been contrariwise.   Today, it is fair to say, the specialized agencies are going to receive relatively more money for their purposes than is the United Nations Organization itself.   And the United Nations Organization's power of coordination is very slight.

Program Budgets of Specialized Agencies.   The coordination of budgets made possible by the Charter is of administrative budgets only.   The major proportion of the budgets of specialized agencies goes to administrative expenses.   But it seems assumed that specialized agencies may have special or operating budgets for special programs, which fall outside the usual arrangements.   So far, the International Refugee Organization offers an example

of this.   In addition to its administrative budget of about 5 million dollars, it has an operating budget of over 150 million dollars
assessed and accepted partly on the basis of benefit.   The United
States and the United Kingdom, which would benefit by the
International Refugee Organization's care of refugees in their
zones of Germany, accepted shares of 43 and 15 per cent, respectively, in its operating budget.   This example shows that it is
possible to distinguish between administrative expenses—justly a
charge on members in accordance with ability to pay—and expenses of special operations chargeable on the basis of benefit.
The practical difficulty of collecting such special assessments is
another matter.

Other specialized agencies also furnish machinery for carrying
out programs of unquestioned, and sometimes striking, importance.   Many problems of human well-being are insoluble on the
national level and readily soluble on the international.   Political
problems of this sort are refugees and trade.   Economic and social
problems are exemplified by inoculation against disease, raising
educational standards, and protecting laborers in undeveloped
areas.   Such projects may be expensive and may require additional funds from members of the specialized agencies.   There
are also programs which are debatable.   The Food and Agriculture Organization's plan for a world food program, very similar
to the United States' own domestic program of financial support
for farmers, was stopped in the Food and Agriculture Organization by pressure from the United States.

The Budgets of the Future

For the smaller members of the United Nations their contribution to the budget is less than the salary of one diplomat marooned
in a minor capital.   For the United States it is less than the cost
of a small bureau in Washington.   Nations can well pay much
more for an organization which provides them with so many services.   They will have to do so in the future.

With the complete publicity that exists and the scrutiny of
fifty to sixty member governments, it is unlikely that any special-

ized agency or the United Nations itself will waste any large amount of money. The publicity is complete and the accountability is strict. The budgets of the United Nations and of the specialized agencies, unlike those of national governments, contain no hidden appropriations used for secret purposes.

Chapter 17. THE INTERNATIONAL COURT
OF JUSTICE

Planning for the Court

The Need of a Court

Any complete government must have a judicial branch, consisting of a court or courts. If the United Nations is to be in any
sense a world government, it must provide a tribunal above all the
nations which can judge them all according to the immutable
principles of law.

This objective is not new. A central international tribunal
existed before the Reformation in the supreme arbitral power
of the Pope. Since the Reformation proposals for a world court
have been frequently made. The Hague Conferences of 1899
and 1907 actually created a sort of international court in the Permanent Court of Arbitration (the "Hague Tribunal") which was
capable of rendering decisions in disputes between nations, though
it was not a court in any conventional sense. Indeed, the United
States delegation to the Second Hague Conference had proposed
the establishment of "permanent tribunal composed of judges who
are judicial officers and nothing else."

The Old "World Court"

When the Covenant of the League of Nations was drawn up,
it included a provision, in Article 14, that the Council should
formulate plans for the establishment of a permanent court of
international justice. At the summons of the Council a group
of distinguished jurists drew up a project for such a court. The
project, after approval by the Council and the Assembly of the
League, was incorporated in a formal protocol offered for sig-

360

nature to members of the League and to states originally invited
to join the League.

In Mr. Elihu Root, its representative in the commission of
jurists, the United States possessed one of the important creators
of the Court, and in particular the author of the plans by which
the interests of both large and small powers were considered in
the election of judges.   The United States never became a member of the Court.   It did, however, provide in succession three
judges for the Court (elected, of course, by the member states)
Mr. Charles Evans Hughes, Mr. Frank B. Kellogg, and Prof.
Manley O. Hudson.

The "World Court," as the Permanent Court of International
Justice was conveniently called, was the one part of the League
of Nations machinery with which none of its participants found
any serious fault.   It had one great weakness: its jurisdiction was
voluntary; no case could be brought before it except after preliminary agreement by the states concerned.   As a result it had
before it, in a quarter century of existence, only a small number
of cases and requests for advisory opinions.   On the other hand
its work was of exceptionally high quality.   It settled some questions that might have led to war.   It showed that something in
the nature of international jurisprudence is possible and it began
to write that jurisprudence.   Case by case it made examinations
of crucial areas of international jurisprudence and in each of
them gave a decision which affected the thinking of national
courts and national statesmen.   Most of its decisions were both
good statesmanship and good law.

The World Court was created by a special protocol embodying
its Statute.   The protocol was signed and ratified separately from
the Covenant of the League.   The Court had a legal and constitutional existence quite apart from any other international organization.   For practical purposes, however, it was tied to the League
of Nations in three ways.   Its judges were elected by the League.
Its budget (drawn up by the Court itself) was paid by the
League. The League might ask advisory opinions of it.   Its
membership (though wider) largely coincided with that of the

League.   At the same time it had its own seat, The Hague, its own officers, and its own registry or secretariat.

After 1939 the work of the Court, like that of the League, was in abeyance.   Judges did not try to reach The Hague.

Planning for the International Court of Justice

When the United Nations was proposed, it was clear that it must have a judicial branch.   It was equally clear that the old Court could not be improved on, except perhaps in detail.   Only one major change seemed useful—that the Court, this time, should be an integral part of the United Nations Organization.   The United Nations, if not monolithic in power, was at least to be monolithic in structure.

The Dumbarton Oaks Proposals merely provided that there should be a court.   On the invitation of the sponsoring powers of the San Francisco Conference, the United Nations Committee of Jurists met in Washington from April 9 to 20, 1945, and drew up a draft statute for a court, based on the Statute of the Permanent Court of International Justice, but leaving a few doubtful questions to be settled at San Francisco.

The San Francisco Conference based its work on this draft statute.   It decided that there should be a new court rather than merely a continuation of the old.   The Statute of the new Court is almost identical with that of the old, however, except in provisions necessary to adjust the Court to the rest of the United Nations Organization.

The Court and the Charter

The Court is incorporated into the structure of the United Nations in an ingenious, if somewhat repetitious, way.   According to Article 7 of the Charter, the Court is established as one of the six "principal organs" of the United Nations.   Chapter XIV of the Charter, a very brief chapter, then states that:

The International Court of Justice shall be the principal judicial organ of the United Nations.   It shall function in accordance with the annexed Statute, which is based upon the Statute of the Permanent Court of International Justice and forms an integral part of the present Charter.

The rest of Chapter XIV deals briefly with basic questions.

As to membership, it says, "All Members of the United Nations are *ipso facto* parties to the Statute" and other states may be admitted by the General Assembly on recommendation of the Security Council.

As to obligation, each member of the United Nations undertakes to comply with decisions of the Court in cases in which it is a party, and all nonmembers must agree to compliance before their cases are heard.

As to jurisdiction, members of the United Nations may use other tribunals if they like.

And, as proved so valuable in the old World Court, the General Assembly and the Security Council may ask the International Court of Justice for advisory opinions on legal questions, and other organs of the United Nations and specialized agencies may do so with the approval of the General Assembly.

This is as far as the Charter goes. But an annex of seventy detailed articles forms the Statute of the Court. The Statute is appended directly to the Charter itself. It forms an integral part of the Charter and was signed and ratified as such.

ORGANIZATION AND JURISDICTION OF THE COURT

Membership of the Court

The Court is composed of fifteen judges, or "members," of whom no two may be nationals of the same state. The judges will be citizens of their own country and elected to the Court as such. It is to be presumed that they will have at least a sentimental attachment to the state from which they come; and by the method of their nomination and election, they are likely to have a more practical connection with it than that. It is assumed, however, that they will be able to conduct themselves as honest and

upright judges, free of effective prejudice. They are to be "independent judges, elected regardless of their nationality from among
persons of high moral character, who possess the qualifications required in their respective countries for appointment to the highest
judicial offices, or are jurisconsults of recognized competence in
international law." Collectively, they are to be chosen so as to
ensure the representation of "the main forms of civilization and
of the principal legal systems of the world."

How are they to be nominated? How is the preliminary selection to be made, the preliminary guarantee to be given, that the
prospective judges are truly qualified? They are nominated by
the national groups that exist for the Permanent Court of Arbitration (or "Hague Tribunal"). These national groups are lists of
four jurists per nation chosen by each government as possible
judges for the Hague Tribunal. Where a state is not a member
of the Hague Tribunal, an equivalent group may nominate for
the Court. These national groups may nominate two of their
own conationals and may also nominate the nationals of other
states.

How are the judges of the International Court of Justice
elected? By concurrent vote of the General Assembly and Security Council of the United Nations. A concurrent vote means
that the two bodies vote independently, but at the same time.
Candidates who receive an absolute majority of votes in both
bodies are declared elected. The Security Council in these elections votes by an ordinary (or numerical) and not by special
majority.

The judges, or members, of the Court are elected for nine years,
their terms being overlapping in units of three years. They make
a solemn declaration to exercise their powers impartially and conscientiously. They are forbidden to engage in any political
activity or to exercise any administrative function or any occupation of a professional nature. In other words, they must be
judges of the International Court of Justice only. And they are
compensated accordingly, for it has been decided that they shall
receive the remuneration of directors of the United Nations Secre-

tariat of the highest rank, plus handsome pension rights and comfortable provisions for leave.

Officers and Machinery of the Court

The Court elects its own officers, a president and vice-president, a registrar and officers of the registry. The seat of the Court is The Hague; it has secured the approval of the Carnegie Foundation for its use of the Peace Palace, which was used by the old World Court.

The Court normally acts through its full membership, a quorum being nine and a simple majority of those sitting on a case being enough to give the decisions. But the Court must annually form a chamber of five judges to hear cases by summary procedure and it may establish chambers of three or more judges for dealing with particular categories of cases.

Perhaps the most peculiar item of the Court's procedure—an item copied from the old World Court—consists in the use of "national" judges. When any case is before the Court, if the two parties each have a judge of its own nationality on the Court, no question arises. But if any state which is a party to a case before the Court is not thus represented, it is entitled to choose an additional judge of its own or some other nationality to sit on the Court during the hearing of the case and to join in the decision.

The expenses of the Court are borne by the United Nations as the General Assembly may direct and consist chiefly of the salaries of judges and officials. As estimated by the Court itself, they are included in the United Nations budget.

The Competence of the Court

The Court is a court in international law, and in that law only states can be persons, capable of suing and being sued. Consequently, only states can be parties to cases before the International Court of Justice. This limits greatly its jurisdiction but ensures the grave importance of the cases which come before it. Normally, the parties to cases before the Court will be members of the United Nations. But nonmember states may use the Court, either as complainants or as respondents, if they agree to accept the decisions of the Court and to carry them out in good faith. The varieties of cases which may be brought to the Court include all cases which the parties wish to refer to it and also all cases which the Charter of the United Nations or other treaties designate as intended for its decision.

Optional versus Compulsory Jurisdiction

The use of the Court is optional. No case may be heard by the Court unless both parties to the case specifically agree to accept the Court's jurisdiction in that particular case. This is, of course, a very serious limitation on the possible activity of the Court. The resultant situation resembles the primitive situation in private law, where courts existed but where persons might refuse to use them, perhaps merely for fear of finding themselves placed in the wrong.

The planners of the old World Court had tried to avoid voluntary jurisdiction by providing that member states could agree to a clause accepting compulsory jurisdiction on a reciprocal basis. If they accepted this clause, they might be brought before the court willy-nilly by any other state which had also accepted compulsory jurisdiction.

The greatest question of policy in the United Nations Conference of Jurists and at San Francisco was the question of compulsory jurisdiction. Many states wished to write it into the Statute. The opposition of the United States and the Soviet Union prevailed. No state can be compelled against its will to appear before the International Court of Justice. At the same time, the Statute of the new Court, like that of the old, includes a provision that states may agree to accept compulsory jurisdiction on a reciprocal basis. Furthermore, agreements to accept the compulsory jurisdiction of the old World Court were extended to cover the new Court. Thirty-four states had by September 21, 1948, accepted compulsory jurisdiction in one way or another, in some cases with reservations. The United States on August 14, 1946, accepted the compulsory jurisdiction of the Court for five years, but with a number of reservations of which the most serious is that the United States reserves the right to determine whether any case falls within its domestic jurisdiction and so outside the competence of the Court.⁵

The Law Applied by the Court

The law applied by the Court is international law, and never has international law been so clearly defined as in Article 38 of the Statute (which is a verbatim reproduction of the language of the old Court's Statute). This article says:

1. The Court, whose function is to decide in accordance with international law such disputes as are submitted to it, shall apply:

a. international conventions, whether general or particular, establishing rules expressly recognized by the contesting states;

b. international custom, as evidence of a general practice accepted as law;

c. the general principles of law recognized by civilized nations;

d. subject to the provisions of Article 59, judicial decisions and the teachings of the most highly qualified publicists of the various nations, as subsidiary means for the determination of rules of law.

The Court also has the power "to decide a case *ex aequo et bono*, if the parties agree thereto" (Article 38.2). This means that the parties may agree to accept the judgment of the Court guided not by law in the strict sense but by the Court's sense of justice.

Advisory Opinions

The Court possesses the power, which may be of great usefulness, of giving an advisory opinion "on any legal question" at the request of any body authorized to request it by the Charter. Requests for advisory opinions are essentially requests for legal advice and not for the settlement of a dispute between two parties. According to Article 96 of the Charter, the General Assembly and the Security Council have the right to ask for advisory opinions on any legal subject. The privilege to ask for such opinions has also been granted by the General Assembly, in accordance with the Charter, to the Economic and Social Council, the Trusteeship Council and, in the agreements with the specialized agencies, to each agency brought into relation with the United Nations. In all these cases the question must be related to the work of the Council or of the agency.

Court procedure on advisory opinions closely resembles court procedure in cases, since any state entitled to appear before the Court may appear and be heard on the question that is raised. Advisory opinions are not binding, even on the organ or agency asking for them. They are merely legal advice from the highest possible source.

In its discussion of the Court in the session of 1947 the General Assembly urged that a wider use of advisory opinions should be made by the organs of the United Nations and by the specialized agencies. This recommendation was opposed by the Soviet Union on the ground that it was undesirable that the Court should exercise the sort of power to interpret the Charter that the Supreme Court of the United States exercises in interpreting the American Constitution. The basic difference of opinion as to who should interpret the Charter—the more or less politically minded organs or the more or less judicially minded Court—is a more fundamental difference of opinion than most Americans can understand. For the ordinary European legislature is generally the final interpreter of its own powers, even under a written constitution, and some self-consciously democratic constitutions, like the Swiss, specifically make the representative body judge of the constitutionality of its own actions.

Procedure

The procedure of the Court is outlined in the Statute and elaborated in the Rules of Court adopted on May 6, 1946. It is the procedure customarily used in cases between nations and is based on Roman rather than common law procedure. This procedure places great emphasis on written pleadings and very little on oral hearings. Consequently, the consideration of a case by the Court will often seem unusually protracted, since the Court must allow for the exchange of written memorials and replies to them. 7

Amendment

The Statute of the Court can be amended by the same procedures as the Charter.

THE ESTABLISHMENT OF THE COURT

Election of Judges

A call for the nomination of judges by the national groups was issued by the Preparatory Commission in London, and the nominations were submitted to the General Assembly and the Security Council in January, 1946.   On February 6 the first elections took place—all fifteen judges being chosen, some for three, some for six, and some for nine years.   As might be expected, a national of each of the five great powers was elected.   They were Hsu Mo of China, Basdevant of France, McNair of the United Kingdom, Hackworth of the United States, and Krylov of the Soviet Union.   There were also elected nationals of four Latin-American states (Alvarez of Chile, Azevedo of Brazil, Guerrero of El Salvador, and Alfaro of Mexico), two Western European states (De Visscher of Belgium and Klaestad of Norway), two Eastern European states (Winiarsky of Poland and Zoricic of Yugoslavia), one Arab League state (Badawi of Egypt), and one British dominion (Read of Canada).   The "main forms of civilization and the principal legal systems of the world" (Article 9 of the Statute) seem to be well-represented, except for the type of Teutonic law which was developed in Germanic countries in the late nineteenth century.

The judges, without exception, have been in the government service of their own countries, some of them in the highest positions.   A few have been judges.   Two of them—Guerrero from 1931 and De Visscher from 1937—had been judges of the old World Court. Zoricic had served as Yugoslav national judge in 1935–1936 in a case involving his country and Hungary.   They all undoubtedly meet the qualifications of the Statute in training and experience, and some of them are jurists of world renown. The American, Mr. Green Hackworth, had been legal adviser to the Department of State for many years. His election made impossible the election to the Court of another American, Prof. Manley O. Hudson, who had been judge of the old World Court since 1936.

When the terms of five judges were due to expire in February, 1949, the General Assembly and the Security Council (on October 22, 1948) reelected all five for the full term of nine years.

Assembling of the Court

The Secretary-General summoned the first meeting of the Court. It met in the Peace Palace at The Hague on April 3, 1946. An impressive inaugural ceremony was held on April 18. The Court continued to sit till May 6. During this month they completed the work of organization. They elected officers— Mr. Guerrero, formerly president of the old World Court, as president; Mr. Basdevant, formerly member of the old Court, as vice-president; Mr. Edvard Hambro of Norway as registrar. They established the summary chamber of the Court, adopted the Rules of Court, organized its registry, and adopted a budget. They also adopted a report proposing diplomatic privileges for their judges and registrar and appropriate immunities for lesser officials.

At the moment when the international Court of Justice held its first meeting on April 3, 1946, the Permanent Court of International Justice was still in existence. Its doors had been closed when Holland was invaded in 1940, though Judge Van Eysinga had managed to protect its archives. Its registry moved to Geneva and functioned nominally there. Two cases before it went unheard. The salaries were not paid. Its judges contemplated the hope of usefulness again when the war should cease. But when the San Francisco Conference decided that they should be superseded and a new court formed, they met at the call of their president at The Hague from October 26 to 31, 1945, and considered ways in which they might help the establishment of the new court by transferring to it their archives and their good will.

The termination of the old Court was a little complicated. The members of the Preparatory Commission (*i.e.*, all the members of the United Nations) agreed in London late in 1945 that, if they were signatories to the Statute of the old Court, they would accept its dissolution and would recommend this dissolution to the League of Nations. The terminal meeting of the Assembly of the League was held in Geneva from April 8 to April 18, 1946. Among its resolutions was one terminating the Permanent Court of International Justice on the day following the conclusion of the Assembly session, that is, on April 19. Consequently, the new Court held its formal inaugural one day before the old Court went out of existence.

One further question determined in 1946 was that of accession to the Statute of the Court by states not members of the United Nations. The question was raised by Switzerland. The General Assembly on recommendation of the Security Council decided that the Court was open to accession by nonmember states who accept its jurisdiction and undertake to comply with its decisions. In accordance with this decision, Switzerland became a signatory to the Statute in 1948. In 1949 Liechtenstein was approved as signatory on the same terms as Switzerland.

In 1947 the Court met for necessary administrative purposes from February 11 to March 14. It shortly received its first case and, later on that year, its first request for an advisory opinion.

In 1949 the Court elected Judge Basdevant as president for three years and Judge Guerrero as vice-president.

THE JURISPRUDENCE OF THE COURT

The Corfu Channel Case

The first case brought before the Court arose from incidents in the channel which lies between the Greek island of Corfu and the Albanian coast. On October 22, 1946, British destroyers were damaged by mines in the channel with loss of life to their crews.

Three weeks later British mine sweepers swept the channel. The British government contended that Albania was responsible for the illegal presence of the mines. The case was heard by the Security Council which recommended that it be referred to the International Court of Justice. On May 22, 1947, the United Kingdom filed an application with the Court. The Albanian government on July 23, 1947, communicated to the Court its willingness to appear. The British case was submitted in a memorial of October 1. The Albanian countermemorial of December 1, 1947, took the form of a protest against the jurisdiction of the Court on the ground that the case had not been submitted by the two parties, nor had Albania accepted the compulsory jurisdiction of the Court.

The first hearing of the case by the Court began on February 26, 1948. Since there was no Albanian national on the Court, a judge *ad hoc* was designated by the Albanian government and sworn in. The Albanian contention and the reply were heard, and on March 25 by a vote of 15 to 1 (the *ad hoc* judge being the one judge in the minority) the Court held that the submission of the case had been proper and that Albania, having agreed to appear before the Court, had voluntarily and unquestionably accepted the Court's jurisdiction.

Thereupon the two governments concerned announced an agreement according to which the Court was asked to decide two questions, first, whether the Albanian government was responsible in international law for the explosions and the damages and loss of life resulting; and, second, whether the United Kingdom had violated Albanian sovereignty by acts of its navy in Albanian waters and whether satisfaction was due.

The judgment of the Court was given on April 9, 1949. It decided by 11 votes to 5 that Albania was responsible for the explosions and the damage and loss of lives. By 10 votes to 6 it reserved the assessment of compensation. By 14 votes to 2 it held that the United Kingdom did not violate Albanian sovereignty on October 22. Unanimously it decided that the United Kingdom did violate Albanian sovereignty by the mine-sweeping expedition and that the declaration of the Court to that effect was in itself appropriate satisfaction.

The dissenting opinions on the first and vital question were given by the Polish, Egyptian, Soviet, Brazilian, and *ad hoc* judges.

Advisory Opinion on Membership

On November 17, 1947, the General Assembly asked the Court for an advisory opinion on two questions relating to membership in the United Nations. The questions were whether or not a member of the United Nations voting on the admission of a new state is "juridically entitled" to make its consent dependent on other conditions than those specifically mentioned in the Charter (Article 4) and in particular whether a member could make its consent dependent on the condition that other states also be admitted to membership at the same time.

Fifteen member states of the United Nations availed themselves of the right to submit written statements on the matter. Twelve of them denied that conditions other than those in the Charter could be imposed. The Soviet Union, the Ukraine, and Yugoslavia expressed the opinion that the questions raised were political and not juridical, and therefore outside the competence of the Court.

Public hearings were held on April 22 to 24, 1948, and the Court delivered its opinion on May 28. By 9 to 6 it voted that the answer to the questions is "No"; that a member cannot make its consent dependent on other than explicit Charter conditions. No sharp ideological divisions can be seen in the decision. The majority of nine included the American, Chinese, Egyptian, Belgian, Norwegian, and Latin-American judges. The minority of six included the British, French, Soviet, Yugoslav, Polish, and Canadian judges.

The majority of the judges held that the requirements for admission enumerated in the Charter were an exhaustive enumeration and must be considered not merely as necessary conditions but as conditions that suffice. Judge Alvarez of Chile, one of the majority, went further and held that any state fulfilling the stated Charter requirements had a right to admission to the United Nations.

Four judges (Basdevant of France, Winiarsky of Poland, McNair of the United Kingdom, and Read of Canada) agreed with the majority that the question was a legal one and that the Court was entitled to give an interpretation of the Charter. But they held on the substantive issue that the decisions of the Security Council and General Assembly on membership were essentially political and that their members might base their votes on political considerations not mentioned in the Charter. The two other dissenting judges, Zoricic and Krylov, gave individual opinions agreeing with the four, but going further in upholding the right of the members of the Security Council to use their discretion.

Advisory Opinion on Reparation for Injuries to United Nations Agents

Disturbed by the assassination of Count Bernadotte, the mediator in Palestine, and of other agents of the United Nations, the General Assembly decided unanimously on December 3, 1948, to ask two questions of the Court:

1. In the event of an agent of the United Nations in the performance of his duties suffering injury in circumstances involving the responsibility of a state, has the United Nations, as an Organization, the capacity to bring an international claim against the responsible *de jure* or *de facto* Government with a view to obtaining the reparation due in respect of the damage caused (a) to the United Nations, (b) to the victim or to persons entitled through him?

2. In the event of an affirmative reply on point 1(b) how is action by the United Nations to be reconciled with such rights as may be possessed by the State of which the victim is a national?

These questions involved not only the specific problem of reparations but the more fundamental problem of whether or not the United Nations Organization possesses an international legal personality entitling it to sue and be sued and otherwise to behave in international law as states may behave.

The unanimous decision of the Court was affirmative on the first question. The Court held that if a United Nations agent suffers injury, the United Nations as an organization has the legal capacity to bring a claim against the responsible *de jure* or *de facto* government to obtain reparation for the damages to the United Nations. It did not distinguish between governments of member and nonmember states.

By an 11 to 4 decision the Court decided that the Organization may bring a claim for reparation for damages to the victim or persons injured through him. In this latter decision the dissents reveal no ideological differences, being made by the American, Soviet, Egyptian, and Polish judges.

Fundamentally the most important effect of the decision was the unanimous agreement that the United Nations Organization has full international legal personality.

The Future of the Court

Up to the present time the International Court of Justice has been by far the least active part of the United Nations Organization. One case decided and two advisory opinions given during a life of four years is certainly a minimum of activity. At the same time, as the experience of the United States Supreme Court shows, it may take many years for sovereign governments to develop trust in a court which is new to them and whose adverse decisions may hurt them politically. Only parties to an issue who think their case is likely to win will place themselves voluntarily and gladly under the jurisdiction of the Court. And if it be suggested that the Permanent Court of Justice, of which the new International Court of Justice is a continuation, existed usefully for twenty-five years, it should be noted that many of the present states of the United Nations were not signatories to the Statute of the old Court and never appeared before it.

Again, in the confused international situation which has prevailed thus far during the existence of the International Court of Justice, many issues between states bearing a legal aspect are at the moment predominantly political, and the Security Council exists to give a political answer to them. It is not unnatural that states have been slow to bring cases to the Court.

The problem of advisory opinions is different. Here, the organs of the United Nations and the specialized agencies might use the Court much more than they have done. But again, each question which arises has political aspects, and the general conference of a specialized agency, for example, may prefer to make its own interpretation of its constitution and of its obligations rather than to ask questions of the Court. Deeper still lies the question, on which (as the opinions in the membership question show) there is real and legitimate difference of opinion, as to whether the interpretations of the Charter and of related documents can best be done by the Court.

Troubled by the small use of the Court, the General Assembly on November 14, 1947, recommended by a large majority that the organs of the United Nations and the specialized agencies should review points of law arising in the course of their activities and, if appropriate, refer them to the Court. It also expressed the view that the Court should be utilized as much as possible "in the progressive development of international law both in regard to legal issues between states and in regard to constitutional interpretations."

Chapter 18. THE FUTURE OF THE UNITED NATIONS

THE UNITED NATIONS SO FAR

The United Nations has not yet fulfilled all the purposes of its founders. Has it therefore "failed"? This question would seem unreasonable were it not so frequently asked. The bitter disappointment of many Americans that the United Nations has not met their ideals for an international organization and the more measured discontent of other peoples and governments do not give the whole answer. Nor does the comparative satisfaction with the Organization felt by officials of many member states (including many Americans) who have taken part in its meetings and deliberations. Can an organization planned to be permanent and to promote international peace, security, and well-being for centuries to come be judged on the basis of its first five years? An evaluation is needed, as dispassionate as possible, though any judgment will inevitably be tinged with nationalistic prejudice. If one examines the work of the Organization so far, in the light of its three purposes—peace and security, well-being, permanency —one can judge its initial effectiveness and speculate reasonably as to its future.

International Peace and Security

In the first and most conspicuous of its functions, the United Nations has won successes and suffered defeats. As an organization to *enforce* peace, it has been helpless, because the whole section of the Charter providing for enforcement has been a dead letter.[1]

As an organization to conciliate disputing or warring govern-

[1] This was written before the Korean crisis of 1950. See the Preface.

ments, the United Nations has sometimes succeeded, sometimes failed. How one strikes a balance must depend on how much one expects of immediate international action and how much one leaves to time and to the nongovernmental forces that influence mankind.

Nevertheless, an honest examination of the efforts of the United Nations to conciliate shows many plusses balanced by many minuses. The problem of Palestine (previously insoluble) seems on the road to solution. Here the United Nations has been the greatest instrument of conciliation, though the final answer will not be precisely what the General Assembly wanted in 1947. In Indonesia and Kashmir the United Nations has mediated with considerable success. It has not been so useful in regard to Spain, Korea, Greece, or South-West Africa. No other agency could have done so much in these areas, but perhaps the United Nations should have done more.

The United Nations has not settled the political struggle between the United States and the Soviet Union, though it is only honest to remember that the Charter assumes great-power unity and that the Security Council was not intended to mediate between great powers or to bring them to book. Nevertheless, the United Nations provides a meeting place, otherwise lacking, where East and West can ventilate their differences in the presence of the enlightened opinion of the world and can, when they wish, agree. And the mediation of Dr. Evatt, Mr. Lie, and the "neutral powers" had a very real effect on the powers involved in the Berlin issue (see Chapter 8). It is to the credit of the Organization that "contact on this issue . . . was reestablished through their United Nations Delegates on United Nations ground." [2]

Well-being

In promoting well-being, a less spectacular purpose, the United Nations has only begun what must be a long and varied program.

[2] *The United Nations: 4 Years of Achievement,* U.S. Department of State, Washington, D.C., 1949.

Perhaps the supervision by the Trusteeship Council of the trust territories is its most effective contribution so far. But we can already note the effectiveness of such specific things as care of refugees, relief for children, inoculation against tuberculosis, control of narcotic drugs—or such broad projects as plans for European recovery and for aid to undeveloped areas. Many important things of a practical sort, such as locating weather ships on the Atlantic, administering wheat quotas, setting standards for commercial airplanes, shifting surplus labor, or regulating devaluations of currency—such tasks are the province of the specialized agencies, but the specialized agencies also are a part of the United Nations system.

The promotion of the general well-being will be the major function of the United Nations in the long run, just as it is the major function of national governments today. But there will be few quick results.

Permanency

In maintaining a general international organization intended to be permanent, the United Nations has so far notably succeeded. In spite of political difficulties, the United Nations, as created at San Francisco and as organized in London, is intact. Not only that, but it has admitted eight new members, some of them like Israel, Pakistan, India, or Sweden conspicuously useful and important members. Bitter dissensions, threats of noncooperation, withdrawals from the work of one organ or another, all are accepted as inevitable in the world in which the United Nations lives. But the work of the Organization goes on. Meetings— almost too numerous—are well-attended. The Secretariat does its work. The budget is frozen at far too low an amount, but the amount permits the level of activity that occurs. There is a general feeling among those who are concerned with the Organization that it is worth the time and trouble. The dangerous period is over. Any American who reads of the early days of the Republic, any Frenchman who reads his country's history in the 1870's, will appreciate the fact that the life of the United

Nations has never been as precarious as was that of the early American or French republic.

To say all this is not to praise the United Nations. Its weakness is that of the governments (and the people behind them) who consciously created an imperfect instrument. We can obtain no more work out of the United Nations than we are willing to pay for. We can secure no more efficiency and no more justice out of the United Nations than we have put into it, and that is very little. We may have put hopes into it, but we have also burdened it with our fears. As of today, the United Nations (in the world in which we have forced it to spend its infancy) has been a surprising success. When it grows to maturity, it may even pay us back something which we need and do not possess.

AMENDING THE CHARTER

No one ever lived under a constitution without wanting to tinker with it. Already there are points where experience indicates that amendment of the Charter would be useful. But can the Charter be amended?

Amending constitutions is difficult. A few constitutions (like that of the United States) include reasonable provisions for change. They are wise to do so. Others may have to submit to change by what is legally revolution—as did England in 1689 or France when the Fourth Republic replaced the Third Republic. Real revision of a constitution is almost inevitably a revolutionary act. And if the United Nations Organization is ever replaced by any of the modifications and substitutes that one hears proposed, it is probable that the Charter process of amendment will not be gone through. Indeed, did not the United Nations Organization itself replace the League of Nations by revolutionary means?

What the Charter Provides

The drafters of the United Nations Charter thought in more limited terms. What did they provide, and how can the Charter be amended?

Chapter XVIII gives the answer, and its Article 108, the essential article, is mostly what the British, American, and Russians worked out at Dumbarton Oaks.

Amendments to the present Charter shall come into force for all Members of the United Nations when they have been adopted by a vote of two thirds of the members of the General Assembly and ratified in accordance with their respective constitutional processes by two thirds of the Members of the United Nations, including all the permanent members of the Security Council.

Is this easy or is it difficult? Is the Charter a flexible constitution or a rigid one? Inflexible, of course, and obviously difficult of amendment in essentials. Certain rigidities in the Charter are intentionally protected by the amendment process. One is the balance of power between five great powers and the fifty-odd small powers. This cannot be changed if any *one* great power objects, or if just over one-third of the small powers object. The other rigidity is the relationship between the great powers themselves. The veto of the great powers is safeguarded in the amendment process. Any one of them can effectively say "No" to any amendment. No one of them can lose anything without its consent.

In view of the Dumbarton Oaks Proposals and the discussions at San Francisco, it would be ridiculous to suggest that the great powers intended to make amendment easy. But their intention appears to have gone further: the Charter of the United Nations was to be all but incapable of amendment. Since from a technical point of view it is a multilateral treaty, and since multilateral treaties cannot be changed without the consent of all the signatories, this is perhaps not surprising. Indeed, in this context, the amendment provision is liberal, since amendment can be made contrary to the will of a minority (say, twenty) of the member states. In view of the counterfact that the United Nations is an organization, presumably liable to growth, development, and change, the difficulty or practical impossibility of amendment is unreasonable. The only precedent that has existed is the League of Nations. The League Covenant was as difficult of amendment (though the provisions were slightly different) and it was never amended during a quarter of a century, except in a few technical respects. Nevertheless, the League Covenant provided that any member which did *not* accept an amendment would cease to be a member of the League.

The Charter is stauncher than this. The Charter does not recognize the power of withdrawal under any conditions, and the small state which objects to a Charter amendment is nevertheless bound by it. To the delegates of the smaller nations at San Francisco this seemed unfair. They, therefore, insisted that the power of withdrawal be recognized. This was done in a statement approved by the Conference. But withdrawal would be at the risk of the dissatisfied member, since the Charter appears to oblige members to enforce the Charter even against nonmembers.

Perhaps these are only "theoretical" considerations, since withdrawal has not yet become a practical matter. Membership seems useful to the veto-protected great powers—even to the Soviet Union which construes the Charter with the same strictness with which the antifederalists used to construe the Constitution of the United States. Though the policies of governments are unpredictable, it seems likely that any one of the Big Five will continue to prefer a privileged position *inside* the Organization to a position of freedom outside it. To the smaller powers, membership on almost any terms is far more useful than isolation, and in dollars it is very cheap. *They* have no choice. They *may* influence decisions if inside; they are *certain* to be trampled upon if outside.

Any consideration of the problem of withdrawal must allow for the possibility that the Soviet abstentions from attendance at the meetings of the organs, which began in January, 1950 (and which continued when this chapter was written), might be permanent. But the Soviet Union has "walked out" before. The Soviet delegate left the Security Council for some weeks in 1946, and the Soviet representative did not attend the Trusteeship Council for the entire first year of its existence.

Amendment at San Francisco

The privileged position of the Big Five in regard to amendment and the corresponding rigidity of the Charter did not escape criticism at San Francisco. Amendment was one of the great problems of the Conference. The Big Five remained adamant in regard to the veto. The lesser powers were obliged to accept the Charter as dictated to them. Believing, however, that a period of peace and good will some years hence might be more favorable to changes in the Charter to suit their views, the lesser powers secured the insertion of the provisions of Article 109 which permit the calling of a conference for proposing amendments.

1. A General Conference of the Members of the United Nations for the purpose of reviewing the present Charter may be held at a date and place to be fixed by a two-thirds vote of the members of the General Assembly and by a vote of any seven members of the Security Council. Each Member of the United Nations shall have one vote in the conference. . . .

3. If such a conference has not been held before the tenth annual session of the General Assembly following the coming into force of the present Charter, the proposal to call such a conference shall be placed on the agenda of that session of the General Assembly, and the conference shall be held if so decided by a majority vote of the members of the General Assembly and by a vote of any seven members of the Security Council.

These added provisions at least make possible a "constitutional convention" or conference to propose amendments to the Charter at any time. And they make it certain that the calling of such a conference shall be considered ten years after the Charter has gone into effect. The General Assembly of 1955 will be obliged to discuss Charter revision. As to acceptance of any amendments which might come out of such a conference, the ratification of such amendments would require the approval of two-thirds of the member states, including all members of the Big Five.

The calling of a conference "for the purpose of reviewing the present Charter" might occur even before the first ten years are up. Its results under world political conditions like the present would be useless. The Western majority would propose measures that would be threatened with a Soviet veto at the ratification stage, and the Soviet Union might press for inclusion in the Charter those proposals concerning atomic energy and disarmament which the United States has rejected.

Persons desiring reasonable changes in the Charter of the United Nations had better not try to secure them by amendment of the Charter.

CAN THE CHARTER BE MODIFIED BY USAGE?

Usages Contrary to the Charter

Constitutions can be modified by usage. So far, the Charter of the United Nations has been modified in two ways which seem contrary to its specific language. One is the practice of not considering abstention in the Security Council as a veto. If Article 27.3 is taken literally, the abstention of a permanent member from a vote is a veto. By practice concurred in by all the great powers, abstention of a permanent member allows an affirmative decision to be made so long as it gets seven affirmative votes and no great-power negative.

The other respect in which the Charter is changed by usage is in regard to trusteeship agreements. The provision that the terms of trusteeship shall be agreed upon by the "states directly concerned" (Article 79) and then approved by the General Assembly (Article 85) is interpreted to mean that the agreement is made between the administering authority, one state, and the General Assembly. This interpretation was objected to in 1946 by the Soviet Union, but tacitly accepted by it when the "agreement" for the Trust Territory of the Pacific Islands was approved by the Security Council in 1947.

These are important, though not comprehensive, amendments and they indicate a process which might continue.

Shifts in Emphasis

Shifts in emphasis are observable. In the long run they may be extremely important. Article 73e has become the basis of an examination of the conduct of colonial administration far more searching than anticipated by those who drafted Article 73. The acceptance of responsibility for the welfare of non-self-governing peoples was a principle of the Charter, but the present use of Article 73e comes close to claiming for the General Assembly an authority which the Charter does not grant. The General Assembly has assumed charge of a number of problems of international peace and security, under the authority of Article 11.2, though the Security Council is given the primary responsibility in that field. Elections to the Councils and to the Commissions of the Economic and Social Council have become political jobs to be divided up by blocs—very possibly a good thing, but not what the Charter intended. High posts in the Secretariat have to be distributed on a basis of national claims.

The Organization tends to add to its powers. A "guard force" is something not foreseen in the Charter, and any strict constructionist of the Charter (even if he be a Russian) may be correct in questioning it. The Russians did not, however, question two enterprises which are clearly outside the letter of the Charter—administration of Trieste under the Security Council and international administration of Jerusalem. Neither of these enterprises is in operation, but both of them are officially decided upon.

Disuse

It is possible to change a constitution by disuse of its provisions. Perhaps it is not too soon to say that the articles providing for the provision of armed forces to be on call by the Security Council have been neglected so long that they can almost be considered null.

Official Interpretation

There is a recognized method of interpretation for any constitution—whether it is a decision by a court (as in the United
States) or by a supreme political authority (as the Swiss National
Assembly) or whether (as seems true in France) each organ in-
terprets its own competence. The authority to give advisory
opinions to the Security Council, the General Assembly, and the
other organs and agencies is granted to the International Court
of Justice. Such a grant suggests that the Court is the authorized
guardian of the Charter. In the one case in which such an interpretation has been given—the advisory opinion asked by the General Assembly in regard to Security Council's voting on membership—the Security Council has failed to be governed by the opinion of the Court. An advisory opinion is, of course, mere advice.
So far, each principal organ of the United Nations has jealously
maintained the position that it alone is the judge of its own authority under the Charter.

Supplementing or Partial Supplanting

The Charter attempts to safeguard its own legal position and
its own primacy as binding law by the provision that "In the
event of a conflict between the obligations of the Members of
the United Nations under the present Charter and their obligations under any other international agreement, their obligations
under the present Charter shall prevail" (Article 103). Consequently, any *other* arrangement made between member states
is legally invalid unless it is consistent with the Charter. The
question has been raised in connection with "regional security
agreements" of which the North Atlantic Treaty is the most conspicuous. This treaty specifically states that it is made in accordance with Article 51 of the Charter, but grave doubt exists in the
minds of many persons as to whether the treaty does not contain
provisions which are contrary not only to the spirit of the Charter
as a whole but to the words of Article 54. Intended by its sponsors to "supplement" or to "implement" the Charter, the treaty

may seem to by-pass it, or to replace it by another system of international organization—stronger, though geographically more limited. Here again there is no supreme interpreter of the Charter. But quite apart from the North Atlantic Treaty, it is possible that the Charter could be pushed to one side by other arrangements.

Other Possible Modifications

For the moment the modification most generally desired by the majority of member states is the liberal admission of new members. It is probable that if left to itself the General Assembly would vote to admit not only those proposed members backed by the United States and vetoed by the Soviet Union, but also those backed by the Soviet Union and failing of seven votes because of Western opposition.

Restrictions on the use of the veto are desired by most member states, though how far any of the five powers that possess the veto would agree to formal limitation of the veto power is still a question.

The control by the United Nations of atomic weapons and the limitation of conventional armaments are both objectives clearly desired by most member states.

REFORM OF THE UNITED NATIONS

If the Charter of the United Nations cannot easily be amended, why not replace it by something different? Those who wish to destroy the United Nations for the benefit of something more or something less may be divided into the radicals and the reactionaries.

The Radical Solution: "World Government"

Many honest supporters of international cooperation work to scrap the United Nations and to replace it by a "world government" or a "world federation." They want a superstate, something which the United Nations is not.

All such proposals have certain common elements. The organization would be stronger than the United Nations, with definite coercive power over the member states and the persons within them. Though the new organization might be a federation, and the existing member states might continue to exist, they would be subordinated much as the states of the American union have been subordinated since 1789. The government of the world state would be more popular and more democratic than the United Nations, since it would be, to some extent, at least, a representative government based on popular election. The effective share that any one nation would have in the world state would be proportioned to its population or its wealth or its power or to all of them.

Some advocates of world government desire a universal and inclusive world state. Others wish to start with what they would consider the more democratic states of Western Europe and of America and the other British dominions beyond the seas—or with the Marshall-plan countries or with the North Atlantic Treaty powers.

A world government, including all or most of the nations included in the United Nations, seems unlikely to be created at once. It seems unlikely, for example, that any plan of representation acceptable to Americans, who are richer and more powerful but much less numerous than many other peoples, would also be acceptable to the rest of the world community.

The more limited type of superstate, composed of nations possessing democratic governments in some Western European sense, would be more practicable. It would not be a general international organization, but rather an alliance—cultural, political, economic, and military. It would unite nations that are mature, Europeanized, industrialized, and predominantly white. It would exclude, and inevitably find itself in opposition to, less mature and less fully Europeanized states, poorer, less highly industrialized, and mostly nonwhite. Power now resides in the Western states, which are richer though less populous, but will it continue to do so in the future? The Charter of the United

Nations, Western as it is in most of its ideas, consciously includes safeguards for native non-European cultures. To non-Europeans any Western world government would look like Western imperialism, cultural if not military.

If some integrated Western federation is necessary to the preservation of Western culture, as many of its proponents believe, the "Western Union" must accept the role of a new Rome holding its frontiers on the Elbe and the Danube against new barbarians. It is just as well for those of us who are descended not from the Romans but from the barbarians who replaced them to ask what good such a policy did for the Rome our ancestors destroyed.

Those who want a strong and centralized world state, which would include everybody, propose an authentic rival to the United Nations. Their appeal is greatest in the United States, because what they propose looks like an adaptation to the international community of a development like that which the United States underwent in shifting from the Articles of Confederation to the Federal Constitution. It may still be doubted, however, whether the United States is ready to give up its sovereignty to a superstate, even if it could be guaranteed a disproportionate voting strength therein. Whether a world government, if established, would be a pleasant government under which to live is a matter of speculation. There is at least a chance that if it were strong enough to maintain law and order it would be strong enough to oppress.

Being for the most part genuine internationalists, the proponents of world government draw away much high-minded support from the United Nations. But they serve a useful purpose by forcing attention on the problem of modernizing the structure and the working of the United Nations, whether by Charter amendment or by usage.

The Reactionary Solution: Alliances

At the opposite extreme are those critics of the United Nations who look backward. Seeing the weaknesses of the United Nations with less pain and surprise than the radicals, they have an equally sharp answer. The United Nations is falling to pieces: let it. Nobody expected it to work. If it fails, say those who hold this view, we can get on well enough without it, for we can put our money and our energy into pursuing our own national interests. At the moment the supporters of this view are either isolationists or are backing various plans for restoring and for arming other groups of countries for their defense. Many Englishmen, many Frenchmen, as well as many Americans belong to this group. If it be suggested that this group takes its ideas too much from general staffs and other military planners, it is wise to remember that general staffs do not plan for us without our consent.

The Functional Solution

One other approach offers real possibilities, though it does not appeal to the impatient. Habitually, organizations improve as they function. The persons least worried about either survival or success for the United Nations are those members of the Secretariat or of the national delegations to the United Nations who spend most of their time on its affairs. The United Nations best approaches the job of establishing itself by doing the duties that fall to it, by going ahead where possible and by drawing back where it is necessary, by assuming a greater future and preparing for it. Every job well done counts in the tally toward better jobs better done in the future. So far the prospects are good. The United Nations will grow by growing, it will succeed by a series of successes.

THE PRESENT SITUATION

The Atmosphere of Crisis

After four years of organized existence the United Nations finds itself still living in a world disturbed and bitterly divided by a struggle for power between two very powerful states and by a struggle between conflicting political ideals.

The struggle for power should be easy to understand. It is merely one of the kinds of rivalry that the existence of the nation-state implies. International politics have always been "power politics." There is nothing new in rivalry for empires, and there is nothing necessarily fatal. In the present rivalry between the United States and the Soviet Union, which is hypostatized more and more as a naked struggle for domination, the United Nations offers a convenient battlefield to the superpowers. But by bringing together, and thereby making effective, the smaller powers, the United Nations becomes a balancing force; it is at least one sort of "third force" for which many believers in freedom have yearned. It might wear out its life as such, but it may also survive the quarrels of the other forces and win out at last by its reasonableness, its persistence, and its vitality.

The ideological struggle is less serious because there are actually three types of political and economic systems in the world today, all sufficiently powerful to be effective rivals. Most of the members of the United Nations are "welfare states" in the sense that their governments take almost complete responsibility for the economic well-being of the people. As such they are, or tend to be, socialist. The moderate socialistic paternalism of the British Labour government is far more nearly what Turks, Ethiopians, Norwegians, and Mexicans want than is the "capitalism" of the United States or the "communism" of the Soviet Union. At present socialistic paternalism cannot mediate between capitalism and communism because it has given hostages to both camps. It is inevitably Marxist, though gradualistic no doubt, and therefore must agree with communists that eventually a United Nations Organization should be replaced by a federated and socialistic world. At the same time, the socialist inherits the democratic liberalism of the nineteenth century and insists on individual freedoms of the sort which the communist disparages as "capitalistic."

Today the socialists are with the capitalists in their opposition to communism, and there seem to be two groupings in conflict with each other. But actually in the organs of the United Nations the conflicts that appear to be between a "capitalistic" United

States and a "communistic" Soviet Union are really struggles for power and not for the success of ideas. Conflict of ideas does play its part in the United Nations. Many votes are cast rather because of a cherished principle than because of a hope of getting material benefit, but the issue is not usually the issue of communism, capitalism, or socialism. Mohammedan states have voted with their coreligionists in questions of Palestine or the Italian colonies. Spanish-American states have felt and exhibited a cultural tie with Spain and a tendency to follow papal leadership in regard to Jerusalem. The differences between colonial powers and anticolonial powers are largely ideological, but they are not struggles between competing economic doctrines. Disagreements in the United Nations are quite as likely to be religious or cultural as economic.

Perhaps it should be noted also that it is not only the United States and the Soviet Union that struggle to attain or to keep power, but that the Arab states, the "emergent nations" of the British Commonwealth, the old colonial powers, and many others, on a lesser scale, do precisely the same thing.

If the members of the United Nations were all satisfied with their position in the world and in relation to each other, meetings of the United Nations would be scenes of harmony rather than of controversy. But in that case the United Nations would serve no particular purpose. For all political organizations of whatever sort, on whatever scale, exist to serve as arenas in which battles can be fought—by political means with political weapons.

Like all organizations the United Nations experiences periods when the antagonists are deadlocked because even the will to try to agree seems to be lacking. Like other governments it may find some problems incapable of satisfactory solution and many others insoluble except by a series of temporary expedients. To make an organization work when it contains conflicting interests requires patience and demands more from those of experience than from those who lack it. It is to be hoped that an exercise of good will on the part of those nations (like the United States) which are rich and strong and self-confident will produce agreement in lesser things with less self-confident opponents, and that the habit of agreement in lesser things will begin to produce agreement in larger affairs.

The Future

After the foregoing exploration of possibilities, prediction should be as safe—or as doubtful—as it ever is in political affairs.

The United Nations might fall into disuse if it should be sufficiently disregarded or if member states should attempt habitually to secure in other ways the ends that (according to the apparent intent of the Charter) should be sought through the United Nations. The United States is sometimes accused of making such an attempt by seeking the economic recovery of Europe outside the United Nations through the Organization for European Economic Cooperation and through the establishing of a military alliance under the North Atlantic Treaty.

The United Nations would disappear in any future major war in which great powers were ranged against each other. Its planners knew this to be true. It was not expected either to prevent or to survive a third world war. If such a war should occur and should end with the world resembling at all the world of today, a new international organization would be started, but it would not be the United Nations.

The United Nations might easily be killed by the United States should that country either pursue a policy of habitual disregard or alternatively refuse to accept its principles in a major situation, as the British and French did with the League in the 1930's. It is hard to see how any other great power or any possible grouping of small powers could have the same destructive effect. If the Soviet Union should withdraw from the United Nations or should boycott it indefinitely, the United Nations would be greatly weakened, precisely as the League of Nations was weakened by the abstention of the United States. But it would not be killed, nor would it be prevented from developing.

If in the future the United States shows half the faith in the United Nations that was needed for the United States to bring it to birth, the United Nations will continue—succeeding here and failing there, developing irregularly and unsurely as any new organization must, but gaining strength from the fact that it serves many useful purposes and will grow by adaptation to its functions. Like the flower planted in a crevice of the barren rock, it makes the soil of internationalism on which it must be nourished.

Americans who object to strong government at home can hardly want too strong a government in the international field. Those who insist that government action in domestic matters must prove itself before it is acceptable cannot assume that international government will be wiser merely because it is international. Not at once—perhaps never—shall any of us be able to work only with those whose ideals and assumptions we completely share. On the contrary, we must expect the advances we desire to be the contributions of many men, many organizations, many governments, and the result of many initially conflicting forces. For this it is necessary not only to work but also to wait and to hope.

The United Nations is an experiment, "as all life is an experiment." It will never completely succeed, because the problems of government are never permanently settled. It will never seem to be a success until the time arises when its success is no longer questioned.

BIBLIOGRAPHICAL NOTE

The headquarters of the United Nations is Lake Success, New York. It maintains information offices in Manhattan and in Washington, D.C. The American agent for its publications is the International Documents Service, Columbia University Press, 2960 Broadway, New York 27. All United Nations publications may be obtained through that agent.

Essential for the Intelligent Citizen and Student

The *Charter* may be obtained in a pocket edition in English from the Department of State (publication 2353) and from the United Nations in all the official languages.

The *United Nations Bulletin,* published twice a month in English, French, and Spanish by the Department of Public Information of the United Nations, gives a continuing and complete account of the work of the United Nations and the specialized agencies. It has a digest of official actions, lists of films, publications, and sources of information. It is very well edited.

Leland M. Goodrich and Edvard Hambro, *The Charter of the United Nations:—Commentary and Documents* (2d edition, World Peace Foundation, Boston, 1949) is the one essential book on the structure of the United Nations, the meaning of the Charter, and the constitutional development of the Organization. It is detailed and scholarly.

Everyman's United Nations is a small volume packed with facts on the structure and activities of the Organization. It was "prepared by the United Nations Department of Public Information" and published by Funk & Wagnalls Company, New York, in association with United Nations World, New York, in 1948.

United Nations Publications

The United Nations is like a government in producing a great quantity of documents difficult to classify. They record all the deliberations and actions of the principal organs of the United Nations and of the subsidiary commissions and committees. The complete collections maintained by a dozen libraries in the United States, and by libraries in other parts of the world, are a necessary source of reference material, but many other American libraries contain the major documents in English.

The simplest form in which United Nations accounts of its own doings appear is the *United Nations Bulletin.* This is the best introduction to the work of the United Nations and the easiest place in which to follow it. Like all publications of the United Nations Secretariat, it must be fair to all member states. The author has relied on it heavily and urges others to do the same.

The Department of Public Information of the United Nations issues a small *United Nations Reporter* (formerly *Newsletter*), monthly, "primarily for organizational and student groups." This can be obtained from James Gray, Inc., 216 East 45th Street, New York.

The *Annual Report of the Secretary-General on the Work of the Organization,* which goes from one July to the next, contains a few introductory comments by the Secretary-General and a summary of the work of the Organization which is the best thing of its sort.

The annual *Reports* of the Security Council, Economic and Social Council, and Trusteeship Council to the General Assembly are similar summaries, but more detailed. All these reports are lacking in emphasis and often fail to emphasize the points in which the reader is interested.

The International Court of Justice issues a *Yearbook* published at The Hague. The Court's documentation is separate from that of the rest of the United Nations.

The *Yearbook of the United Nations,* published by the Department of Public Information, Lake Success, is a huge volume containing accounts of structure, organization, and actions of the organs and their subordinate groups and of the various specialized agencies. It has lists of names and diagrams. It is an all-inclusive work of reference. The first volume (1946–1947) covered 1946 and the first half of 1947, and the second and subsequent volumes (1947–1948, etc.) each cover a year. Though not light reading, the *Yearbook* contains all the essential records of every sort. The 1947–1948 volume contained 1,126 pages.

The ordinary reader will have little occasion to consult the detailed records of the debates of the General Assembly or of the other organs. The reports of the various committees and commissions, for example, the reports of the United Nations Special Committee on Palestine or of the Administrative and Budgetary Committee, will interest students of special subjects.

Special volumes contain the resolutions of the General Assembly. The important resolutions are always printed in the *Bulletin.*

United States Government Publications

(To be obtained from Superintendent of Documents, Washington 25, D.C.)

The Department of State publishes annually the *Report by the President to Congress* on the work of the American delegation to the United Nations. It is entitled *The United States and the United Nations* for the years 1946 (two reports) and 1947. Since then it is called *United States Participation in the United Nations.* These reports are assembled and edited by an able editor from drafts made by officers of the Department who took part in the work. Though written from the United States point of view, they give a good summary of the work of the Organization. They contain appendixes with important speeches and resolutions. They are honest and fair.

The Department of State *Bulletin* (weekly) and its *Documents and State Papers* (monthly) contain many valuable articles on United Nations affairs by experts.

The Department of State also issues, in its Conference series and otherwise, a large number of pamphlets of uneven value explaining the American position on individual matters.

Periodicals

International Organization, published quarterly by the World Peace Foundation, Boston, is devoted largely to articles on the United Nations and to summaries of the work of the United Nations and the specialized agencies. It is edited by Leland H. Goodrich and a group most of whom were at San Francisco.

International Conciliation, published monthly except July and August by the Carnegie Endowment for International Peace (405 West 117th Street, New York), devotes most of its space to substantial articles on United Nations activities.

The *Foreign Policy Reports,* published by the Foreign Policy Association, Inc. (22 East 38th Street, New York) are often very valuable.

The *United Nations World,* published monthly (319 East 44th Street,

New York), is a semipopular magazine with emphasis on spectacular aspects of United Nations action and international political problems.

A variety of news and propaganda sheets and pamphlets are issued, some of them reliable. The Rotary International publishes an excellent monthly newssheet, *Report on United Nations: by Rotary International,* which is attractively edited, informative, and honest (35 East Wacker Drive, Chicago).

The *American Journal of International Law* (700 Jackson Place, N.W., Washington, D.C.) is full of analysis and comment.

The *American Political Science Review* has contained many articles by reliable and informed political scientists.

Books

The United Nations is discussed, sometimes at length, in all recent books on international organization, law, or relations. Books specifically on the United Nations are as yet rare, and most of them are not very useful.

In a selective bibliographical note one should mention:

For the San Francisco Conference and earlier:

The only book published so far which gives any real understanding of the political and diplomatic background of the San Francisco Conference is Edward R. Stettinius, Jr., *Roosevelt and the Russians: The Yalta Conference* (Doubleday & Company, Inc., New York, 1949). The Department of State produced its own account of its planning for the Charter in *Postwar Foreign Policy Preparation: 1939–1945* (written by Harley A. Notter, Department of State Publication 3580, U.S. Government Printing Office, Washington, 1949).

Sigrid Arne, *United Nations Primer* (revised edition, Rinehart & Company, Inc., New York, 1948) is an excellent journalistic account of the conferences that preceded San Francisco.

The documents of the San Francisco Conference are available in two forms:

The United Nations Conference on International Organization: San Francisco . . . Selected Documents (One volume. Department of State Publication 2490, U.S. Government Printing Office, Washington, 1946).

Documents of the United Nation Conference on International Organization, San Francisco 1945 (Sixteen volumes published in cooperation with the Library of Congress by the United Nations Information Organization, 1945–1946).

After San Francisco:

Raymond Dennett and Robert K. Turner, Eds., *Documents on American Foreign Relations* . . . [1945–1946] (World Peace Foundation, Boston) contains many documents.

Herbert Vere Evatt, *The United Nations* (revised edition, Harvard University Press, Cambridge, Mass., 1949) contains important comments by a great statesman.

Herbert Vere Evatt, *The Task of Nations* (Duell, Sloan & Pearce, Inc., New York, 1949) is a discussion of the Assembly in 1948–1949.

Quincy Wright, Ed., *The World Community* (University of Chicago Press, Chicago, 1948) is a series of studies.

Clyde Eagleton, *Annual Review of United Nations Affairs: 1949* is the report of discussions by United Nations officials and others.

Bibliographies

Bibliographies are to be found in each United Nations *Yearbook*. They are so good as hardly to need supplementing.

The World Peace Foundation in its quarterly *Documents of International Organizations* gives a more comprehensive survey and much more detail about *all* international organizations. This publication supplements its excellent *International Organization* listed above.

The United Nations Headquarters Library has begun a bibliographical series. The first number is a *Selected Bibliography of the Specialized Agencies Related to the United Nations* (Lake Success, 1949).

The Specialized Agencies

The specialized agencies have separate headquarters and documentation.

Headquarters	*United States Office*
International Labour Organisation	
Geneva, Switzerland	1825 Jefferson Place, N.W.
	Washington, D.C.
Food and Agriculture Organization	
Temporary:	
1201 Connecticut Avenue, N.W.	
Washington, D.C.	
Permanent:	
Villa Borghese	
Rome, Italy	

Headquarters   *United States Office*

United Nations Educational, Scientific, and Cultural Organization
10 Avenue Kléber   405 East 42d Street
Paris 16, France   New York, N.Y.

International Civil Aviation Organization
1017 Dominion Square Building
Montreal, Canada

International Bank for Reconstruction and Development
1818 H Street
Washington 25, D.C.

International Monetary Fund
1818 H Street
Washington 25, D.C.

Universal Postal Union
Schwarztorstrasse 38
Bern, Switzerland

World Health Organization
Palais des Nations   350 Fifth Avenue
Geneva, Switzerland   New York, N.Y.

International Refugee Organization
Palais des Nations   1344 Connecticut Avenue, N.W.
Geneva, Switzerland   Washington 25, D.C.

International Telecommunications Union
Palais Wilson
Geneva, Switzerland

Inter-Governmental Maritime Consultative Organization
c/o United Nations
Lake Success, N.Y.

International Trade Organization
Palais des Nations
Geneva, Switzerland

World Meteorological Organization
Rue Etraz 5
Lausanne, Switzerland

The United Nations

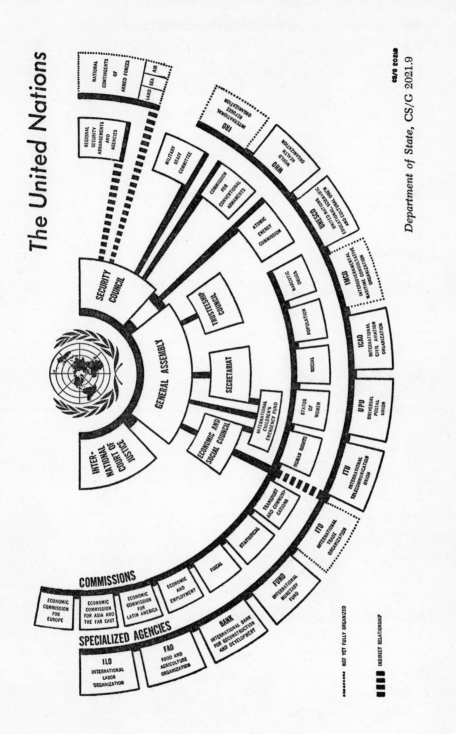

National Contingents of Armed Forces — LAND · SEA · AIR

Regional Security Arrangements and Agencies

SECURITY COUNCIL

Military Staff Committee

Commission for Conventional Armaments

Atomic Energy Commission

TRUSTEESHIP COUNCIL

GENERAL ASSEMBLY

SECRETARIAT

INTER-NATIONAL COURT OF JUSTICE

ECONOMIC AND SOCIAL COUNCIL

International Children's Emergency Fund

Narcotic Drugs

Population

Social

Status of Women

Human Rights

Transport and Communications

Statistical

Fiscal

Economic and Employment

COMMISSIONS

Economic Commission for Europe

Economic Commission for Asia and the Far East

Economic Commission for Latin America

SPECIALIZED AGENCIES

ITO INTERNATIONAL TRADE ORGANIZATION

FUND INTERNATIONAL MONETARY FUND

BANK INTERNATIONAL BANK FOR RECONSTRUCTION AND DEVELOPMENT

FAO FOOD AND AGRICULTURE ORGANIZATION

ILO INTERNATIONAL LABOR ORGANIZATION

ITU INTERNATIONAL TELECOMMUNICATION UNION

UPU UNIVERSAL POSTAL UNION

ICAO INTERNATIONAL CIVIL AVIATION ORGANIZATION

IMCO INTERGOVERNMENTAL MARITIME CONSULTATIVE ORGANIZATION

UNESCO UNITED NATIONS EDUCATIONAL, SCIENTIFIC AND CULTURAL ORGANIZATION

WHO WORLD HEALTH ORGANIZATION

IRO INTERNATIONAL REFUGEE ORGANIZATION

········· NOT YET FULLY ORGANIZED

▬▬▬ INDIRECT RELATIONSHIP

Department of State, CS/G 2021.9

CHARTER OF THE UNITED NATIONS
SAN FRANCISCO, 1945*

WE THE PEOPLES OF THE UNITED NATIONS
DETERMINED

>to save succeeding generations from the scourge of war, which twice in our lifetime has brought untold sorrow to mankind, and
>
>to reaffirm faith in fundamental human rights, in the dignity and worth of the human person, in the equal rights of men and women and of nations large and small, and
>
>to establish conditions under which justice and respect for the obligations arising from treaties and other sources of international law can be maintained, and
>
>to promote social progress and better standards of life in larger freedom,

AND FOR THESE ENDS

>to practice tolerance and live together in peace with one another as good neighbors, and
>
>to unite our strength to maintain international peace and security, and
>
>to ensure, by the acceptance of principles and the institution of methods, that armed force shall not be used, save in the common interest, and
>
>to employ international machinery for the promotion of the economic and social advancement of all peoples,

* Department of State Publication 2368, Conference Series 76.

HAVE RESOLVED TO COMBINE OUR EFFORTS
TO ACCOMPLISH THESE AIMS.

Accordingly, our respective Governments, through representatives assembled in the city of San Francisco, who have exhibited their full powers found to be in good and due form, have agreed to the present Charter of the United Nations and do hereby establish an international organization to be known as the United Nations.

CHAPTER I

PURPOSES AND PRINCIPLES

Article 1

The Purposes of the United Nations are:

1. To maintain international peace and security, and to that end: to take effective collective measures for the prevention and removal of threats to the peace, and for the suppression of acts of aggression or other breaches of the peace, and to bring about by peaceful means, and in conformity with the principles of justice and international law, adjustment or settlement of international disputes or situations which might lead to a breach of the peace;

2. To develop friendly relations among nations based on respect for the principle of equal rights and self-determination of peoples, and to take other appropriate measures to strengthen universal peace;

3. To achieve international cooperation in solving international problems of an economic, social, cultural, or humanitarian character, and in promoting and encouraging respect for human rights and for fundamental freedoms for all without distinction as to race, sex, language, or religion; and

4. To be a center for harmonizing the actions of nations in the attainment of these common ends.

Article 2

The Organization and its Members, in pursuit of the Purposes stated in Article 1, shall act in accordance with the following Principles.

1. The Organization is based on the principle of the sovereign equality of all its Members.

2. All Members, in order to ensure to all of them the rights and

benefits resulting from membership, shall fulfil in good faith the obligations assumed by them in accordance with the present Charter.

3. All Members shall settle their international disputes by peaceful means in such a manner that international peace and security, and justice, are not endangered.

4. All Members shall refrain in their international relations from the threat or use of force against the territorial integrity or political independence of any state, or in any other manner inconsistent with the Purposes of the United Nations.

5. All Members shall give the United Nations every assistance in any action it takes in accordance with the present Charter, and shall refrain from giving assistance to any state against which the United Nations is taking preventive or enforcement action.

6. The Organization shall ensure that states which are not Members of the United Nations act in accordance with these Principles so far as may be necessary for the maintenance of international peace and security.

7. Nothing contained in the present Charter shall authorize the United Nations to intervene in matters which are essentially within the domestic jurisdiction of any state or shall require the Members to submit such matters to settlement under the present Charter; but this principle shall not prejudice the application of enforcement measures under Chapter VII.

CHAPTER II

MEMBERSHIP

Article 3

The original Members of the United Nations shall be the states which, having participated in the United Nations Conference on International Organization at San Francisco, or having previously signed the Declaration by United Nations of January 1, 1942, sign the present Charter and ratify it in accordance with Article 110.

Article 4

1. Membership in the United Nations is open to all other peace-loving states which accept the obligations contained in the present

Charter and, in the judgment of the Organization, are able and willing to carry out these obligations.

2. The admission of any such state to membership in the United Nations will be effected by a decision of the General Assembly upon the recommendation of the Security Council.

Article 5

A Member of the United Nations against which preventive or enforcement action has been taken by the Security Council may be suspended from the exercise of the rights and privileges of membership by the General Assembly upon the recommendation of the Security Council. The exercise of these rights and privileges may be restored by the Security Council.

Article 6

A Member of the United Nations which has persistently violated the Principles contained in the present Charter may be expelled from the Organization by the General Assembly upon the recommendation of the Security Council.

CHAPTER III

ORGANS

Article 7

1. There are established as the principal organs of the United Nations: a General Assembly, a Security Council, an Economic and Social Council, a Trusteeship Council, an International Court of Justice, and a Secretariat.

2. Such subsidiary organs as may be found necessary may be established in accordance with the present Charter.

Article 8

The United Nations shall place no restrictions on the eligibility of men and women to participate in any capacity and under conditions of equality in its principal and subsidiary organs.

CHAPTER IV

THE GENERAL ASSEMBLY

Composition

Article 9

1. The General Assembly shall consist of all the Members of the United Nations.

2. Each Member shall have not more than five representatives in the General Assembly.

Functions and Powers

Article 10

The General Assembly may discuss any questions or any matters within the scope of the present Charter or relating to the powers and functions of any organs provided for in the present Charter, and, except as provided in Article 12, may make recommendations to the Members of the United Nations or to the Security Council or to both on any such questions or matters.

Article 11

1. The General Assembly may consider the general principles of cooperation in the maintenance of international peace and security, including the principles governing disarmament and the regulation of armaments, and may make recommendations with regard to such principles to the Members or to the Security Council or to both.

2. The General Assembly may discuss any questions relating to the maintenance of international peace and security brought before it by any Member of the United Nations, or by the Security Council, or by a state which is not a Member of the United Nations in accordance with Article 35, paragraph 2, and, except as provided in Article 12, may make recommendations with regard to any such questions to the state or states concerned or to the Security Council or to both. Any such question on which action is necessary shall be referred to the Security Council by the General Assembly either before or after discussion.

3. The General Assembly may call the attention of the Security Council to situations which are likely to endanger international peace and security.

4. The powers of the General Assembly set forth in this Article shall not limit the general scope of Article 10.

Article 12

1. While the Security Council is exercising in respect of any dispute or situation the functions assigned to it in the present Charter, the General Assembly shall not make any recommendation with regard to that dispute or situation unless the Security Council so requests.

2. The Secretary-General, with the consent of the Security Council, shall notify the General Assembly at each session of any matters relative to the maintenance of international peace and security which are being dealt with by the Security Council and shall similarly notify the General Assembly, or the Members of the United Nations if the General Assembly is not in session, immediately the Security Council ceases to deal with such matters.

Article 13

1. The General Assembly shall initiate studies and make recommendations for the purpose of:

a. promoting international cooperation in the political field and encouraging the progressive development of international law and its codification;

b. promoting international cooperation in the economic, social, cultural, educational, and health fields, and assisting in the realization of human rights and fundamental freedoms for all without distinction as to race, sex, language, or religion.

2. The further responsibilities, functions, and powers of the General Assembly with respect to matters mentioned in paragraph 1(b) above are set forth in Chapters IX and X.

Article 14

Subject to the provisions of Article 12, the General Assembly may recommend measures for the peaceful adjustment of any situation, regardless of origin, which it deems likely to impair the general welfare or friendly relations among nations, including situations resulting from a violation of the provisions of the present Charter setting forth the Purposes and Principles of the United Nations.

Article 15

1. The General Assembly shall receive and consider annual and special reports from the Security Council; these reports shall include an account of the measures that the Security Council has decided upon or taken to maintain international peace and security.

2. The General Assembly shall receive and consider reports from the other organs of the United Nations.

Article 16

The General Assembly shall perform such functions with respect to the international trusteeship system as are assigned to it under Chapters XII and XIII, including the approval of the trusteeship agreements for areas not designated as strategic.

Article 17

1. The General Assembly shall consider and approve the budget of the Organization.

2. The expenses of the Organization shall be borne by the Members as apportioned by the General Assembly.

3. The General Assembly shall consider and approve any financial and budgetary arrangements with specialized agencies referred to in Article 57 and shall examine the administrative budgets of such specialized agencies with a view to making recommendations to the agencies concerned.

Voting

Article 18

1. Each member of the General Assembly shall have one vote.

2. Decisions of the General Assembly on important questions shall be made by a two-thirds majority of the members present and voting. These questions shall include: recommendations with respect to the maintenance of international peace and security, the election of the non-permanent members of the Security Council, the election of the members of the Economic and Social Council, the election of members of the Trusteeship Council in accordance with paragraph 1(c) of

Article 86, the admission of new Members to the United Nations, the suspension of the rights and privileges of membership, the expulsion of Members, questions relating to the operation of the trusteeship system, and budgetary questions.

3. Decisions on other questions, including the determination of additional categories of questions to be decided by a two-thirds majority, shall be made by a majority of the members present and voting.

Article 19

A Member of the United Nations which is in arrears in the payment of its financial contributions to the Organization shall have no vote in the General Assembly if the amount of its arrears equals or exceeds the amount of the contributions due from it for the preceding two full years. The General Assembly may, nevertheless, permit such a Member to vote if it is satisfied that the failure to pay is due to conditions beyond the control of the Member.

Procedure

Article 20

The General Assembly shall meet in regular annual sessions and in such special sessions as occasion may require. Special sessions shall be convoked by the Secretary-General at the request of the Security Council or of a majority of the Members of the United Nations.

Article 21

The General Assembly shall adopt its own rules of procedure. It shall elect its President for each session.

Article 22

The General Assembly may establish such subsidiary organs as it deems necessary for the performance of its functions.

CHAPTER V

THE SECURITY COUNCIL

Composition

Article 23

1. The Security Council shall consist of eleven Members of the United Nations. The Republic of China, France, the Union of Soviet

Socialist Republics, the United Kingdom of Great Britain and Northern Ireland, and the United States of America shall be permanent members of the Security Council. The General Assembly shall elect six other Members of the United Nations to be non-permanent members of the Security Council, due regard being specially paid, in the first instance to the contribution of Members of the United Nations to the maintenance of international peace and security and to the other purposes of the Organization, and also to equitable geographical distribution.

2. The non-permanent members of the Security Council shall be elected for a term of two years. In the first election of the non-permanent members, however, three shall be chosen for a term of one year. A retiring member shall not be eligible for immediate re-election.

3. Each member of the Security Council shall have one representative.

Functions and Powers

Article 24

1. In order to ensure prompt and effective action by the United Nations, its Members confer on the Security Council primary responsibility for the maintenance of international peace and security, and agree that in carrying out its duties under this responsibility the Security Council acts on their behalf.

2. In discharging these duties the Security Council shall act in accordance with the Purposes and Principles of the United Nations. The specific powers granted to the Security Council for the discharge of these duties are laid down in Chapters VI, VII, VIII, and XII.

3. The Security Council shall submit annual and, when necessary, special reports to the General Assembly for its consideration.

Article 25

The Members of the United Nations agree to accept and carry out the decisions of the Security Council in accordance with the present Charter.

Article 26

In order to promote the establishment and maintenance of international peace and security with the least diversion for armaments of the world's human and economic resources, the Security Council shall be responsible for formulating, with the assistance of the Military Staff

Committee referred to in Article 47, plans to be submitted to the Members of the United Nations for the establishment of a system for the regulation of armaments.

Voting

Article 27

1. Each member of the Security Council shall have one vote.

2. Decisions of the Security Council on procedural matters shall be made by an affirmative vote of seven members.

3. Decisions of the Security Council on all other matters shall be made by an affirmative vote of seven members including the concurring votes of the permanent members; provided that, in decisions under Chapter VI, and under paragraph 3 of Article 52, a party to a dispute shall abstain from voting.

Procedure

Article 28

1. The Security Council shall be so organized as to be able to function continuously. Each member of the Security Council shall for this purpose be represented at all times at the seat of the Organization.

2. The Security Council shall hold periodic meetings at which each of its members may, if it so desires, be represented by a member of the government or by some other specially designated representative.

3. The Security Council may hold meetings at such places other than the seat of the Organization as in its judgment will best facilitate its work.

Article 29

The Security Council may establish such subsidiary organs as it deems necessary for the performance of its functions.

Article 30

The Security Council shall adopt its own rules of procedure, including the method of selecting its President.

Article 31

Any Member of the United Nations which is not a member of the Security Council may participate, without vote, in the discussion of any question brought before the Security Council whenever the latter considers that the interests of that Member are specially affected.

Article 32

Any Member of the United Nations which is not a member of the Security Council or any state which is not a Member of the United Nations, if it is a party to a dispute under consideration by the Security Council, shall be invited to participate, without vote, in the discussion relating to the dispute. The Security Council shall lay down such conditions as it deems just for the participation of a state which is not a Member of the United Nations.

CHAPTER VI

PACIFIC SETTLEMENT OF DISPUTES

Article 33

1. The parties to any disputes, the continuance of which is likely to endanger the maintenance of international peace and security, shall, first of all, seek a solution by negotiation, enquiry, mediation, conciliation, arbitration, judicial settlement, resort to regional agencies or arrangements, or other peaceful means of their own choice.

2. The Security Council shall, when it deems necessary, call upon the parties to settle their dispute by such means.

Article 34

The Security Council may investigate any dispute, or any situation which might lead to international friction or give rise to a dispute, in order to determine whether the continuance of the dispute or situation is likely to endanger the maintenance of international peace and security.

Article 35

1. Any Member of the United Nations may bring any dispute, or any situation of the nature referred to in Article 34, to the attention of the Security Council or of the General Assembly.

2. A state which is not a Member of the United Nations may bring to the attention of the Security Council or of the General Assembly any dispute to which it is a party if it accepts in advance, for the pur-

poses of the dispute, the obligations of pacific settlement provided in the present Charter.

3. The proceedings of the General Assembly in respect of matters brought to its attention under this Article will be subject to the provisions of Articles 11 and 12.

Article 36

1. The Security Council may, at any stage of a dispute of the nature referred to in Article 33 or of a situation of like nature, recommend appropriate procedures or methods of adjustment.

2. The Security Council should take into consideration any procedures for the settlement of the dispute which have already been adopted by the parties.

3. In making recommendations under this Article the Security Council should also take into consideration that legal disputes should as a general rule be referred by the parties to the International Court of Justice in accordance with the provisions of the Statute of the Court.

Article 37

1. Should the parties to a dispute of the nature referred to in Article 33 fail to settle it by the means indicated in that Article, they shall refer it to the Security Council.

2. If the Security Council deems that the continuance of the dispute is in fact likely to endanger the maintenance of international peace and security, it shall decide whether to take action under Article 36 or to recommend such terms of settlement as it may consider appropriate.

Article 38

Without prejudice to the provisions of Articles 33 to 37, the Security Council may, if all the parties to any dispute so request, make recommendations to the parties with a view to a pacific settlement of the dispute.

CHAPTER VII

ACTION WITH RESPECT TO THREATS TO THE PEACE, BREACHES OF THE PEACE, AND ACTS OF AGGRESSION

Article 39

The Security Council shall determine the existence of any threat to the peace, breach of the peace, or act of aggression and shall make recommendations, or decide what measures shall be taken in accordance with Articles 41 and 42, to maintain or restore international peace and security.

Article 40

In order to prevent an aggravation of the situation, the Security Council may, before making the recommendations or deciding upon the measures provided for in Article 39, call upon the parties concerned to comply with such provisional measures as it deems necessary or desirable. Such provisional measures shall be without prejudice to the rights, claims, or position of the parties concerned. The Security Council shall duly take account of failure to comply with such provisional measures.

Article 41

The Security Council may decide what measures not involving the use of armed force are to be employed to give effect to its decisions, and it may call upon the Members of the United Nations to apply such measures. These may include complete or partial interruption of economic relations and of rail, sea, air, postal, telegraphic, radio, and other means of communication, and the severance of diplomatic relations.

Article 42

Should the Security Council consider that measures provided for in Article 41 would be inadequate or have proved to be inadequate, it may take such action by air, sea, or land forces as may be necessary to maintain or restore international peace and security. Such action may include demonstrations, blockade, and other operations by air, sea, or land forces of Members of the United Nations.

Article 43

1. All Members of the United Nations, in order to contribute to the maintenance of international peace and security, undertake to make available to the Security Council, on its call and in accordance with a special agreement or agreements, armed forces, assistance, and facilities, including rights of passage, necessary for the purpose of maintaining international peace and security.

2. Such agreement or agreements shall govern the numbers and types of forces, their degree of readiness and general location, and the nature of the facilities and assistance to be provided.

3. The agreement or agreements shall be negotiated as soon as possible on the initiative of the Security Council. They shall be concluded between the Security Council and Members or between the Security Council and groups of Members and shall be subject to ratification by the signatory states in accordance with their respective constitutional processes.

Article 44

When the Security Council has decided to use force it shall, before calling upon a Member not represented on it to provide armed forces in fulfillment of the obligations assumed under Article 43, invite that Member, if the Member so desires, to participate in the decisions of the Security Council concerning the employment of contingents of that Member's armed forces.

Article 45

In order to enable the United Nations to take urgent military measures, Members shall hold immediately available national air-force contingents for combined international enforcement action. The strength and degree of readiness of these contingents and plans for their combined action shall be determined, within the limits laid down in the special agreement or agreements referred to in Article 43, by the Security Council with the assistance of the Military Staff Committee.

Article 46

Plans for the application of armed force shall be made by the Security Council with the assistance of the Military Staff Committee.

Article 47

1. There shall be established a Military Staff Committee to advise and assist the Security Council on all questions relating to the Security Council's military requirements for the maintenance of international peace and security, the employment and command of forces placed at its disposal, the regulation of armaments, and possible disarmament.

2. The Military Staff Committee shall consist of the Chiefs of Staff of the permanent members of the Security Council or their representatives. Any Member of the United Nations not permanently represented on the Committee shall be invited by the Committee to be associated with it when the efficient discharge of the Committee's responsibilities requires the participation of that Member in its work.

3. The Military Staff Committee shall be responsible under the Security Council for the strategic direction of any armed forces placed at the disposal of the Security Council. Questions relating to the command of such forces shall be worked out subsequently.

4. The Military Staff Committee, with the authorization of the Security Council and after consultation with appropriate regional agencies, may establish regional subcommittees.

Article 48

1. The action required to carry out the decisions of the Security Council for the maintenance of international peace and security shall be taken by all the Members of the United Nations or by some of them, as the Security Council may determine.

2. Such decisions shall be carried out by the Members of the United Nations directly and through their action in the appropriate international agencies of which they are members.

Article 49

The Members of the United Nations shall join in affording mutual assistance in carrying out the measures decided upon by the Security Council.

Article 50

If preventive or enforcement measures against any state are taken by the Security Council, any other state, whether a Member of the United Nations or not, which finds itself confronted with special economic problems arising from the carrying out of those measures shall have the right to consult the Security Council with regard to a solution of those problems.

Article 51

Nothing in the present Charter shall impair the inherent right of individual or collective self-defense if an armed attack occurs against a Member of the United Nations, until the Security Council has taken the measures necessary to maintain international peace and security. Measures taken by Members in the exercise of this right of self-defense shall be immediately reported to the Security Council and shall not in any way affect the authority and responsibility of the Security Council under the present Charter to take at any time such action as it deems necessary in order to maintain or restore international peace and security.

CHAPTER VIII

REGIONAL ARRANGEMENTS

Article 52

1. Nothing in the present Charter precludes the existence of regional arrangements or agencies for dealing with such matters relating to the maintenance of international peace and security as are appropriate for regional action, provided that such arrangements or agencies and their activities are consistent with the Purposes and Principles of the United Nations.

2. The Members of the United Nations entering into such arrangements or constituting such agencies shall make every effort to achieve pacific settlement of local disputes through such regional arrangements or by such regional agencies before referring them to the Security Council.

3. The Security Council shall encourage the development of pacific settlement of local disputes through such regional arrangements or by such regional agencies either on the initiative of the states concerned or by reference from the Security Council.

4. This Article in no way impairs the application of Articles 34 and 35.

Article 53

1. The Security Council shall, where appropriate, utilize such regional arrangements or agencies for enforcement action under its authority. But no enforcement action shall be taken under regional arrangements or by regional agencies without the authorization of the Security Council, with the exception of measures against any enemy state, as defined in paragraph 2 of this Article, provided for pursuant to Article 107 or in regional arrangements directed against renewal of aggressive policy on the part of any such state, until such time as the Organization may, on request of the Governments concerned, be charged with the responsibility for preventing further aggression by such a state.

2. The term enemy state as used in paragraph 1 of this Article applies to any state which during the Second World War has been an enemy of any signatory of the present Charter.

Article 54

The Security Council shall at all times be kept fully informed of activities undertaken or in contemplation under regional arrangements or by regional agencies for the maintenance of international peace and security.

CHAPTER IX

INTERNATIONAL ECONOMIC AND SOCIAL COOPERATION

Article 55

With a view to the creation of conditions of stability and well-being which are necessary for peaceful and friendly relations among nations based on respect for the principle of equal rights and self-determination of peoples, the United Nations shall promote:

a. higher standards of living, full employment, and conditions of economic and social progress and development;

b. solutions of international economic, social, health, and related problems; and international cultural and educational cooperation; and

c. universal respect for, and observance of, human rights and fundamental freedoms for all without distinction as to race, sex, language, or religion.

Article 56

All Members pledge themselves to take joint and separate action in cooperation with the Organization for the achievement of the purposes set forth in Article 55.

Article 57

1. The various specialized agencies, established by intergovernmental agreement and having wide international responsibilities, as defined in their basic instruments, in economic, social, cultural, educational, health, and related fields, shall be brought into relationship with the United Nations in accordance with the provisions of Article 63.

2. Such agencies thus brought into relationship with the United Nations are hereinafter referred to as specialized agencies.

Article 58

The Organization shall make recommendations for the coordination of the policies and activities of the specialized agencies.

Article 59

The Organization shall, where appropriate, initiate negotiations among the states concerned for the creation of any new specialized agencies required for the accomplishment of the purposes set forth in Article 55.

Article 60

Responsibility for the discharge of the functions of the Organization set forth in this Chapter shall be vested in the General Assembly and, under the authority of the General Assembly, in the Economic and Social Council, which shall have for this purpose the powers set forth in Chapter X.

CHAPTER X

THE ECONOMIC AND SOCIAL COUNCIL

Composition

Article 61

1. The Economic and Social Council shall consist of eighteen Members of the United Nations elected by the General Assembly.

2. Subject to the provisions of paragraph 3, six members of the Economic and Social Council shall be elected each year for a term of three years. A retiring member shall be eligible for immediate re-election.

3. At the first election, eighteen members of the Economic and Social Council shall be chosen. The term of office of six members so chosen shall expire at the end of one year, and of six other members at the end of two years, in accordance with arrangements made by the General Assembly.

4. Each member of the Economic and Social Council shall have one representative.

Functions and Powers

Article 62

1. The Economic and Social Council may make or initiate studies and reports with respect to international economic, social, cultural, educational, health, and related matters and may make recommendations with respect to any such matters to the General Assembly, to the Members of the United Nations, and to the specialized agencies concerned.

2. It may make recommendations for the purpose of promoting respect for, and observance of, human rights and fundamental freedoms for all.

3. It may prepare draft conventions for submission to the General Assembly, with respect to matters falling within its competence.

4. It may call, in accordance with the rules prescribed by the United Nations, international conferences on matters falling within its competence.

Article 63

1. The Economic and Social Council may enter into agreements with any of the agencies referred to in Article 57, defining the terms on which the agency concerned shall be brought into relationship with the United Nations. Such agreements shall be subject to approval by the General Assembly.

2. It may coordinate the activities of the specialized agencies through consultation with and recommendations to such agencies and through recommendations to the General Assembly and to the Members of the United Nations.

Article 64

1. The Economic and Social Council may take appropriate steps to obtain regular reports from the specialized agencies. It may make arrangements with the Members of the United Nations and with the specialized agencies to obtain reports on the steps taken to give effect to its own recommendations and to recommendations on matters falling within its competence made by the General Assembly.

2. It may communicate its observations on these reports to the General Assembly.

Article 65

The Economic and Social Council may furnish information to the Security Council and shall assist the Security Council upon its request.

Article 66

1. The Economic and Social Council shall perform such functions as fall within its competence in connection with the carrying out of the recommendations of the General Assembly.

2. It may, with the approval of the General Assembly, perform services at the request of Members of the United Nations and at the request of specialized agencies.

3. It shall perform such other functions as are specified elsewhere in the present Charter or as may be assigned to it by the General Assembly.

Voting

Article 67

1. Each member of the Economic and Social Council shall have one vote.

2. Decisions of the Economic and Social Council shall be made by a majority of the members present and voting.

Procedure

Article 68

The Economic and Social Council shall set up commissions in economic and social fields and for the promotion of human rights, and such other commissions as may be required for the performance of its functions.

Article 69

The Economic and Social Council shall invite any Member of the United Nations to participate, without vote, in its deliberations on any matter of particular concern to that Member.

Article 70

The Economic and Social Council may make arrangements for representatives of the specialized agencies to participate, without vote, in its deliberations and in those of the commissions established by it, and for its representatives to participate in the deliberations of the specialized agencies.

Article 71

The Economic and Social Council may make suitable arrangements for consultation with non-governmental organizations which are concerned with matters within its competence.   Such arrangements may be made with international organizations and, where appropriate, with national organizations after consultation with the Member of the United Nations concerned.

Article 72

1. The Economic and Social Council shall adopt its own rules of procedure, including the method of selecting its President.

2. The Economic and Social Council shall meet as required in accordance with its rules, which shall include provision for the convening of meetings on the request of a majority of its members.

CHAPTER XI

DECLARATION REGARDING NON–SELF–GOVERNING TERRITORIES

Article 73

Members of the United Nations which have or assume responsibilities for the administration of territories whose peoples have not yet attained a full measure of self-government recognize the principle that the interests of the inhabitants of these territories are paramount, and accept as a sacred trust the obligation to promote to the utmost, within the system of international peace and security established by the present Charter, the well-being of the inhabitants of these territories, and, to this end:

a. to ensure, with due respect for the culture of the peoples concerned, their political, economic, social, and educational advancement, their just treatment, and their protection against abuses;

b. to develop self-government, to take due account of the political aspirations of the peoples, and to assist them in the progressive development of their free political institutions, according to the particular circumstances of each territory and its peoples and their varying stages of advancement;

c. to further international peace and security;

d. to promote constructive measures of development, to encourage research, and to cooperate with one another and, when and where appropriate, with specialized international bodies with a view to the practical achievement of the social, economic, and scientific purposes set forth in this Article; and

e. to transmit regularly to the Secretary-General for information purposes, subject to such limitation as security and constitutional considerations may require, statistical and other information of a technical nature relating to economic, social, and educational conditions in the territories for which they are respectively responsible other than those territories to which Chapters XII and XIII apply.

Article 74

Members of the United Nations also agree that their policy in respect of the territories to which this Chapter applies, no less than in respect of their metropolitan areas, must be based on the general principle of good-neighborliness, due account being taken of the interests and well-being of the rest of the world, in social, economic, and commercial matters.

CHAPTER XII

INTERNATIONAL TRUSTEESHIP SYSTEM

Article 75

The United Nations shall establish under its authority an international trusteeship system for the administration and supervision of such territories as may be placed thereunder by subsequent individual agreements. These territories are hereinafter referred to as trust territories.

Article 76

The basic objectives of the trusteeship system, in accordance with the Purposes of the United Nations laid down in Article 1 of the present Charter, shall be:

a. to further international peace and security;

b. to promote the political, economic, social, and educational advancement of the inhabitants of the trust territories, and their progressive development towards self-government or independence as may be appropriate to the particular circumstances of each territory and its peoples and the freely expressed wishes of the peoples concerned, and as may be provided by the terms of each trusteeship agreement;

c. to encourage respect for human rights and for fundamental freedoms for all without distinction as to race, sex, language, or religion, and to encourage recognition of the interdependence of the peoples of the world; and

d. to ensure equal treatment in social, economic, and commercial matters for all Members of the United Nations and their nationals, and also equal treatment for the latter in the administration of justice, without prejudice to the attainment of the foregoing objectives and subject to the provisions of Article 80.

Article 77

1. The trusteeship system shall apply to such territories in the following categories as may be placed thereunder by means of trusteeship agreements:

a. territories now held under mandate;

b. territories which may be detached from enemy states as a result of the Second World War; and

c. territories voluntarily placed under the system by states responsible for their administration.

2. It will be a matter for subsequent agreement as to which territories in the foregoing categories will be brought under the trusteeship system and upon what terms.

Article 78

The trusteeship system shall not apply to territories which have become Members of the United Nations, relationship among which shall be based on respect for the principle of sovereign equality.

Article 79

The terms of trusteeship for each territory to be placed under the trusteeship system, including any alteration or amendment, shall be agreed upon by the states directly concerned, including the mandatory power in the case of territories held under mandate by a Member of the United Nations, and shall be approved as provided for in Articles 83 and 85.

Article 80

1. Except as may be agreed upon in individual trusteeship agreements, made under Articles 77, 79, and 81, placing each territory under the trusteeship system, and until such agreements have been concluded, nothing in this Chapter shall be construed in or of itself to alter in any manner the rights whatsoever of any states or any peoples or the terms of existing international instruments to which Members of the United Nations may respectively be parties.

2. Paragraph 1 of this Article shall not be interpreted as giving grounds for delay or postponement of the negotiation and conclusion of agreements for placing mandated and other territories under the trusteeship system as provided for in Article 77.

Article 81

The trusteeship agreement shall in each case include the terms under which the trust territory will be administered and designate the authority which will exercise the administration of the trust territory. Such authority, hereinafter called the administering authority, may be one or more states or the Organization itself.

Article 82

There may be designated, in any trusteeship agreement, a strategic area or areas which may include part or all of the trust territory to which the agreement applies, without prejudice to any special agreement or agreements made under Article 43.

Article 83

1. All functions of the United Nations relating to strategic areas, including the approval of the terms of the trusteeship agreements and of their alteration or amendment, shall be exercised by the Security Council.

2. The basic objectives set forth in Article 76 shall be applicable to the people of each strategic area.

3. The Security Council shall, subject to the provisions of the trusteeship agreements and without prejudice to security considerations, avail itself of the assistance of the Trusteeship Council to perform those functions of the United Nations under the trusteeship system relating to political, economic, social, and educational matters in the strategic areas.

Article 84

It shall be the duty of the administering authority to ensure that the trust territory shall play its part in the maintenance of international peace and security. To this end the administering authority may make use of volunteer forces, facilities, and assistance from the trust territory in carrying out the obligations towards the Security Council undertaken in this regard by the administering authority, as well as for local defense and the maintenance of law and order within the trust territory.

Article 85

1. The functions of the United Nations with regard to trusteeship agreements for all areas not designated as strategic, including the approval of the terms of the trusteeship agreements and of their alteration or amendment, shall be exercised by the General Assembly.

2. The Trusteeship Council, operating under the authority of the General Assembly, shall assist the General Assembly in carrying out these functions.

CHAPTER XIII

THE TRUSTEESHIP COUNCIL

Composition

Article 86

1. The Trusteeship Council shall consist of the following Members of the United Nations:

    a. those Members administering trust territories;

    b. such of those Members mentioned by name in Article 23 as are not administering trust territories; and

c. as many other Members elected for three-year terms by the General Assembly as may be necessary to ensure that the total number of members of the Trusteeship Council is equally divided between those Members of the United Nations which administer trust territories and those which do not.

2. Each member of the Trusteeship Council shall designate one specially qualified person to represent it therein.

Functions and Powers

Article 87

The General Assembly and, under its authority, the Trusteeship Council, in carrying out their functions, may:

a. consider reports submitted by the administering authority;

b. accept petitions and examine them in consultation with the administering authority;

c. provide for periodic visits to the respective trust territories at times agreed upon with the administering authority; and

d. take these and other actions in conformity with the terms of the trusteeship agreements.

Article 88

The Trusteeship Council shall formulate a questionnaire on the political, economic, social, and educational advancement of the inhabitants of each trust territory, and the administering authority for each trust territory within the competence of the General Assembly shall make an annual report to the General Assembly upon the basis of such questionnaire.

Voting

Article 89

1. Each member of the Trusteeship Council shall have one vote.

2. Decisions of the Trusteeship Council shall be made by a majority of the members present and voting.

Procedure

Article 90

1. The Trusteeship Council shall adopt its own rules of procedure, including the method of selecting its President.

2. The Trusteeship Council shall meet as required in accordance with its rules, which shall include provision for the convening of meetings on the request of a majority of its members.

Article 91

The Trusteeship Council shall, when appropriate, avail itself of the assistance of the Economic and Social Council and of the specialized agencies in regard to matters with which they are respectively concerned.

CHAPTER XIV

THE INTERNATIONAL COURT OF JUSTICE

Article 92

The International Court of Justice shall be the principal judicial organ of the United Nations. It shall function in accordance with the annexed Statute, which is based upon the Statute of the Permanent Court of International Justice and forms an integral part of the present Charter.

Article 93

1. All Members of the United Nations are *ipso facto* parties to the Statute of the International Court of Justice.

2. A state which is not a Member of the United Nations may become a party to the Statute of the International Court of Justice on conditions to be determined in each case by the General Assembly upon the recommendation of the Security Council.

Article 94

1. Each Member of the United Nations undertakes to comply with the decision of the International Court of Justice in any case to which it is a party.

2. If any party to a case fails to perform the obligations incumbent upon it under a judgment rendered by the Court, the other party may have recourse to the Security Council, which may, if it deems necessary, make recommendations or decide upon measures to be taken to give effect to the judgment.

Article 95

Nothing in the present Charter shall prevent Members of the United Nations from entrusting the solution of their differences to other tribunals by virtue of agreements already in existence or which may be concluded in the future.

Article 96

1. The General Assembly or the Security Council may request the International Court of Justice to give an advisory opinion on any legal question.

2. Other organs of the United Nations and specialized agencies, which may at any time be so authorized by the General Assembly, may also request advisory opinions of the Court on legal questions arising within the scope of their activities.

CHAPTER XV

THE SECRETARIAT

Article 97

The Secretariat shall comprise a Secretary-General and such staff as the Organization may require. The Secretary-General shall be appointed by the General Assembly upon the recommendation of the Security Council. He shall be the chief administrative officer of the Organization.

Article 98

The Secretary-General shall act in that capacity in all meetings of the General Assembly, of the Security Council, of the Economic and Social Council, and of the Trusteeship Council, and shall perform such other functions as are entrusted to him by these organs. The Secretary-General shall make an annual report to the General Assembly on the work of the Organization.

Article 99

The Secretary-General may bring to the attention of the Security Council any matter which in his opinion may threaten the maintenance of international peace and security.

Article 100

1. In the performance of their duties the Secretary-General and the staff shall not seek or receive instructions from any government or from any other authority external to the Organization. They shall refrain from any action which might reflect on their position as international officials responsible only to the Organization.

2. Each Member of the United Nations undertakes to respect the exclusively international character of the responsibilities of the Secretary-General and the staff and not to seek to influence them in the discharge of their responsibilities.

Article 101

1. The staff shall be appointed by the Secretary-General under regulations established by the General Assembly.

2. Appropriate staffs shall be permanently assigned to the Economic and Social Council, the Trusteeship Council, and, as required, to other organs of the United Nations. These staffs shall form a part of the Secretariat.

3. The paramount consideration in the employment of the staff and in the determination of the conditions of service shall be the necessity of securing the highest standards of efficiency, competence, and integrity. Due regard shall be paid to the importance of recruiting the staff on as wide a geographical basis as possible.

CHAPTER XVI

MISCELLANEOUS PROVISIONS

Article 102

1. Every treaty and every international agreement entered into by any Member of the United Nations after the present Charter comes into force shall as soon as possible be registered with the Secretariat and published by it.

2. No party to any such treaty or international agreement which has not been registered in accordance with the provisions of paragraph 1 of this Article may invoke that treaty or agreement before any organ of the United Nations.

Article 103

In the event of a conflict between the obligations of the Members of the United Nations under the present Charter and their obligations under any other international agreement, their obligations under the present Charter shall prevail.

Article 104

The Organization shall enjoy in the territory of each of its Members such legal capacity as may be necessary for the exercise of its functions and the fulfillment of its purposes.

Article 105

1. The Organization shall enjoy in the territory of each of its Members such privileges and immunities as are necessary for the fulfillment of its purposes.

2. Representatives of the Members of the United Nations and officials of the Organization shall similarly enjoy such privileges and immunities as are necessary for the independent exercise of their functions in connection with the Organization.

3. The General Assembly may make recommendations with a view to determining the details of the application of paragraphs 1 and 2 of this Article or may propose conventions to the Members of the United Nations for this purpose.

CHAPTER XVII

TRANSITIONAL SECURITY ARRANGEMENTS

Article 106

Pending the coming into force of such special agreements referred to in Article 43 as in the opinion of the Security Council enable it to begin the exercise of its responsibilities under Article 42, the parties to the Four-Nation Declaration, signed at Moscow, October 30, 1943, and France, shall, in accordance with the provisions of paragraph 5 of that Declaration, consult with one another and as occasion requires with other Members of the United Nations with a view to such joint action on behalf of the Organization as may be necessary for the purpose of maintaining international peace and security.

Article 107

Nothing in the present Charter shall invalidate or preclude action, in relation to any state which during the Second World War has been an enemy of any signatory to the present Charter, taken or authorized as a result of that war by the Governments having responsibility for such action.

CHAPTER XVIII

AMENDMENTS

Article 108

Amendments to the present Charter shall come into force for all Members of the United Nations when they have been adopted by a vote of two thirds of the members of the General Assembly and ratified in accordance with their respective constitutional processes by two thirds of the Members of the United Nations, including all the permanent members of the Security Council.

Article 109

1. A General Conference of the Members of the United Nations for the purpose of reviewing the present Charter may be held at a date and place to be fixed by a two-thirds vote of the members of the General Assembly and by a vote·of any seven members of the Security Council. Each Member of the United Nations shall have one vote in the conference.

2. Any alteration of the present Charter recommended by a two-thirds vote of the conference shall take effect when ratified in accordance with their respective constitutional processes by two thirds of the Members of the United Nations including all the permanent members of the Security Council.

3. If such a conference has not been held before the tenth annual session of the General Assembly following the coming into force of the present Charter, the proposal to call such a conference shall be placed on the agenda of that session of the General Assembly, and the conference shall be held if so decided by a majority vote of the members of the General Assembly and by a vote of any seven members of the Security Council.

CHAPTER XIX

RATIFICATION AND SIGNATURE

Article 110

1. The present Charter shall be ratified by the signatory states in accordance with their respective constitutional processes.

2. The ratifications shall be deposited with the Government of the United States of America, which shall notify all the signatory states of each deposit as well as the Secretary-General of the Organization when he has been appointed.

3. The present Charter shall come into force upon the deposit of ratifications by the Republic of China, France, the Union of Soviet Socialist Republics, the United Kingdom of Great Britain and Northern Ireland, and the United States of America, and by a majority of the other signatory states. A protocol of the ratifications deposited shall thereupon be drawn up by the Government of the United States of America which shall communicate copies thereof to all the signatory states.

4. The states signatory to the present Charter which ratify it after it has come into force will become original Members of the United Nations on the date of the deposit of their respective ratifications.

Article 111

The present Charter, of which the Chinese, French, Russian, English, and Spanish texts are equally authentic, shall remain deposited in the archives of the Government of the United States of America. Duly certified copies thereof shall be transmitted by that Government to the Governments of the other signatory states.

IN FAITH WHEREOF the representatives of the Governments of the United Nations have signed the present Charter.

DONE at the city of San Francisco the twenty-sixth day of June, one thousand nine hundred and forty-five.

STATUTE OF THE INTERNATIONAL
COURT OF JUSTICE
SAN FRANCISCO, 1945*

Article 1

The International Court of Justice established by the Charter of the United Nations as the principal judicial organ of the United Nations shall be constituted and shall function in accordance with the provisions of the present Statute.

CHAPTER I

ORGANIZATION OF THE COURT

Article 2

The Court shall be composed of a body of independent judges, elected regardless of their nationality from among persons of high moral character, who possess the qualifications required in their respective countries for appointment to the highest judicial offices, or are jurisconsults of recognized competence in international law.

Article 3

1. The Court shall consist of fifteen members, no two of whom may be nationals of the same state.

2. A person who for the purposes of membership in the Court could be regarded as a national of more than one state shall be deemed to be a national of the one in which he ordinarily exercises civil and political rights.

Article 4

1. The members of the Court shall be elected by the General Assembly and by the Security Council from a list of persons nominated by

* Department of State Publication 2368, Conference Series 76.

the national groups in the Permanent Court of Arbitration, in accordance with the following provisions.

2. In the case of Members of the United Nations not represented in the Permanent Court of Arbitration, candidates shall be nominated by national groups appointed for this purpose by their governments under the same conditions as those prescribed for members of the Permanent Court of Arbitration by Article 44 of the Convention of The Hague of 1907 for the pacific settlement of international disputes.

3. The conditions under which a state which is a party to the present Statute but is not a Member of the United Nations may participate in electing the members of the Court shall, in the absence of a special agreement, be laid down by the General Assembly upon recommendation of the Security Council.

Article 5

1. At least three months before the date of the election, the Secretary-General of the United Nations shall address a written request to the members of the Permanent Court of Arbitration belonging to the states which are parties to the present Statute, and to the members of the national groups appointed under Article 4, paragraph 2, inviting them to undertake, within a given time, by national groups, the nomination of persons in a position to accept the duties of a member of the Court.

2. No group may nominate more than four persons, not more than two of whom shall be of their own nationality. In no case may the number of candidates nominated by a group be more than double the number of seats to be filled.

Article 6

Before making these nominations, each national group is recommended to consult its highest court of justice, its legal faculties and schools of law, and its national academies and national sections of international academies devoted to the study of law.

Article 7

1. The Secretary-General shall prepare a list in alphabetical order of all the persons thus nominated. Save as provided in Article 12, paragraph 2, these shall be the only persons eligible.

2. The Secretary-General shall submit this list to the General Assembly and to the Security Council.

Article 8

The General Assembly and the Security Council shall proceed independently of one another to elect the members of the Court.

Article 9

At every election, the electors shall bear in mind not only that the persons to be elected should individually possess the qualifications required, but also that in the body as a whole the representation of the main forms of civilization and of the principal legal systems of the world should be assured.

Article 10

1. Those candidates who obtain an absolute majority of votes in the General Assembly and in the Security Council shall be considered as elected.

2. Any vote of the Security Council, whether for the election of judges or for the appointment of members of the conference envisaged in Article 12, shall be taken without any distinction between permanent and non-permanent members of the Security Council.

3. In the event of more than one national of the same state obtaining an absolute majority of the votes both of the General Assembly and of the Security Council, the eldest of these only shall be considered as elected.

Article 11

If, after the first meeting held for the purpose of the election, one or more seats remain to be filled, a second and, if necessary, a third meeting shall take place.

Article 12

1. If, after the third meeting, one or more seats still remain unfilled, a joint conference consisting of six members, three appointed by the General Assembly and three by the Security Council, may be formed at any time at the request of either the General Assembly or the Security Council, for the purpose of choosing by the vote of an absolute

majority one name for each seat still vacant, to submit to the General Assembly and the Security Council for their respective acceptance.

2. If the joint conference is unanimously agreed upon any person who fulfils the required conditions, he may be included in its list, even though he was not included in the list of nominations referred to in Article 7.

3. If the joint conference is satisfied that it will not be successful in procuring an election, those members of the Court who have already been elected shall, within a period to be fixed by the Security Council, proceed to fill the vacant seats by selection from among those candidates who have obtained votes either in the General Assembly or in the Security Council.

4. In the event of an equality of votes among the judges, the eldest judge shall have a casting vote.

Article 13

1. The members of the Court shall be elected for nine years and may be re-elected; provided, however, that of the judges elected at the first election, the terms of five judges shall expire at the end of three years and the terms of five more judges shall expire at the end of six years.

2. The judges whose terms are to expire at the end of the above-mentioned initial periods of three and six years shall be chosen by lot to be drawn by the Secretary-General immediately after the first election has been completed.

3. The members of the Court shall continue to discharge their duties until their places have been filled. Though replaced, they shall finish any cases which they may have begun.

4. In the case of the resignation of a member of the Court, the resignation shall be addressed to the President of the Court for transmission to the Secretary-General. This last notification makes the place vacant.

Article 14

Vacancies shall be filled by the same method as that laid down for the first election, subject to the following provision: the Secretary-General shall, within one month of the occurrence of the vacancy, proceed to issue the invitations provided for in Article 5, and the date of the election shall be fixed by the Security Council.

Article 15

A member of the Court elected to replace a member whose term of office has not expired shall hold office for the remainder of his predecessor's term.

Article 16

1. No member of the Court may exercise any political or administrative function, or engage in any other occupation of a professional nature.

2. Any doubt on this point shall be settled by the decision of the Court.

Article 17

1. No member of the Court may act as agent, counsel, or advocate in any case.

2. No member may participate in the decision of any case in which he has previously taken part as agent, counsel, or advocate for one of the parties, or as a member of a national or international court, or of a commission of enquiry, or in any other capacity.

3. Any doubt on this point shall be settled by the decision of the Court.

Article 18

1. No member of the Court can be dismissed unless, in the unanimous opinion of the other members, he has ceased to fulfil the required conditions.

2. Formal notification thereof shall be made to the Secretary-General by the Registrar.

3. This notification makes the place vacant.

Article 19

The members of the Court, when engaged on the business of the Court, shall enjoy diplomatic privileges and immunities.

Article 20

Every member of the Court shall, before taking up his duties, make a solemn declaration in open court that he will exercise his powers impartially and conscientiously.

Article 21

1. The Court shall elect its President and Vice-President for three years; they may be re-elected.

2. The Court shall appoint its Registrar and may provide for the appointment of such other officers as may be necessary.

Article 22

1. The seat of the Court shall be established at The Hague. This, however, shall not prevent the Court from sitting and exercising its functions elsewhere whenever the Court considers it desirable.

2. The President and the Registrar shall reside at the seat of the Court.

Article 23

1. The Court shall remain permanently in session, except during the judicial vacations, the dates and duration of which shall be fixed by the Court.

2. Members of the Court are entitled to periodic leave, the dates and duration of which shall be fixed by the Court, having in mind the distance between The Hague and the home of each judge.

3. Members of the Court shall be bound, unless they are on leave or prevented from attending by illness or other serious reasons duly explained to the President, to hold themselves permanently at the disposal of the Court.

Article 24

1. If, for some special reason, a member of the Court considers that he should not take part in the decision of a particular case, he shall so inform the President.

2. If the President considers that for some special reason one of the members of the Court should not sit in a particular case, he shall give him notice accordingly.

3. If in any such case the member of the Court and the President disagree, the matter shall be settled by the decision of the Court.

Article 25

1. The full Court shall sit except when it is expressly provided otherwise in the present Statute.

2. Subject to the condition that the number of judges available to constitute the Court is not thereby reduced below eleven, the Rules of the Court may provide for allowing one or more judges, according to circumstances and in rotation, to be dispensed from sitting.

3. A quorum of nine judges shall suffice to constitute the Court.

Article 26

1. The Court may from time to time form one or more chambers, composed of three or more judges as the Court may determine, for dealing with particular categories of cases; for example, labor cases and cases relating to transit and communications.

2. The Court may at any time form a chamber for dealing with a particular case. The number of judges to constitute such a chamber shall be determined by the Court with the approval of the parties.

3. Cases shall be heard and determined by the chambers provided for in this Article if the parties so request.

Article 27

A judgment given by any of the chambers provided for in Articles 26 and 29 shall be considered as rendered by the Court.

Article 28

The chambers provided for in Articles 26 and 29 may, with the consent of the parties, sit and exercise their functions elsewhere than at The Hague.

Article 29

With a view to the speedy despatch of business, the Court shall form annually a chamber composed of five judges which, at the request of the parties, may hear and determine cases by summary procedure. In addition, two judges shall be selected for the purpose of replacing judges who find it impossible to sit.

Article 30

1. The Court shall frame rules for carrying out its functions. In particular, it shall lay down rules of procedure.

2. The Rules of the Court may provide for assessors to sit with the Court or with any of its chambers, without the right to vote.

Article 31

1. Judges of the nationality of each of the parties shall retain their right to sit in the case before the Court.

2. If the Court includes upon the Bench a judge of the nationality of one of the parties, any other party may choose a person to sit as judge. Such person shall be chosen preferably from among those persons who have been nominated as candidates as provided in Articles 4 and 5.

3. If the Court includes upon the Bench no judge of the nationality of the parties, each of these parties may proceed to choose a judge as provided in paragraph 2 of this Article.

4. The provisions of this Article shall apply to the case of Articles 26 and 29. In such cases, the President shall request one or, if necessary, two of the members of the Court forming the chamber to give place to the members of the Court of the nationality of the parties concerned, and, failing such, or if they are unable to be present, to the judges specially chosen by the parties.

5. Should there be several parties in the same interest, they shall, for the purpose of the preceding provisions, be reckoned as one party only. Any doubt upon this point shall be settled by the decision of the Court.

6. Judges chosen as laid down in paragraphs 2, 3, and 4 of this Article shall fulfil the conditions required by Articles 2, 17 (paragraph 2), 20, and 24 of the present Statute. They shall take part in the decision on terms of complete equality with their colleagues.

Article 32

1. Each member of the Court shall receive an annual salary.

2. The President shall receive a special annual allowance.

3. The Vice-President shall receive a special allowance for every day on which he acts as President.

4. The judges chosen under Article 31, other than members of the Court, shall receive compensation for each day on which they exercise their functions.

5. These salaries, allowances, and compensation shall be fixed by the General Assembly. They may not be decreased during the term of office.

6. The salary of the Registrar shall be fixed by the General Assembly on the proposal of the Court.

7. Regulations made by the General Assembly shall fix the conditions under which retirement pensions may be given to members of the Court and to the Registrar, and the conditions under which members of the Court and the Registrar shall have their traveling expenses refunded.

8. The above salaries, allowances, and compensation shall be free of all taxation.

Article 33

The expenses of the Court shall be borne by the United Nations in such a manner as shall be decided by the General Assembly.

CHAPTER II

COMPETENCE OF THE COURT

Article 34

1. Only states may be parties in cases before the Court.

2. The Court, subject to and in conformity with its Rules, may request of public international organizations information relevant to cases before it, and shall receive such information presented by such organizations on their own initiative.

3. Whenever the construction of the constituent instrument of a public international organization or of an international convention adopted thereunder is in question in a case before the Court, the Registrar shall so notify the public international organization concerned and shall communicate to it copies of all the written proceedings.

Article 35

1. The Court shall be open to the states parties to the present Statute.

2. The conditions under which the Court shall be open to other states shall, subject to the special provisions contained in treaties in force, be laid down by the Security Council, but in no case shall such conditions place the parties in a position of inequality before the Court.

3. When a state which is not a Member of the United Nations is a party to a case, the Court shall fix the amount which that party is to contribute towards the expenses of the Court. This provision shall not apply if such state is bearing a share of the expenses of the Court.

Article 36

1. The jurisdiction of the Court comprises all cases which the parties refer to it and all matters specially provided for in the Charter of the United Nations or in treaties and conventions in force.

2. The states parties to the present Statute may at any time declare that they recognize as compulsory *ipso facto* and without special agreement, in relation to any other state accepting the same obligation, the jurisdiction of the Court in all legal disputes concerning:

    a. the interpretation of a treaty;

    b. any question of international law;

    c. the existence of any fact which, if established, would constitute a breach of an international obligation;

    d. the nature or extent of the reparation to be made for the breach of an international obligation.

3. The declarations referred to above may be made unconditionally or on condition of reciprocity on the part of several or certain states, or for a certain time.

4. Such declarations shall be deposited with the Secretary-General of the United Nations, who shall transmit copies thereof to the parties to the Statute and to the Registrar of the Court.

5. Declarations made under Article 36 of the Statute of the Permanent Court of International Justice and which are still in force shall be deemed, as between the parties to the present Statute, to be acceptances of the compulsory jurisdiction of the International Court of Justice for the period which they still have to run and in accordance with their terms.

6. In the event of a dispute as to whether the Court has jurisdiction, the matter shall be settled by the decision of the Court.

Article 37

Whenever a treaty or convention in force provides for reference of a matter to a tribunal to have been instituted by the League of Nations, or to the Permanent Court of International Justice, the matter shall, as between the parties to the present Statute, be referred to the International Court of Justice.

Article 38

1. The Court, whose function is to decide in accordance with international law such disputes as are submitted to it, shall apply:

a. international conventions, whether general or particular, establishing rules expressly recognized by the contesting states;

b. international custom, as evidence of a general practice accepted as law;

c. the general principles of law recognized by civilized nations;

d. subject to the provisions of Article 59, judicial decisions and the teachings of the most highly qualified publicists of the various nations, as subsidiary means for the determination of rules of law.

2. This provision shall not prejudice the power of the Court to decide a case *ex aequo et bono*, if the parties agree thereto.

CHAPTER III

PROCEDURE

Article 39

1. The official languages of the Court shall be French and English. If the parties agree that the case shall be conducted in French, the judgment shall be delivered in French. If the parties agree that the case shall be conducted in English, the judgment shall be delivered in English.

2. In the absence of an agreement as to which language shall be employed, each party may, in the pleadings, use the language which it prefers; the decision of the Court shall be given in French and English. In this case the Court shall at the same time determine which of the two texts shall be considered as authoritative.

3. The Court shall, at the request of any party, authorize a language other than French or English to be used by that party.

Article 40

1. Cases are brought before the Court, as the case may be, either by the notification of the special agreement or by a written application addressed to the Registrar. In either case the subject of the dispute and the parties shall be indicated.

2. The Registrar shall forthwith communicate the application to all concerned.

3. He shall also notify the Members of the United Nations through the Secretary-General, and also any other states entitled to appear before the Court.

Article 41

1. The Court shall have the power to indicate, if it considers that circumstances so require, any provisional measures which ought to be taken to preserve the respective rights of either party.

2. Pending the final decision, notice of the measures suggested shall forthwith be given to the parties and to the Security Council.

Article 42

1. The parties shall be represented by agents.

2. They may have the assistance of counsel or advocates before the Court.

3. The agents, counsel, and advocates of parties before the Court shall enjoy the privileges and immunities necessary to the independent exercise of their duties.

Article 43

1. The procedure shall consist of two parts: written and oral.

2. The written proceedings shall consist of the communication to the Court and to the parties of memorials, counter-memorials and, if necessary, replies; also all papers and documents in support.

3. These communications shall be made through the Registrar, in the order and within the time fixed by the Court.

4. A certified copy of every document produced by one party shall be communicated to the other party.

5. The oral proceedings shall consist of the hearing by the Court of witnesses, experts, agents, counsel, and advocates.

Article 44

1. For the service of all notices upon persons other than the agents, counsel, and advocates, the Court shall apply direct to the government of the state upon whose territory the notice has to be served.

2. The same provision shall apply whenever steps are to be taken to procure evidence on the spot.

Article 45

The hearing shall be under the control of the President or, if he is unable to preside, of the Vice-President; if neither is able to preside, the senior judge present shall preside.

Article 46

The hearing in Court shall be public, unless the Court shall decide otherwise, or unless the parties demand that the public be not admitted.

Article 47

1. Minutes shall be made at each hearing and signed by the Registrar and the President.
2. These minutes alone shall be authentic.

Article 48

The Court shall make orders for the conduct of the case, shall decide the form and time in which each party must conclude its arguments, and make all arrangements connected with the taking of evidence.

Article 49

The Court may, even before the hearing begins, call upon the agents to produce any document or to supply any explanations.   Formal note shall be taken of any refusal.

Article 50

The Court may, at any time, entrust any individual, body, bureau, commission, or other organization that it may select, with the task of carrying out an enquiry or giving an expert opinion.

Article 51

During the hearing any relevant questions are to be put to the witnesses and experts under the conditions laid down by the Court in the rules of procedure referred to in Article 30.

Article 52

After the Court has received the proofs and evidence within the time specified for the purpose, it may refuse to accept any further oral or written evidence that one party may desire to present unless the other side consents.

Article 53

1. Whenever one of the parties does not appear before the Court, or fails to defend its case, the other party may call upon the Court to decide in favor of its claim.

2. The Court must, before doing so, satisfy itself, not only that it has jurisdiction in accordance with Articles 36 and 37, but also that the claim is well founded in fact and law.

Article 54

1. When, subject to the control of the Court, the agents, counsel, and advocates have completed their presentation of the case, the President shall declare the hearing closed.

2. The Court shall withdraw to consider the judgment.

3. The deliberations of the Court shall take place in private and remain secret.

Article 55

1. All questions shall be decided by a majority of the judges present.

2. In the event of an equality of votes, the President or the judge who acts in his place shall have a casting vote.

Article 56

1. The judgment shall state the reasons on which it is based.

2. It shall contain the names of the judges who have taken part in the decision.

Article 57

If the judgment does not represent in whole or in part the unanimous opinion of the judges, any judge shall be entitled to deliver a separate opinion.

Article 58

The judgment shall be signed by the President and by the Registrar. It shall be read in open court, due notice having been given to the agents.

Article 59

The decision of the Court has no binding force except between the parties and in respect of that particular case.

Article 60

The judgment is final and without appeal. In the event of dispute as to the meaning or scope of the judgment. the Court shall construe it upon the request of any party.

Article 61

1. An application for revision of a judgment may be made only when it is based upon the discovery of some fact of such a nature as to be a decisive factor, which fact was, when the judgment was given, unknown to the Court and also to the party claiming revision, always provided that such ignorance was not due to negligence.

2. The proceedings for revision shall be opened by a judgment of the Court expressly recording the existence of the new fact, recognizing that it has such a character as to lay the case open to revision, and declaring the application admissible on this ground.

3. The Court may require previous compliance with the terms of the judgment before it admits proceedings in revision.

4. The application for revision must be made at latest within six months of the discovery of the new fact.

5. No application for revision may be made after the lapse of ten years from the date of the judgment.

Article 62

1. Should a state consider that it has an interest of a legal nature which may be affected by the decision in the case, it may submit a request to the Court to be permitted to intervene.

2. It shall be for the Court to decide upon this request.

Article 63

1. Whenever the construction of a convention to which states other than those concerned in the case are parties is in question, the Registrar shall notify all such states forthwith.

2. Every state so notified has the right to intervene in the proceedings; but if it uses this right, the construction given by the judgment will be equally binding upon it.

Article 64

Unless otherwise decided by the Court, each party shall bear its own costs.

CHAPTER IV

ADVISORY OPINIONS

Article 65

1. The Court may give an advisory opinion on any legal question at the request of whatever body may be authorized by or in accordance with the Charter of the United Nations to make such a request.

2. Questions upon which the advisory opinion of the Court is asked shall be laid before the Court by means of a written request containing an exact statement of the question upon which an opinion is required, and accompanied by all documents likely to throw light upon the question.

Article 66

1. The Registrar shall forthwith give notice of the request for an advisory opinion to all states entitled to appear before the Court.

2. The Registrar shall also, by means of a special and direct communication, notify any state entitled to appear before the Court or international organization considered by the Court, or, should it not be sitting, by the President, as likely to be able to furnish information on the question, that the Court will be prepared to receive, within a time limit to be fixed by the President, written statements, or to hear, at a public sitting to be held for the purpose, oral statements relating to the question.

3. Should any such state entitled to appear before the Court have failed to receive the special communication referred to in paragraph 2 of this Article, such state may express a desire to submit a written statement or to be heard; and the Court will decide.

4. States and organizations having presented written or oral statements or both shall be permitted to comment on the statements made by other states or organizations in the form, to the extent, and within the time limits which the Court, or, should it not be sitting, the President, shall decide in each particular case. Accordingly, the Registrar shall in due time communicate any such written statements to states and organizations having submitted similar statements.

Article 67

The Court shall deliver its advisory opinions in open court, notice having been given to the Secretary-General and to the representatives of Members of the United Nations, of other states and of international organizations immediately concerned.

Article 68

In the exercise of its advisory functions the Court shall further be guided by the provisions of the present Statute which apply in contentious cases to the extent to which it recognizes them to be applicable.

CHAPTER V

AMENDMENT

Article 69

Amendments to the present Statute shall be effected by the same procedure as is provided by the Charter of the United Nations for amendments to that Charter, subject however to any provisions which the General Assembly upon recommendation of the Security Council may adopt concerning the participation of states which are parties to the present Statute but are not Members of the United Nations.

Article 70

The Court shall have power to propose such amendments to the present Statute as it may deem necessary, through written communications to the Secretary-General, for consideration in conformity with the provisions of Article 69.

INDEX

A

Acheson-Lilienthal report, 121, 220
Afghanistan, 94, 107
Albania, 114
  as applicant for membership, 107
  and Greek question, 190–191
  (*See also* Corfu Channel question)
Alfaro, Ricardo J., 369, 370
Alvarez, Alejandro, 369–370, 373–374
American Republics, Conference of, in
  1945, 35
Anglo-Egyptian dispute, 195, 200
Arab Higher Committee, 147, 150, 156
Arab League, 55, 84, 99, 146, 148, 150,
  156, 200, 202
Aranha, Oswaldo, 100, 103, 339
Arce, José, 103, 339
  on abstention, 181
Argentina, member Security Council,
  170
  member Trusteeship Council, 305
  at San Francisco, 35, 56
Armaments, 205–228
  1946 resolution on, 96, 121
  in 1948 General Assembly, 121–123
  1949 proposals, 133
Armstrong, Hamilton Fish, 21
Atlantic Charter, 14, 17, 22, 301
Atomic energy, 130
  Acheson-Lilienthal report, 220
  Smyth report, 221
Atomic Energy Commission, 85–88,
  121–123, 133, 207–209, 213–214,
  218–226
Attlee, Clement, 46, 50, 53, 218, 264
Austin, Warren R., 20, 171, 179
Australia, 28, 41, 170
  on colonial problems, 60
  on Indonesia, 192
  influence of, on Charter, 52
  on Palestine, 148–149
  at San Francisco, 47, 56
Australian-New Zealand Agreement of
  1944, 47, 317, 328

B

Austria as applicant for membership,
  107
Axis, 14
Azevedo, José, 369–370

Badawi Pasha, Abdel Hamid, 369–370
Balfour declaration, 140–142
Balkans (*see* Greek question)
Baruch, Bernard, 220, 221
Basdevant, Jules, 89, 369–371
Bases, international, 210, 215–217
Bech, Joseph, 47, 51
Belgium, 47, 170
Berlin, Congress of, in 1878, 9
Berlin blockade, 120–121, 124–125,
  128–129, 197–198, 378
Bernadotte, Count Folke, assassination
  of, 121, 127, 161, 374
  as mediator in Palestine, 159–161
Bevin, Ernest, 119, 120
  and Palestine, 145, 146
Bidault, Georges, 46, 51, 100
Big Five, 148, 233
  and amendments, 383–384
  position of, safeguarded, 176
  ratification of Charter by, 63
  at San Francisco, 15, 53, 55, 59
  and Secretary-General, 85
  and trusteeship, 60
Big Three, 32, 43
Black, Eugene R., 261
Bloom, Sol, 44
Boncour, Paul, 59
Bramulgia, Juan A., 100, 125
Brazil, 41, 170
Budgets, 379
  coordination of, 356–357
  of Court, 365
  of specialized agencies, 250, 259,
    277, 281–282, 349, 354–359
  of United Nations, 86, 92–93, 105,
    349–359
Bulgaria, 114

Sayre, Francis B., 305, 308
Schuman, Robert, 100, 120
Scott, Michael, 134
Secretariat, 337–350
  and budget, 350–351
  Charter provisions for, 341–343
  duties of, 330, 338–344, 348
  establishment of, 86, 343
  and finance, 349
  influence of, 337, 340–341, 347–348
  organization of, 89–90, 343–345
  and other organs, 340
  personnel of, 345–346
  as planned, 74–75
  salaries of, 345
  Secretary-General (see Secretary-General)
  Secretaries-General, Assistant, 343–344
  weaknesses of, 346–349
Secretary-General, 74–75
  annual reports by, 101, 198, 208, 396
  appointment of Secretariat by, 342–344
  election of, 85, 185
Security Council, 167–204
  abstention in, 180–182, 384
  and amendments to Charter, 186
  authority of, 59–60, 67, 70, 71, 174
  Committee of Experts of, 86–87, 172, 187
  conciliator, 198–201
  elections to, 84
  establishment of, 84, 86–87
  and forces, 205–217
  functions of, 69–71, 86–87
    directive, 184–188
    electoral, 184–186
  members of, 57, 66–67, 168–170, 174–175
  and membership in UN, 66, 87, 106–109
  organization of, 170–172
  origins of, 167–169
  and Pacific Islands, 187, 302–303
  presidency of, 172–173
  procedure of, 86, 172–174
  situations and disputes in, 188–198
  special agreements, 211–212, 215
  and Trieste, 187–188

Security Council, voting in, 128, 174–184
  (See also Veto)
  (See also Atomic Energy Commission; Commission on Conventional Armaments; Military Staff Committee)
Shotwell, James T., 224
Siam, 94, 106
Small powers at San Francisco, 55–58
Smuts, Jan C., 47, 56, 59, 231
  on race question, 99
Smyth, H. D., 221
Sobolev, Arcady A., 343
South Pacific regional commission, 290, 327–328
South-West Africa, discussion of, in 1949, 134
  as mandate, 126, 287
  problem of, 117, 126, 298, 300, 308, 311–312, 323
  referred to International Court of Justice, 134
  reports on, 126
Sovereignty, 6–7
Soviet bloc, 55, 99, 100, 126, 130–131
Spaak, Paul-Henri, 47, 83, 100, 103, 120, 339
Spain, 10
  exclusion of, from specialized agencies, 248, 266
    from United Nations, 94–95, 108, 115
Spanish question, 194
Specialized agencies, 230, 232, 235–236, 246–283
  budgets of, 93, 277, 281–282, 349, 354–359
  coordination of, 276–281
  definition of, 248–249
  and dependent areas, 322, 325
  development of, 274–276
  headquarters of, 277–278, 399–400
  membership in, 277
  programs of, 282–283
  relationship of, with United Nations, 249–250
  success of, 379
  (See also specific agencies)
Spitzbergen, 323
Sponsoring powers, 15, 41, 55, 58
  statement on voting, 178–180